JF 229.V

M. J. C. Vile

CONSTITUTIONALISM

AND THE

SEPARATION OF POWERS

M. J. C. Vile

SECOND EDITION

LIBERTY FUND

Indianapolis

This book is published by Liberty Fund, Inc., a foundation
established to encourage study of the ideal of a society
of free and responsible individuals.

⌈✷⌉ 𝄐⋏⫤

The cuneiform inscription that serves as our logo and as the design motif for
our endpapers is the earliest-known written appearance of the word
"freedom" (*amagi*), or "liberty." It is taken from a clay document written
about 2300 B.C. in the Sumerian city-state of Lagash.

Originally published in 1967 by Oxford University Press

Frontispiece photograph by Alfie and Trish Jarvis LMPA, Canterbury, Kent

Library of Congress Cataloging-in-Publication Data
Vile, M. J. C.
Constitutionalism and the separation of powers / M.J.C. Vile. — 2nd ed.
p.   cm.
Includes bibliographical references and index.
ISBN 0-86597-174-9 (hardcover). —ISBN 0-86597-175-7 (pbk.)
1. Separation of powers.   I. Title.
JF229.V5   1998
320.473'04—dc21   97-29369

02 01 00 99 98 C 5 4 3 2 1
02 01 00 99 98 P 5 4 3 2 1

LIBERTY FUND, INC.
8335 Allison Pointe Trail, Suite 300
Indianapolis, IN 46250-1687

CONTENTS

PREFACE
TO THE SECOND EDITION

This work concentrates upon the history and analysis of a strand of constitutional thought which attempts to balance the freedom of the individual citizen with the necessary exercise of governmental power—a dilemma facing us as much today as at any time in our history. I believe that the study of the ways in which this problem has been approached in the past can provide invaluable lessons for today.

In this new edition, appearing thirty years after the first, I have not attempted to revise the text of the original. This is due in part to the fact that so much has been published in the interim and in part because I have since come across a great deal of which I was previously unaware. Thus, any attempt to take all this into account would mean writing a completely new work. At the same time, although I could easily add more material, I do not believe that doing so would necessarily alter the broad outlines of the book, nor would it alter the argument it presents. I have, however, taken the opportunity to add an Epilogue in which the major developments of the past thirty years in Britain and the United States are surveyed, and an attempt has been made to carry the essence of the theory of the separation of powers forward to meet the conditions of government at the end of the twentieth century. I have also added a bibliography, a serious omission from the first edition. Although it can hardly claim to be comprehensive, this bibliography includes many works which were not referred to in the text but which will perhaps assist students who wish to pursue the subject further.

ONE

The Doctrine of the Separation of Powers and Institutional Theory

T HE HISTORY OF Western political thought portrays the development and elaboration of a set of values—justice, liberty, equality, and the sanctity of property—the implications of which have been examined and debated down through the centuries; but just as important is the history of the debates about the institutional structures and procedures which are necessary if these values are to be realized in practice, and reconciled with each other. For the values that characterize Western thought are not self-executing. They have never been universally accepted in the societies most closely identified with them, nor are their implications by any means so clear and unambiguous that the course to be followed in particular situations is self-evident. On the contrary, these values are potentially contradictory, and the clash of interests to be found in the real world is so sharp that the nature of the governmental structures through which decisions are arrived at is critically important for the actual content of these decisions. There has therefore been, since earliest times, a continuous concern with the articulation of the institutions of the political system, and with the extent to which they have promoted those values that are considered central to the "polity."

Western institutional theorists have concerned themselves with the problem of ensuring that the exercise of governmental power, which is essential to the realization of the values of their societies, should be controlled in order that it should not itself be destructive of the values it was intended to promote. The great theme of the advocates of constitutionalism, in contrast either to theorists of utopianism, or of absolutism, of the right or of the left, has been the frank acknowledgment of the role of government in society, linked with the determination to bring that government under control and to place limits on the exercise of its power. Of the theories of government which have attempted to provide a solution to this dilemma, the doctrine of the separation of powers has, in modern times, been the most significant, both intellectually and in terms of its influence upon institutional structures. It stands alongside that other great pillar of Western political thought—the concept of representative government—as the major support for systems of government which are labelled "constitutional." For even at a time when the doctrine of the separation of powers as a guide to the proper organization of government is rejected by a great body of opinion, it remains, in some form or other, the most useful tool for the analysis of Western systems of government, and the most effective embodiment of the spirit which lies behind those systems. Such a claim, of course, requires qualification as well as justification. The "doctrine of the separation of powers" is by no means a simple and immediately recognizable, unambiguous set of concepts. On the contrary it represents an area of political thought in which there has been an extraordinary confusion in the definition and use of terms. Furthermore, much of the specific content of the writings of earlier centuries is quite inappropriate to the problems of the mid twentieth century. The doctrine of the separation of powers, standing alone as a theory of government, has, as will be demonstrated later, uniformly failed to provide an adequate basis for an effective, stable political system. It has therefore been combined with other political ideas, the theory of mixed government, the idea of balance, the concept of checks and balances, to form the complex constitutional theories that provided the basis of modern Western political systems. Nevertheless, when all the necessary qualifications have been made, the essential ideas behind the doctrine remain as vital ingredients of Western political thought and practice today. To substantiate this view it will be necessary to attempt to define and use terms in a more precise way than has been generally the case in the past, and to review the evolution and history of the doctrine, important enough in itself, in order to understand its significance in the past and its relevance today. In spite of the criticisms which can be made of the idea of the separation of powers, perhaps the most important conclusion to be drawn from such a review is that the problems of earlier centuries remain the problems of today; although the context is different, and the dimensions of the problem have changed, it is nevertheless the continuity of political thought, and of the needs of political man, which emerges as the most striking aspect of the history of institutional thought.

The doctrine of the separation of powers finds its roots in the ancient world, where the concepts of governmental functions, and the theories of mixed and balanced government, were evolved. These were essential elements in the development of the doctrine of the separation of powers. Their transmission through medieval writings, to provide the basis of the ideas of constitutionalism in England, enabled the doctrine of the separation of powers to emerge as an alternative, but closely related, formulation of the proper articulation of the parts of government. Yet if we define the doctrine in the terms suggested below, it was in seventeenth-century England that it emerged for the first time as a coherent theory of government, explicitly set out, and urged as the "grand secret of liberty and good government."[1] In the upheaval of civil war the doctrine emerged as a response to the need for a new constitutional theory, when a system of government based upon a "mixture" of King, Lords, and Commons seemed no longer relevant. Growing out of the more ancient theory, the doctrine of the separation of powers became both a rival to it, and also a means of broadening and developing it into the eighteenth-century theory of the balanced constitution. Thus began the complex interaction between the separation of powers and other constitutional theories which dominated the eighteenth century. In England, France, and America this pattern of attraction and

---

1. *A True State of the Case of the Commonwealth*, London, 1654, p. 10; see below, pp. 53–57.

repulsion between related yet potentially incompatible theories of government provided the fabric into which was woven the varied combinations of institutional theories that characterized the thought of these countries in that eventful century. The revolutionary potentialities of the doctrine of the separation of powers in the hands of the opponents of aristocratic privilege and monarchical power were fully realized in America and France, and its viability as a theory of government was tested in those countries in a way which all too clearly revealed its weaknesses. Nevertheless, the separation of powers, although rejected in its extreme form, remained in all three countries an essential element in constitutional thought, and a useful, if vague, guide for institutional development. That this once revolutionary idea could also become in the course of time a bulwark of conservatism, is understandable, for this is the fate of many political ideas.

As the nineteenth century developed the social environment became less and less favourable for the ideas which had been embodied in the pure doctrine of the separation of powers. The attack upon the doctrine came in two waves. First, the group which in earlier years had most fervently supported the separation of powers, the middle class, now saw within its reach the control of political power through the extension of the franchise, and the need for a theory that was essentially a challenge to the power of an aristocracy diminished. However, the lessened enthusiasm for the doctrine took the form, in the period up until the Second Reform Act in England, of a re-examination and reformulation of the doctrine rather than an outright rejection of it. Any suggestion of an *extreme* separation of powers had to be denied, but the importance of the idea as a part of the newly emerging theory of parliamentary government was readily acknowledged. The idea of balance, which was now transferred from the earlier theory of the balanced constitution to become an integral part of the new theory, required still a separation of organs and functions, but with a different set of concepts that had to be fitted into the framework of constitutional theory. The second wave of attack upon the doctrine of the separation of powers came with what Dicey labelled "the age of collectivism." Yet paradoxically it was the middle-class defenders of the mid-nineteenth-century *status quo* who, for reasons which will become apparent at a later stage, laid the ground for the virtual eclipse of the separation of powers as a coherent doctrine in England. The rise and fall of the classical theory of parliamentary government is, therefore, an integral part of the story of the separation of powers. At the centre of this development stands the figure of Walter Bagehot, whose work represents a turning-point in the history of English constitutional thought.

Changing ideas about the role of government and its structure were accompanied by a changing emphasis in ideas about the nature of sovereignty. In earlier centuries the stress upon the necessity of a single, omnipotent source of power was in general the resort of theorists of absolutism, strongly rejected by liberal constitutionalists. The defenders of liberty against arbitrary government stressed the division of power, and the limitations upon power imposed by the constitution or by a higher law. Rousseau's association of the idea of unlimited sovereignty with the people, rather than with a monarch, led, however, to a reorientation of ideas. If absolute power were in the hands of the people, or their representatives, then it could be stripped of its associations with arbitrary government and formed into an instrument of democratic power. If the franchise could be restricted to those with a stake in the community then the idea of an unlimited, indivisible sovereign power became for the liberal individualist not a threat, but a safeguard. It became, in the hands of Bentham and Austin, not a means of arbitrary rule but an instrument for the reform of government which would *increase* the freedom of the individual. That it could equally well become the instrument of another class, and of a different philosophy of government, was a possibility that, if they acknowledged it, did not prevent them from attacking the earlier ideas of the division and limitation of power. It is one of the great ironies of intellectual history that those who were most concerned to establish *laissez-faire* busied themselves with the fashioning of those weapons which were to be used most powerfully to destroy it.

The general context of political development during the nineteenth and early twentieth centuries provided, therefore, the framework for a sharp reappraisal of the doctrine of the separation of powers, but there were other equally important, and related, intellectual challenges to the doctrine. The desire for a unified system of government, whether to achieve reform or for purposes of positive State action, led to a rediscovery of the role of discretion and prerogative in government. The idea of a "mere executive power" which had never been wholly accepted in England, except by extreme radicals, was now specifically rejected. The attack upon the Montesquieu formulation of the triad of government powers, initiated by Bentham and Austin, was taken up by the writers on parliamentary government, and further developed in Germany, France, and America, so that by the early decades of the twentieth century the beautiful simplicity of the eighteenth-century view of the functions of government lay mangled and shattered. And yet, although the attack seemed overwhelming, it was so far a merely negative criticism that no coherent formulation of the structure of government and the articulation of its parts rose up to take the place of the earlier theory. As a result the vocabulary of an earlier age continued in use *faute de mieux*. It was much more than a problem merely of usage, however, for the persistence of the concepts and terminology of an earlier age reflected the fact that Western society in the mid twentieth century continued to value the ideas which had been an integral part of constitutionalism for three centuries, but wished to modify them in the light of new conditions, and new needs. The result of this critical onslaught was, therefore, to leave unrelated fragments of earlier constitutional theories without a new synthesis to fill the gap.

The realization that the functional concepts of the doctrine of the separation of powers were inadequate to describe and explain the operations of government was heightened by the emerging awareness of the nature of bureaucracy. The impact of Prussian bureaucracy upon the nineteenth-century writers, the establishment of a non-political civil service in England, the dissatisfaction with the spoils system in the United States, and the development of the Weberian theory of bureaucracy, led to a complete reassessment of the "executive" function. Thus the demand for the establishment of "harmony" between legislature and government, which characterized the theory of parliamentary government in Britain and France, and the Progressive movement in the United States, was accompanied by a new "separation of powers"—that between the "political" branches of government and the bureaucracy. The distinction between *"Regierung"* and *"Verwaltung,"* or between "politics" and "administration" was, paradoxically, to open a new chapter in the establishment of semi-autonomous branches of government in an age which stressed unity and cohesion.

The credibility of the doctrine of the separation of powers, particularly in the extreme forms that had characterized the Constitution of Pennsylvania in 1776, or the Constitution of France in 1791,[2] already diminished by these social and institutional developments, was further undermined by the new approaches to the study of politics which characterized the twentieth century. If not everyone was prepared to relegate the study of political institutions to the sphere of mere "superstructure" that Marxist thought seemed to demand, the new concentration upon the "real forces" of politics, upon economics and class interest, led to a discounting of theories that seemed concerned only with constitutional and legal considerations. The now discarded theory of mixed government had at least had a social basis for its view of a desirable governmental system, whereas the separation of powers had, quite deliberately, been formulated as a constitutional theory devoid of class bias. There was a diminution of belief in the efficacy of constitutional barriers to the exercise of power, and students of politics demonstrated how legal rules could be evaded or employed to produce an effect directly opposite to that intended. A concentration upon the facts of "politics" rather than of law, leading to a concern with political parties and pressure-groups, directed attention away from the role of constitutions in the political system. The general attack upon "political theory," which suggested that it was merely the expression of opinion or prejudice, tended to depreciate those theories that historically had been strongly empirical in content, along with more metaphysical philosophizing. It was suggested that it was not possible to deduce from a general theory of politics specific unequivocal solutions to particular problems, and that therefore it was probably more fruitful to adopt a pragmatic approach to these individual problems, rather than to attempt wide-ranging generalizations.

The weight of the attack upon the doctrine of the separation of powers

---

2. The role of the separation of powers in these Constitutions is discussed in Chs. 6 and 7 below.

was thus seemingly overwhelming. Yet the examination of the history of the doctrine is not merely an academic exercise, of historical interest only. In spite of the attacks upon the form, and upon the content, of the doctrine there is a sense in which the problems the theorists of the separation of powers set out to solve are more than ever critical today. The recognition of the fact that modern society must meet demands unknown in earlier centuries may make the form of the earlier doctrine irrelevant, but the values it represented are still an essential part of the content of "Western democracy." An examination of the history of the past centuries reveals that for all its inadequacy there is a stubborn quality about the doctrine of the separation of powers. It persistently reappears in differing forms, often in the very work of those who see themselves as its most bitter critics. As will be suggested at a later stage, this is no mere coincidence; it is a recognition of the fact that in some form, a division of power, and a separation of function, lie at the very heart of our systems of government. An idea that finds its roots in ancient constitutionalism, and which in the seventeenth century became a central feature of a system of limited government, has obviously to be reformulated if it is to serve as an instrument of modern political thought, but it can only be rejected altogether if we are prepared to discard also the values that called it into being. The study of the history of constitutional theory can show us, therefore, the extent to which the doctrine remains important, and the extent to which the concepts upon which it rests have become outmoded. The importance of such an investigation hardly needs to be stressed, when we recall that the current institutional structures of two of the three countries with which we are here concerned are overtly based upon the acceptance of the doctrine of the separation of powers; and it will be argued that an approach to the study of British government that rules out all reference to the "separation of powers" is an inadequate one.

But what is "constitutional theory"? It is at once both more than and less than the study of political institutions. It is based upon the assumption that not all States are "constitutional regimes," for in the constitutional State there must be a set of rules which *effectively* restrains the exercise of governmental power. "Constitutionalism" consists in the *advocacy* of certain types of institutional arrangement, on the grounds that certain ends will be achieved in this way, and there is therefore introduced into the discussion a normative element; but it is a normative element based upon the belief that there are certain demonstrable relationships between given types of institutional arrangement and the safeguarding of important values. Thus on the one hand constitutional theory has to grapple with the problems of the existence of nominal or façade constitutions, and on the other with the assumptions implicit in the extreme versions of the modern behaviourist approach, which, with its emphasis upon informal processes, tends to suggest that formal structures have little or no significance.[3] It is therefore a type of political theory that is essentially empirical, yet which overtly recognizes the importance of certain values and of the means by which they can be safeguarded. Yet in this respect perhaps constitutionalism and constitutional theory are not so far removed from the general stream of political science as might at first be supposed. In the twentieth century the study of politics has become more empirically oriented, less overtly concerned with the justification of particular patterns of values. Nevertheless, the close relationship between the description and explanation of political institutions and of the justification of the values they reflect is an inescapable one. However strong the urge towards objectivity on the part of the student of politics, it is impossible for his work to be wholly detached from the problem of what is a "just," "desirable," or "efficient" political system, for the work must inevitably reveal the values that infuse the politics of the countries he studies and the results which their political systems produce. The more theoretical and general his approach the more likely he is, even if only through the means of classification he adopts, to take up a stance of approval or disapproval. This can be seen very clearly in many modern American works on political science.[4] There is, in fact, a complex interrelationship between the study of political institutions and the justification of particular types of governmental systems.

The doctrine of the separation of powers was for centuries the main

3. See the discussion by Giovanni Sartori, "Constitutionalism: A Preliminary Discussion," *A.P.S.R.*, Vol. LVI, No. 4, Dec. 1962.

4. See the discussion of Almond and Coleman, *The Politics of the Developing Areas*, in Ch. 10 below.

constitutional theory which claimed to be able to distinguish the institutional structures of free societies from those of non-free societies. It was by no means a value-free or neutral theory of politics, but it did claim to be based upon a demonstrable empirical proof. In the mid twentieth century, however, the doctrine has largely been rejected, either as a prescription for the creation of an efficient, free system of government suited to modern circumstances, or as a set of concepts which provides a useful vocabulary for the investigation and description of systems of government. Yet little has been offered in place of this relatively coherent body of political doctrine as a framework for the analysis of political systems. Indeed, the modern attempts to provide generalized statements about the articulation of the parts of government depend very heavily upon just those concepts of function and balance which characterized earlier constitutional theories. Clearly, however, the extent to which these earlier constitutional theories concentrated attention upon the formal structures of government, especially upon the formal relationships between executive, legislature, and judiciary, made it impossible to handle effectively the problems of distinguishing nominal from effective constitutions, and failed to give a complete picture of "constitutional government" in operation. A discussion of the nature of a limited government must encompass parties and groups, and the results of behavioural studies, as well as the operation of those structures which have traditionally occupied political theorists. At the same time we must not minimize the importance of these political institutions. The emphasis upon the study of certain aspects of behaviour has been taken, at the extreme, to suggest that "institutions" are merely formal and insignificant pieces of window-dressing, whereas in fact political institutions are the framework of rules within which the actors in political situations must normally operate and which students of behaviour tend to take for granted.

The history of the doctrine of the separation of powers provides a panorama of the complex evolution of an idea, and of the role it has played, and continues to play, in the political systems of Western countries; but, equally important, it helps us better to understand the concepts still in use today in the discussion of government, even though many of the assumptions which originally gave rise to these concepts have changed. We still talk of the legislative function or of the relation between legislation and execution, although the meaning we attach to such concepts is very different from that of earlier ages. To understand the way in which these concepts developed is an essential prerequisite for a critical reappraisal of them, in order more clearly to understand how we can best approach the analysis of political systems. Thus the idea of "function," an essential element in the doctrine, has given rise to considerable confusion in the past, and has been bitterly attacked, yet it still plays a part in our everyday vocabulary of political analysis. The apparent rejection of the doctrine of the separation of powers cannot hide the fact that many practical problems of twentieth-century government are essentially problems with which the doctrine claimed to deal, and we have seen the emergence of terms such as "quasi-judicial," "delegated legislation," or "administrative justice," which represent attempts to adapt the older categories to new problems. The truth is that we face today serious problems, both in political analysis, and in matters of practical significance in the field of government functions and their division among the agencies of government, as well as in terms of the relationships between these agencies. We are not prepared to accept that government can become, on the grounds of "efficiency," or for any other reason, a single undifferentiated monolithic structure, nor can we assume that government can be allowed to become simply an accidental agglomeration of purely pragmatic relationships. Some broad ideas about "structure" must guide us in determining what is a "desirable" organization for government.

Yet it is not simply the need to attain an academic "understanding" of the ideas and institutions of contemporary Western society that may lead us to explore the history, and analyse the content, of the doctrine of the separation of powers. For today there are practical problems of the control of government every bit as important and difficult as in the days of Locke, Montesquieu, or the Founding Fathers. Although we may be much more sceptical than they were of constitutional theories which claim to be able to set limits to the exercise of governmental power, nevertheless we cannot merely accept without question the view that the continued concentration of power into the hands of cabinets and presidents is inevitable and cannot be restrained. The concentration of *more* power into such hands, or of certain sorts of power, may be "inevitable," given certain assumptions about the military, social, and economic needs of modern societies, but which powers, how much of them, and how they can be effectively limited, are the questions we should be asking. The detail of the theories of constitutionalism may be rejected as no longer applicable, but the *ethos* of constitutionalism remains; we still believe in "limited government," but we do not yet see how the limits are to be applied in modern circumstances.

In some ways the modern problems of limiting government power are much more subtle and difficult than those of earlier centuries, when liberal constitutionalists took up the cause of freedom from the exercise of arbitrary power. Today, in the West at least, there are no absolute monarchs wielding an oppressive personal power for their own aggrandizement. If there is a danger, it is rather from a process of erosion than from a direct assault upon liberty. There is no conspiracy of power-hungry men attempting to usurp our governmental systems, and the reaction that is called for from us is not the hysterical denunciation of tyranny. The instruments of the extension of government power, both politicians and civil servants, are sincere men who see merely complex practical problems that have to be solved, and which require strong and efficient government action for their solution. A protagonist of "constitutional government" cannot simply adopt the attitude that such problems must remain unsolved in the cause of "liberty"; indeed the modern liberal constitutionalist is likely to be much embarrassed by the support of many who wish to use the banner of "constitutional liberty" to restrain government action that conflicts with their own programmes, yet who are only too ready to use such governmental power, when they themselves control it, for their own ends. Yet the problem of the control of government remains.

In this work, then, the intention is to examine one great current of constitutional thought, the doctrine of the separation of powers, together with its associated theories of mixed government and checks and balances. The history of the doctrine, fascinating in itself, can tell us much about the forces that gave it birth and shape, and by tracing its various formulations light can be thrown upon the problems with which it has attempted to grapple over the years. Following upon the history of the doctrine, an attempt will be made to analyse its content and to discuss the working institutions of Britain and the United States in the light of this analysis. In this way, it is hoped, we shall be able to disentangle the elements of the doctrine which still have relevance today for the understanding of our political systems, and the value of its recommendations for modern society. Such an investigation may lay the foundation for a wider approach to the discussion of governmental structure of the kind referred to above.

A major problem in an approach to the literature on the doctrine of the separation of powers is that few writers define exactly what they mean by the doctrine, what are its essential elements, and how it relates to other ideas. Thus the discussions about its origin are often confused because the exact nature of the claims being made for one thinker or another are not measured against any clear definition. Some kind of preliminary analysis of the doctrine and its elements is therefore necessary before we step into the vast mass of material that history presents to us. The process of definition of a "pure doctrine" of the separation of powers will of necessity have an arbitrary quality, and no doubt other opinions can be put forward as to what constitutes the "essential doctrine," on the one hand, and what are modifications of, and deviations from, it, on the other. However, no value judgement is intended in putting forward a particular definition, except to say that it is considered the most useful formulation for the purposes we have in mind. It is labelled the "pure doctrine" simply to indicate that it represents a coherent, interrelated set of ideas, with the complicating factors of related theories removed.

An initial problem in any attempt to make a clear statement of the theory of the separation of powers is the ambiguity which attaches to the word "power" in the literature. It has been used to mean the possession of the ability through force or persuasion to attain certain ends, the legal authority to do certain acts, the "function" of legislating, executing, or judging, the agencies or branches of government, or the persons who compose these agencies. A word that is used in at least five different ways within one context is clearly more of a liability than an asset in any attempt to achieve clear thinking, so that we shall as far as possible avoid its use. Wherever possible in the discussion of the ideas of political writers we shall substitute for the word "power" the appropriate synonym of person, agency, or function, according to the context but, of course, when reporting their views we shall by no means be able to do away with the term altogether. It is also difficult to avoid the use of the word in the sense of an ability, through force or influence, to achieve certain ends, and we shall use it in this sense.

A "pure doctrine" of the separation of powers might be formulated in the following way: It is essential for the establishment and maintenance of political liberty that the government be divided into three branches or departments, the legislature, the executive, and the judiciary. To each of these three branches there is a corresponding identifiable function of government, legislative, executive, or judicial. Each branch of the government must be confined to the exercise of its own function and not allowed to encroach upon the functions of the other branches. Furthermore, the persons who compose these three agencies of government must be kept separate and distinct, no individual being allowed to be at the same time a member of more than one branch. In this way each of the branches will be a check to the others and no single group of people will be able to control the machinery of the State.

This stark, extreme doctrine we shall then label the "pure doctrine," and other aspects of the thought of individual writers will be seen as modifications of, or deviations from, it. It is true, of course, that the doctrine has rarely been held in this extreme form, and even more rarely been put into practice, but it does represent a "bench-mark," or an "ideal-type," which will enable us to observe the changing development of the historical doctrine, with all its ramifications and modifications, by referring to this constant "pure doctrine." We shall not go as far as to say that only a thinker who fully subscribes to the above formulation is a "separation of powers theorist," for this would exclude most of those who have written on the subject and whose intentions were closely in line with the general *ethos* of the doctrine, but clearly all these elements must be present *to some extent* for a writer to be considered in this category. Many writers have of course contributed to the development of the theory by evolving one or more elements of it, without being separation of powers theorists—indeed, whilst rejecting the doctrine. Thus the idea of the functions of government has been evolved in large part by the theorists who implicitly or explicitly rejected other essential elements of the doctrine.

The first problem presented by the theory outlined above is its commitment to "political liberty," or the exclusion of "arbitrary power." Clearly the viability of the whole approach may turn upon the definition of liberty chosen. Thus perhaps one of the most persuasive general criticisms of the doctrine is that it has been associated with an essentially negative view of political liberty, one too concerned with the view of freedom as absence of restraint, rather than with a more positive approach to freedom. The concern to prevent the government from encroaching upon individual liberty leads to measures which weaken it to the point where it is unable to act in order to provide those prerequisites of social and economic life which are essential if an individual is to be able to make proper use of his faculties. The decline in the popularity of the doctrine in the twentieth century, both in the United States and in Britain, is closely related to the recognition of the need for "collectivist" activities on the part of government, which require a co-ordinated programme of action by all parts of the government machine. The doctrine of the separation of powers is clearly committed to a view of political liberty an essential part of which is the restraint of governmental power, and that this can best be achieved by setting up divisions within the government to prevent the concentration of such power in the hands of a single group of men. Restraints upon government are an essential part of the view of political liberty enshrined in this approach, but we shall have to consider the extent to which the proponents of the doctrine also recognized that a minimum degree of "strong government" was also necessary to political liberty, and the possible ways in which the tenets of the doctrine are compatible with the minimum needs of government action in the twentieth century. Indeed it will be assumed that the recognition of the need for government action to provide the necessary environment for individual growth and development is complementary to, not incompatible with, the view that restraints upon government are an essential part of a theory of political liberty.

The first element of the doctrine is the assertion of a division of the agencies of government into three categories: the legislature, the executive, and the judiciary. The earliest versions of the doctrine were, in fact, based upon a twofold division of government, or at any rate upon a twofold division of government functions, but since the mid eighteenth century the threefold division has been generally accepted as the basic necessity for constitutional government.[5] We may not today take the scriptural authority that John Sadler in 1649 propounded as the basis for a threefold division — "And why may not the Sacred Trinity be shaddowed out in Bodies Politick, as well as in Naturall?"[6] — but something of a mystical quality seems still to surround this method of organizing the agencies of government. In the eighteenth century the idea of a balance or equilibrium in the system of government which depended upon the ability of any two of King, Lords, and Commons being able to prevent the third from exceeding the proper limits of its power, provided a basis for the idea, at any rate, of an odd number, rather than an even number, of governmental agencies, but today such a justification seems to have disappeared entirely,[7] and in fact it is often difficult to force the manifold agencies of a modern system of government into these three categories. Nevertheless this division does reflect important, continuing elements in liberal democratic theory. The growth of three separate branches of the government system in Britain reflected in part the needs of the division of labour and specialization, and partly the demand for different sets of values to be embodied in the procedures of the different agencies, and in the representation of varying interests in the separate branches. This aspect of the doctrine, although usually assumed by political theorists rather than explicitly developed, is clearly central to the whole pattern of Western constitutionalism. The diffusion of authority among different centres of decision-making is the antithesis of totalitarianism or absolutism. Thus in the totalitarian State every aspect of the State machine is seen merely as an extension of the party apparatus, and subor-

5. As far as the actual institutional development is concerned, of course, the basis of the threefold structure had been laid in England by the thirteenth century. See F. W. Maitland, *The Constitutional History of England*, Cambridge, 1961, p. 20; see also E. Klimowsky, *Die englische Gewaltenteilungslehre bis zu Montesquieu*, Berlin, 1927.

6. *Rights of the Kingdom*, London, 1649, p. 86.

7. The connection between the theories of mixed government, of the balanced constitution, and the emergence of the threefold separation of powers is discussed in Ch. 3.

dinate to it. A continuous effort has to be made to prevent any division of the machine from developing its own interest, or from creating a degree of autonomy in the taking of decisions. In practice the pressures which operate against this attempt to maintain a single monolithic structure are too strong, for the price in inefficiency which has to be paid is too high, and of necessity rival centres emerge in the bureaucracy and in industry or elsewhere. But the "ideal" of the totalitarian state is that of a single all-embracing agency of government.

The "separation of agencies," therefore, is an essential element in a theory which assumes that the government must be checked internally by the creation of autonomous centres of power that will develop an institutional interest. Without the other elements of the doctrine of the separation of powers being present we might still expect some limitation on the ability of a single group to dominate the government if separate agencies are established. Even if the personnel of the agencies overlap, powerful influences may arise to create divergences of interest within the government. Differing procedures introduce differing values and different restraints; the emergence of an "institutional interest," the development of professionalism, the influence of colleagues and traditions, all provide the possibility, at least, of internal checks. Separate agencies, composed of distinct bodies of men even where functions are shared can be made representative of different groups in the community, and so, as with bicameral legislatures, provide the basis of a check upon the activities of each of them.

The second element in the doctrine is the assertion that there are three specific "functions" of government. Unlike the first element, which *recommends* that there should be three branches of government, this second part of the doctrine asserts a sociological truth or "law," that there are in all governmental situations three necessary functions to be performed, whether or not they are in fact all performed by one person or group, or whether there is a division of these functions among two or more agencies of government. *All* government acts, it is claimed, can be classified as an exercise of the legislative, executive, or judicial functions. The recommendation then follows that each of these functions should be entrusted solely to the appropriate, or "proper," branch of the government. This view of the "functions" of government is extremely abstract, and some of the attempts to justify this threefold division have reached a very high degree of abstraction indeed. It must be distinguished from the very different view of the functions of government which enumerates them as, for example, the duty of keeping the peace, of building roads, or of providing for defence. These we might label the "tasks" of government in order to distinguish them from the more abstract notion of function. In the period before Locke and Montesquieu firmly established this abstract view of the functions of government there were two main streams of thought, in one of which the word "power" was used to describe the function of legislating, or executing the law, and in the other a more practical view was taken of the multiplicity of government acts by dividing up the "attributes of sovereignty" into six, seven, or more categories, which included, as well as making laws, such tasks as the control of the coinage, or the appointment of standard weights and measures.[8] The triumph of the more abstract conception of the "powers" or functions of government in the eighteenth century, and its later development and ramification, was of great importance for the way in which later writers approached the problems of government structure. In the twentieth century this view of the nature of the functions of government has been subjected to severely critical analysis, but the vocabulary of the doctrine still dominates our everyday usage and our way of thinking about the nature of the operations of government.

The third element in the doctrine, and the one which sets the separation of powers theorists apart from those who subscribe to the general themes set out above but are not themselves advocates of the separation of powers, is what, for want of a better phrase, we shall describe as the "separation of persons." This is the recommendation that the three branches of government shall be composed of quite separate and distinct groups of people, with no overlapping membership. It is perfectly possible to envisage distinct agencies of government exercising separate functions, but manned by the same persons; the pure doctrine here argues, however, that separation of agencies and functions is not enough. These functions must be separated

8. See Ch. 2 below.

in distinct hands if freedom is to be assured. This is the most dramatic characteristic of the pure doctrine, and is often in a loose way equated with the separation of powers. The final element in the doctrine is the idea that if the recommendations with regard to agencies, functions, and persons are followed then each branch of the government will act as a check to the exercise of arbitrary power by the others, and that each branch, because it is restricted to the exercise of its own function will be unable to exercise an undue control or influence over the others. Thus there will be a check to the exercise of the power of government over "the people" because attempts by one branch to exercise an undue degree of power will be bound to fail. This is, of course, the whole aim and purpose of the doctrine, but it is just here that the greatest theoretical difficulty is to be found; and as a result what we have termed the pure doctrine has therefore been modified by combining it with some rather different doctrine to produce a complex amalgam of ideas about the limitations to be placed upon government authorities. The pure doctrine as we have described it embodies what might be called a "negative" approach to the checking of the power of the agencies of government. The mere existence of several autonomous decision-taking bodies with specific functions is considered to be a sufficient brake upon the concentration of power. Nothing more is needed. They do not actively exercise checks upon each other, for to do so would be to "interfere" in the functions of another branch. However, the theory does not indicate how an agency, or the group of persons who wields its authority, are to be restrained if they do attempt to exercise power improperly by encroaching upon the functions of another branch. The inadequacy of the controls which this negative approach to the checking of arbitrary rule provides, leads on to the adaptation of other ideas to complement the doctrine of the separation of powers and so to modify it.

The most important of these modifications lies in the amalgamation of the doctrine with the theory of mixed government, or with its later form, the theory of checks and balances. The connections between these theories will be examined more fully in the ensuing chapters; from an analytical point of view the main consideration is that these theories were used to import the idea of a set of *positive* checks to the exercise of power into the doctrine of the separation of powers. That is to say that each branch was given the power to exercise a degree of *direct* control over the others by authorizing it to play a part, although only a limited part, in the exercise of the other's functions. Thus the executive branch was given a veto power over legislation, or the legislative branch was given the power of impeachment. The important point is that this power to "interfere" was only a limited one, so that the basic idea of a division of functions remained, modified by the view that each of the branches could exercise *some* authority in the field of all three functions. This is the amalgam of the doctrine of the separation of powers with the theory of checks and balances which formed the basis of the United States Constitution. Related to this, and to its predecessor in time, is an amalgam of the doctrine of the separation of powers with the theory of mixed government to produce a *partial separation of functions.* That is to say that one function, the legislative, was to be shared, but other functions were to be kept strictly separate. This was a basic element in eighteenth-century English constitutionalism, the theory of balanced government. These modifications of the doctrine have of course been much more influential than the doctrine in its pure form.

The idea of a *partial* separation of functions is an important one, for it does not cease to be significant simply because it is partial. We shall consider the objections made against Montesquieu, for example, on the grounds that he did not believe in the separation of powers because he gave to the branches of government certain powers over each other which amounted to a participation in the exercise of the functions of another branch. But Montesquieu did not give each branch an *equal* part to play in the exercise of each function of government—far from it; he set up a basic division of functions and then imposed certain control mechanisms upon this fundamental division. A similar modification of the pure doctrine can be seen in the area of the separation of persons. The pure doctrine demands the complete separation of the personnel of the three branches of government, but this can be modified to introduce a *partial separation of persons.* That is to say that some people may be allowed to be members of more than one branch of the government, although a complete identity of personnel in the various branches will be forbidden. Again, as with the separation of functions, such an approach does not mean that the idea of the separation of powers has been wholly jettisoned. The *degree* of separation will become important. How many people are to be allowed to be members of more than one branch, who will they be, and what will be their function and authority? The answers given to these questions in the mid nineteenth century provided the basis of the parliamentary system of government. Thus we can see the pure doctrine as an ideal for an extreme separation of "powers," but we can then introduce various modifications and discuss their effects, and try to determine the points at which the doctrine no longer plays a significant part in the resulting amalgam.

Two further concepts must be mentioned which have not figured to any great extent in the literature on the separation of powers, but whose relation to the doctrine is of great importance. The first, an extremely ancient concept, is the idea of procedure as a check to the exercise of power. The belief that "due process" is an essential part of constitutional government is of great antiquity, and it runs parallel with ideas of mixed government and the separation of powers, but has relatively rarely been explicitly linked with those ideas and made an integral part of those theories. The second notion, a much more modern one, is the idea of *process* in government. This term, although used in different ways, indicates an awareness that government and politics do not consist in the automatic operation of formal procedures, but that there is a whole complex of activities around these procedures which determines the exact way in which they will be operated, sometimes in fact bringing about through the medium of the procedure exactly the reverse of what the procedure was intended to achieve. The concern of political studies with the role which political parties and groups play in the processes of government makes it impossible any longer to discuss a theory like that of the separation of powers purely in terms of the more formal, legal institutions of government. If the theory has anything to offer it must be able to cope with the complexities of "politics" as well as the structure of governments.

The long history of the doctrine of the separation of powers reflects the developing aspirations of men over the centuries for a system of government in which the exercise of governmental power is subject to control. It illustrates how this basic aspiration towards limited government has had to be modified and adapted to changing circumstances and needs. It offers a rich mass of material, of human thought and experience, on a subject which remains today a matter of vital importance. To follow the course of this history should be of interest in itself, but it is also an essential step towards the understanding of the ideas of the past which have helped to shape our own, and towards the reformulation of these ideas into a more coherent theoretical approach to the nature of modern constitutional government.

TWO

The Foundation of the Doctrine

THE MODERN VIEW that there are three functions of government, legislative, executive, and judicial, evolved slowly over many centuries, and it is important to realize that the categories which today form the basis for much of our thinking about the structure of government and its operation are the result of a gradual development of ideas that reflects problems concerning the nature of government, first clearly perceived in seventeenth-century England, and still today in process of being worked out. These "functions" of government reflect the response to particular problems in Western societies, and the demand for particular sets of values to be embodied in institutional structures and procedures. The roots of these ideas are to be found in the ancient world, where thinkers wrestled with similar problems, although not unnaturally their responses were somewhat different. Nevertheless the ideas of the ancients about the nature of law, and about the means of controlling power in civil societies, provided much of the basic material to which writers in later ages were to turn for ammunition in the great battles over the control of the machinery of the State.

There is an essential connection between the notion of government according to law and the concept of the functions of government. This connection forms the basis of the concern with function down through the ages, and is the explanation of the persistence of this concept in spite of the many attacks made upon it. Government according to law presupposes at least two distinct operations, the making of law, and putting it into effect. Otherwise we are left with a formless and unstable set of events which gives no basis for a constitution, or in the Greek context, for a moderate government. Thus Aristotle divided political science into two parts: legislative science, which is the concern of the law-giver, and politics, which is a matter of action and deliberation, or policy; the second part he subdivided into deliberative and juridical science.[1] The major division here between legislation and action was not the modern distinction between legislative and executive, for the Greeks did not envisage the continuous or even frequent creation of new law which is implicit in the modern view of the legislative function. The work of a divinely-inspired legislator who set the foundations of a legal system might need to be amended from time to time to meet new conditions, but this must be done only infrequently and with great caution, for frequent change could lead to the undermining of the general respect for law.[2] When he distinguished the three elements in every constitution which the good legislator must consider, Aristotle described them as the deliberative element, the element of the magistracies, and the judicial element.[3] The function of the deliberative element here did have some relation to the modern notion of the legislative function, for Aristotle described it as being dominant in the enacting of laws, and being concerned with common affairs, but this must be seen within the general view of the nature of legislation mentioned above. Furthermore, the deliberative element was also concerned with what we should call judicial and executive functions.

When we turn from the idea of distinct functions to the view that these should be entrusted to distinct groups of people, we find little to support it in Aristotle. It is true that in the *Constitution of Athens*, attributed to him, the impropriety was stressed of the execution by the council of a citizen

1. *Ethics*, VI, 8, translation by J. A. K. Thomson, London, 1955, p. 181.
2. *Politics*, II, 8, ed. by Sir Ernest Barker, New York, 1958, p. 73; and Plato's *Laws*, Book VII.
3. Ibid., IV, 14, p. 189.

who had not been tried in a law-court,[4] but this was a matter of attributing certain tasks to the proper agency, a matter of due process, rather than the assertion of a doctrine of the separation of persons. In fact the guiding principle of the Athenian Constitution, the direct participation of all citizens in all functions of government,[5] was directly opposed to any such doctrine. Thus Aristotle asserted that "Whether these functions—war, justice and deliberation—belong to separate groups, or to a single group, is a matter which makes no difference to the argument. It often falls to the same persons both to serve in the army and to till the fields"; and more specifically, "The same persons, for example, may serve as soldiers, farmers and craftsmen; the same persons again, may act both as a deliberative council and a judicial court."[6] Thus the major concern of ancient theorists of constitutionalism was to attain a balance between the various classes of society and so to emphasize that the different interests in the community, reflected in the organs of the government, should each have a part to play in the exercise of the deliberative, magisterial, and judicial functions alike. The characteristic theory of Greece and Rome was that of mixed government, not the separation of powers.[7]

The greatest contribution of ancient thought in the sphere in which we are concerned, was its emphasis upon the rule of law, upon the sovereignty of law over the ruler. It emphasized the necessity of settled rules of law which would govern the life of the State, give it stability and assure "justice for equals." "He who commands that law should rule may thus be regarded as commanding that God and reason alone should rule; he who commands that a man should rule adds the character of the beast."[8] This emphasis upon law, upon the importance of settled rules, was essential to the thought

4. *The Constitution of Athens*, Ch. 45, ed. by K. von Fritz and E. Kapp, New York, 1950, p. 118.

5. G. M. Calhoun, *Introduction to Greek Legal Science*, Oxford, 1944, pp. 32–33.

6. *Politics*, IV, 6, p. 166; see also Plato's *Laws*. See, however, the discussion by Aristotle of the division of functions among different groups on the grounds of the division of labour: *Politics*, VII, 9, pp. 300–3.

7. See Kurt von Fritz, *The Theory of the Mixed Constitution in Antiquity*, New York, 1954, p. 205; and Sir Paul Vinogradoff, *Outlines of Historical Jurisprudence*, Oxford, 1922, Vol. II, p. 128.

8. *Politics*, III, 16, p. 146.

of the Greeks, for they were deeply convinced of the importance of making proper arrangements for the way in which the State should go about its business. Constitutional provisions had for them a real significance in determining the impact of the government upon the citizen, and were not, as some modern writers seem to suggest, of little importance in determining the outcome of political situations. As a corollary of the rule of law was the assertion, in both Greek and Roman thought, of the generality of law. Aristotle insisted that "law should be sovereign on every issue, and the magistrates and the citizen body should only decide about details";[9] "law can do no more than generalize."[10] The same attitude was expressed by the Roman rule in the code of the XII Tables that no law may be passed against an individual.[11] But if the law can deal only with generalities, then there must be provision for giving discretion to those who have to apply the law to individual cases, or who have to make decisions on issues on which the law-giver, because of the generality of the language he must use, was unable to pronounce.[12] As we have seen above, the distinctions drawn here by Aristotle do not correspond exactly with the distinction between the legislative and executive functions defined in later ages, but they do deal with the difference between making a general rule on the one hand, and judging particular instances, on the other. When the conception of law as a relatively unchanging pattern was later replaced by the idea of a system of law subject to human control, then the basis of a twofold division of the functions of government was ready to hand.

The connection between modern theories of law and sovereignty and the emergence of the concepts of the legislative, executive, and judicial functions of government is very close. The idea of an autonomous "legislative power" is dependent upon the emergence of the idea that law could be *made* by human agency, that there was a real power to make law, to legislate. In the early medieval period this idea of making law by human agency

9. *Politics*, IV, 4, p. 169.
10. *Ethics*, V, 10, p. 167.
11. See H. F. Jolowicz, *Historical Introduction to the Study of Roman Law*, Cambridge, 1954, p. 25.
12. *Ethics*, V, 10, pp. 166–7; *Politics*, III, 16, pp. 145–8.

was subordinated to the view that law was a fixed unchanging pattern of divinely-inspired custom, which could be applied and interpreted by man, but not *changed* by him. In so far as men were concerned with "legislation" they were in fact declaring the law, clarifying what the law really was, not creating it. Legislation was in fact part of the judicial procedure.[13] Law was seen as the embodiment of the law of God in the custom of the community, and the actions of the King in his Council making formal statements of the law were seen as clarificatory acts. There could, therefore, be only one "function" of government—the judicial function; all acts of government were in some way justified as aspects of the application and interpretation of the law. The participation of Parliament in the promulgation of law was seen as an aspect of this judicial function of government; the High Court of Parliament advised the King upon the issues which came before him for decision, and declared the law as a court declares it, but in a more formal way, and usually, but not always, in general terms.[14] Of course, this is not to say that there was a medieval or early modern view of a "judicial function" equivalent to our modern view of that function. Rather it was a way of looking at government which encompassed the whole range of governmental acts, whilst recognizing that there were differing agencies involved, differing tasks to be performed, and differing procedures to be employed. This recognition formed the basis for the lists of the "parts of sovereignty" that were later evolved by writers on government, and again at a later stage provided the starting-point for the formulation of new distinctions of the functions of government.

Authorities differ upon the extent to which this view carried over into the later medieval and early modern periods of English history. McIlwain argues that it is a view which prevailed, among lawyers at least, as late as the assembling of the Long Parliament,[15] and certainly references to Parliament as a court are to be found throughout the seventeenth century.

13. Ewart Lewis, *Medieval Political Ideas,* London, 1954, Vol. I, pp. 4–5.

14. Ibid., Vol. I, p. 4; and C. H. McIlwain, *The High Court of Parliament and Its Supremacy,* New Haven, 1910, pp. 109–10.

15. Op. cit., p. 110. See also A. von Mehren, "The Judicial Concept of Legislation in Tudor England," in P. Sayre (ed.), *Interpretations of Modern Legal Philosophies,* New York, 1947, p. 751.

However, Professor Plucknett points out that as early as the first half of the fourteenth century the English judges frankly faced the fact that law was being made by statute, and that their decisions created generally applicable rules. There was, however, no clear distinction drawn between legislative and judicial activities, nor did they work out anything which resembled a theory of law or legislation.[16] Certainly the idea of the creation of *new* law by Parliament was well understood in the seventeenth century, although the vocabulary of an earlier age persisted. A manual of parliamentary practice of 1628 stated the position thus:[17] "In this Court of Parliament, they doe make new positive Laws or Statutes, and sometimes they inlarge some of them." The author then observed that "the Judges doe say that they may not make any interpretation against the express words of the Statute."[18] By the time of the English Civil War it is clear that one of the things which is being contended for is a "legislative power" to make or unmake the positive laws of England. Nevertheless, the fundamental conception of the government as an instrument for distributing justice persisted, for this was in fact still the major aspect of government from the point of view of the citizens. Thus when in the seventeenth century the distinction between the legislative and executive "powers" was more clearly formulated in the context of the battle between King and Parliament, it was as subdivisions of the basic judicial function of government that these two "powers" were seen. Even in 1655 Sir Henry Vane still saw the legislative and executive powers as elements of the "supreme judicature or visible sovereignty."[19]

The impulse for the emergence of a "legislative power" was given by the development of the command theory of law, the view that law is essentially the expression of an order or prohibition rather than an unchanging pattern of custom, a view that was reinforced by the emergence of the modern notion of sovereignty as the repository of the power to issue final commands. The basis for the idea of a division of functions existed in medi-

16. T. F. T. Plucknett, *Statutes and their Interpretation in the First Half of the Fourteenth Century,* Cambridge, 1922, pp. 22–25 and 31.

17. *The Priviledges and Practice of Parliaments in England,* 1628, p. 42.

18. Ibid., p. 43.

19. *A Healing Question . . . ,* London, 1655, in *Somers Tracts,* Vol. VI, pp. 310–12.

eval thought, for the idea of function played an important part in the papal theory of the division of labour among the offices of the Church,[20] and the foundation for a twofold division of government function was to be found in the division of royal power into *gubernaculum* and *juridictio*, the powers of government and jurisdiction.[21] In the exercise of the former the King was unrestrained, but in the latter he had to abide by the law. The problem of the exact articulation of these aspects of the royal power, and the desire to limit the monarch by subjecting him to a law which he did not himself make, provided the basis for the evolution of a "legislative power" independent of the will of the King. As a corollary, there emerged the idea of an executive power in the King, by virtue of which he ensured that the law was put into effect. The doctrine of popular sovereignty, which finds its roots deep in the medieval period, provided the stimulus for the progressive clarification of the idea of a legislative function, the function of delineating that law by which the ruler will be bound. The enunciation of the doctrine of sovereignty by Bodin sharpened the image of the power which was being contended. Reacting against the medieval view of the King as essentially a judge interpreting an unchanging law, a view which was still dominant in France in the sixteenth century, among lawyers at any rate,[22] Bodin asserted that the monarch had the authority to give new laws to his people, and that this was the first and chief mark of sovereignty.[23] Thus the stage was set for a seventeenth-century contest for the control of the "legislative power."

The work of Marsilius of Padua in the fourteenth century shows clearly this connection between the emergence of the concept of the legislative and executive functions and the ending of the medieval approach to the nature of law. A little earlier, Aquinas had used the distinction, taken from Aristotle and Cicero, between the ruler's functions of laying down the law and

20. W. Ullmann, *Principles of Government and Politics in the Middle Ages*, London, 1961, pp. 66–67.

21. C. H. McIlwain, *Constitutionalism, Ancient and Modern*, Ithaca, 1947, pp. 77–82.

22. W. F. Church, *Constitutional Thought in Sixteenth-Century France*, Harvard, 1941, Ch. IV.

23. Jean Bodin, *The Six Bookes of a Commonweale*, the Knolles edition of 1606, ed. by K. D. McRae, Harvard, 1962, p. 159.

of administering the political community,[24] but Marsilius went much further by placing the legislative power clearly in the people, and by rejecting the view that positive law must conform to a higher law. The legislative power thus becomes a genuine power to make laws, laws which are seen as the commands of the law-making authority. "The primary and proper efficient cause of the law," said Marsilius, "is the people . . . commanding or determining that something be done or omitted with regard to human civil acts, under a temporal pain or punishment."[25] This power to command meant that, by authority of the people, the laws must "undergo addition, subtraction, complete change, interpretation or suspension, in so far as the exigencies of time or place or other circumstances make any such action opportune for the common benefit."[26] This essentially modern view of law led Marsilius to make a distinction between the legislator and the ruler, but a distinction which was still cast in a medieval mould. For Marsilius still saw the over-all function of government as judicial, the settlement of disputes,[27] but he distinguished the "parts" of the State in a way that was quite different from that of earlier writers. Marsilius in fact provided a transition, from the classification of the parts of the State by a mere echoing of Aristotle, to a classification of government functions which forms the basis of modern thought, and which remained essentially intact until the time of Montesquieu.[28]

Initially Marsilius restated Aristotle's "parts of the State"—the agricultural, the artisan, the military, the financial, the priestly, and the judicial or deliberative, and emphasized the distinction between the priestly, the warrior, and the judicial parts and the others, the former being parts of the

24. T. Gilby, *Principality and Polity*, London, 1958, p. 292.

25. *Defensor Pacis*, translated by A. Gewirth, *Marsilius of Padua: The Defender of Peace*, New York, 1951, Vol. II, p. 45.

26. Ibid.

27. Gewirth, Vol. I, p. 173. Note that it is Marsilius' origin in the Italian republic of Padua which gives him the background for the development of a view which is so in advance of the rest of European thought. See C. W. Previté-Orton, "Marsiglio of Padua, Part II. Doctrines," *English Historical Review*, Vol. XXXVIII, No. 149, Jan. 1923, pp. 14–15, and Gewirth, Vol. I, p. 229.

28. For Marsilius' influence on later thought see Previté-Orton, op. cit., pp. 14–15; and Gewirth, Vol. I, pp. 303–5.

State "in the strict sense."[29] But then, having clarified his view of law and the role of the people as the effective legislative body, Marsilius switched to a classification of government *functions,* although one still related to Aristotle's analysis of political science in the *Ethics.*[30] "The primary efficient cause [which establishes and determines the other parts or offices of the State] is the legislator; the secondary, as it were the instrumental or executive cause, we say is the ruler through the authority granted to him for this purpose by the legislator." The execution of legal provisions is effected more conveniently by the ruler than by the entire multitude of citizens, said Marsilius, "since in this function one or a few rulers suffice."[31] Marsilius had a clear distinction of functions in mind, and he placed them in distinct hands, but his concern was with the division of labour on grounds of efficiency, not with an attempt to limit the power of government by setting up internal divisions; he was not, therefore, directly concerned with the "separation of powers" as we have defined it.[32]

An essential point about the use of the term *executive* by Marsilius, and its use by most writers until the end of the seventeenth century, is that Marsilius meant by this essentially what we should describe as the judicial function, the function of the courts headed by the ruler, which put the law into effect. He did not distinguish between the judicial and the executive functions, and indeed the idea of a separate executive function is a relatively modern notion, not being fully developed until the end of the eighteenth century. Marsilius saw the legislative and "executive" functions as branches of the over-all judicial function. This usage becomes extremely important in the seventeenth century, when the idea emerged of placing distinct functions in separate hands for the purpose of limiting the government. Although, as we shall see, the roots of the idea of a judicial "power" distinct from the executive go a long way back into seventeenth-century England, nevertheless the dominant view of the division of government

---

29. *Politics,* VII, 8, p. 299; *Defensor,* I, 5.
30. For a full discussion of this point see Gewirth, Vol. I, pp. 229–33.
31. *Defensor,* I, 15.
32. See Gewirth, Vol. I, p. 235.

functions remained a twofold division into "legislative" and "executive." The modern notion of an executive power distinct from the machinery of law enforcement through the courts, could hardly be envisaged in an age when almost the only impact of government upon the ordinary citizen was through the courts and the law-enforcement officers. The "executive power" meant, then, either the function of administering justice under the law, or the machinery by which the law was put into effect. Bishop John Poynet, in 1554, expressed this conception very clearly in his *Short Treatise of Politicke Power*. Writing of the authority to make laws and of the power of the magistrates to execute them, he commented that "lawes without execution, be no more profitable, than belles without clappers." James Harrington in 1656 defined the "executive order" as that part of the science of government which is styled "of the frame, and course of courts or judicatories,"[33] and Algernon Sidney, writing as late as 1680, defined the executive function in terms which we should today consider purely judicial. He divided government between "the sword of war" and "the sword of Justice." "The Sword of Justice comprehends the legislative and executive Power: the one is exercised in making Laws, the other in judging controversies according to such as are made."[34] Milton wrote of the need for the execution of law by local county courts so that the people "shall have Justice in their own hands, Law executed fully and finally in their own counties and precincts,"[35] and in 1656 Marchamont Nedham defined those who held the executive power as the constant administrators and dispensers of law and justice.[36]

It is not clear how far seventeenth-century writers included in the "executive power" aspects of the government machine other than the courts, or included ideas about those functions of government which we should today label "executive" or "administrative," rather than "judicial." Certainly many writers mention non-judicial officials and non-judicial functions of

33. *The Commonwealth of Oceana*, London, 1656, p. 27.

34. *Discourses Concerning Government*, London, 1698, III, 10, p. 295.

35. *The Ready and Easy Way to Establish a Free Commonwealth*, in *Works*, Amsterdam, 1698, Vol. II, p. 795.

36. *The Excellencie of a Free State*, London, 1656, p. 212.

the prince. In 1576 Bodin had listed nine major "powers of sovereignty," including the power to declare war or peace, to coin money, and to tax,[37] and in ensuing years similar lists were provided by other writers. Sir Walter Ralegh in producing his list made a distinction between judges and other "magistrates," such as "lieutenants of shires, marshals, masters of horse, admirals, etc."[38] However, the only consistent, abstract formulation of the "powers of government" was the same basic legislative-executive division that Marsilius had made. These lists produced by Bodin, Ralegh, Hobbes, and Pufendorf, among others, provided perhaps a more realistic and practical approach to the listing of the functions of government than the more abstract categories which finally triumphed under the influence of Locke and Montesquieu, but it was clearly an essential step in the development of the doctrine of the separation of powers for the "powers of government" to be consolidated into a few categories rather than to comprise an extensive list which would also include what we have called the "tasks" of government. Broadly speaking, then, we must see the seventeenth-century abstraction of the functions of government as a twofold one in which "executive" was generally synonymous with our use of "judicial," and in fact in the latter part of the century the two words were used synonymously.[39] Let us then turn, appropriately enough, to John Milton to sum up the dominant seventeenth-century view of the functions of government: "In all wise Nations the Legislative power, and the judicial execution of that power have bin most commonly distinct, and in several hands. . . . If then the King be only set up to execute the Law, which is indeed the highest of his Office, he ought no more to make or forbidd the making of any law agreed upon in Parliament; then other inferior Judges, who are his Deputies."[40]

This is essentially a hierarchical view of government functions in which the over-all judicial function is divided into the legislative and "executive" functions. Such a view naturally tends to inhibit the development of the idea of a threefold division, with a judicial "power" and an execu-

---

37. *Six Bookes*, I, 10.
38. *The Prince, or Maxims of State*, in *Somers Tracts*, Vol. III, p. 286.
39. See for example Sidney's use of the terms, *Discourses*, III, 10, p. 296.
40. *Eikonoklastes*, London, 1649, p. 57.

tive "power" ranged alongside a legislative "power," because in one sense judicial and executive are virtually synonymous, and in another sense the executive function is derived from and subordinate to the fundamental judicial power. It took a century, from the English Civil War until the mid eighteenth century, for a threefold division to emerge fully and to take over from the earlier twofold division. However, the notion of an independent "judicial power," at any rate in the sense of the independence of the judges, goes back beyond the seventeenth century, and during the English Civil War the basis was laid for a threefold division which never quite managed fully to materialize. The need for independent judges had, of course, been emphasized in the sixteenth century, by George Buchanan in 1579,[41] and by Richard Hooker who asserted that the King ought not to be the judge in cases of felony or treason, because in such cases he is himself a party to the suit.[42] In the seventeenth century both Philip Hunton and Sidney, among others, asserted the need for an independent judiciary, but the view that there were three distinct "powers" of government seems to have emerged during the English Civil War.

At this time there was a great deal of discussion both about the position of the judges, and (rather more) about the judicial powers of the two Houses of Parliament. Thus in 1647 Henry Ireton argued that "the two great powers of this kingdom are divided betwixt the Lords and the Commons, and it is most probable to me that it was so that the judicial power was in the Lords principally . . . the legislative power principally in the Commons."[43] A tract of 1654 demanded a form of government in which Parliament would refrain from the exercise of that "jurisdictive power" which they had taken upon themselves or their committees for "the judgement of particular causes concerning mens persons and estates,"[44] and the *Humble Petition and Advice* of 1657 placed limits upon the exercise of judi-

41. *De Jure Regni apud Scotos,* English edn. of 1680, p. 50.
42. *The Laws of Ecclesiastical Polity,* VIII, 7, ed. by B. Hanbury, London, 1830, Vol. III, p. 317.
43. In the Putney Debates; see *Puritanism and Liberty,* ed. by A. S. P. Woodhouse, London, 1950, p. 119.
44. *The Declaration of the Free and Well-Affected People of England,* in *Memorials of the English Affairs,* 1682, p. 601.

cial power by the "other House."[45] The problem of the "judicial power" clearly agitated men's minds, and the well-known division of legal writs into original, judicial, and executive provided some sort of analogy for the situation which faced them. In 1649 John Sadler used the analogy of the writs to develop a threefold category of government functions, legislative or original, judicial, and executive: "If I may not grant, yet I cannot deny, Originall Power to the Commons, Judiciall to the Lords; Executive to the King."[46] In 1657 the most effective use of the analogy was made by George Lawson who also formulated the threefold legislative, judicial, and executive division of functions and argued it out to a much greater extent than Sadler.[47] The use of these terms by Sadler and Lawson was, however, far from the modern usage. They saw the judicial and executive functions, respectively, in terms of judgement, and the carrying out of the sentence of the Court, and in this connection it is interesting to note that for this reason both placed the judicial function *before* the executive, as is only logical, whereas in the later threefold division of the functions of government it is usual to arrange them with the executive second and the judicial last.

A rather more remarkable attempt to refashion the pattern of thought about the functions of government was made in a work dated 1648, entitled *The Royalists Defence,* and attributed to Charles Dallison, Recorder of Lincoln, and a moderate royalist. Dallison made a clear distinction between the "soveraigne power of government," which is in the King, and the authority to judge the law. "The Judges of the Realme declare by what Law the King governs, and so both King and people [are] regulated by a known law,"[48] and he justified this division of functions on the ground that the judges are "unconcerned." Dallison avoided the use of the term "executive power," for

45. Article 5. S. R. Gardiner, *Constitutional Documents of the Puritan Revolution,* Oxford, 1906, p. 452.

46. *Rights of the Kingdom,* London, 1649, p. 86. F. D. Wormuth describes this as a "political sport," but in view of the context in which it occurs and the other writings which occur at this time it is difficult to see it quite in this light. See *The Origins of Modern Constitutionalism,* New York, 1949, pp. 60–61.

47. *An Examination of the Political Part of Mr. Hobbs his Leviathan,* London, 1657, p. 8. This work is more fully discussed in Ch. 3.

48. *The Royalists Defence,* p. A2.

he was in fact splitting the seventeenth-century executive function into two parts, the functions of governing and of judging. In addition, Parliament had the function of making the law, so he arrived at a threefold division of government functions very close to that which came to be generally accepted a century later. "It is one thing to have power to make Lawes, another to expound the Law, and to governe the people is different from both."[49] We shall return to this work when we come to look more closely at the other elements in the development of the doctrine of the separation of powers, but for the moment it is sufficient to note that the cauldron of the Civil War had hastened the evolution of the ideas of the functions of government and formed them into two main streams. The dominant conception was still the twofold division of executive and legislative which reflected an older tradition about the functions of government, but the first elements of a new basis for ideas about these functions were being developed. Although after the Restoration Locke adhered to the older tradition, it was with modifications, and the ideas of the Civil War were not lost, for the elements in Sadler, Lawson, and Dallison all reappear in the theory of the balanced constitution at the opening of the eighteenth century.

By the time of the English Civil War one of the fundamental elements in the doctrine of the separation of powers, an abstract classification of the functions of government into two or three categories, had been developed to a high degree under the impact of the contest between King and Parliament. However, something more was needed before the doctrine of the separation of powers could be fully developed, that is to say the idea that these functions must be placed in distinct hands, in those of separate people or groups of people. This idea did not spring into men's minds from nowhere; they were led into it through the process of adapting the familiar, age-old theory of mixed government to the problems they faced, and finally, when they found this theory to be no longer relevant to their situation, they replaced it with the new ideas it had fathered. It is therefore to the theory of mixed government that we shall now turn our attention.

The theory of mixed government is logically quite distinct from the doc-

49. Ibid., p. 70.

trine of the separation of powers, yet these two theories have been closely connected with each other over much of their history. The theory of mixed government is much the older of the two, as old as political theory itself, and it remained a part of English political thought well into the nineteenth century. The two doctrines are not merely logically distinct, but to a considerable extent they conflict with each other. The theory of mixed government was based upon the belief that the major interests in society must be allowed to take part jointly in the functions of government, so preventing any one interest from being able to impose its will upon the others, whereas the theory of the separation of powers, in its pure form, divides the functions of government among the parts of the government and restricts each of them to the exercise of its appropriate function. Furthermore the class basis of the theory of mixed government is overtly lacking from the doctrine of the separation of powers. But it would be quite untrue to say that the latter does not have any class *bias*. The theory of mixed government had as its central theme a blending of monarchy, aristocracy, and democracy, and, as we shall see, there is a tendency to equate these, in some stages of the development of the doctrine of the separation of powers, respectively with the executive, judicial, and legislative "powers." The latter doctrine assumes that the legislature will, or may, be taken over entirely by the democratic element, and that checks upon "mob rule" will therefore have to be applied by branches of the government largely or wholly outside the legislature. The battle for the control of the "chief mark of sovereignty," the legislative power, may be won by the proponents of popular rule, but there are methods of ensuring that this power is subjected to limitations, one of them being the maintenance of the bicameral system, another the decentralization of the government under a federal constitution, and the third the separation of functions among different agencies so that movements of popular opinion in the legislature can be slowed down by the other branches of government.

This is the "shift" which took place between the two doctrines, but of course it was not achieved overnight. The succession was effected extremely slowly, as slowly in fact as the success of "democracy" in the make-up of the legislature was recognized. In mid-seventeenth-century England,

the later doctrine was quickly born and adopted in the revolutionary conditions which temporarily destroyed the monarchy and the House of Lords,
but this was a situation too far ahead of its time to be maintained. The
Restoration introduced a long period in which the two doctrines were combined in an amalgam which recognized the class element in the control of
the legislative power. When democratic movements gained the ascendency
the theory of mixed government dropped out, and the theory of the separation of powers became the major theory of constitutional government, but
only rarely in its pure form. In the Constitution of the United States we find
it combined with the idea of "checks and balances," the old theory of mixed
government stripped of its class connotations, and now in a subordinate
role. The later history of the relationship between the doctrine and democratic theory became more and more involved as the twentieth century accepted the principle of democracy, only to find that the centre of power had
again moved away from legislative bodies towards the executive branch.

Though the theory of mixed government is not logically connected with
the theory of the separation of powers, the former theory provided sug-
gestive ideas which formed the basis of the new doctrine. Both theories
are concerned with the limitation of power by instituting internal checks
within the government. The terminology of the "powers" of government
came to be applied both to the representative organs of mixed government,
and to the functionally divided agencies of the separation of powers. The
threefold mixture of monarchy, aristocracy, and democracy was a particular case of a general theory of limited government, in which the people
exercised a check upon the monarch, or some other combination of powers
prevented the dominance of a single person or group.[50] In the ancient world
the theory of mixed government figured principally in the work of Aristotle, Plato, and Polybius. Plato emphasized the belief in moderation and
compromise which is the basis of the theory. Too much power concentrated
in one place, either in nature or in the State, leads to the "wantonness of

50. See Otto von Gierke, *Natural Law and the Theory of Society*, ed. by Sir Ernest Barker,
Boston, 1957, pp. 238–9; C. M. Walsh, *The Political Science of John Adams*, New York, 1915, pp.
25–26; and M. L. Levin, *The Political Doctrine of Montesquieu's Esprit des Lois: Its Classical Background*, New York, 1936, pp. 127–30.

excess"; only in the observance of the mean can arbitrary rule be avoided.[51] The preservation of Sparta was the consequence of its constitution, which consisted of a dual kingship, a council of Elders, and the Ephors elected by lot, and was thus "compounded of the right elements and duly moderated."[52] Later Plato asserted that democracy and monarchy are the "two mother forms of states from which the rest may be truly said to be derived." Both forms of these are required in some measure.[53] He emphasized the basic element of the theory of mixed government—its frank recognition of the class basis of society. But the classes, with their potentially conflicting interests, must be harmonized through a constitutional structure ensuring that each class can play a part in the control of those decisions in which its interests will be affected.[54]

Aristotle criticized Plato's formulation of the theory by insisting that we shall "come nearer the truth" if we seek to combine more than two of the basic forms in a State, for "a constitution is better when it is composed of more numerous elements,"[55] although Aristotle himself wrote elsewhere of the best form of State as a combination of democracy and oligarchy.[56] He placed even more emphasis than Plato upon the value of the mean in politics, and upon the need for each part of the State to have a proportionate share in government: "Proportion is as necessary to a constitution as it is (let us say) to a nose."[57] Indeed it is a criterion of a proper mixture of democracy and oligarchy that it should be capable of being described indifferently as either.[58] Aristotle also made a closer examination of the class basis of the mixed constitution, stressing the moderating influence of a middle class, and equating the feasibility of establishing a successful mixed constitution with the existence of an extensive middle class in the State.[59]

---

51. *Laws*, III, *The Dialogues of Plato*, translated by B. Jowett, 3rd edn., Oxford, 1892, V, 72.
52. Ibid., V, 73.
53. Ibid., V, 75.
54. *Laws*, IV; ibid., V, 98.
55. *Politics*, II, 6, pp. 60–61.
56. Ibid., IV, 9, p. 178.
57. Ibid., V, 9, p. 232.
58. Ibid., IV, 9, p. 177.
59. Ibid., IV, 11, pp. 180–4.

Polybius, in his analysis of the Roman Republic, developed the theory to a greater degree than his predecessors, and, by adapting the theory to encompass the elected consuls of Rome as the "monarchical" element, he provided the pattern for the transformation of the theory of mixed government into a theory of checks and balances, in which the agencies of government might not all have a distinct "class" to represent, but might, of themselves, provide an institutional check within the government structure.[60]

The importance of the ancient theory of mixed government for our theme, therefore, is its insistence upon the necessity for a number of separate branches of government if arbitrary rule is to be avoided. This view of the "separation of agencies" was not based upon the efficiency to be achieved by the division of labour, nor upon the functions which are "proper" to different branches of the government. The various branches were expected to play a part in all the tasks of government, but their representative character enabled them to prevent the use of that power in ways which would be prejudicial to the interests they represented. As we have seen, this "separation of agencies" is an essential part also of the doctrine of the separation of powers. The theory of mixed government opposed absolutism by the prevention of the concentration of power in one organ of the State, and the doctrine of the separation of powers starts from the same assumption. The vitally important step in the emergence of the latter doctrine is the attribution of distinct functions to the agencies of government, and in this respect the critical difficulty of the transition from one to the other is that the three agencies of the mixed government, King, aristocratic assembly, and popular assembly, do not correspond to the executive, legislature, and judiciary in the doctrine of the separation of powers. The transition takes a long while in the development of the theory, and is the explanation of much of the confusion about the nature of the functions of government that we have to some extent already observed.

There are, therefore, two major steps to be noted in the transformation of this ancient theory into the modern doctrine of the separation of powers.

60. For a full discussion of Polybius see K. von Fritz, *The Theory of the Mixed Constitution in Antiquity*, New York, 1954. Von Fritz points out that it is impossible to separate the interests of the consuls from those of the aristocracy at the time with which Polybius is concerned.

First, the insistence that particular agencies should be restricted to particular functions. Second, the emergence of a recognition of an independent judicial branch, which will take its place alongside King, Lords, and Commons. The first of these is achieved in the seventeenth century, the second is fully attained only in the eighteenth. It is these developments we must now trace.

The ancient tradition of mixed government was transmitted to medieval Europe, was echoed and restated, and was used to support the view that royal power should be subjected to feudal and popular restraints. In the thirteenth century Aquinas reproduced the Aristotelian concept of mixed government as a *regimen bene commixtum* of monarchy, aristocracy, and democracy. He did so, however, in a very formal way, and the medieval references to the theory seem to have little depth or reality until in England the institutional and political developments provided a factual basis for the theory to work upon.[61] With the development of representative institutions in England, however, the idea of the best system of government as a combination in which King, Lords, and Commons shared the power of government developed, until the theory of mixed government became, in seventeenth-century England, the dominant political theory of the age. In the late fifteenth century Sir John Fortescue saw three kinds of government: *dominium regale,* absolute monarchy, *dominium politicum,* republican government, and *dominium politicum et regale,* a mixed form, which was the pattern of English government.[62] Bishop Poynet, in 1556, asserted that men had long judged "a mixte state" to be the best of all, and that where it had been established it had been the most stable form of government.[63] Sir Thomas Smith, a few years later, saw the English system as a threefold mixture. The Commonwealth of England is "governed, administered, and manured by three sortes of persons"—the Prince, the gentle-

61. In this connection note Janet's remark that Aquinas reproduces the theory of mixed government "sans la bien comprendre." (Janet, *Histoire de la science politique,* Paris, 1887, Vol. II, p. 376.) Wormuth describes the doctrine during the medieval period as "a literary tradition which only occasionally . . . touched the political life of the time." (Op. cit., pp. 30–31.)

62. *The Governance of England: The Difference between Absolute and Limited Monarchy,* ed. by C. Plummer, Oxford, 1885.

63. *A Short Treatise of Politicke Power,* Strasbourg, 1556.

men, and the yeomanry.[64] However, neither Fortescue, Poynet, nor Smith was fired by the desire to limit the power of the monarch to the exercise of only one specific function of government. For it is this demand, the requirement that the monarch be limited to the execution of the law, which is the beginning of the doctrine of the separation of powers, and at the same time the beginning of the end for the doctrine of mixed government. At the end of the sixteenth century it was in France rather than in England that this demand seemed to be on the point of being formulated, for in France the extreme difficulties of the Huguenots were such as to stimulate such an approach. François Hotman, writing in 1573, insisted that the French system had historically been a mixed government, that the power of making laws had, till a century earlier, been entrusted to a "public annual council of the nation," later called the three estates, and he seemed to be on the verge of demanding that the King be limited to the "administration of the Kingdom."[65] The authors of the *Vindiciae contra Tyrannos* were also striving towards a similar position.[66]

In mid-seventeenth-century England the theory of mixed government became a commonplace of political writers, until, indeed, in 1648 Sir Robert Filmer, himself the strongest opponent of the theory, could write: "There is scarce the meanest man of the multitude but can now in these daies tell us that the government of the Kingdome of England is a Limited and Mixed Monarchy."[67] Charles I made an acknowledgment of the doctrine in his reply to the Nineteen Propositions of 1642. It was at the height of the theory's popularity that the attempt to make it fit the circumstances after 1641 brought forth a new and different theory, the separation of powers. The theory of mixed government was from the earliest times intended to

64. *De Republica Anglorum*, ed. by L. Alston, Cambridge, 1906, pp. 46–47. Smith wrote the book in the 1560's but it was first published posthumously in 1583. See also J. W. Allen, *A History of Political Thought in the Sixteenth Century*, Part II, Ch. X, especially the references to Sir John Hayward and Sir Thomas Craig.

65. *Franco-Gallia*, 2nd English edn., London, 1721, pp. 64–65 and 77.

66. See G. P. Gooch, *English Democratic Ideas in the Seventeenth Century*, New York, 1959, p. 17.

67. *The Anarchy of a Limited or Mixed Monarchy*, London, 1648, p. 1. On the importance of the theory in this period see Z. S. Fink, *The Classical Republicans*, Evanston, 1945.

provide a check to the exercise of arbitrary power by the balancing of the "powers of government" in a constitution. But before the intense political activity of the mid seventeenth century, the exact articulation of the elements of a system of mixed government had not been explored. The outbreak of open hostilities between King and Parliament prompted attempts by the protagonists of the theory to define the relative functions of the elements of the government. The failure in the sphere of practical politics of the attempt to find a workable compromise resulted in the creation of conditions in which mixed government seemed irrelevant, and the way was clear for the new doctrine.

The impact upon constitutional thought of the dispute between King and Parliament can be seen in the way in which two major theories of government, which were to act and react upon each other for the next two centuries, were formulated in the 1640's and rapidly developed into impressive schools of thought. The theory of mixed government, which earlier had been rather vague and lacking in articulation, was refashioned in Charles I's *Answer to the Nineteen Propositions* into the basis of the later theory of the balanced constitution. Published in 1642, some months before hostilities actually started, the *Answer* presented a combination of mixed government and a division of the tasks of government among its parts in such a way that they might each check the power of the others.[68] At the same time Parliament's supporters were evolving a theory of government that placed less stress upon mixed government, and which depended heavily upon an abstract formulation of the powers of government and the allocation of these functions, in fact the basis of the theory of the separation of powers.

The starting point in a discussion of the "transition" from the theory of mixed government to the doctrine of the separation of powers may begin with the work of Charles Herle, a supporter of the Parliamentary cause. Writing in 1642, Herle made quite explicit the scattered suggestions in the earlier literature that the three elements of the mixed constitution, King,

---

68. On the *Answer* see Corinne Comstock Weston, *English Constitutional Theory and the House of Lords, 1556–1832*, London, 1965, pp. 23 ff.

Lords, and Commons, had a *co-ordinate* status.[69] But did this mean that all three were co-ordinate in the exercise of all the functions of government? Dr. H. Ferne, Herle's opponent, asked if Herle was asserting that the two Houses were co-ordinate in both the enacting and the execution of law.[70] In reply Herle took the position that whilst the two Houses had a status superior to the King's in the exercise of the legislative power, and the representative character of the Commons gave it the "largest share" of this power, it was above all in the execution of the laws that the Houses had a status co-ordinate with the King's. Of what use, Herle asked, is the co-ordinate status of the Houses in the making of law, if they have not the power to ensure the execution of the laws?[71] Herle, of course, was not proposing a division of functions into distinct hands; quite the reverse. He was using the ancient idea of a fusion of the functions of government, rather than their separation, in order to justify the action of Parliament in taking up arms against the King. However, the emphasis he placed upon the co-ordinate status of King, Lords, and Commons, was to be reflected in later writing, where the problem was to ensure that the person entrusted with the executive power was not merely a subordinate official but had a position and autonomy of his own. He was also one of the first to raise the basic problem of any theory which divides functions among agencies: if the legislature were restricted solely to passing legislation, what guarantee would it have that its commands would be properly carried out?

In 1643 one of the most competent of Parliament's supporters, Philip Hunton, undertook in his *Treatise of Monarchy* to clarify the theory of mixed government and the relationships between the parts of the mixed State. Hunton was the most sophisticated and systematic of the supporters of mixed government in this period, working out in detail its differing categories, although it should be mentioned that he started from a belief in the indivisibility of the "power of magistracie."[72] Hunton took a rather different line from Herle's, a line which led him much closer to a theory

69. C. Herle, *A Fuller Answer to a Treatise Written by Dr. Ferne.*
70. *Conscience Satisfied . . .* , Oxford, 1643, pp. 13–14.
71. *An Answer to Dr. Ferne's Reply*, London, 1643, pp. 29–30 and 35.
72. *A Treatise of Monarchy*, London, 1643, p. 5.

of functionally divided agencies of government. First, he established the difference between "mixed government" and a "mixed monarchy." Governments can be simple or mixed, limited or absolute. Mixed governments are always limited governments, although the reverse is not true. The general term "a mixed State" is, however, only appropriate when "the highest command in a state by the first constitution of it is equally seated" in all three of the elements of the government.[73] This, then, is broadly what Herle had been describing. However, a more stable State is likely if one of the three elements is "predominant," and where this is so the predominant element "gives the denomination to the whole." Thus England is a "mixed monarchy."[74] In such a mixed monarchy the sovereign power must be originally in all three elements, for this is the reason for the mixture, that "they might confine each other from exhorbitance."[75] Nevertheless, if it is to be a stable mixed *monarchy*, then there cannot be full equality in the three estates. "A power then must be sought wherewith the Monarch must be invested, which is not so great as to destroy the mixture; nor so titular as to destroy the Monarchy."[76]

Hunton's answer to this problem was to suggest a number of powers which, vested in the King, would give him this position of limited dominance. The first of these, and the most important, was the executive power. The "power of magistracie," said Hunton, has two degrees; it is "Nomotheticall or Architectonicall and Gubernative or Executive."[77] The King can be made "head and fountain of the power which governs and executes the established laws, so that both the other States . . . be his sworn subjects, and owe obedience to his commands, which are according to established lawes."[78] The King is, then, to be the executive, but what of the legislative power? Hunton argued that in England the legislative (as well as the taxing) power is "mixed," and that all three agencies of government must take part in the "making and authentick expounding of lawes,"[79] but he did suggest that the King should suspend the use of his "negative voice" in legislation.[80] Herle had made a similar demand, but this taken together with Hunton's

---

73. Ibid., p. 25.
76. Ibid., pp. 25–26.
79. Ibid., p. 46.

74. Ibid.
77. Ibid., p. 5.
80. Ibid., p. 79.

75. Ibid.
78. Ibid., p. 26.

investing the King with the sole executive function, leads to a theory of the separation of powers and is the end of mixed government as formerly understood. Hunton intended this as a purely temporary measure, for elsewhere he was quite definite about the legislative role of the monarch, but this antagonism to the royal veto power was soon to swell into a demand for the abolition of all participation by the King in the process of legislation.

Hunton experienced difficulty with just those problems which were also to perplex later ages; for here we see emerging the first attempts to evolve that peculiarly English approach to the idea of sovereignty which has so often been misunderstood. In England the acceptance of the idea of a single source of sovereign power led to the concept of parliamentary supremacy, but this did not mean, and never has meant except during the reign of the Long Parliament, that the *representative element* of Parliament exercised an unrestrained power to carry out all the tasks of government. Parliamentary supremacy is not the same as *gouvernement d'assemblée,* for the "King-in-Parliament" has always been composed of a number of distinct elements with certain autonomous powers. There is a real sense in which, even today, the spirit of "mixed government" lives on in the British system of government, through the recognition of the autonomous position of the government in relation to the elected representatives of the people or of the political parties. In the seventeenth century Hunton attempted to formulate his own reconciliation between the idea of a single source of sovereign power and the need to divide authority between the King and the members of the legislature. He argued that the supreme power is *either* "the Legislative or the Gubernative," but that the legislative is the chief of the two.[81] The title of supremacy attaching to the King, he asserted, is fully justified by his being the *sole* fountain of executive power, whilst retaining a share of the legislative.[82] Four years later Filmer was to maintain that by requiring the King to govern according to the law Hunton relegated him "from the legislative to the executive power only."[83] The argument that Hunton formulated, however, confused though it may be, is one of the basic ele-

81. Ibid., p. 26.
82. *A Vindication of the Treatise of Monarchy,* London, 1644, pp. 38–39.
83. Op. cit., p. 24.

ments in the constitutional theory which became firmly established after the Revolution of 1688–9. Locke and the theorists of the early eighteenth century faced exactly the same problem that Hunton had tackled, and basically their solution was the same as his, except that their emphasis was upon the supremacy of Parliament, whereas Hunton had looked for a formula to satisfy a "supreme monarch."

Herle and Hunton were writing during the early stages of the Civil War, when it was thought that some such formula could be found; a formula which would leave the basic constitutional position of the monarchy unaltered. The emphasis upon the executive role of the monarch was intended to make sure that the law was supreme, an empire of laws and not of men, as Harrington was later to express it. But as time went on Charles's intransigence gave rise to the demands for greater restraints upon royal power, and ever more insistent came the demand that the royal veto should be restrained, suspended, or abolished. In 1647 the House of Commons resolved that the King was bound "for the time being . . . by the duty of his office, to give his assent to all such laws as by the Lords and Commons assembled in Parliament, shall be adjudged to be for the good of the kingdom."[84] The Levellers and others put forward the view that the King's coronation oath bound him to execute the law, and that his participation in the passage of legislation was a breach of this oath.[85] Milton put it more strongly still. "We may conclude that the Kings negative voice was never any law, but an absurd and reasonless Custom, begott'n and grown up either from the flattery of basest times, or the usurpation of immoderat Princes."[86] Thus the demand that the King be the sole executive was transformed into the very different demand that he be solely concerned with execution.

The idea that the King should be limited to the exercise of the executive function was now well understood. However, the momentous years of 1648 and 1649 introduced ideas which were to ensure that it was not

84. S. R. Gardiner, *History of the Great Civil War, 1642–1649*, London, 1901, Vol. IV, p. 9.

85. Wildman in the Putney debates of 1647: see *Puritanism and Liberty*, p. 109; also John Selden, *An Historical and Political Discourse of the Laws and Government of England*, edn. of 1688/9, p. 53.

86. *Eikonoklastes*, London, 1649, p. 53.

merely a doctrine of undiluted legislative supremacy which was to emerge from the Revolution. It was no longer possible to see the problems of England as simply King versus Parliament. The divisions within the parliamentary camp were deep and serious. Presbyterians, Independents, and Levellers, were deeply hostile to each other, and other sectarian divisions loomed ominously. The use of the power of Parliament by one group of its supporters to threaten other groups had shown to men who had previously seen only the royal power as a danger, that a parliament could be as tyrannical as a king. Men who had previously been Parliament's strongest supporters became its strongest critics. Milton in his *Character of the Long Parliament,* probably written in the late 1640's but not published until 1681, expressed bitter disappointment with the rule of the Presbyterians who dominated the Long Parliament;[87] that Parliament governed the country by appointing a host of committees dealing with all the affairs of state, confiscating property, summoning people before them, and dealing with them in a summary fashion.[88]

The second stage in this development, therefore, was the realization that legislatures must also be subjected to restriction if individual freedom was not to be invaded; restricted not so much in the exercise of a genuinely legislative function, but in their attempts to *govern* and so to interfere with the lives and property of individuals who displeased the members of the legislature. Ireton expressed this distrust of legislatures in the Whitehall debates of 1649,[89] and, from a different point of view, the authors of the *Agreement of the People* of 1648 demanded that the "Representatives intermeddle not with the execution of laws, nor give judgement upon any mans person or estate, where no law hath been before provided."[90] One bitter opponent of this aspect of Parliament's activities was the Leveller leader, John Lilburne, who had come personally into conflict with Parliament and its committees. In a tract aimed at the Commons he proposed that "whereas

87. For a discussion of the authenticity and dating of this short work see Fink, op. cit., Appendix B, pp. 193–4.

88. See E. Jenks, *The Constitutional Experiments of the Commonwealth,* Cambridge, 1890, pp. 4 and 11–12.

89. *Puritanism and Liberty,* p. 172.

90. *Foundations of Freedom: or an Agreement of the People,* London, 1648, article VI, 6.

there are multitudes of complaints of oppression, by committees of this House, determining particular matters, which properly appertains to the cognizance of the ordinary Courts of Justice . . . therefore henceforth, no particular cause, whether criminal or other, which comes under the cognizance of the ordinary Courts of Justice, may be determined by this House or any Committee thereof. . . ."[91] In a later pamphlet directed against the Council of State he asserted that "the House itself was never (neither now, nor in any age before) betrusted with a Law executing power, but only with a Law making power."[92] It was true that Parliament had the power to set up courts of justice, but only "provided that the Judges consist of persons that are not members of their House, and provided that the power they give them be universal," not a power directed at particular individuals.[93] This is a new and vitally important element, which resulted from the experience of the Long Parliament during the Civil War. The assertion of the generality of law is thousands of years old, but this was something more. Not only was law to be couched in general terms, but also the *legislature* must be restricted to the making of law, and not itself meddle with particular cases. This was indeed a major step in the development of the separation of powers. The Levellers also made the same demand for the exclusion of placemen from the legislature which was to characterize the eighteenth century, and which is an essential aspect of the doctrine.

All the elements of the pure doctrine of the separation of powers were now present in the minds of the men who witnessed the struggle between King and Parliament, and who had come to fear the arbitrary rule of either. The idea of two or three abstractly-defined, inclusive functions of government was well known; the desire to place limits to the power of both King and Parliament was strong in the minds of men of very different points of view. All that was needed for the doctrine was the idea that the agencies of government should be restrained by each being confined to the exercise of its own appropriate function. We have already quoted Milton's remark

91. *The Ernest Petition of Many Free-born People*, reprinted in *A Declaration of Some Proceedings*, London, 1648, pp. 28–29.
92. *The Picture of the Councel of State*, 1649, p. 6.
93. Ibid., p. 8.

in the *Eikonoklastes* that in all wise nations the legislative and executive powers "have bin most commonly distinct and in several hands,"[94] and in *The Rights of the Kingdom* John Sadler, later Master of Magdalene College, Cambridge, argued that the three Estates should be "more exactly bounded in their severall sphers."[95] The three powers of government, legislative, judicial, and executive, "should be in Distinct Subjects; by the Law of Nature, for if Lawmakers be judges, of those that break their Laws; they seem to be Judge in their own cause: which our Law, and Nature it self, so much avoideth and abhorreth, so it seemeth also to forbid, both the Lawmaker, and the Judge to Execute. . . ."[96] Sadler's view of the executive function was, as we have seen, not our modern one, but in other respects his grasp of the principles of the doctrine of the separation of powers was clear.

However, important as are the sources of the ideas we have examined, so far all of them are fragmentary, with little coherent theoretical development or elaboration. Probably the first person to undertake an extended treatment of this kind was Charles Dallison, if he is indeed the author of the remarkable work *The Royalists Defence* of 1648. Dallison not only had a threefold division of functions in mind, but the whole of this work was devoted to the argument that a satisfactory system of government can result only from the placing of these distinct functions of government in separate hands so that "every one is limited, and kept within his owne bounds."[97] His work may be seen as an attempt to combine the theory of mixed government as it had been set out in Charles I's *Answer to the Nineteen Propositions,* with the emphasis upon the more abstract and thoroughgoing separation of functions which had been stressed by parliamentary writers. It represented perhaps the clearest and most comprehensive statement that had then been made of the relationship between separating the functions of government, placing them in different hands, and balancing the parts of government. Dallison argued that the King must retain the "sovereign power of government" but he must not have the authority to judge the laws. "The Judges of the Realme declare by what law the King

94. Op. cit., p. 57.
96. Ibid., p. 87.

95. Op. cit., p. 86.
97. *The Royalists Defence*, p. 126.

governs, and so both King and people [are] regulated by a known law."[98] Neither does Parliament have the power to determine individual points of law. It is neither fit for such work, nor was it instituted for that purpose. "Those things . . . are the office of the Judges of the Realme."[99] Parliament's function is "only to make new laws,"[100] whilst the King is "our onely Supream Governour."[101] Dallison echoed Hunton's argument that the King's supremacy is assured by his having the sole executive authority, using the rather strange argument that "neither the making, declaring or expounding the Law, is any part of Sovereignty."[102]

There are thus three agencies of government, each with its appropriate function. Furthermore, it is because the branches of government retain "their own proper authority without clashing with, or encroaching each upon other" that both King and subjects are preserved in their just rights.[103] "Whilst the Supremacy, the Power to Judge the Law, and the Authority to make new Lawes, are kept in severall hands, the known Law is preserved, but united it is vanished, instantly thereupon, and Arbitrary and Tyrannicall power is introduced."[104] Dallison's objection to the concentration of power in the hands of Parliament was just as strong as his objection to the King's governing outside the known law. Attempts by Parliament to govern are as inefficient as they are improper.[105] The Parliament has established a tyrannical regime by attempting to govern, and to judge individual causes. The only remedy is to restore the King, and the "foresaid Authorities are returned into their proper places, and againe divided into severall hands." At once "every Court, Assembly and person, not only enjoyes its own Authority, but is limited within its own bounds; no man then is permitted to be both Judge and Party."[106]

The Royalists Defence was, then, a lengthy and well-developed plea for the separation of powers, but it was not the pure doctrine as we have defined it, for in one major respect it adhered to the theory of mixed government. The King was to retain the authority with the assent of the two

98. Ibid., p. A2.
101. Ibid., p. 60.
104. Ibid., p. 80.

99. Ibid., pp. 47–48.
102. Ibid., p. 70.
105. Ibid., pp. 84–85.

100. Ibid., p. 56.
103. Ibid., p. 63.
106. Ibid., p. 136.

Houses, to alter the law and to make new laws.[107] The King, therefore, played an essential part in the exercise of the legislative function, although Dallison for the most part, but not consistently, wrote of him as if he were outside, and separate from the Parliament. In this respect Dallison's book is closely related to the theory of the balanced constitution of the eighteenth century, except that he had a clear view of the independence of the judges, exercising a quite distinct function of government, whereas the later writings are much less clear upon this point.

By the year of the execution of Charles I, then, the doctrine of the separation of powers, in one form or another, had emerged in England, but as yet it was still closely related to the theory of mixed government. It had been born of the latter theory but had not yet torn itself away to live an independent life. For a short time, in the years of the Protectorate, it did achieve this independent existence, although in an atmosphere so rarified and unreal that it soon returned to its parent for succour. The execution of the King, and the abolition of the House of Lords, destroyed the institutional basis of the theory of mixed government, and any justification of the new constitution which was to be framed for England would have to rest upon a different theoretical basis. In 1653 the *Instrument of Government* instituted England's first written Constitution, and in the official defence of this constitution, entitled *A True State of the Case of the Commonwealth,* we find the doctrine of the separation of powers standing on its own feet, claiming to be the only true basis for a constitutional government. The Cromwellian Constitution embodied, on paper at least, a separation of persons and functions. The supreme legislative authority was vested in a Lord Protector and the people assembled in Parliament;[108] but although this seemed to echo the old theory of mixed government in relation to the legislative function, the role of the Protector in legislation was limited to a suspensive veto of twenty days. If after that period the Lord Protector "hath not consented nor given satisfaction," then, upon a declaration of Parliament, bills became law without his consent.[109] Thus, formally, the legislative function was placed squarely in the hands of Par-

107. Ibid., p. 60.   108. Art. I.   109. Art. XXIV.

liament. However, the Protector was given the power to pass ordinances between the sittings of Parliament, and in practice this gave him the power to rule without Parliament's prior consent. Article II of the *Instrument* provided that "the exercise of the chief magistracy and the administration of the government . . . shall be in the Lord Protector, assisted with a council." The Protector was given only a limited power of dissolution, provision was made for the automatic calling of Parliaments every three years, even if the Protector failed to issue the summonses, the great officers of state were to be chosen with the approbation of Parliament, and the Parliament did not have the power to alter the fundamental structure of the Constitution.

The broad outlines of the *Instrument* reflect, therefore, the earlier dissatisfaction with both a tyrannical King and a tyrannical Parliament, and set up a legislature and an executive, each with a degree of independence of the other, each with its proper function. The major aspect of the *Instrument* that clashed with the doctrine of the separation of powers was the position of the Council of State, for this body was entrusted with a part in the exercise of the executive "power," but there was nothing to prevent its members being drawn from among the members of the legislature. Major-General John Lambert, who is usually credited with being the foremost author of the *Instrument*, was both a member of the first Parliament of the Protectorate, and of the Council of State. This reflects a general tendency during the seventeenth century and the early eighteenth century to concentrate upon the head of the executive in discussions of the separation of functions, and to pay less attention to the people who served him.

The defence of the *Instrument*, published in 1654, no doubt had official backing, for Cromwell shortly afterwards made an approving reference to it in a speech before Parliament.[110] Although the title-page refers to "divers persons" as the source of the work, its authorship was contemporaneously attributed to Marchamont Nedham,[111] a journalist who was apparently prepared to write in support of any cause if the price was right, or if cir-

110. *His Highness Speech to the Parliament*, Jan. 1655, p. 20.
111. In *Sighs for Righteousness* . . . , London, 1654, p. 24, the authorship of *The State of the Case* is attributed to "*Mercurius Politicus,* the more than supposed author thereof." This was the name of the newspaper which Nedham edited at the time, and was his pseudonym.

cumstances made it prudent. Undoubtedly the work paints a rosier picture of the *Instrument* than the facts warranted, but this is not our main concern. We are interested rather in the justification that was put forward, and the ideas upon which it was based.

The tract commenced with a justification of the Army, first in the execution of the King for his tyrannous ambitions, and second in dissolving the Parliament, which contrary to their hopes had "wholly perverted the end of Parliaments," largely by their "unlimited arbitrary decisions at Committees."[112] The recently proposed Biennial Bill would, if passed, not merely have kept the supreme authority in Parliament constantly in session, but would have offended against "the grand secret of liberty and good government" by placing in the same hands the supreme power of making laws and of putting them into execution, "which placing the legislative and executive powers in the same persons, is a marvellous in-let of corruption and tyranny."[113] The secret of liberty is "the keeping of these two apart, flowing in distinct channels, so that they may never meet in one (save upon some transitory extraordinary occasion)."[114] The combination of these two powers in a single person is tyranny enough, but the consequences are abundantly more pernicious when they are in the hands of an assembly, for such a multitude can more easily escape responsibility. The ancient wisdom of the English had been to "temper" their government by placing the supreme law-making power in the people in Parliament, and entrusting the execution of law, "with the mysteries of government," in the hands of a single person and his council.[115]

Each of the two arms of government, the writer insisted, must be limited to its proper sphere. The continuance of military government would have been dangerous because it would have left both the instituting and executing of the law "to the arbitrary discretion of the souldier," who would be apt to execute his own will in place of law, without check or control.[116] On the other hand Parliament should not meddle in the executive sphere. It is

112. *A True State of the Case of the Commonwealth,* London, 1654, p. 9.
113. Ibid., p. 10.
114. Ibid.
115. Ibid., pp. 10–11.
116. Ibid., p. 22.

contrary to the nature of Parliament, whose great work is to make laws, to take upon itself the administration of law and justice.[117] "The ordinary preventive physick in a state against growing maladies, is execution and administration of law and justice, which must be left to its officers."[118] Parliaments were never intended to execute the law, "it being the peculiar task of inferior courts."[119] In future the government would be managed by an elected person, so that all power, both legislative and executive, will flow from the community.[120]

This, then, was no mere casual reference but a well-developed theory of government. It did not have the *finesse* of Dallison's work of six years before, but in part this is because it was a starker doctrine, closer in many ways to our ideal type of the pure doctrine. The analysis is, it is true, in terms of two functions of government only, with little or no realization of the importance of a judiciary independent of the executive. It was almost completely stripped of the paraphernalia of mixed government; only in the final paragraph of the fifty-two-page document is a passing appeal made to the ancient theory. The author then in his final words returned to his main theme, emphasizing in the clearest possible way the theory of government upon which he relied: "And whereas in the present Constitution, the Legislative and Executive Powers are separated. . . ." However, no consideration was given to the dual role the Council was to play in this Constitution, as the adviser to the Protector in the exercise of the executive function, and as the only control by Parliament over the Protector. This work came very near indeed to a purely negative view of the constitutional checks necessary to prevent arbitrary rule. The complicated inter-relationships which characterized the work of Montesquieu a century later were almost completely absent.

In 1656 Marchamont Nedham published *The Excellencie of a Free State*, in which the same argument was developed in words that echo the *True State of the Case*. This is a full-length work on government and the discussion of the separation of powers is no longer the central peg upon which the book hangs, but is merely one of the principles upon which it says a

117. Ibid., p. 17.
119. Ibid., p. 25.

118. Ibid., p. 23.
120. Ibid., pp. 28–29.

free state must be built. "A fifth Errour in Policy hath been this, viz. a permitting of the Legislative and Executive Powers of a State, to vest in one and the same hands and persons."[121] The reason is evident, for if the law-makers "should be also the constant administrators and dispensers of law and justice, then (by consequence) the people would be left without remedy in case of injustice."[122] The book was not without importance, for it was reprinted in France during the Revolution and was, according to John Adams, well-known in colonial America.[123] In the same year Harrington published his *Commonwealth of Oceana,* in which he formulated a separation of functions among the agencies of government. The Senate, composed of an aristocracy of merit, must propose the laws, which are then to be affirmed or rejected by the people or their representatives. Harrington continued: "Wherefore as these two orders of a Common-wealth, namely the Senate and the People are Legislative, so of necessity there must be a third to be executive of the Lawes made, and this is the Magistracy." Thus The "Common-wealth" consisted of "the Senate proposing, the People resolving, and the Magistracy executing."[124] In contrast, however, to the political theory of the *Instrument of Government,* Harrington's emphasis lay upon mixed government, and for all its revolutionary overtones, was more in sympathy with Charles I's *Answer,* or Hunton's *Treatise,* than with Nedham's *True State of the Case of the Commonwealth.* Nevertheless, in a petition of 1659, which Toland attributes to Harrington, the vocabulary of the mid-seventeenth-century doctrine of the separation of powers was clearly deployed,[125] and, indeed, by that year, when the future constitution of England was being so hotly debated, the doctrine of a twofold separation of powers had become a commonplace.[126]

121. *The Excellencie of a Free State,* London, 1656, p. 212.

122. Ibid., p. 213.

123. P. Zagorin, *A History of Political Thought in the English Revolution,* London, 1954, pp. 124–5.

124. Op. cit., p. 15.

125. *The Humble Petition of Divers Well-affected Persons . . . ,* London, 1659, pp. 7–9.

126. See for example: *Lilburn's Ghost . . . ,* London, 1659, pp. 5–6; *A Declaration of the Parliament Assembled at Westminster,* London, 1660, pp. 4–10; *A Needful Corrective or Ballance in Popular Government,* p. 5; *XXV Queries: Modestly and Humbly . . . ,* London, 1659, p. 13.

Thus, some thirty years before the publication of Locke's *Second Treatise*, the doctrine of the separation of powers had been evolved as a response to the problems of the Civil War and the Commonwealth, and had, in its seventeenth-century formulation reached a high degree of development. But the Protectorate failed and the *Instrument of Government* itself had failed long before the end of the Protectorate, being replaced by a much more monarchical constitution, the *Humble Petition and Advice* of 1657. With the Restoration there was a return to the theory of mixed government as the basic constitutional pattern of England, but from then on the doctrine of the separation of powers could not be ignored; it had become a part of the intellectual climate of Western constitutionalism. A few years later John Locke's treatment of the "powers of government" must be seen in the light of an assumption that his readers were well acquainted with such a doctrine, rather than as if he were hesitantly presenting a new concept of government.

The doctrine of the separation of powers was well developed by the end of the Protectorate, but it was a relatively unsophisticated doctrine, the bare essentials without much appreciation of the complex inter-relationships of a system of government the functions of which are divided up among several agencies. During the ensuing century it was to be combined with its related theories to produce a much more complex theory of constitutionalism, but in the mid seventeenth century it suffered from the fact that no real attempt was made to work out the arrangements needed to ensure that deadlock did not result from the separation of functions in separate hands. In this respect the doctrine reflected the realities of politics under the Protectorate. The systems of influence or party, which made a set of functionally divided institutions workable at a later date, could not operate in the bitterly divided England of the period just before the Restoration. It had been proved that neither a Protector nor a Parliament could govern alone, and that neither could develop the necessary relationships with the other that would have made the system workable. The politics of deadlock, implicit in the pure doctrine of the separation of powers, made people look to a version of the traditional system of government, but a version in which the elements of the newer doctrine must have a place.

THREE

The Theory of the Balanced Constitution

THE DOCTRINE OF the separation of powers was born and developed in the particular circumstances of the Civil War and the Commonwealth, but with the Restoration, such an extreme theory, which had no necessary place for a King with a share in the legislative power, nor any place for a House of Lords, would of necessity have to be replaced with a view of the nature of government more suited to the restored monarchy. The materials for such a refurbishing of constitutional theory lay to hand. The old doctrine of mixed government, temporarily cast aside, could be rehabilitated. But it could never again be held in the simple undifferentiated version of the pre–Civil War era. The battle between King and Parliament had resulted in two fundamentally important modifications of this doctrine. First, the King, although he still had powerful and important prerogatives, must acknowledge the supremacy of the law, and, therefore, of the legislature. It is true that he formed an essential part of the legislature, and could at least have a veto upon the proposed laws to which he would have to conform, but the principle of legislative supremacy was, by the end of the seventeenth century, a firmly established fact of English government and of English political thought. The installation by Parliament of William and Mary was an impressive confirmation of the extent of the power of the legislature. Furthermore, it was a legislature which clearly made and unmade the law of England, in spite of the archaic language sometimes used to describe its composition and procedures. Second, the basic ideas of the doctrine of the separation of powers (although, of course, it was not known by that name) were part of the general currency of English political thought. The "pure doctrine" had, naturally, to be rejected, but its main points were not forgotten. They had to be woven into the constitutional theory, which became a complex amalgam of mixed government, legislative supremacy, and the separation of powers. Potentially contradictory though these ideas might be, it was the achievement of the years between 1660 and 1750 that they were blended into a widely accepted theory of English government—the theory of the balanced constitution. This theory dominated the eighteenth century in England and formed the basis for the views Montesquieu put forward in his chapter of the *Esprit des Loix* on the English Constitution.

A major problem in the reconciliation of the theory of mixed government with the doctrine of the separation of powers lay in the fact that, in its initial formulations during the Commonwealth period, the latter had been expressed in the vocabulary of the prevailing legislative-executive division of functions, whereas the theory of mixed government, which dealt principally with the *agencies* of government, propounded a threefold division into King, Lords, and Commons. Charles I in his *Answer to the Nineteen Propositions* had associated a distribution of the tasks of government between its parts, with control over the exercise of power, distinguishing also between the making of laws, and "the Government according to these laws" which was entrusted to the King. At the same time Charles had stressed the importance of the "judicatorie power" of the House of Lords. On the other hand, the development by the anti-royalists of a theory of government which was independent of the theory of mixed government had been based largely upon the two abstractly-defined functions of legislating and executing. If the ancient theory of mixed government was now to be closely associated with some form of abstract functional differentiation, then at least three functions were necessary. The gradual emergence of the judges as an independent branch of government merely complicated matters, for there was no place for them in the theory of mixed government, and they constituted a *fourth* agency. Nevertheless, the idea of an autonomous "judiciary power" continued to develop on the basis of the discussions of the judicial functions of Parliament, and particularly of the Lords, which had figured so large in the mid seventeenth century. It is the irony of this period, therefore, that the emergence of separate judicial and executive "powers" was not associated very closely with the establishment of the independence of the judges, formally achieved in 1701 with the Act of Settlement, but rather the judicial function came to be associated with the House of Lords as a final court of appeal and as the court in which impeachments should be tried. The requirements of the theory of mixed government virtually demand this solution. The importance of this aspect of the problem can be seen in the work of the Reverend George Lawson, produced just as the Protectorate was dying.

Lawson's work is extremely important in the understanding of the way in which the old twofold division of government functions was broken up into three categories. It is a complicated story. The old view of the "executive power" was fundamentally a conception of the carrying of the law into effect through the machinery of the courts, with the ruler at the head of the system. Since Bodin there had been a clearer view of the fact that more than this was involved in government, and clearly there was a pressure for a reformulation of the "powers" of government. Lawson drew upon the idea of a judicatory power in the Lords, upon the analogy of the judicial writs that Sadler had used, and upon the idea of "government," the power of the sword, which Dallison had developed, and which had, of course, a long history, reaching back to the medieval notion of *gubernaculum*. In 1657 and 1660 George Lawson published two important works on politics, in which he developed the threefold division of the functions of government. "There is a threefold power civil, or rather three degrees of that power. The first is legislative. The second judicial. The third executive."[1] But Lawson acknowledged that the term "executive power" was used in two quite distinct

1. *An Examination of the Political Part of Mr. Hobbs his Leviathan*, London, 1657, p. 8.

senses. He formulated two "acts of Majestie." These were *legislation* and *the execution of laws made.*[2] This was the traditional division of powers. But then he distinguished the two senses of *execution*. The second act of Majesty, he said, "is not the execution of the Judges sentence, for that follows as a distinct act of Jurisdiction." Execution understood as an act of Majesty has a far wider connotation, reaching "all acts that tend to the execution of the Lawes." As "Officers" and "Judgement" are essential to this, therefore the executive power comprehends both the right of appointing officers and the "administration of justice."[3] The latter is the "Power of Jurisdiction," and this he sub-divided again into, first, "acts of Judgement, more strictly so called," which are the hearing and decision of causes upon evidence, and, second, execution. The latter includes the infliction of penalties, dispensations of judgement, suspension of execution, and pardons.[4] "From all this it is evident," said Lawson, "that all *Jura Majestatis* may be reduced to the Legislative, Judicial and Executive Power, if we understand Judicial and Executive in a larger sense, than they are commonly taken."[5] In his earlier work, Lawson had elaborated on the need for an executive power in this second sense. The supreme power to command presupposes three things—understanding, practical judgement, and an "executive power and a coactive force" that would ensure the obedience of the subject to laws and judgements made under them.[6] In all government there must be a sword, which is "an outward coactive strength and force," for "Legislation, Judgement and Execution by the Sword, are the three essential acts of supreme Power civil in the administration of the State."[7]

Thus Lawson had split up the old "executive power" into two, and had given the name "executive" to that part of the functions of government concerned with the carrying out of judgements, rather than the carrying into effect of the law as a whole. He wrote of "execution by the sword" in a way which conjures up a picture of the headman's axe. Thus he distin-

2. *Politica Sacra et Civilis,* London, 1660, p. 38.
3. Ibid., p. 39.
4. Ibid., p. 41.
5. Ibid.
6. *An Examination of . . . Leviathan,* p. 7.
7. Ibid., p. 8.

guished between two ways of viewing punishment; either "as defined by the judge on judicial evidence," or "as inflicted by the minister of execution."[8] This was the power of punishing of which Pufendorf wrote a few years later in 1672, and which his French translator, Barbeyrac, rendered as *le pouvoir coactif.*[9] The term "coactive power," the power to coerce, which both Lawson and Barbeyrac use, had long had currency in both France and England. Lawson had developed, therefore, a new view of the functions of government, closer to the present-day view than the older twofold division, but still a long way from our present conception of the executive function, for he still saw it as essentially a step in the judicial procedure of applying largely penal laws. He also foreshadowed the division of the internal and external functions of the Crown that Locke made although he did not give them the status of separate "powers" of government. Like Locke, however, he insisted that these two aspects of the executive power should be in the same hands. "One and the same sword must protect from enemies without and unjust subjects within. For the sword of war and justice are but one sword."[10]

Lawson's views about the distribution of these functions among the agencies of government show a rather strange inconsistency. In his *Examination of . . . Leviathan* published in 1657 Lawson saw clearly the distinction between mixed government and a separation of functions among distinct agencies of government. He rejected the idea of a mixed monarchy, although there might be a mixture in the *exercise* of the three powers of government by which a monarch might be limited. It seemed to Lawson to be irrational to place the legislative power in three co-ordinate parties, each with a negative vote, for to do so would "retard all businesses." It is much more "agreeable to the rules of reason" to place "the universal power originally in the general assembly without any negative, the judicial in the Lords, and the executive in the King."[11] In his *Politica Sacra et Civilis,* how-

8. Ibid., p. 114.

9. *Le Droit de la Nature et des Gens,* VII, 4, translated by J. Barbeyrac, Amsterdam, 1712, Vol. II, p. 260. Pufendorf lists a number of other parts of sovereignty, but the first three are the legislative power, the power of punishing, and the judicial power, in that order.

10. *An Examination of . . . Leviathan,* p. 8.

11. Ibid., pp. 141–2.

ever, published in 1660, Lawson stated the view that the proper constitution of England was one in which the *Jura Majestatis* were not divided between King, Lords, and Commons but rather one in which "the personal Majesty primary was in King, Peers and Commons joyntly: in the whole assembly as one body."[12] Lawson here emphasized that the legislative power was jointly held by all three parts of the government, and portrayed this as the mark of a free State.[13] It is difficult to make any assumptions about the relation of this change of view to the political events of the time, because the *Politica*, although published after the *Examination of . . . Leviathan*, was first written *before* the earlier published work, but may well have been revised for publication in 1660.[14] Nevertheless, Lawson's work does provide an important bridge between the ideas of the Civil War and Protectorate and the theory of the balanced constitution of the eighteenth century. He emphasized the supremacy of the legislative power—"the foundation and rule of all acts of administration"[15] and all the major elements of that later theory are to be found in these two works, though by no means fully related in the eighteenth-century fashion. Thus Lawson's main contribution to the transition to the modern conception of government lay in the relationships between mixed government and the separation of powers; the next step in the development towards the theory of the balanced constitution was the reconciliation of legislative supremacy with the ideas of the separation of powers. This step was taken by John Locke.

In discussions of the origin of the doctrine of the separation of powers the argument as to whether Locke or Montesquieu was the founder of the doctrine has dominated the scene. It is clear, however, that neither of these great thinkers can claim to be the source of the doctrine, although by incorporating it into their works in one form or another they placed the great

---

12. *Politica*, p. 95.

13. Ibid., p. 97.

14. See the Preface to the *Examination of . . . Leviathan*. A. H. Maclean argues that the date of the composition of *Politica* must have been 1657, or, more probably, "a year or two earlier." ("George Lawson and John Locke," *The Cambridge Historical Journal*, Vol. IX, No. 1, 1947.) However, the work might well have been revised in or after 1657. See, for example, the reference to the *Humble Petition and Advice* of 1657 on p. 109.

15. *Politica*, p. 97.

weight of their influence behind it, and so gave it a place in political theory that otherwise it might not have attained. Part of the difficulty experienced in assessing the importance of the elements of the doctrine of the separation of powers in Locke's work is that the antecedent thought upon this subject has not been given its full weight. Mr. Peter Laslett in his recent Introduction to Locke's *Treatises* argues that Locke was not concerned to put forward a theory of the defence of liberty by the placing of distinct functions in separate hands, and that Montesquieu and the American Founding Fathers took him up in a sense he had not intended to convey.[16] It is, of course, certainly true that Locke did not maintain the "pure doctrine" of the separation of powers, but combined it with other elements of his theory that modify it very considerably. However, if we approach the *Second Treatise* afresh, with the ideas of Hunton, *The State of the Case*, Lawson, and others, in mind, the role of the elements of the doctrine, all of which are to be found in Locke's work, will be more clearly seen, for it is suggested that the ideas behind the doctrine are an essential part of his thought, and that there is no reason to believe that the Founding Fathers did not understand what he had to say.

The inter-relationship of the "powers" of government may be considered to be one of the central considerations of Locke's theory. The crucial middle chapters of the *Second Treatise* are taken up with a discussion of this problem. Clearly the establishing of different categories of governmental authority and function is at the heart of what Locke has to say. He, like Marsilius, was concerned to establish over-all popular control of government, and to subject the magistrate to the law. At the same time, like Marsilius, he recognized that the day-to-day concerns of government cannot be dealt with efficiently by the people or their representatives. The demand that the ruler must conform to known established laws, and that these laws derive their authority from the consent of the people, leads inevitably to the old division of functions, the making of law and its execution. Locke found the origin of the legislative and executive authority in the powers man had in the state of nature. The first of these was to do whatever he

16. *Two Treatises of Government*, ed. by P. Laslett, Cambridge, 1960, pp. 117–19.

thought fit for the preservation of himself and others within the limits of the Law of Nature. This was the origin of the legislative power.[17] The second power man had in the state of nature was the power to punish crimes committed against the Law of Nature. This was the origin of the executive power.[18] However, man's inability effectively to exercise these rights led to the establishment of civil society. For the state of nature was deficient in certain crucial respects. There was no established, settled, known law, there was no known and indifferent judge with authority to determine differences according to the established law, and there was no "power to back and support the sentence when right and to give it due execution."[19] This threefold division of legislation, judgement, and execution is in conception an exact parallel of the categories George Lawson had developed, but for the most part in the earlier chapters of the *Second Treatise* Locke remained true to the older twofold division of functions and authority. Thus when the inconveniences of the state of nature give rise to civil society, said Locke, the legislative and executive powers are established: the former when men give up the power of doing whatever they think fit for their own preservation, to be regulated instead by the laws of the society; the latter by their giving up their power to punish others, in order to create a power to enforce these laws.[20] Locke still saw the main function of the State as essentially judicial; the function of the legislature was to "dispense justice," and the State was, therefore, the judge which had been lacking in the state of nature, so that, like earlier writers, Locke had an equivocal view of the judicial function. He emphasized very strongly the need for independent, impartial judges, and the distinction between giving judgement and the execution of judgement is clearly seen; but when at a later stage he made an all-inclusive statement about the "powers of government" he did not formulate a separate judicial power alongside the legislative and executive powers, or, more accurately, he did not divide the functions of the enforcement of the law into two independent "powers" as Lawson had done.

17. Op. cit., IX, 128–9, and VII, paras. 87–88.
18. Ibid., IX, paras. 128 and 130.
19. Ibid., IX, paras. 124–6.
20. Ibid., IX, paras. 130–1.

Locke's most important modification of the conception of the functions of government lies in his attempt to divide up the "executive power" in a different way, that is to take into account the different nature of the internal and external responsibilities of the government. The power of making war and peace, and of entering into alliances, was the second mark of sovereignty, according to Bodin's formulation,[21] and Lawson and Sidney had both distinguished the sword of war from the sword of justice. Locke distinguished a third "power," the federative power, "which one may call natural, because it is that which answers to the power every man naturally had before he entred into society."[22] The federative power contains the "Power of War and Peace, Leagues and Alliances, and all the Transactions, with all Persons and Communities without the Commonwealth."[23] Locke made it quite clear that the distinction between the executive authority proper, and that part of it which he labels "federative," is one of *function* only, for he immediately insisted that though they "be really distinct in themselves, yet they are hardly to be separated, and placed, at the same time, in the hands of distinct Persons."[24] Why then bother to make this distinction? The importance of what Locke has to say here has generally been overlooked, and the failure, particularly on the part of Montesquieu, to take up this point, has contributed greatly to the inadequacy of the classification of government functions. Locke was writing at a time when the supremacy of the legislature over the policy of the government *in internal affairs* was being established. The King must rule according to law. But Locke realized, as did others before him, that the control of internal affairs, particularly taxation, presented very different problems from those of external affairs. In matters of war, and of treaties with foreign powers, it was not possible, and still is not possible today, to subject the government to the sort of prior control that is possible in domestic matters. As Locke put it, "Though this federative Power in the well or ill management of it be of great moment to the commonwealth, yet it is much less capable to be directed by antecedent, standing, positive Laws, than the Executive."[25] Thomas Jefferson was later

21. *Six Bookes,* I, 10.   22. *Second Treatise,* XII, para. 145.
23. Ibid., XII, para. 146.   24. Ibid., XII, para. 148.
25. Ibid., XII, para. 147.

to say, "Foreign affairs is executive altogether," for by then the distinction Locke had in mind was already almost lost. The point Locke insists upon is that in foreign affairs the government is *not* "executing," it is *not* putting law into effect, it is carrying out a quite distinct function. This function is in the hands of the "executive," which gets its name from *one* of its major functions, that of putting the law into effect, so that, as Locke says, the two functions "are always almost united"; but that they are very distinct and very different functions cannot be too strongly emphasized.

Thus far, then, the emphasis is upon the division of the functions of government, and the general approach is not very different from the doctrine stated by Marsilius three and a half centuries earlier. Like Marsilius, Locke argued that the legislative and executive powers should be placed in separate hands for the sake of efficiency, on the grounds of the division of labour. Laws which take only a short time to pass need "perpetual execution," and therefore there must be an executive always in being.[26] The representative nature of the legislature renders it too large, and therefore too slow, for the execution of the law.[27] But Locke was writing shortly after the experiences of the Civil War and the Interregnum, and his view of the "separation of powers" went a great deal further than that of Marsilius of Padua. All that Locke writes is redolent of the experiences and writings of the period since 1640.

There is some confusion in the *Second Treatise* which makes it seem as if Locke was unconcerned about the form a government might take, arguing that the community might dispose of the powers of government in any way that it pleased. Yet there can be no doubt that Locke accepted the seventeenth-century version of the doctrine of the separation of powers, that the legislative and executive powers must be placed in distinct hands if liberty is to be preserved. He was quite emphatic about this. He asserted that "in all moderated Monarchies, and well-framed Governments" the legislative and executive powers are in distinct hands.[28] He made this idea the central point for the rejection of absolute monarchy, because the absolute monarch, "being supposed to have all, both Legislative and Ex-

26. Ibid., XII, para. 144.   27. Ibid., XIV, para. 160.
28. Ibid., XIV, para. 159.

ecutive Power in himself alone, there is no Judge to be found, no Appeal lies open to any one, who may fairly, and indifferently, and with Authority decide."[29] The very nature of limited government required that these two functions and authorities should not be in one man's hands. Nor was it safe to place both in the hands of a representative legislature. There must be a separate executive power, for, Locke frequently insisted, the legislature must only concern itself with the passing of general rules, and it should not be constantly in session. "Constant frequent meetings of the Legislative, and long Continuations of their Assemblies . . . could not but be burthensome to the People, and must necessarily in time produce more dangerous inconveniences."[30] If the legislature does not limit itself to the promulgation of standing laws, but assumes to itself the power to rule by "extemporary Arbitrary Decrees," then the purpose of the creation of the State, the ending of the situation in which everyone is "Judge, Interpreter and Executioner" of the Law of Nature, is confounded.[31] "In Governments, where the Legislative is in one lasting Assembly always in being, or in one Man, as in Absolute Monarchies, there is danger still, that they will think themselves to have a distinct interest from the rest of the Community."[32] Locke had that distrust both of Kings and of legislatures which made him unwilling to see power concentrated in the hands of either of them. For this reason, as well as for reasons of efficiency and convenience, he concluded that the legislative and executive powers should be in separate hands. "It may be too great a temptation to humane frailty, apt to grasp at Power, for the same Persons who have the power of making Laws, to have also in their hands the power to execute them, whereby they may exempt themselves from Obedience to the Laws they make, and suit the Law, both in its making and execution, to their own private advantage."[33] There could hardly be a clearer statement than this of the essence of the doctrine of the separation of powers.

However, the main objection to seeing Locke as a proponent of the doctrine, even in a modified form, is his emphatic assertion of legislative

29. Ibid., VII, paras. 90–91.
31. Ibid., XI, para. 136.
33. Ibid., XII, para. 143.

30. Ibid., XIII, para. 156.
32. Ibid., XI, para. 138.

supremacy. "There can be but one supream power, which is the legislative, to which all the rest are and must be subordinate."[34] Is this view consistent with the doctrine, which not merely places the separate functions in distinct hands, but implies a certain co-ordinate status for the *agencies* of government? The *complete* subordination of one agency of the government to another is surely inconsistent with the doctrine. In fact Locke took great pains to make it clear that no single agency of government is omnipotent, that the two main branches of the government, the legislature and the executive, do have an autonomous status.

Part of the difficulty here arises simply from the ambiguity of the term "power," which Locke used in two senses in this context, and also because he used "legislative" both as an adjective and as a noun. When he insisted upon the supremacy of the legislative power, Locke was clearly making two distinct points. First, the legislative function is prior to the executive, and the latter must be exercised according to the rules which result from the exercise of the former. This is, of course, an essential part of democratic theory. The supremacy of the *law* is certainly a part of the doctrine of the separation of powers. Second, Locke was saying that there is a clear sense in which the executive branch must be subordinate to the legislature. "For what can give Laws to another, must needs be superior to him."[35] Again this is perfectly consistent with the doctrine; the executive must not make laws, he must carry out the commands of the legislature. But this is as far as Locke goes. By legislative supremacy he does not mean that the executive is a mere office-boy, to be completely subordinated to the legislature *in the exercise of his own functions.* On the contrary the power of the legislature is itself limited to the exercise of *its* own proper functions.

Locke, and his contemporaries, argued that although the "legislative power" is supreme, even absolute, it is not arbitrary and unlimited. Locke listed four bounds to the extent of the legislative authority, and the most important of these for our purposes is his assertion that "the legislative, or supream authority, cannot assume to its self a power to rule by extemporary arbitrary decrees, but is bound to dispense justice, and decide the

34. Ibid., XIII, para. 149.   35. Ibid., XIII, para. 150.

rights of the subject by promulgated standing laws, and known authoris'd Judges."[36] This is exactly the objection to the activities of the Long Parliament that formed the basis of the distrust of legislatures in and after the Civil War. The nature of the legislative authority is tied to settled procedures of legislation, and does not extend to "extemporary dictates and undetermined resolutions."[37] The legislative authority is the authority *to act in a particular way.* Furthermore, Locke argued, those who wield this authority should make *only* general rules, "They are to govern by promulgated establish'd Laws, not to be varied in particular cases."[38] Locke stressed the fact that the legislative power was delegated from the people, and developed what was later to become in the United States the doctrine that the delegation of legislative power to non-legislative bodies is unconstitutional.[39] Thus "legislative supremacy" for Locke was clearly very different from the right of a legislature to do anything it wished in any way that it wished.

The other side of the coin was the position of the executive agency. Locke emphasized the independent autonomous elements in the position of the executive. For this purpose he drew upon the same ideas that we found in the work of Philip Hunton. To be sure Locke did not place a great deal of emphasis upon the theory of mixed government. He acknowledged that the community may "make compounded and mixed Forms of Government, as they think good,"[40] but for the most part his analysis was in terms of the relationships between the legislature and the executive, with little reference to the House of Lords. It was only when he discussed the "dissolution of government" that he assumed a legislature composed of a single hereditary person, an assembly of hereditary nobility, and an assembly of representatives, as a hypothetical framework for the system of government.[41] Though he placed relatively little emphasis upon mixed government, Locke, with the restored monarchy in mind, gave a share in the exercise of the legislative function to the King, and it is here that he made use of Hunton's ideas

---

36. Ibid., XI, para. 136.
38. Ibid., XI, para. 142.
40. Ibid., X, para. 132.

37. Ibid., XI, para. 137.
39. Ibid., XI, para. 141.
41. Ibid., XIX, para. 213.

in order to raise the executive branch from a position of subordination to a status co-ordinate with the representative parts of the government.

In some commonwealths, says Locke, where the "Executive is vested in a single Person, who has also a share in the legislative; there that single Person in a very tolerable sense may also be called Supream." Not because he has all the supreme power, "which is that of Law-making," but because "he has in him the Supream Execution, from whom all inferiour Magistrates derive all their several subordinate Powers."[42] If the executive power is placed anywhere other than in a person who has a share of the legislative power, then the executive is "visibly subordinate and accountable to it." The supreme executive power can only be co-ordinate ("exempt from subordination" in Locke's words) if the person in whom that power is vested has also a share of the legislative power.[43] In this way the Executive must agree to the laws to which he will have to conform, so that "he is no more subordinate than he himself shall think fit, which one may certainly conclude will be but very little."[44] This seemingly rather tortured argument can only be fully understood in the light of the events which had preceded the composition of the *Second Treatise* and of the writings of Hunton and others who had grappled with the problems of reconciling the "negative voice" of the King with his being subject to the law and limited to carrying it out. Locke was emphasizing that the King's primary function is to execute the law, but that some way must be found of giving him a degree of independence that will place him on some level of equality with the two Houses of Parliament, and this his veto power will achieve. But Locke, like the Founding Fathers, saw the role of the "Executive" in this respect as essentially a negative one. The formal power of the King is to assent to, or withhold his assent from, legislation passed by the two Houses. His assertion of the co-ordinate status of the executive branch did not stop there. He devoted a chapter to the discussion of the prerogative which constitutes "the discretion of him, that has the Executive Power."[45] Legislators are not able to foresee, and provide for, all the things necessary for the good of the

42. Ibid., XIII, para. 151.
44. Ibid.

43. Ibid., XIII, para. 152.
45. Ibid., XIV, para. 159.

community. There are many things for which the law can "by no means" provide. Accidents may happen and strict adherence to the laws may do harm. For all these reasons the executive has "the Power to act according to discretion, for the publick good, without the prescription of the Law, and sometimes even against it."[46] Only the flexibility that this discretion gives enables the proper execution of the laws and provides for changing conditions. The prerogative is ultimately under the control of the legislature, but it also includes a certain authority over the legislature, that is the right to determine the precise time, duration, and meeting-place of Parliaments.[47]

Locke's theory of government, therefore, embodied the essential elements of the doctrine of the separation of powers, but it was not the pure doctrine. The *legislature,* in its widest sense, included the person who had the sole executive power. This did not mean, however, that there was a "fusion of powers" in the system. The basic division of function was clear. The King could not legislate, but only accede to legislation. The Parliament supervised the execution of the law, but must not itself execute. This was the basis of the theory of the balanced constitution, a theory which we may label as a *partial* separation of functions, for there was a sharing of the legislative authority, but a fundamental division of function between executive and legislature. The extent to which Locke may be described as "the Father of the United States Constitution" should now be somewhat clearer. Fundamentally this partial separation of functions is the theory upon which the relationship between the President and Congress was established. The legislative function was given to Congress, the executive function to the President, but the President had a veto over legislation. Apart from the fact that the President's veto could be overridden, the major difference between the Americans and Locke on this point was that the Constitution gave the President a share of the legislative function without his being in the legislature, whereas in England the position of the King as a member of the legislative *branch* seemed to give a very different flavour to the relationship. But did it? If the King's legislative function was confined to a veto, just as is the President's, then whether he was formally a member of the

---

46. Ibid., XIV, para. 160.   47. Ibid., XIV, para. 167.

legislative branch or not is unimportant. What is much more important is the power of King or President to influence or coerce the legislature. But neither Locke nor the Founding Fathers saw the executive as a "legislative leader" who would actively make the law in this way. Locke strongly condemned corruption in elections, and the use by the executive of bribery to ensure that legislators would support a particular point of view. "To prepare such an Assembly as this, and endeavour to set up the declared Abettors of his own Will . . . is certainly a great breach of trust. . . ."[48] Nor should we see Locke as a theorist of cabinet government, for when he was writing, the idea of "a single person" as the executive dominated men's minds. True, the "single person," whether King or Protector, needed ministers and advisers, and subordinate magistrates, but it mattered little whether or not they were members of either House of Parliament, except in so far as the practical needs of government required. It was the single person who was to be subjected to control, not his subordinates, who were simply his instruments. The separation of persons did not much interest Locke, therefore, because the ministers' membership of the legislature was not so important to him as their ability to control it by corrupt means. As the seventeenth century closed and the eighteenth began, however, the building up of the cabinet focused much more attention on this aspect of government; and the complete exclusion of officeholders, enacted in the Act of Settlement of 1701, if it had not been later amended, would have created a system of government in Britain not far removed from that which was later to be established in France, under the Constitution of 1791, as a consequence of deference to the idea of the separation of powers.

We have, then, already in Locke some of the major elements of the theory of balanced government, the sharing of the legislative authority, and the division of the functions of government. A major difference between Locke and the eighteenth-century writers, both in England and later in the United States, was his neglect of the judicial function. Locke did not attribute, as Lawson had done, an autonomous judicial function to the House of Lords. If we add this further dimension, plus a greater emphasis

---

48. Ibid., XIX, para. 222.

upon mixed government than Locke had given, the theory of the balanced constitution is almost complete; but this greater emphasis upon mixed government in eighteenth-century theory is important, for it is true to say that the doctrine of the separation of powers shows a much clearer influence in the work of Locke than it does in early eighteenth-century writings in England. In the latter the doctrine was subordinated to the theory of mixed government, whereas John Locke's vocabulary and approach were much nearer those of his contemporaries who had personally experienced a system of government without King or House of Lords.

The relatively clear division of the functions of government that had been evolved in the later seventeenth century became somewhat blurred as the theory of the balanced constitution was established in the eighteenth. The strong emphasis upon the legislative and executive functions which we find in the work of Locke and his predecessors was closely related to the seventeenth-century need to set limits upon royal power, and to a lesser extent upon the power of Parliament; but with the relatively firm position achieved for the monarchy by the Revolution Settlement a completely new situation arose. The dominant political theory was a conservative one, a concern to maintain the "perfect balance" which it was believed had been achieved within the system of government. As Dean Swift wrote in 1701: "I see no other course to be taken in a settled state, than a steady constant resolution in those, to whom the rest of the balance is entrusted, never to give way so far to popular clamours, as to make the least breach in the constitution."[49] As a result there was a tendency to place the emphasis once again upon a list of the "parts of sovereignty" similar to those that had earlier been put forward by writers who were more interested in enumerating the contents of sovereign power than in settling limits to arbitrary rule. The fact is that a straightforward classification into two or even three "powers" of government was inadequate for the theory of the balanced constitution, for this was firmly based upon two propositions: first, that the legislative authority was shared between King, Lords,

---

49. Jonathan Swift, *A Discourse of the Contests and Dissentions between the Nobles and Commons in Athens and Rome*, 1701, in *Works*, London, 1766, Vol. III, p. 52.

and Commons; second, that each of these had, in the words of John Toland, "their peculiar Priviledges and Prerogatives."[50] Thus there must be three distinct sets of "powers and priviledges" *in addition* to the legislative power. The parts of the sovereign power were parcelled out, therefore, among the three branches of government. Thus William Stephens in 1699 divided up the powers of government, other than the legislative, giving the executive power the power of making war and peace, and the power over the mint to the King, the "last appeal" in all cases of law to the Lords, and the power of raising money for the support of the government to the Commons.[51]

In the first half of the eighteenth century the theory of mixed government was in the ascendency again, more so, indeed, than ever before. But it was no longer the undifferentiated theory of mixed government that had preceded the Civil War. The ideas behind the separation of powers were added to it so that each element of the mixed government might wield an independent and co-ordinate authority that gave it the ability to check the exercise of power by the other branches. Thus the principle of functionally differentiated agencies became an integral part of the theory of the balanced constitution, and the exact articulation of their functions, and the interrelationships of the agencies and their members, became a major concern of political writers; for "in order to preserve the balance in a mixed state, the limits of power deposited with each party ought to be ascertained, and generally known."[52]

This theory of the constitution was stated in 1701 by Sir Humphrey Mackworth in terms little different from those used by Charles I in 1642.[53] The mixed constitution is essential to a happy and secure State, but in this constitution the legislative authority is shared, whilst the other functions of government are divided so that there is "a prudent distribution of power."[54] The three branches of the supreme authority must have "several particular powers lodged in them," in order that each may prevent the en-

---

50. *The Art of Governing by Partys,* London, 1701, p. 31.
51. *A Letter to His Most Excellent Majesty King William III,* 3rd edn., London, 1699, pp. 12–13.
52. Swift, op. cit., Vol. III, p. 17.
53. *A Vindication of the Rights of the Commons of England,* London, 1701.
54. Ibid., p. 2.

croachment of the others. The King must have the power of making war and peace, of command of the forces, of the calling and dissolving of parliaments, and of the appointment of all officers, ecclesiastical, civil, and military. The particular powers of the Commons are the levying of money and the impeachment of Ministers, while the Lords are entrusted with the "right of judicature." Thus within the umbrella of the legislative power the three branches exercise separate powers that enable each of them to check the others.[55] Each of these branches must be "limited and bounded by one another, in such a manner that one may not be allowed to encroach on the other." This is the "infallible touchstone" of a happy constitution.[56]

This was the basic pattern of the early-eighteenth-century theory of the constitution, and, in spite of a very poor prose style, Mackworth set it forth faithfully. Discussions about the nature of the constitution took place *within* this framework, which was itself rarely questioned. Bitter differences of opinion arose, based upon the political issues of the day, but the arguments were couched in terms of the proper articulation of the parts of this constitution, in terms of the details of its "proper" working, not of its own adequacy, or inadequacy. The first half of the eighteenth century in England was not a period of great political writers, and we must look for these arguments about the constitution in the occasional pieces that resulted from the clashes over particular issues of the day. These reveal some of the problems of the theory of the balanced constitution, and of the mechanisms it involved, which were reflected later in the practical working of the Constitution of the United States.

The Peerage Bill of 1719 provoked perhaps the most interesting discussion of the nature of the balanced constitution and the role of the "partial separation of functions" in this constitution. The Peerage Bill represented an attempt by Whig leaders to "freeze" the size of the House of Lords at 235 peers, and as they at the time controlled the House of Lords, so to continue this control indefinitely. The royal prerogative to create new peers was to be limited to the replacement of peerages which became ex-

55. Ibid., pp. 2–3. Mackworth is at pains to restrict the use of the term, the "power of judicature," to the Lords' power to try impeachments.
56. Ibid., p. 4.

tinct through failure of issue. In this way the Whig leaders, who feared that the succession of the Prince of Wales to the throne would bring about a new, and to them unfavourable, attitude in the monarchy, hoped to retain control of the government; and perhaps by repealing the Septennial Act also to preserve the existing House of Commons.[57] The proposal to limit the size of the House of Lords involved a considerable change in the royal authority and provoked a bitter altercation between rival pamphleteers concerning the extent to which this was compatible with the over-all philosophy of the British Constitution. Each side claimed that its position on the Peerage Bill was compatible with that constitution, and indeed that their view was the only one possible that would preserve the constitution. We are thus presented with an extensive discussion of the relationship between King, Lords, and Commons.[58]

The proponents of the Bill argued that the proposed alteration was necessary in order to give to the House of Lords that degree of independence of the monarch that would enable it to play its proper role as the moderator of disputes between the King and the Commons, and to act as a safeguard for the constitution should the other two branches unite against it. This role could only be safeguarded if the Lords were to be free from the threat of the creation of sufficient new peerages to swamp the existing majority. The existence of this threat rendered it a subordinate branch of the government, not a co-ordinate member as required both by the basic doctrine of mixed government and by the constitutional balance; for these required a threefold, not a twofold, division of governmental power if any one branch was to have a casting vote in disputes. In defence of the Bill Addison wrote: "It is necessary that these three branches should be entirely separate and distinct from each other, so that no one of them may lie too much under the influence and controul of either of the collateral branches."[59] The opponents of the Bill, led by Sir Robert Walpole, argued, however, that although

57. See E. R. Turner, "The Peerage Bill of 1719," *English Historical Review,* Vol. 28, 1913, pp. 243–59.

58. See the collection of pamphlets in the Bodleian Library entitled *On the Peerage,* 1719, Hope 8°, 766.

59. *The Old Whig,* No. I, London, 1719, p. 2.

each of the branches must be independent of the others, nevertheless it was essential that each branch should exercise a check to the power of the others, if the balance were to be maintained. If the King had the Commons' power to raise money, then the monarchy would be absolute. If the power of dissolution were to be abolished, then the Commons would "devolve into an ill-contrived democracy,"[60] and if the prerogative of creating peers were removed the Lords would become an unrestrained aristocracy. It was pointed out also that those who supported the independence of the Lords were not at the same time proposing a means by which the independence of the Commons would be safeguarded from control through "influence." Steele summed up the fundamental objection to the complete independence of the branches of the government: "The unhappy consequence that must ensue would be that if any discord shou'd arise betwixt them, and each remain inflexibly resolv'd, here the constitution would want a casting power."[61] Thus deadlock would ensue, and would result in the resolution of the problem by violence, as no other means would be open.

It is not to be supposed that those who proposed the Peerage Bill really believed in the perfect independence of all three branches of the government, for their plan depended upon their being able to control the House of Commons through the system of influence; the discussion does reveal, however, the two possible approaches to the element of the separation of powers doctrine that we find embedded in this eighteenth-century view of the constitution. Given separate branches of the government exercising distinct but interlocking functions, or sharing in the exercise of a particular function, should the independence-of-each-other of these three branches be as great as possible, or should care be taken to ensure that the independence of each, although real, should be limited by powers in the others to prevent that independence from being allowed to wreck the operation of government altogether? This dispute was a curtain-raiser for the different views about the doctrine of the separation of powers, which were to characterize French and American attitudes later in the century. In the English political disputes of the first half of the eighteenth century the ideas

60. *The Thoughts of a Member of the Lower House, etc.*, London, 1719, p. 7.
61. *The Plebian*, No. II, London, 1719, p. 11.

of the doctrine of the separation of powers were applied to the theory of mixed government, and the result was a theory of checks and balances, which was very different from the earlier theory of mixed government; for in the latter the branches of the government were intended to share in the exercise of its functions. In the new doctrine each branch, it is true, was to share in the supreme legislative power, but each was also to have a basis of its own distinctive functions that would give it independence, and at the same time would give it the power to modify positively the attitudes of the other branches of government. In England this theory was applied to the institutions of a mixed monarchy, but it was quite capable of being adapted at a later date to a different set of institutions in which a monarch and a hereditary aristocracy played no part.

The great political issue of this period was, of course, the use of "influence" in politics, the bribery of electors and the corruption of members of the House of Commons in order to gain a majority favourable to the Ministry. This system of influence can be seen as the first of the links between the executive and legislative branches that formed the basis of the newly developing pattern of cabinet government. In an age when party allegiance alone was not a reliable means of ensuring the support of members of parliament for government policies, the system of influence provided a useful alternative. At the same time corruption can be seen as a means of subverting the balance of the constitution, of uniting powers that should be divided, and reducing to subordination in practice a branch of the government which in theory was co-ordinate in power. The eighteenth century was, therefore, both the age of the emergence of cabinet government, and the age of place-bills, proposed in an attempt to maintain the division between parliament and the executive. The success of the British Constitution can perhaps be attributed to the fact that in the end those who wanted to control the Commons and those who wished the Commons to be free of office-holders were *both* partially successful.

The greatest opponent of the system of corruption was Henry St. John, Viscount Bolingbroke, who for many years defended his concept of the balanced constitution against the "ministerial system" of Sir Robert Walpole. Bolingbroke was well acquainted with Montesquieu, and the latter undoubtedly gained much of his knowledge of the separation of powers doctrine from Bolingbroke and his writings.[62] Walpole in his fight against the Peerage Bill had argued that too much independence in the branches of the government would create "a state of war, instead of a civil state,"[63] and the later defenders of his own ministerial system argued that business could not be carried on or a government subsist "by several powers absolutely distinct and absolutely independent."[64] Bolingbroke reported the views of his opponents that corruption was necessary to "oil the wheels of government, and to render the Administration more smooth and easy."[65] These men, he said, present the constitution in a ridiculous and contemptible light. For them the constitution is "no better than a jumble of incompatible powers, which would separate and fall to pieces of themselves" without the cement of corruption.[66] Bolingbroke's statement of the essence of the constitution is remarkably clear:[67]

> A King of Great Britain is that supreme magistrate, who has a negative voice in the legislature. He is entrusted with the executive power, and several other powers and privileges, which we call prerogative, are annex'd to this trust. The two Houses of Parliament have their rights and privileges, some of which are common to both; others particular to each. They prepare, they pass bills, or they refuse to pass such as are sent to them. They address, represent, advise, remonstrate. The supreme judicature resides in the Lords. The Commons are the grand inquest of the nation; and to them it belongs to judge of national expences, and to give supplies accordingly.

Bolingbroke emphasized that the division of powers between the three branches was an essential element in this structure. If the King had the legislative as well as the executive powers he would be absolute, and if either of the Houses had both we should have an aristocracy or a democracy. "It is this division of power, these distinct privileges attributed to the King, to the Lords and to the Commons which constitute a limited mon-

62. See R. Shackleton, *Montesquieu: A Critical Biography*, Oxford, 1961, pp. 298–300.
63. *Some Reflections upon a Pamphlet called the Old Whig*, London, 1719, p. 16.
64. *The London Journal*, 4 July 1730, quoted by Shackleton op. cit., p. 299.
65. *A Dissertation upon Parties*, 2nd edn., London, 1735, p. 119.
66. *Of the Constitution of Great Britain*, in *A Collection of Political Tracts*, London, 1748, p. 251.
67. *Remarks on the History of England*, London, 1743, p. 82.

archy."[68] Thus a partial sharing and a partial separation of the functions of government among distinct bodies of persons was the fundamental characteristic of the English system of government. Bolingbroke then presented a defence of his view that the independence of the parts of the government, which is subverted by the system of corruption, was perfectly compatible with their "mutual dependency." The parts of the government have each the power to exercise some control over the others, and they are therefore mutually dependent. This does not mean that they cannot and should not be independent of each other also. Indeed the independence of the branches is a necessary prerequisite to their being interdependent, for if it were not so then "mutual dependency is that moment changed into a particular, constant dependency of one part" on the others.[69] Thus there would be no balance at all.

Here then, set out with great clarity, is the English mid-eighteenth-century amalgam of mixed government, legislative supremacy, and the separation of powers. Although playing a subordinate role in this theory, the ideas of the separation of powers doctrine are essential to it. The division of the functions of government among distinct agencies is there, but neither the functions nor the agencies follow the categories of the pure doctrine of the separation of powers, and in one vital function the authority is shared, not divided. The idea of the separation of persons is also very important, demanding at least a partial separation among the agencies of government. There were recurrent attempts to rid the Commons of office-holders and pensioners. In the Act of Settlement provision was made for the exclusion from the House of Commons of all office-holders, which, if it had not been repealed before coming into effect, would have made a very considerable difference to the British system of government. The idea of checks to the exercise of power, through the opposition of functionally divided agencies of government in distinct hands, is there, but it is a much more positive view of the necessary checks to the exercise of power than the pure doctrine envisaged.

From the point of view of the development of the pure theory of the

68. Ibid.   69. Ibid., p. 84.

separation of powers, therefore, the first half of the eighteenth century represented a retreat from the positions reached in the Civil War and in the work of John Locke. The more revolutionary theory had been assimilated by, and subordinated to, the older theory of mixed government, and the English attitude towards the Constitution was long to remain in this mould. But of the two doctrines, the doctrine of the separation of powers represented the thought of the future, the theory of mixed government the thought of the past. The ascendency of the doctrine of the separation of powers in America and on the continent of Europe was to come as the result of the work of Montesquieu, and on the wave of new revolutions which again swept away the assumptions underlying the theory of mixed government, just as they had been swept away in England, for a time at least, when Charles I laid his head upon the block.

FOUR

Montesquieu

T HE NAME most associated with the doctrine of the separation of powers is that of Charles Louis de Secondat, Baron Montesquieu. His influence upon later thought and upon the development of institutions far outstrips, in this connection, that of any of the earlier writers we have considered. It is clear, however, that Montesquieu did not invent the doctrine of the separation of powers, and that much of what he had to say in Book XI Chapter 6 of the *De l'Esprit des Loix* was taken over from contemporary English writers, and from John Locke.[1] Montesquieu, it is true, contributed new ideas to the doctrine; he emphasized certain elements in it that had not previously received such attention, particularly in relation to the judiciary, and he accorded the doctrine a more important position than did most previous writers. However, the influence of Montesquieu cannot be ascribed to his originality in this respect, but rather to the manner and timing of the doctrine's development in his hands.

Long before the publication of *De l'Esprit des Loix* Montesquieu had become widely known and respected through the publication of the *Lettres persanes* and the *Considérations sur les causes de la grandeur des Romains.*

---

1. On the English origin of Montesquieu's ideas, see J. Dedieu, *Montesquieu et la tradition politique anglaise en France,* Paris, 1902.

The appearance of his great work was awaited with impatience, and, once published, it quickly ran through several editions. When the work appeared it was clearly not a piece of transient political propaganda, as had been many of the writings we have so far surveyed—it was the result of twenty years of preparation, and was intended as a scientific study of government, encompassing the whole length and breadth of history, and accounting for all the factors affecting the political life of man. Montesquieu, in his Preface, made it clear what the work contained:[2] "I have laid down the first principles, and have found that the particular cases follow naturally from them; that the histories of all nations are only consequences of them; and that every particular law is connected with another law, or depends on some other of a more general extent." These principles are not drawn from the writer's prejudices, but "from the nature of things." Montesquieu intends to show the way in which the laws of each State are related to the nature and principles of its form of government, to the climate, soil, and economy of the country, and to its manners and customs.[3] Such a scientific approach rules out the expression of personal likes and dislikes: "Every nation will here find the reasons on which its maxims are founded." No absolute solutions are proposed, only the necessary relationships between the form of government and the laws are exposed. This claim to scientific detachment gives to Montesquieu's work a status that no political pamphleteer could claim. The doctrine of the separation of powers is embedded in this examination of cause and effect in the political system. It is no longer an isolated doctrine, taken up when political advantage makes it expedient, and put off when no longer needed; it is part of the relationships of a particular type of legal system; and furthermore, it is a necessary characteristic of that system which has political liberty as its direct aim. *De l'Esprit des Loix* was hailed as the first systematic treatise on politics since Aristotle; not a desiccated, boring treatise for the expert alone, but rather as a work the brilliant style of which made it an object of attention for all educated men. Indeed,

2. The standard edition of *De l'Esprit des Loix* is by J. Brette de la Gressaye, Paris, 1950, 4 vols. Quotations are from the translation by Thomas Nugent, ed. by F. Neumann, New York, 1949.

3. *De l'Esprit des Loix*, Book I, Ch. 3.

Voltaire caustically remarked that it was Montesquieu's style alone which retrieved a work so full of error.[4]

De l'Esprit des Loix was published in 1748, and so became available at the beginning of a period of great change and development in Europe and America. Ideas which had blossomed in the English Civil War, but which had been premature and unrealistic in terms of the then existing society, could now find fertile ground in the British colonies of North America and in France. Within the next fifty years men were to be called upon to create new institutions, to attempt to establish new systems of government. Where better look for help than in a manual where the principles of all governments were set out, and where none were more sympathetically treated than those forms of government that set bounds to the exercise of arbitrary power. For although Montesquieu claimed to be disinterested, his affection for moderate government shines through the whole work, whether it be a moderate monarchy or a moderate republic he is describing. But Montesquieu's approach did lead to a good deal of confused speculation about his own loyalties. Was he advocating monarchy as the best system of government, or did he believe in a mixed system, or was he a good republican? Evidence for all these points of view can be found in his great work, and, indeed, it was the very fact that the *De l'Esprit des Loix* can be pressed into service in support of widely differing views that added to its influence. By the end of the eighteenth century Montesquieu was being quoted as an authority in England, France, and America, as conclusive evidence of the rightness of very different systems of government.

Montesquieu started from a rather gloomy view of human nature, in which he saw man as exhibiting a general tendency towards evil, a tendency that manifests itself in selfishness, pride, envy, and the seeking after power.[5] Man, though a reasoning animal, is led by his desires into immoderate acts. Of the English, Montesquieu wrote that "A people like this, being always in ferment, are more easily conducted by their passions than

4. *L'ABC*, quoted by W. Struck—*Montesquieu als Politiker*, Berlin, 1933, p. 4.

5. See the discussion of Montesquieu's concept of human nature in W. Stark, *Montesquieu: Pioneer of the Sociology of Knowledge*, London, 1960, Ch. IV.

by reason, which never produced any great effect in the mind of man."[6] In the realm of politics this is of the greatest consequence: "Constant experience shows us that every man invested with power is apt to abuse it, and to carry his authority as far as it will go."[7] However, this tendency towards the abuse of power can be moderated by the constitution of the government and by the laws, for, although by no means a starry-eyed utopian, Montesquieu, like the Greeks, believed that the nature of the State's constitution is of the greatest consequence. Thus Montesquieu commenced his work with a description of the three different types of government, their nature and their principles, for if he could establish these, then the laws would "flow thence as from their source."[8] Let us look at the way in which Montesquieu dealt with this problem of the control of power.

He defined three types of government: republican, monarchical, and despotic. In the first the people is possessed of the supreme power; in a monarchy a single person governs by fixed and established laws; in a despotic government a single person directs everything by his own will and caprice.[9] Republican government can be subdivided into aristocracy and democracy, the former being a State in which the supreme power is in the hands of a part of the people, not, as in a democracy, in the body of the people. In a despotic government there can be no check to the power of the prince, no limitations to safeguard the individual—the idea of the separation of powers in any form is foreign to despotic governments. In an aristocracy also, though it be a moderate government, the legislative and executive authority are in the same hands.[10] However, in a democracy, Montesquieu argued, the corruption of the government sets in when the people attempt to govern directly and try "to debate for the senate, to execute for the magistrate, and to decide for the judges."[11] Montesquieu implied, then, that some form of separation of powers is necessary to a democracy, but he did not develop this point. The relevance of this to modern states is in any case rather slight, as Montesquieu believed that democracy was only suitable

6. *De l'Esprit des Loix*, XIX, 27.   7. Ibid., XI, 4.
8. Ibid., I, 3.   9. Ibid., II, 1.
10. Ibid., II, 3.   11. Ibid., VIII, 2.

to small societies.[12] The most extended treatment he gives of institutional checks to power, therefore, is to be found in his discussion of monarchy and of the English Constitution. These two discussions, though obviously connected in spirit, seem to be drawn from quite different sources, and to depend upon different principles. Each system is praised for its virtues, but it is difficult to say that Montesquieu clearly favoured one above the other. Here we have the source of the confusions on this subject.

The different elements in Montesquieu's approach to the control of power can be attributed to his two major sources of inspiration. On the one hand the influence of English writers, especially Locke and Bolingbroke, is clear.[13] From the time of the Civil War onwards the volume of translations of English works on politics, and of French commentaries on England, had grown, until in the early eighteenth century it reached large proportions. Dedieu points to the importance of the exiled Huguenot journalists, lauding the virtues of the Glorious Revolution, to the writings of anglophile Frenchmen, and to the work of historians who emphasized the role of the English Parliament as a balance to the power of the Crown.[14] In particular Rapin-Thoyras, in his *Histoire d'Angleterre* in 1717, emphasized the importance of a balanced constitution and mixed government. Voltaire in 1734 published a French edition of his *English Letters,* in which he wrote of the "mélange dans le gouvernement d'Angleterre, ce concert entre les Communes, les Lords et le Roy."[15] These, together with Montesquieu's travels in England, his acquaintance with Bolingbroke, and his knowledge of the writings in the *Craftsman,* the paper for which Bolingbroke wrote,[16] are the sources of the main ideas to be found in his chapter on the English Constitution.

There are other sources, nearer at home, however, for Montesquieu's

12. Ibid., VIII, 16.
13. On Locke see Dedieu, op. cit., Ch. VI; on Bolingbroke see Robert Shackleton, "Montesquieu, Bolingbroke and the Separation of Powers," *French Studies,* Vol. III, 1949.
14. See Dedieu, op. cit., p. 71 for a list of French historical works on England 1689–1748, and pp. 73–74 for a list of English political works translated into French during the same period.
15. *Lettres sur les Anglois,* Basle, 1734, p. 56.
16. Shackleton, op. cit.

attitude towards monarchy. Here, as in his description of the English Constitution, Montesquieu was concerned with the control of arbitrary power, but in a different way, and in a different context. As an aristocrat, and *président à mortier* of the *parlement* of Bordeaux, he could look back upon a long tradition of French resistance to the idea of despotism, not along the lines of the English developments, but in terms of the power of the *parlements,* and of the aristocracy and clergy of France as checks upon the royal authority.[17] Bodin, though asserting the indivisibility of the sovereign power of the King, nevertheless had advocated that the *parlements* should have the power of remonstrance and of enregistering royal enactments, so that they might judge these in the light of justice and equity.[18] The *parlements* had from time to time asserted their right to refuse to register royal edicts, especially the *parlement* of Bordeaux, of which Montesquieu later became a *président à mortier.*[19] Boulainvilliers in 1727 had argued that all the unhappiness of France was due to the way in which the nobility had declined in power, and it was in defence of a similar thesis that Montesquieu approached the problem of the French monarchy.[20] Thus when Montesquieu defined monarchy, as opposed to despotism, as a system in which "intermediate, subordinate, and dependent powers" played an essential role, and named these intermediate powers as the nobility, the clergy, and the *parlements,* he was following a well-trodden path in French thought.

It is Bodin, however, more than any other thinker, who would seem to have provided the pattern for Montesquieu's idea of monarchy; and if this is so, it is of great importance, for Bodin's views on sovereignty are bound to colour the whole nature of the approach to the monarchical system.[21] Bodin had, it is true, been concerned to champion a strong monarchy, and to stress the concentration of power in the hands of the monarch, but he also stressed the difference between a tyranny and a "royal" or "legitimate"

17. See W. F. Church, *Constitutional Thought in Sixteenth-Century France,* Harvard, 1941, esp. Ch. I.

18. Church, op. cit., p. 221.

19. Shackleton, *Montesquieu,* pp. 280–1.

20. See Neumann's Introduction, pp. xxiv–xxvii.

21. For a general discussion of Bodin and Montesquieu see A. Gardot, "De Bodin à Montesquieu," in *La pensée politique et constitutionnelle de Montesquieu,* Paris, 1952.

monarchy. The latter is one in which the king "yieldeth himself as obedient unto the laws of nature as he desireth his subjects to be towards himselfe, leaving unto every man his naturall libertie, and the proprietie of his own goods."[22] He accorded a role in the government, even if only a subordinate one, to the States-General and the *parlements*. The pattern of Bodin's royal monarchy is very close to Montesquieu's view of monarchy, and there is little evidence to suggest that the latter saw any real modification in the structure of this form of government that would approximate to a "separation of powers." It is true that Montesquieu writes that to form a "moderate government," which of course includes monarchy, it is "necessary to combine the several powers; to regulate, temper, and set them in motion; to give, as it were, ballast to one, in order to enable it to counterpoise the other."[23] However, it is difficult to place much weight upon this statement as an indication of Montesquieu's belief in a "separation of powers" in a moderate government, for as it stands it applies also to aristocracy, which Montesquieu specifically characterizes as a system in which the legislative and executive powers are in the same hands, and there is no other indication of a belief in the separation of powers in a "monarchy." On the contrary, Montesquieu clearly asserted the indivisibility of the supreme power in the hands of the monarch,[24] and the subordination of the "intermediary powers."[25] We must, therefore, see Montesquieu's moderate monarchy as governed by law, but not as a limited monarchy in the English sense, nor as a system of mixed government or the separation of powers.

Monarchy for Montesquieu was government by the law, through the recognized channels by which the royal power must flow. The idea of a separation of agencies and functions, in part at least, is implicit and explicit in his treatment of monarchy. The judges must be the depository of the laws; the monarch must never himself be a judge, for in this way the "de-

22. *Six Bookes*, II, 3, p. 204.

23. *De l'Esprit des Loix*, V, 14.

24. Ibid., II, 4.

25. Shackleton, in *Montesquieu*, p. 279, describes how the emphasis upon the subordinate character of the intermediary powers was a later insertion in the text by Montesquieu, perhaps as a precaution against royal displeasure. However, this insertion would seem to be in the general spirit of Montesquieu's view of monarchy.

pendent intermediate powers" would be annihilated.[26] The king's ministers ought not to sit as judges, because they would lack the necessary detachment and coolness requisite to a judge.[27] There must be many "formalities" in the legal process in a monarchy in order to leave the defendant all possible means of making his defence,[28] and the judges must conform to the law.[29] In the monarchy, then, power is exercised in a controlled way, but it is not the separation of powers in the sense in which we have used this term, at any rate as far as the legislative and executive powers are concerned. There is considerable emphasis upon the role of the judges, but "the prince is the source of all power," and he clearly exercises both the legislative and executive powers within the fundamental constitution.[30] The checks upon the royal power operate as a result of the existence of the various orders of society through which that power must be channelled, but these "intermediate powers" do not even include a body of representatives of the people. The people's safeguard is in the principle of monarchy, honour, which, by definition, infuses the rule of the monarch over his people.[31] This, then, is what Montesquieu seems to have considered best for France; it is the ancestral constitution that had been for a time subverted, a constitution in which the King did not exercise a capricious and arbitrary power, but not a constitution that can be described as embodying the separation of powers. Indeed we must not be confused by the terminology Montesquieu uses. Undoubtedly today his "monarchy" would be described as a despotism, if a benevolent one. His constitutional monarch was in the tradition of French, not English, thought. It certainly is not the monarchy that the seventeenth-century constitutional battles produced in England. Even Charles I could hardly have hoped that a King of England would exercise the power Montesquieu accords his monarch.[32]

26. *De l'Esprit des Loix*, VI, 5.

27. Ibid., VI, 6.

28. Ibid., VI, 2.

29. Ibid., VI, 3.

30. Ibid., II, 4, and V, 10.

31. Ibid., III, 10.

32. Thus K. von Raumer argues that Montesquieu saw, even in the France of Louis XV, the idea of freedom embodied in Europe, as opposed to the slavery of Asia. Although this freedom

When we turn from the description of the monarchy to the discussion of the English Constitution we must first consider two difficulties. What were Montesquieu's views on mixed government, and what form of government did he believe England to have? Montesquieu's treatment of mixed government is characteristic of the problems of interpretation he presents. At the beginning of his work, when enumerating the types of government, he did not consider mixed government at all. There is no direct mention of this idea which had been so important in English political thought for centuries, and which had also figured in the work of Hotman and others in France. Montesquieu writes of "moderate" governments, but these are the uncorrupted forms of monarchy and republic. At one point he seems to be saying that a mixed constitution is impossible, or at least that he knows of none that exists.[33] Again the parallel with Bodin is striking. When Montesquieu turns in Book XI to his discussion of England, however, he adopts a very different approach.

In this form of government the executive power should be in the hands of a monarch, and the legislative power committed to the body of the nobles and to that body which represents the people, "each having their assemblies and deliberations apart, each their separate views and interests."[34] This is the fundamental constitution of a free state: "The legislative body being composed of two parts, they check one another by the mutual privilege of rejecting. They are both restrained by the executive power, as the executive is by the legislative." Montesquieu immediately follows this sentence with a reference to "these three powers," by which he seems to mean King, Lords, and Commons, not legislature, executive, and judiciary. This is clearly a system of mixed government, and in the rest of Book XI Montesquieu refers to mixed systems in glowing terms, whether in reference

---

was threatened it was still a reality, such that France was still a moderate monarchy, not a tyranny. ("Absoluter Staat, korporative Libertät; persönliche Freiheit," *Historische Zeitschrift*, Vol. 183, Munich, 1957, p. 59.)

33. Ibid., VIII, 21. W. Struck argues that Montesquieu's principles of the three forms of government are by definition incapable of being blended into a mixed form. *Montesquieu als Politiker, Historische Studien*, 228, Berlin, 1933, pp. 68–69.

34. All further quotations in this chapter are from Book XI, Ch. 6 of *De l'Esprit des Loix* unless otherwise noted.

to the Gothic constitutions of Europe, or to the harmony of power in the government of Rome when it consisted of a mixture of monarchy, aristocracy, and democracy.[35] How do we reconcile these references with the earlier chapters of the work? One answer, perhaps, is simply to say that they are irreconcilable and leave it at that. Montesquieu drew his inspiration from diverse sources and was unable to integrate all his ideas into a single theoretical framework. It is hardly surprising that he failed to reconcile completely the two models of government that he drew from Bodin and from Bolingbroke. A rather different approach is to view Montesquieu's descriptions of despotism, monarchy, and republic as "ideal types" to which governments in practice would only imperfectly conform, so that imperfect examples of actual governments might contain elements of more than one type. There is some evidence that Montesquieu was thinking in this way. For example he writes: "The nearer a government approaches towards a republic, the more the manner of judging becomes settled and fixed."[36] And in Book VIII, where he discusses the way in which the principles of the three forms of government can be corrupted, he clearly envisages that States can exist that only imperfectly conform to the principles of these three forms. Again, reference to Bodin may help us here. Bodin tells us that his three forms of commonwealth are "ideal types."[37] He rejects altogether the idea of a mixed form of *State*, because of the logical and practical impossibility of the division of the sovereign power; but he distinguishes between forms of State and forms of government, allowing that the form of government may differ from the form of State in which it operates, so that a monarchy may, in reality, operate as an aristocracy or democracy, and also that combinations of forms of *government* are possible.[38] Montesquieu seems to view England in this light. Thus he refers to it as "a nation that may be justly called a republic, disguised under the form of a monarchy";[39] and again, he says that England "having been for-

---

35. Ibid., XI, 12.
36. *De l'Esprit des Loix*, VI, 3.
37. *Six Bookes*, II, 1, p. 183.
38. Ibid., II, 12, pp. 199–200; and II, 7, pp. 249–50.
39. *De l'Esprit des Loix*, V, 19.

merly subject to an arbitrary power, on many occasions preserves the style of it, in such a manner as to let us frequently see upon the foundation of a free government the form of an absolute monarchy."[40]

However, the problem is further complicated by the view that, in Book XI, Chapter 6, Montesquieu was creating an ideal type of a "constitution of liberty," with England as its source, but that he was not *describing* the English Constitution as it actually existed. When Montesquieu wrote of "England" here he was writing of an imaginary country, as in the *Lettres persanes*: *"l'Angleterre de Montesquieu c'est l'Utopie, c'est un pays de rêve."*[41] Thus in certain respects Montesquieu's statements in this chapter differ considerably from what he actually knew to be the case in England. For example, he writes of the judiciary as if it contained no professional judges, as if juries were judges of both fact and law. The reality of English life was, as Montesquieu himself notes elsewhere, quite different from the ideal situation depicted in XI, 6.[42] If, therefore, this chapter also constructs an "ideal type," we must consider it on its merits, and not concern ourselves with the long controversy over the correctness of Montesquieu's description of the early-eighteenth-century constitution of England.[43] But how does this ideal type relate to his ideal types of monarchy, despotism, and republic? Is it a fourth and quite distinct category, or a sub-category of one of them? These questions are no doubt unanswerable, for they demand from Montesquieu a consistency he does not have. We must accept these inconsistencies, and make the best of them.

This, then, is the framework within which is set the famous chapter on the English Constitution, which has had greater influence than any other part of the *De l'Esprit des Loix*, the chapter which further evolves the doctrine of the separation of powers. As with all the previous writers we have surveyed, it is still not a "doctrine," nor does the term "separa-

---

40. Ibid., XIX, 27. In this reference and the preceding one Montesquieu does not refer to England by name, but it is generally accepted that it was to England that he was referring.

41. B. Mirkine-Guetzévitch, in *La pensée politique et constitutionnelle de Montesquieu*, p. 14. Mirkine-Guetzévitch asserts that none of Montesquieu's contemporaries thought that he was writing of the reality of English political life.

42. Ibid.

43. Franz Neumann's introduction to *The Spirit of the Laws*, New York, 1949, pp. liv–lv.

tion of powers" appear in the text, although Montesquieu does assert that liberty is lost if the three powers are not "separated."[44] What does Montesquieu have to say about the separation of powers? A remarkable degree of disagreement exists about what Montesquieu actually did say. Two broad streams of interpretation of his thought since the latter part of the eighteenth century can be detected. One, largely associated with the continent of Europe, and with jurists rather than political theorists, sees what we have called "the pure doctrine of the separation of powers," a thoroughgoing separation of agencies, functions, and persons. The other, represented principally by the Fathers of the American Constitution, French writers such as Benjamin Constant, and in a rather different way the English commentators of the eighteenth and nineteenth centuries, has seen some form of a *partial* separation of powers, that is the pure doctrine modified by a system of checks and balances.[45] Some writers go further and claim that the term "separation of powers" as applied to Montesquieu's thought is an exaggeration or misrepresentation, that he was concerned only with the establishment of the "non-confusion" of powers,[46] that he was trying to establish only the *juridical* independence of the legislature and the government and not a separation of functions or persons,[47] or that he demanded only the "harmonious integration" of the powers of government.[48] Let us take each strand of the doctrine and of the idea of checks and balances in order to assess what Montesquieu has to say in the *De l'Esprit des Loix*.

Montesquieu's approach to the definition of the functions of government resembles a review of the history of the uses of these concepts. Chapter 6 of Book XI begins: "In every government there are three sorts of power, the legislative; the executive in respect to things dependent on the law of nations; and the executive in regard to matters that depend on the civil law."

44. "Il n'y a point encore de liberté si la puissance de juger n'est pas séparée de la puissance législative et de l'exécutrice."

45. See the discussion by Charles Eisenmann, in *La pensée politique et constitutionnelle de Montesquieu*, pp. 135 ff.

46. M. Barckhausen, *Montesquieu, ses Idées et ses Oeuvres*, Paris, 1907, p. 95.

47. C. Eisenmann, *L'Esprit des Lois et la séparation des pouvoirs* in *Mélanges R. Carré de Malberg*, Paris, 1933, pp. 166 ff.

48. Stark, op. cit., p. 21.

This is clearly a restatement of Locke's division of government functions, except that Montesquieu does not use the term "federative power" for the executive power in regard to external affairs. He still uses the term "executive" to cover all internal affairs, both governmental and judicial; in other words he adopts, though only momentarily, the twofold division of functions into legislative and executive so familiar to the seventeenth century and earlier. Montesquieu then immediately redefines his terms. He affirms that he intends to use the term "executive power" exclusively to cover the function of the magistrates to make peace or war, send or receive embassies, establish the public security, and provide against invasions. He now seems to wish to confine the term "executive power" to foreign affairs, for he does not make it at all clear that the power to "establish the public security" has any internal connotation—in other words, for Locke's "federative power" read "executive power." Furthermore, Montesquieu announces that he will call the third power, by which the magistrate punishes criminals or decides disputes between individuals, the "power of judging."[49] This appears to represent an attempt to reconcile the authority of Locke with the heightened appreciation of the separate existence of the judicial power as distinct from the royal power which had emerged in the early eighteenth century. But this formulation leaves out of account any "executive" acts other than foreign affairs, for the judicial power is confined to disputes between the prince and the individual, and between individuals. Montesquieu has not so far, then, managed to reconcile the seventeenth-century vocabulary with the facts of eighteenth-century government; the vital distinction between the internal acts of the executive and the acts of the judiciary is obscured. However, when he goes on to use these terms he drops both definitions and uses them in a very much more modern way; the three powers are now "that of enacting laws, that of executing the public resolutions, and of trying the causes of individuals," clearly including internal as well as external affairs in the executive power. It is in this final sense that Montesquieu discusses the relationships between the powers of government, and it is, of course, basically the modern use of these terms. The importance of this

---

49. Montesquieu always uses *"la puissance de juger,"* not *"le pouvoir judiciaire."*

transition in his use of words cannot be overemphasized. Not only does he bridge the gap between early modern and later modern terminology, but he also obscures one of the basic problems of a threefold definition of government functions. Locke and others had been bothered by the fact that the "ruler" had two aspects to his function. He had to carry out the law where it was clear and easily stated, principally in internal affairs, but he had also to act in areas where the law could not be laid down in detail and where his prerogative must remain almost wholly untrammelled, that is to say largely in external affairs. Thus between them Locke and Montesquieu state at least *four* functions of government, not three: the legislative, the executive, the "prerogative," and the judicial. To bring the two middle ones together as "executive" obscures the fact that in large areas of government activity those responsible for day-to-day government decisions will not be "executing the law," but exercising a very wide discretion. However, the idea that there are *three,* and only three, functions of government, was now established, except perhaps in the minds of those English lawyers who had actively to define the prerogative powers of the Crown.

The most important aspect of Montesquieu's treatment of the functions of government is that he completes the transition from the old usage of "executive" to a new "power of judging," distinct from the putting of the law into effect, which becomes the new executive function. However, it is in his treatment of the "power of judging" that Montesquieu's greatest innovatory importance lies. He treats the *puissance de juger* as on a par, analytically, with the other two functions of government, and so fixes quite firmly the trinity of legislative, executive, and judicial which is to characterize modern thought. Vitally important also is the fact that he detaches this power from the aristocratic part of the legislature and vests it unequivocally in the ordinary courts of the land, although the noble house of the legislature is to have the role of a court of appeal. However, he still does not give the courts the position they were soon to achieve in American thought; he does not accord the judicial *branch* an exactly equal status with the legislative and executive branches, although he clearly intends the judiciary to be independent of the other two. He sees these two agencies as permanent bodies of magistrates,[50] which represent real social forces, the monarch, the nobility, and the people. The judiciary, however, "so terrible to mankind," should not be annexed to any particular class (*état*) or profession, and so becomes, in some sense, no social force at all—*"en quelque façon nulle"*—representing everyone and no one.[51] The judiciary, therefore, is to be wholly independent of the clash of interests in the State, and this emphasis upon judicial independence is extremely important for the development of the doctrine.

Montesquieu devotes considerable attention to the nature and composition of the judiciary, but his approach to this problem is very much a reflection of his general scheme, and does not bear much relation to the actual practice in England. In Book VI he had developed his ideas about the judicial function in the differing forms of State. In a despotic government the caprice of the prince is the basis of the law, and judging will be an arbitrary process without rules. In a monarchy, however, the prince rules according to the laws; these must be relatively stable and applied in a cool, aloof fashion. The judges in a monarchy, therefore (and Montesquieu is clearly thinking of the *parlements*), must be learned in the law, professional, and skilled in the reconciliation of potentially conflicting rules. But the closer the form of government approaches that of a republic, the more fixed and settled are the rules of law, and the more the judges must follow the letter of the law.[52] In Rome, he avers, the judges had only to decide matters of fact, and then the punishment was clearly to be found in the laws. In England the jury gives its verdict on the facts and the judge pronounces the punishment inflicted by the law, "and for this he needs only to open his eyes."[53] In Book XI he describes a judicial system without professional judges. He rejects the idea of the judiciary power being lodged in a "standing senate," and affirms that it should be exercised by persons drawn

50. He justifies this stability in the legislative and executive powers by declaring that "they are not exercised on any private subject."

51. Franz Neumann, op. cit., p. lviii.

52. *De l'Esprit des Loix*, VI, 3.

53. Ibid.

(*tirées*) from the people, on an *ad hoc* basis for fixed periods of short duration. In other words a system of juries, which would apparently be judges of both fact and law, because the laws would be so clear and explicit as to require no professional knowledge in the judges.

Two further aspects of Montesquieu's treatment of the judiciary require emphasis. First, his insistence that in republics the judges must abide by the letter of the law is of great importance for later views of the judicial function. In England in medieval times the judges were well aware that they "interpreted" the law, and from time to time were aware that they were making law through "interpretation." The role of the judges in making the law was also recognized in the seventeenth century. But Montesquieu insists that to allow the judges to exercise discretion is to expose the people to the danger that the private opinions of the judges might render the laws uncertain, and that people would then live in society "without exactly knowing the nature of their obligations." The judges must be "no more than the mouth that pronounces the words of the law, mere passive beings, incapable of moderating either its force or rigour." This mechanical view of the proper role of the judges can be found in the writings of Lilburne and Harrington during the Civil War in England, and it is perhaps from the latter that Montesquieu obtained this notion. Its influence in the nineteenth century and in the early part of the twentieth, until the rise of the "sociological" school of jurisprudence, was a formidable one indeed. Second, he emphasizes the importance of judicial procedures as a protection for the individual. The speedy decision of cases may be cheaper and easier, but the set forms of justice with all their expense and delay, even the very dangers of the judicial procedure, are "the price that each subject pays for his liberty." In despotic governments speed is the only consideration, but in moderate governments long inquiries and many formalities are necessary before a man is stripped of his honour or property, or of his life. This insistence upon "due process," a phrase Montesquieu does not use but which again was current in seventeenth-century England, is of the essence of the doctrine of constitutionalism, in the development of which his thought forms such an important step.

By 1748, therefore, he had formulated the tripartite division of government functions in a recognizably modern form. A good deal of change still had to take place in the ensuing two hundred years in the exact connotation of these concepts, but basically the pattern was now set. To legislate is to make the law; to execute is to put it into effect; the judicial power is the announcing of what the law is by the settlement of disputes. These functions exhaust all the "powers" of government, and they can be clearly differentiated from each other. Every government act can be put into one or other of these categories. He also established the idea of three *branches* of government—executive, legislature, and judiciary. So much for the analytical separation of agencies and functions. But to demonstrate that Montesquieu had a "theory of the separation of powers" in one sense or another we must go further. We must show that he maintained that each function should be exercised by the appropriate agency of government, and that he furthermore believed that the personnel of the three branches should not coincide. It will become quite clear at a later stage that he did not maintain the pure doctrine of the separation of powers, for he combined with it the ideas of mixed government and checks and balances; however, that he did advocate that each agency should exercise, in the main, only its own functions, is also perfectly clear. He was quite explicit here:

> When the legislative and executive powers are united in the same person, or in the same body of magistrates, there can be no liberty. . . . Again, there is no liberty, if the judiciary power be not separated from the legislative and executive. Were it joined with the legislative, the life and liberty of the subject would be exposed to arbitrary control; for the judge would then be the legislator. Were it joined to the executive power, the judge might behave with violence and oppression. There would be an end to everything, were the same man, or the same body, whether of the nobles or of the people, to exercise those three powers, that of enacting laws, that of executing the public resolutions, and of trying the causes of individuals.

The representative body ought not to exercise the executive function, because it is not suited to it. The legislature ought not to be able to arraign the person entrusted with the executive power, for this would turn the legislature into a body with arbitrary power. One cannot ignore the clear meaning of these words. Montesquieu believed that the various functions of government should be entrusted to distinct agencies of government, which would be largely independent of each other in the exercise of these functions. The problem of the extent to which each of these agencies should be able to control the others will be considered later.

We have seen that even given the attribution of distinct functions to separate agencies there still arises the problem of personnel. Should the personnel of the agencies be quite distinct, or should a degree of over-lapping be allowed, or does it not matter at all? Montesquieu is less clear on this point than on the other elements, although there are strong in-dications of his line of thought. When writing of monarchy he does not envisage a separation of legislative and executive functions in practice, so the question of personnel does not arise; however, he does express shock at the idea that royal ministers should also sit as judges. There is, he says, a sort of "contradiction" between the prince's council and the courts of judi-cature. The former requires a certain passion in the conduct of its affairs by a few men who identify themselves with its business, whereas the courts demand a certain *"sang-froid"* and a measure of indifference on the part of the judges.[54] Once again we have this emphasis upon the impartiality of the judiciary. In his discussion of the judiciary in Book XI, he is less explicit, but the nature of the selection of the judges, or rather juries, is such that the problem of whether or not they should simultaneously be legislators, or in the service of the king, hardly seems to arise. These *ad hoc* juries are so impermanent that the problem of the overlapping of membership with the more professional and permanent members of the other branches does not arise.

The problem of the separation of the personnel of the legislative and executive branches in the constitution of liberty was also very obliquely dealt with by Montesquieu. He paid little attention to the servants of the king, other than ministers, and so there was no great scope for discussions of the extent to which they should be allowed to be legislators as well. He did, however, echo the English writers who condemn corruption of legis-lators—the English State will perish "when the legislative power shall be

54. *De l'Esprit des Loix*, VI, 6.

more corrupt than the executive." However, one very important change from the contemporary English theory that he made, concerning the composition of the executive and legislative branches, must be noted here. The English writers saw the legislative power as held jointly by King, Lords, and Commons, even though the King's role might be seen as only a negative one. This sharing of the legislative power was the foundation of their theory of the balanced constitution, and it continued to be so even after Montesquieu's work had received general acclaim as a eulogy of the English Constitution. They therefore wrote of "the King-in-Parliament." Montesquieu, however, looked at the problem in a slightly different way. He wrote of the "legislative body" as composed of "two parts," with the executive separated from them. He did give to the executive a veto power, which he described as having a share in legislation (*prendre part à la législation*), but the emphasis of his usage is important. Whereas the English writers saw the King as an essential part of the legislative *branch* itself, he saw the executive as a separate branch which has a part to play in the exercise of the legislative function. The importance of this difference of emphasis becomes clear when we compare the differing approaches of the English and American writers at the end of the eighteenth century. This would suggest, then, that Montesquieu saw the King, "the person entrusted with the executive power," as outside the legislature; if, therefore, the King really makes the decisions, and provided that he cannot corrupt the legislature, it does not matter whether or not his subordinates are members of the legislature or not. This view is supported by the fact that Montesquieu argued that if the executive power is *not* in the hands of a monarch, but is committed "to a certain number of persons selected from the legislative body, there would be an end then of liberty; by reason the two powers would be united, as the same persons would sometimes possess, and would be always able to possess, a share in both." This would seem to be a reference to the ministerial system in England, and to the view that if the monarch were no longer head of the executive, or perhaps became a mere figurehead, with real power in the hands of his ministers, then the concentration of power would be a genuine danger. Those who accuse Montesquieu of being wholly unaware of the contemporary development of cabinet government in England seem to overlook this passage. It should be borne in mind that when he wrote, the King still exercised considerable power—Montesquieu looked forward to a period when this would, perhaps, no longer be the case.

He did not, therefore, work out in detail the problem of the overlapping of the personnel of the agencies of government, and he certainly did not issue a general prohibition. It is strange that he made no direct reference to the problem of place-bills, which had been so important in England. But the spirit of what he had to say seems clear enough; whenever it is a question of the exercise of real power the agencies of government should not come under the control of a single person or group of persons. "When the legislative and executive powers are united in the same person, or in the same body of magistrates, there can be no liberty." Detailed analysis of Montesquieu's words should not be allowed to blind us to what he had to say.

Having shown that all the elements of the pure doctrine of the separation of powers are to be found, if not always clearly worked out, in Montesquieu's thought, can we simply label him as a protagonist of the pure doctrine? Clearly not, for he went further, and added to these ideas the further dimension of a theory of checks and balances between the legislative and executive powers, drawn largely from the theory of mixed government. He did not rely upon a concept of negative checks to the exercise of power, checks dependent upon the mere existence of potentially antagonistic agencies, charged with different functions of government—again he went further, and advocated positive checks by placing powers of control over the other branches in the hands of each of them. Perhaps the first important point to note about his theory of checks and balances is that in Book XI it does not involve the judiciary or "the power of judging" at all. The judiciary is not given any power over the other branches. Equally, its independence is absolute, for it is not subject to control by the other branches, except that the legislature can be a supreme court of appeal in order to mitigate the sentence of the law. The courts, in other words, being merely the mouthpiece of the law, being *en quelque façon nulle,* and not representing any social force in the State, are not seen as a check, nor is it necessary to check them. The difference between this view of judicial power and that of Chief Justice Marshall in *Marbury* v. *Madison,* fifty-five years later, is of great interest although it is true that Montesquieu elsewhere saw the French *par-lements* with their rights of remonstrance as checks to the legislative power.

The relationships between the executive and legislative branches, how-ever, exhibit clearly the characteristics of the idea of checks and balances that we saw in the English theory of the balanced constitution. The execu-tive officer ought to have a share in the legislative power by a veto over legislation, but he ought not to have the power to enter positively into the making of legislation. The executive should have the power of calling and fixing the duration of meetings of the legislative body. In this way the executive branch will be able to prevent the encroachments of the legis-lature on its authority, thus ensuring that the legislature will not become despotic. The legislature should not, however, have the right to stay (*ar-rêter*) the executive, but it should have the power to examine the manner in which its laws have been executed. Whatever the results of this ex-amination, the legislature should not be able to judge the person, or the conduct of the person, who executes the law. However, the counsellors upon whose advice unwise policies are adopted may be punished, and for this purpose the power of impeachment must lie in the legislature, with the Lower House accusing, and the Upper House judging. "Here, then, is the fundamental constitution of the government we are treating of. The legislative body being composed of two parts, they check one another by the mutual privilege of rejecting. They are both restrained by the execu-tive power, as the executive is by the legislative." Montesquieu, though he had great faith in the power of constitutions to mould the public character of a State, was nevertheless sufficiently aware of sociological necessity to see the importance of having the essential parts of the State as representa-tive of different interests in society; and so he adapted the theory of mixed government to the underpinning of a system of divided powers, in order that the varying "passions and interests" of the different classes of society should ensure that no one man or group of men gained arbitrary power. This does not mean that he threw overboard the notion of the separation of powers. It still remained as the foundation of the constitution of liberty, as he frequently reasserted, but certain quite specific and limited powers were attributed to the executive to enable it to control the legislature, and to the legislature to control the subordinate members of the executive. These control mechanisms did not constitute a "fusion" of powers; they were links between the branches of government, each restricted to the exercise of its appropriate function. The practical problems of these controls, the extent to which they embodied an opportunity for co-ordination, or alternatively for deadlock, between the branches, was not yet clearly perceived, although Montesquieu at a later stage devoted some time to a discussion of the nature of party politics in England, with its division of the legislative and executive powers.[55] Thus Montesquieu clearly did see a broad separation of functions among distinct agencies of government, with a separation of personnel, to which was added the need for a set of positive checks to the exercise of power by each of the two major, permanent, agencies of government to prevent them from abusing the power entrusted to them. The ideas of independence and interdependence which Bolingbroke developed are useful here for the understanding of this system. Without a high degree of *independent* power in the hands of each branch they cannot be said to be *interdependent*, for this requires that neither shall be subordinate to the other. At the same time a degree of interdependence does not destroy the essential independence of the branches.

Montesquieu was aware of the problem of ensuring that a system of government so nicely balanced should not result in complete deadlock, that the three bodies, King, Lords, and Commons, by being poised in opposition to each other should not produce merely a state of "repose or inaction." But he dismissed the problem by arguing that in the nature of things they are forced to move (*par le mouvement nécessaire des choses*), and forced to move in concert. The question of whether he saw the State as an organic unity in which the articulated parts formed a single unit exercising the sovereign power, or whether he destroyed the unity of sovereignty by dividing it up into parts which were to be distributed among quite distinct, autonomous bodies, related to each other in a mechanistic fashion only, is probably impossible to answer, because it is doubtful if he ever formulated

55. XIX, 27.

the problem in either of these ways.[56] He seems to have a unitary view of the supreme power when he is discussing his three forms of State in the initial books of *De l'Esprit des Loix*, but there is little clue to his attitude in Book XI, Chapter 6. On the question of legislative supremacy he seems, though less explicitly, to hold much the same position that we attributed above to John Locke. The legislative function is logically prior to the rest in the sense that the executive and judicial functions are concerned with putting the law into effect; but the legislative branch must be limited in its power to interfere with the acts of the executive branch, otherwise the former will be able to wield arbitrary power. Montesquieu does not, however, emphasize the supremacy of the law, or of the legislative function, to anything like the extent Locke had done, and as a consequence there seems to be a good deal more disagreement between them on this point than was probably the case.

What then did Montesquieu add to seventeenth- and early-eighteenth-century English thought on the separation of powers? Clearly his view of the functions of government was much closer to modern usage than his predecessors'—he was one of the first writers to use "executive" in a recognizably modern sense in juxtaposition with the legislative and judicial functions. His emphasis upon the judicial function and upon the equality of this function with the other functions of government, though (as we have seen) by no means altogether new, was nevertheless of great importance. The judiciary had a position of independence in his thought greater than that of earlier English writers, and greater than it was in practice at that time in England. Although he used the idea of mixed government he did not allow it to dominate his thought, as had the writers on the balanced constitution in England; consequently he articulated the elements of the constitution in a different way, and a clearer view of the separation of legislative and executive branches was now possible. He had gone a long way, in fact, towards the transformation of the theory of mixed govern-

56. Stark, op. cit., Ch. I, discusses this problem, arguing that Montesquieu had a semi-organic rather than a mechanistic concept of the State.

ment from its position as a doctrine in its own right into a set of checks and balances in a system of agencies separated on a functional basis. Perhaps the most significant difference between Bolingbroke and Montesquieu is that the latter placed the King outside the legislature. In some ways, then, Montesquieu moved back towards the emphasis that was placed during the Protectorate upon separate and distinct powers; he was certainly closer to the pure doctrine than his English contemporaries, but he did not go all the way. He had a more realistic, more articulated system, with an amalgam of seventeenth- and eighteenth-century ideas woven into a new fabric. Sometimes it is difficult to know whether the changes he introduced into the stream of political thought on constitutionalism were wholly intentional, or whether they resulted rather from his method of writing. We shall never know—but it does not matter. The very defects of his style gave him an influence which a more precise and less interesting thinker would never have achieved, but more important than this is the fact that by changing the emphasis that English writers of the preceding half century had placed upon legislative supremacy and the mixed constitution, he paved the way for the doctrine of the separation of powers to emerge again as an autonomous theory of government. This theory was to develop in very different ways in Britain, in America, and on the continent of Europe, but from this time on, the doctrine of the separation of powers was no longer an English theory; it had become a universal criterion of a constitutional government.

FIVE

The Matchless Constitution
and Its Enemies

A LITTLE OVER a century after the outbreak of the English Civil War two major theories of constitutionalism had been developed, closely related to each other in their evolution and their logic, yet capable of becoming the intellectual weapons of two different schools of thought, bitterly divided on the "proper" constitution of government. The theory of the balanced constitution had been evolved from the ancient theory of mixed government, which held, as the basis of its opposition to the exercise of arbitrary power, the belief that power could only be checked by the creation of a system of government in which the three classes of society were nicely balanced against each other. The transformation of the theory of mixed government into the theory of the balanced constitution, in which King, Lords, and Commons operated a complex system of checks and balances upon each other, demanded, however, a second theorem. This demand was met by the theory of the separation of powers, with the assertion that the functions of government could be divided up among the parts of the system in such a way that each branch could be limited to the exercise of its "proper function," and the balance was completed by allowing each branch a limited right of interference in the functions of the others in order to prevent the encroachment of any one of them upon the function of any other. Thus the separation of powers was a subordinate but essential element in the theory of the balanced constitution. This subordinate theory was, however, capable of a life of its own, rejecting the class basis of the theory of the balanced constitution, and emerging as a theory of constitutionalism which, overtly at any rate, was based exclusively upon a functional approach to the division of power, recognizing only the right of the democratic branch of government in the making of law, relegating the "ruler" to a purely executive role, and, in so far as the aristocratic element was recognized at all, assimilating it to the judiciary.

These two theories, the balanced constitution and the separation of powers, formed a pattern of constitutional theory for the two hundred years following 1640, linked to each other in a curious relationship of mutual attraction and repulsion. The separation of powers was essential to the balanced constitution, for the notion of a *balance* necessarily assumed a basis of *separation*, but this necessity imposed upon the theory of the balanced constitution the burden of maintaining the source of its own destruction; for the separation of powers was eminently suited to the needs of the rising middle class, which was attacking monarchic and aristocratic power, but wished to maintain limits to the exercise of government power even when the government was dominated by an elected legislature. Thus movements towards a greater degree of democracy had the effect of stripping away the monarchical and aristocratic elements of the theory of the balanced constitution, leaving the separation of powers as the only basis of a theory of constitutional government. At each outbreak of democratic fervour the proponents of the balanced constitution were faced with the need to resist the onslaught of a theory they could not wholly reject, and to argue the merits of their complex theory of the constitution against the relatively simple and clear-cut theory of the separation of powers. Only when the evolution of new forms of republican and parliamentary government enabled the checks and balances of the balanced constitution to be applied to governmental systems largely divested of class characteristics (except in their franchise qualifications) was this fierce antagonism brought to an end.

It is to be expected that the conflict between these two constitutional theories would be at its height in a revolutionary situation where the middle class was engaged in wresting privileges from king and nobles, and that in such a situation the theory of the separation of powers would supersede the balanced constitution, and would be tested as a practical means of constituting a system of government. In the years following 1640 in England the first of these revolutionary confrontations took place with the evolution and temporary supremacy of the theory of the separation of powers over the theory of mixed government, only to give way to the establishment of the eighteenth-century theory of the balanced constitution. Over the next two hundred years four other revolutionary or potentially revolutionary confrontations were to take place in America, France, and Britain. The American Revolution, and the French Revolutions of 1789 and 1848 show the pattern very clearly. In England the latent revolution of the period 1770 to 1832 shows a similar pattern, and gives a hint of what might have happened in Britain had a revolution actually broken out. Of course the pattern is not exactly repeated in these five situations; there are important differences due to the exact developments in constitutional thought and the particular circumstances of each event, but the same fundamental elements of constitutional thought are present, and they are related to each other in the same general fashion. The period of constitutional thought from 1640 to 1848 has within it, therefore, an essential unity, a unity based upon the development in these three countries of the same social groups, cherishing similar values, and, in particular, holding the same view of the nature of political liberty.

The eighteenth century ended in England, as it had begun, with eulogies on the mixed and balanced constitution. Robert Nares in 1792, or Francis Plowden in 1794, had essentially the same constitutional theory as Swift or Mackworth in 1701.[1] There is a stability, a changeless quality, about the dominant strands of English political thought in the eighteenth century which only serves, however, to mask the great changes that were taking place. In 1701 the proponents of the balanced constitution were expounding a newly-established delicate balance, which could still be overthrown

---

1. R. Nares, *Principles of Government Deduced from Reason*, London, 1792; and F. Plowden, *A Short History of the British Empire*, London, 1794.

---

by a resurgence of Stuart absolutism; but in 1794 their spiritual beneficia-
ries were fighting a rearguard action against the onrushing tide of "democracy," however narrowly that term might be conceived at the end of the
eighteenth century. The impact of the American and French Revolutions,
together with the popular clamour for parliamentary reform, presented a
challenge to the accepted doctrine of the British Constitution which would
eventually prove irresistible; the wonder is that the theory of the balanced
constitution retained its appeal well into the nineteenth century. The attack
upon a constitutional theory based upon a mixture of monarchy, aristocracy, and democracy began in earnest in the 1770's, and was strongly maintained until the Reform Act brought some respite to the political scene.
The attack took several forms; the idea of balance in politics was ridiculed
as a logical fallacy, as a false description of the English Constitution, or as
a sham theory to hide the real monarchical or aristocratic nature of the
constitution. Over a century before, the theory of mixed government had
failed to meet the demands posed by the changing conditions of English
politics, and the theory of the separation of powers had emerged as an alternative, for a time replacing the older theory altogether. In the potentially
revolutionary situation at the end of the eighteenth century the theory of
mixed and balanced government was again challenged as an adequate basis
for a constitution, and we might expect a similar resurgence of the doctrine
of the separation of powers, following the examples of America and France.
There was indeed a resurgence of interest in the separation of powers
among Englishmen interested in constitutional reform, and had revolution
provided the occasion in England for constitution-making, who knows how
important the doctrine might have become? But the revolution in England
was staved off; the theory of mixed government, although strongly challenged, maintained its influence till well after the passage of the Reform
Act, and a smooth transition to a new theory of balance in a parliamentary
government was developed. However, though unsuccessful, the intellectual
challenge was a strong one, and in the pattern of English political thought
from 1770 to 1830 we find the same interaction between mixed government and the separation of powers so important in America and in France.

The chapter on the English Constitution in Montesquieu's *De l'Esprit des Loix* reflected as its major source the writings of English thinkers on the balanced constitution, yet it is clear that Montesquieu gave an emphasis to the importance of the separation of powers very different from that of any major English writer since Locke. For most English thinkers the separation of powers was essentially a subordinate aspect of their constitutional doctrine, necessary to the maintenance of limits to the power of the three branches of the government—King, Lords, and Commons—but less important than the over-all balance of the "powers" of government maintained by the share each of them had in the legislative function. Montesquieu stressed the separation of powers, and placed that theory in a position of equality with mixed government in his constitutional theory. Furthermore, Montesquieu's formulation of the judicial power was very different from that of Bolingbroke and his contemporaries in the extraparliamentary character he gave to the judicial function. Thus, although there is a considerable continuity between pre- and post-Montesquieu writers on the English Constitution, these changes of emphasis are extremely important in the texture of the late-eighteenth-century constitutional writings. Montesquieu's "description" of the English Constitution, if closely examined, does not correspond with the constitution which the eulogists of the late eighteenth century were defending, but his words, taken out of context, could be used as unqualified praise of the existing constitution. Montesquieu was flattered by a host of English imitators, who used his work either as a source of inspiration or simply as a mine of material for the most flagrant plagiarism.[2] The most important of Montesquieu's disciples in England were Blackstone, de Lolme, and Paley. All three eulogized the English Constitution, but each of them, by his differing emphasis and interpretation, provided the basis for different approaches to the "Matchless Constitution," and consequently each had a quite different influence upon differing sections of political thought in the late eighteenth century and afterwards, both at home and abroad.

Blackstone was not a very original thinker, and his debt to Montesquieu, other than in the field of the common law, has overshadowed his own con-

2. For a full discussion of Montesquieu's imitators see F. T. H. Fletcher, *Montesquieu and English Politics (1750–1800)*, London, 1939.

tribution to constitutional theory, to a point where he has been considered no more than a reflection of the master. This debt was indeed great. It has been said that Blackstone's plagiarism "would be nauseating if it were not comic,"[3] and it would certainly be tedious to enumerate here Blackstone's repetitions of Montesquieu; but it would be quite wrong to suggest that Blackstone's exposition of the constitution differed in no important respects from that of Montesquieu, or that those differences had no relation to later developments in political thought. There were modifications of Montesquieu's thought in the *Commentaries on the Laws of England*, which appeared in 1765–9, and as the Commentaries were regarded as authoritative in the American colonies as well as in England, it was often through Blackstone's eyes that the colonists saw the Montesquieu theory.[4]

It was Blackstone's task to assimilate as much of Montesquieu as possible and to domesticate him; to acknowledge the fact that the separation of powers was an essential part of the constitutional theory of England, but to effect a reconciliation of the separation of powers with the dominant concept of the balanced constitution to a greater degree than had ever been done before. Montesquieu himself never quite achieved this reconciliation. As we have seen, the two theories lie side by side in his work, but they are not really united. However, it is possible to draw from Montesquieu's words the sense of what "he must have meant," and this Blackstone did. His emphasis upon mixed government and its superiority over the three simple types was clear and unmistakable; he had none of Montesquieu's difficulties with methodology—the British system was simply a happy exception to the general rule that such a mixture could not exist.[5] He accepted unhesitatingly Montesquieu's view of the necessity for the separation of the legislative and executive powers.[6] But Blackstone was aware of the potential conflict between this idea and the theory of mixed government, and he resolved it by stating clearly what was no doubt implicit in Montesquieu but never explicitly revealed. It is necessary, said Blackstone, that the

3. Ibid., p. 121.
4. See the essay on Blackstone in Sir Ernest Barker's *Essays on Government*, Oxford, 1945.
5. *Commentaries,* Intro., Sect. 2, p. 50.
6. Ibid., I, 2, p. 146.

executive power should be a branch, but not the whole of the legislature. "The total union of them, we have seen, would be productive of tyranny; the total disjunction of them for the present would in the end produce the same effects by causing that union against which it seems to provide. The legislative would soon become tyrannical, by making continual encroachments and gradually assuming to itself the rights of the executive power."[7] Blackstone was expounding here the idea of a partial separation of persons and functions which for him was the basis of a balanced constitution, and a few years later, with some change of emphasis, basically the same doctrine was used by Madison to explain the nature of the Federal Constitution of the United States.[8] It can perhaps hardly be claimed that Blackstone made a great contribution to political theory here. What he says differs only slightly from the quotation from Bolingbroke given in an earlier chapter.[9] But he has adapted the traditional English theory to the language of Montesquieu and has formulated more precisely than any of his predecessors the essential kernel of this constitutional theory.

The most important "domestication" of Montesquieu's theory, however, came in the sphere of the judicial power. We have seen that the independence of the judges had been a matter of concern to Englishmen for well over a century and a half before Blackstone, and that the idea of a separate "judicial power" had begun in mid-seventeenth-century England. However, the early-eighteenth-century writers on the constitution placed this "power" in the House of Lords, as did Bolingbroke in the quotation mentioned above. It was left to Montesquieu to assert again the importance of an independent judicial power, separate from the legislature and from the executive alike. But Montesquieu had an equivocal view of the position of the judiciary. Only when discussing his monarchical form of government did he see the judiciary as a standing body of professional judges. When writing of the English Constitution he thought in terms of a republican *régime* in which there would be no standing judiciary, only *ad hoc* juries. Blackstone gathered up the threads of Montesquieu's varying statements and firmly combined them into an affirmation of the necessity

7. Ibid., I, 2, p. 154.   8. See Ch. 6 below.   9. p. 80 above.

for an independent judicial power, along the lines of that which actually existed in England. The courts were "the grand depositories of the fundamental laws of the kingdom,"[10] a phrase which Montesquieu had used only for the *parlements*. In England the courts were staffed by professional judges learned in the law, and Blackstone emphasized the importance of the status and tenure conferred by the Act of Settlement upon the English judges, whereas Montesquieu had defended the venality of judicial office in the French monarchy. Finally, Blackstone roundly used the term "judicial power" to describe the function of the judiciary, whilst Montesquieu, in Book XI, Chapter 6, had used simply the term *le pouvoir de juger*, the power of judging, because the courts in his constitution of liberty had merely to announce the law. Blackstone's judges had behind them the whole weight and majesty of the common law of England developing through judge-made precedents, and the function of the judges was to decide "in all cases of doubt."[11] Thus Blackstone wove the judicial power into something different from, and greater than, Montesquieu's conception of it, and different also from the "judicative power" of his compatriots of the early eighteenth century. "In this distinct and separate existence of the judicial power in a peculiar body of men, nominated indeed, but not removable at pleasure by the Crown, consists one main preservative of the public liberty which cannot subsist long in any state unless the administration of common justice be in some degree separated both from the legislative and from the executive power."[12] Thus was the basis laid for the position of the judicial power in the Constitution of the United States; Blackstone was an essential link between Montesquieu and Chief Justice Marshall, for although he did not advocate judicial review of legislation, the American view of the judiciary owes more to Blackstone than it does to Montesquieu.

In other respects Blackstone followed Locke rather than Montesquieu. He emphasized the supremacy of parliament in strong terms,[13] but did not place upon the legislative power the limits which Locke has so strongly urged. He discussed the royal prerogative at length, and seeming to con-

10. *Commentaries*, I, 7, p. 267.   11. Ibid., Intro., p. 69.
12. Ibid., I, 7, p. 269.   13. Ibid., Intro., p. 91.

found both Locke and Montesquieu he roundly equated the prerogative with the executive power of government.[14]

Blackstone, then, was a disciple and plagiarist of Montesquieu, but he was something more than this. He made an essentially English interpretation of Montesquieu, and gave new direction to aspects of English thought which were to play an important part in American constitutional development. Jean Louis de Lolme, on the other hand, in his *Constitution of England*, first published in French in 1771, gave an interpretation to the English system of government which, by attempting a much more "logical" analysis, failed almost entirely to give an impression of the interrelationships between the parts of the machinery of English government. De Lolme, a Genevan who made his home in England for many years, devoted a full-length work to the subject of Montesquieu's single chapter, and is credited with a greater influence on the continent of Europe than Montesquieu himself.[15] De Lolme, like Blackstone, eulogized the balanced constitution, but his emphasis was very different. He stressed the separation of the branches of government much more than the English writers. He emphasized the need to restrain both legislature and executive, but, except for the royal negative over legislation, he did not stress the checks and balances of the constitution; rather he relied, in an almost seventeenth-century sense, upon the division of functions to safeguard liberty.[16] He argued that the division of the legislative branch into three parts and the unity of the executive branch were essential to the restraint of each of them. This found an echo in the United States Federal Convention, where James Wilson used this argument to justify a single executive and the bicameral system. But de Lolme was, in 1771, further out of touch with the realities of English politics than Montesquieu had been twenty-three years earlier. Blackstone had used a mechanical analogy by likening King, Lords, and Commons to "three distinct powers in mechanics" which "jointly impel the machine of government in a direction different from what either,

14. Ibid., I, 8, p. 281.

15. See the interesting work by Edith Ruff: *Jean Louis de Lolme und sein Werk über die Verfassung Englands* in *Historische Studien,* Vol. 240, Berlin, 1934, p. 48.

16. 4th edn. (1784), p. 275.

acting by itself would have done; but at the same time in a direction partaking of each, and formed out of all,"[17] but de Lolme pushed the mechanistic analogy to the point where deadlock—he uses the term "equilibrium"—becomes a virtue.[18] The beauty of the English system was that "the chance that no changes will be made is greatly increased."[19] Complete stagnation became the prerequisite of political liberty. However, this view of English politics, if it could ever have had any validity, was now quite archaic. If we can forgive Montesquieu for underestimating the importance of the King's Ministers, there can be no excuse for de Lolme. As the editions of his work came unheeding off the press the turmoil of discussion in political life centred on the cabinet and its role in English government.

William Paley seemed to be equally unconcerned with the role of the cabinet, but he at least was anxious to discuss the practice of the constitution rather than its "theory," including a frank discussion of the importance of the system of influence.[20] Paley, in 1785, presented perhaps the best eighteenth-century statement of the mixed and balanced constitution, using all the emphasis upon judicial independence and the separation of legislative and executive power which had become since Montesquieu an essential part of constitutional theory. At the same time he defended the system of influence as a necessary part of the constitutional scheme, without which the deadlock implicit in the theories of Montesquieu and de Lolme would certainly have been realized. Paley drew upon the same argument that David Hume had developed in his essay *Of the Independency of Parliament.* The potential power of the Commons, Hume said, was so great that only by the use of influence could the Lower House be prevented from becoming the only effective branch of the government. For Hume, and for Paley, the very power of the House of Commons necessitated a system of patronage by which the Crown and the House of Lords could defend themselves, and so maintain a genuinely mixed constitution: a truly independent

17. *Commentaries,* I, 2, p. 155.
18. Op. cit., p. 171.
19. Ibid., p. 214.
20. *The Principles of Moral and Political Philosophy.*

Commons would be inconsistent with the very existence of the monarchy.[21] Paley's defence of the *status quo* was not couched in terms of its historical longevity or the sacred prescription of tradition, but upon expediency. Those who advocated reform must bear the onus of proving that the alternatives to the existing constitution would contribute better to the sum total of public welfare and happiness. Paley set out, clearly and in a reasoned argument, the case for seeing the balanced constitution as the best and most desirable system of government that the mind of man had so far devised. Thus whilst the legalistic interpretation of Blackstone carried most weight in America, and de Lolme's "logical" view of English government was influential on the Continent, in England it was Paley's pragmatic defence of the balanced constitution that formed the basis of the resistance to reform.

Paley's brand of reasoned conservatism had great appeal for the opponents of reform. A remarkably good example of this style is provided by a work of the Reverend D. M. Peacock. In his *Considerations on the Structure of the House of Commons* of 1794 he skilfully wove into a pattern the fundamental necessity of a separation of powers, of a division of functions between the branches of government, and the need for reciprocal controls between those branches. The elements of a mixed government, he said, must be "weighed out in their just proportions with the utmost nicety and exactness, and worked up together by the most skilful and delicate hand." Should any one of these elements predominate it would destroy the others, and if the branches were not properly combined the mixture would act upon the political body like a violent and destructive poison. Thus there was required in the political system not a subordination of the Commons, but "a nice proportion of influence" which would serve to maintain the proper balance of power. However, the patterns of perfect government worked by Blackstone, Paley, and their followers, were met by a mounting tide of discussion in which the doctrine of the separation of powers played a larger and larger role.

In the sixty years from 1770 there were three major areas of thought in which the relationship of the separation of powers to the dominant

21. Ibid., p. 442.

---

constitutional theory was under discussion. First, those who operated the existing political system, including those who favoured moderate reform, were involved in day-to-day battles wherein the theory of the separation of powers was used as a weapon with which political enemies could be castigated. For these people the theory was mostly a tactical weapon, to be used as the movements of the political battle-lines made it seem appropriate to particular issues in dispute. Second, there were those who, opposing a system based upon corrupt and unrepresentative parliaments, mounted an attack upon the basis of the system, mixed government, and were led into a discussion of the separation of powers as an alternative. Third, there were those radical opponents of the existing system, and particularly of the role of the cabinet in it, who adopted a thoroughgoing version of the separation of powers as the basis of their attack.

The support of the doctrine was invoked in many of the political struggles of this period. The expulsion of Wilkes by the House of Commons was attacked by George Grenville in 1769 as an attempt by the House "to blend the executive and judicial powers of the state with the legislative,"[22] and Burke joined in the condemnation of the role which the Crown was seen to play in a judicial matter by means of legislative influence.[23] The Regency Bill of 1788 was attacked as an attempt by the Commons to take over the executive power,[24] and the appointment of Lord Chief Justice Ellenborough to the Cabinet in 1806 was opposed as a serious breach of the doctrine.[25] The greatest issue of all, however, was the proper role of the cabinet under the Constitution, and the problems that this posed for the theory of mixed government. The system of patronage and influence had, of course, long been the object of bitter attacks as the means of breaking down the independence of the "popular" branch of the legislature, but now this issue was subsumed under the greater one of the part that Ministers should play in the balanced constitution and of the use they should be able to make of this influence. The idea of a cabinet responsible to the King but also de-

22. *The Speech of a Right Honourable Gentleman . . .* , 1769, p. 52.
23. On the separation of powers in these disputes see Fletcher, op. cit., Ch. VIII.
24. *Reflections on the Formation of a Regency,* London, 1788, pp. 15–18.
25. *Annual Register for 1806,* pp. 28–29.

pendent in the long run upon maintaining support in Parliament did not fit at all well into the traditional theory of an independent trio of King, Lords, and Commons. When, furthermore, the possibility was glimpsed of a cabinet responsible to the King only in name, but really dependent upon the support of a faction in Parliament, the theory of mixed government and its subordinate division of functions was almost lost to view. Burke in the *Present Discontents* charged the Ministry with having abandoned the no longer effective fortress of prerogative and of having entered into Parliament to execute their whole programme, so robbing Parliament of any possibility of controlling the Crown, because Parliament was thereby made "to partake in every considerable act of government." The old "check" of impeachment was in danger of disappearing. Burke emphasized the need for an independent House of Commons that would be able to return again to its "old office of control." But when Burke in the same work himself argued that Ministers should be dependent upon "party" support and not merely on that of the King, he was developing a doctrine which cut at the roots of the "balanced constitution," however much in later years he asserted that he had consistently defended it.[26]

The assertion by Charles James Fox in 1784 of the right of the Commons to a negative on the choice of Ministers was characterized by Pitt as an attempt to transfer the executive power of the Crown to the House,[27] and in the same year George Rous used the authority of Montesquieu to condemn the notion of an executive selected by the legislature.[28] The nomination of Ministers by the Commons, said Rous, would remove all possibility of holding Ministers responsible, for then "no accusers remained to the guilty."[29] It is interesting that what we have come now to term "responsible government" was attacked in this period as the antithesis of responsibility, for if the "executive" and the "legislature" were so closely linked as to be jointly responsible for government acts, who was left to

26. For a discussion of this period see C. P. Courtney, *Montesquieu and Burke*, Oxford, 1963, pp. 78–82.

27. Ibid., pp. 121–2.

28. G. Rous, *A Candid Investigation . . .* , London, 1784, pp. 21–22.

29. Ibid., p. 6.

exercise the function of control? George Rous was one of the most consistent proponents in this period of the separation of powers as an essential element in the balanced constitution. He used the doctrine to attack the nomination of Ministers by the House, and to characterize the Regency Bill as an encroachment on the executive;[30] in 1784 he attacked the "mixture of executive government which corrupt Ministers have introduced into the House of Commons,"[31] and later turned to a defence of the French Constitution of 1791 as embodying the total separation of the legislative and executive powers, compared with the "unnatural mixture of executive government" in England.[32]

The moderate reformers used the theory of the balanced constitution as emphatically as the opponents of reform, arguing that the constitutional balance had been destroyed by the exercise of influence over the Commons. The only means of maintaining the reality of the "glorious triplicity" of the Constitution was to assure the independence of the Commons. Thus an appeal could be made to Blackstone's dictum that "when the independence of one of the three branches of the British legislature is lost, or becomes subservient to the other two, there would be an end of the constitution," against Paley's defence of a corrupt and unrepresentative legislature.[33] Those who wished for reform *within* the context of the mixed constitution might be expected to use the separation of powers as a weapon to attack the *status quo.* In 1812 Walter Yate in his *Political and Historical Arguments in Favour of Reform*,[34] whilst stressing that the three branches of the legislature must operate in concord, insisted that the functions of Crown and Parliament must be kept distinct,[35] and emphasized the importance of the separation of powers as an essential principle of free government.[36] Indeed he went far towards stripping away the mixed constitution

30. *A Letter to The Right Honourable Edmund Burke,* London, 1791, pp. 93–95.
31. *The Claim of the House of Commons . . .* , 1784.
32. *A Letter to the Right Honourable . . .* , pp. 96, 99, and 103.
33. See *Defence of the Constitution,* Birmingham, 1822, pp. 21 and 44–45, attributed to Sir Peter Payne.
34. *The Biographical Dictionary of the Living Authors,* London, 1816, p. 403, states: "This was written by Captain Ashe, who sold the MS. for £300."
35. Ibid., p. 85.
36. Ibid., p. 19.

altogether, and relying solely on the separation of powers, when he asked "What is the necessity of a *check* on the power of the Commons by King and Lords?"[37] Provided that "the people of property are free and happy" Yate saw the need only for "an adequate representation of the people, unchecked and uninfluenced by any thing, but the common interest; and that they appoint responsible men for the execution of the laws." If properly constituted annual parliaments were to be held he foresaw the possibility of an executive more permanent than in the existing system, for then the executive would be obliged to act according to justice and the public interest.[38]

The "moderate" proponent of reform within the existing Constitution could easily slide into a much more radical position. "Friends of Reform — Foes of Revolution" is a slogan which has within it the threat of an easy transition to a completely different position if the aims of reformers are baulked. The defence of a perfectly balanced constitution could slip from a eulogy on the French *Charte* of 1830, as a system of government in which "the Commons are triumphant, the peers subordinate, and the king only the premier, or first public minister," to the outright assertion that British government was based upon "the impossible theory of three equal coexisting branches of the legislature."[39] There was therefore implicit in the demands for reform the threat of an all-out attack upon privilege which would sweep away altogether the old system. What the result might have been is suggested in the writings of those radical opponents of the balanced constitution who openly rejected its basic assumption of a mixture of monarchy, aristocracy, and democracy.

The outright attack upon the basis of the balanced constitution in England burst out with the rejection of the established theory of the constitution in America. The upsurge of democratic feeling was reflected in the rejection by the radicals of all monarchic or aristocratic privilege. Many of these radical opponents of mixed government were also bitterly opposed to the cabinet system, which they saw as the instrument of royal or aristo-

37. Ibid., p. 242.
38. Ibid., p. 238.
39. *The Black Book: An Exposition of Abuses in Church and State,* London, 1832, edn. of 1835, p. 625.

cratic oppression. Tom Paine, in *Common Sense,* first published in America in 1776, launched the attack on mixed government and the balanced constitution. "To say that the Constitution of England is a *union* of three powers, reciprocally *checking* each other is farcical; either the words have no meaning, or they are flat contradictions."[40] In practice, wrote Paine, the corrupt influence of the Crown had made England nearly as monarchical as France or Spain. In the first part of the *Rights of Man* Paine turned his attack from the King to the cabinet. "What is supposed to be the King in a mixed government, is the Cabinet."[41] The members of the cabinet, in their dual capacity as members of parliament and servants of the Crown, justify in one capacity the measures that they advise and carry out in another. The system could only be maintained by corrupt means, so that eventually it resolved into a government by committee, "in which the advisers, the actors, the approvers, the justifiers, the persons responsible and the persons not responsible, are the same persons."[42] The antagonism of the radicals to the cabinet system was so great that they preferred to appeal for support to the theory of balanced government of de Lolme or Blackstone rather than accept the idea of a cabinet responsible to the Commons. Thus as late as 1807 Cobbett and other writers in the *Political Register* demanded the complete exclusion of office-holders from the Commons, quoting the Act of Settlement as a precedent, and using the idea of checks and balances as a justification;[43] for whilst the separation of powers clearly played a role in the theory of the balanced constitution, it seemed to them to have no place at all in the evolving theory of ministerial responsibility to parliament.

If the radical reformers saw the English Constitution, in the words of David Williams, as "one of the most awkward and unmanageable fabrics which has ever been produced by human folly,"[44] what did they intend to put in its place? Paine, his energies bent upon slashing criticism, was relatively little concerned with constructive ideas, but for him, like most of the

40. Op. cit., edn. of 1819, p. 8.
41. Edn. of 1819, p. 107.
42. Ibid.
43. *Political Register,* 1807, XI, 518, 558, 585; XII, 587, 990.
44. *Letters on Political Liberty,* London, 1782, p. 9.

others, the example of America, and, for a time at least, of France, was of vital importance. In his own words, "the American Constitutions were to liberty what grammar is to language."[45] The radicals, despairing of getting Parliament to reform itself, turned against the idea of parliamentary supremacy and looked to a constitution that would subordinate Parliament to popular control. Paine's gibe that Britain had no constitution led many to assert that the real constitution, as opposed to the sham system of government then operating, could be found by reaching back to the Saxon institutions of England that had flourished before the Norman feudal yoke had imposed upon the people the crushing burden of aristocracy. Jeremy Bentham, on the other hand, was led to compose a *Constitutional Code*, from first principles, which would regulate the exercise of all power, and in which the legislature would be subject to control.

The evolution of Bentham's thought is of great interest in illustrating the way in which the thought of English radicals might provide a parallel to the constitutional developments of America and France. Bentham's political views underwent a good deal of change with the passage of the years, and in his earlier work he was relatively little concerned with the problems of political organization. In 1776 he, like Paine, attacked the dominant constitutional theory, ridiculing Blackstone's description of the English system of government with a "theorem" which proved that mixed government must be all-weak, all-foolish, and all-knavish,[46] and in the *Book of Fallacies*, first published in 1824, Bentham developed an attack upon the very notion of a "balance" in politics.[47] Although Bentham attacked the notion of the balanced constitution, this did not mean that he accepted the doctrine of the separation of powers as an alternative. Both ideas were subjected to attack as intellectually unsound. In the *Fragment* he doubted that Blackstone, or anyone else, had given enough thought to the terms *legislative power* and *executive power*, which they used so freely, and so vaguely,[48] and in the *General View of a Complete Code of Laws*, published in French

45. *Rights of Man, Part I*, edn. of 1819, p. 65.
46. *A Fragment on Government*, in *Works*, ed. by John Bowring, Edinburgh, 1843, Vol. I, p. 282.
47. *Works*, Vol. II, pp. 445–7.
48. *Works*, Vol. I, pp. 278–9.

in 1802, Bentham criticized the usually-adopted divisions of government functions as "in a state of confusion and disorder."[49] In this work he made the fundamental point that the usual distinction between the legislative power and the judicial power, which defined the former as concerned only with generalities and the latter only with particular acts, was a false one. He developed a distinction between the two powers, largely based upon their procedural characteristics,[50] but he preferred to create his own classification of political powers, seven of them, which he believed would remove the confusions inherent in any attempt to apply the terminology of one system of government when describing another, and so obviate "the torment of those who have had to give an account of a foreign constitution."[51] Bentham was also critical of any theoretical approach to the structure of government that divided the powers of government in a way which would make them separate and independent, for this would be to introduce anarchy into a State. There must always be an authority, superior to all others, which "receives no law, but only gives it, and which remains master even of the rules themselves which it imposes upon its manner of acting."[52]

This last phrase suggests a commitment to an unqualified legislative supremacy, yet elsewhere Bentham showed a considerable concern that *any* exercise of governmental power should be subject to checks. "To the welfare of the governed . . . it is highly conducive at least, if not . . . altogether necessary, that in whatsoever hands power be lodged, checks to it, in some shape or other, should, throughout the whole field of its exercise, be applying themselves."[53] It is in the *Constitutional Code*, published in 1827–30, that Bentham, for the first time, really faced the constitutional problems of a representative democracy. In this work he clearly rejected parliamentary supremacy, explicitly adopting the principle of the French Constitution of 1791, which had been announced by Sieyès, of a constituent authority to which the other authorities of the State—*les autorités constituées*—in-

---

49. Ibid., Vol. III, p. 198.
50. Ibid.
51. Ibid., Vol. III, p. 196.
52. Ibid., Vol. I, pp. 570–1.
53. *The Elements of the Art of Packing*, in *Works*, Vol. V, p. 69.

---

cluding the legislative, were to be subordinated.[54] His basic principle was, however, a hierarchy of powers, rather than the separation of equal powers which the Constituent Assembly adopted in France. The legislative power is subordinate to the supreme constitutive power, the "supreme executive" is subordinate to the legislature, and the executive chief is "superordinate" to the Minister of Justice, who heads the judiciary.[55]

The most striking aspect of the *Constitutional Code* is the admiration Bentham there expresses for the example which the United States has set in the Constitution. His work was based, of course, upon the essential principle of the greatest happiness of the greatest number, but he easily reconciled this philosophic principle with constant appeals to American experience, by simply stating that the American Constitution "has for its object the greatest happiness of the greatest number."[56] It is hardly surprising, therefore, that Bentham's scheme shows clearly the influence of the Federal Constitution, or that, in spite of the hierarchical principle he adopted, some aspects of the separation of powers, in particular in respect of the personnel of government, crept in by the back door. Except for the overriding authority of the constituent power, the people, Bentham's legislature was omnicompetent. He rejected Montesquieu's theory of the separation or division of power because "it is destitute of all reference to the greatest happiness of the greatest number"; yet he praised the *Federalist*.[57] The function of executive and judicial officers was to carry out the orders of the legislature, and no more. If they failed to do this the legislature would be able to intervene in their affairs to ensure compliance.[58] However Bentham felt that the legislature ought not to intervene in this way except in extreme and abnormal situations, and his legislators were required to make an inaugural declaration that they would refrain from interfering "without necessity" in the work of the subordinate departments of the government, for, wrote Bentham, "nothing but disobedience, tardiness, inaptitude, or casual and momentary want of time, on the part of subordinates, can create, on the part of the Supreme Legislature, any such necessity as that of

54. *Works,* Vol. IX, p. 96.
55. Ibid.
56. Ibid., Vol. IX, p. 9.
57. Ibid., Vol. IX, p. 123.
58. Ibid., Vol. IX, p. 124.

assuming to itself, in the whole or in part, business belonging to any one of their several departments."[59]

The dangers of legislative interference with executive and judicial functions were discussed by Bentham, as we should expect, as matters of expediency rather than principle. Yet when he came to the relations between legislature and executive he rejected the parliamentary system in favour of an arrangement which was something of a hybrid between the American Constitution and the French Constitution of 1791. The office of Prime Minister he modelled upon that of the American President, in so far as the latter, according to Bentham, was "on purpose, and to a very wise purpose, placed at a perpetual distance from Congress."[60] This meant that the Prime Minister had no place in the legislature, with which he might communicate only by message.[61] The other Ministers, although they might sit in the legislative chamber and propose motions, could not vote.[62]

Bentham's thought, then, shows clearly the dilemma of the radical reformer, who, having faced the need to replace the existing constitution with a representative democracy, nevertheless recoiled at the idea of a Long Parliament or a Convention of 1792. Whatever the theoretical objections, some form of separation of powers becomes the only refuge. Bentham was chary of giving any real independence to his executive, but his contemporaries in America and France, once having themselves experienced the dangers of government by convention, were much less prepared to entrust "omnicompetent power" to the legislature.

One further strain of thought in England regarding the separation of powers remains to be considered. This is that branch of radical thought which, rejecting all suggestion of the mixed and balanced constitution, looked back to pre-Norman institutions as they were presumed to have operated. This attachment to the Saxon Constitution is reminiscent of the English Civil War, and we find in the advocates of this view a preference for Harrington and Sadler over Montesquieu and Bolingbroke, and a view of government organization more attuned to the simplicity of the *Instrument*

59. Ibid., Vol. IX, p. 203.
61. Ibid., Vol. IX, p. 206.
60. Ibid., Vol. IX, p. 204.
62. Ibid., Vol. IX, p. 316.

of Government than to the complexities of the eighteenth-century constitution. This attachment to "Saxon" principles was closely related to a belief in the strict functional division of powers between the branches of government. The author of *An Historical Essay on the English Constitution,* which was published in 1771 and formed the basis of much of the radical attack in England and America upon aristocratic and monarchical power, argued that three things were necessary for a Saxon government—a court of council, a court of law, and a chief magistrate vested with the executive authority.[63] The best exponents of this style were David Williams and John Cartwright.

David Williams, a friend of Franklin and of Brissot, and founder of the Royal Literary Fund, published in 1782 his *Letters on Political Liberty,* in which he looked back to the Saxon Constitution "beautiful in its general structure, though defective in important parts," and insisted that all the branches of government should be subject to popular control when they transgress their proper boundaries.[64] In 1789 there followed his *Lectures on Political Principles,* an extensive commentary on the *De l'Esprit des Loix.*[65] He was highly critical of Montesquieu's work, and in particular he had a boundless contempt for all the attributes of the mixed and balanced constitution, except for the separation of powers, which remained as the residue when the force of his invective had melted away the checks and balances of monarchy and aristocracy. The idea of a balance in a governmental system, he said, is "puerile and fantastical."[66] To suggest that the several branches of government are independent is to invest them with a trust which they are able to violate with impunity. The only remedy is to constitute the government in such a way that all abuses of power can be corrected by the people. The example of North America gives some hope that "the formation of commonwealths on deliberate plans" may provide

63. Op. cit., p. 29. However, at a later stage this author refers to aspects of the balanced constitution with approval—see pp. 111–12 and 115.

64. Op. cit., p. 17.

65. In the Preface, Williams states that he is being provocative in these lectures in order to stimulate his students to discussion, but there is no reason to believe that he was not in fact stating his real views, and merely attempting in the Preface to avoid some of the possible consequences of his extreme position.

66. Op. cit., p. 149.

the remedy.[67] Williams, like the author of the *True State of the Case of the Commonwealth* in 1654, saw the legislative and executive powers independent of each other, yet with their power flowing directly from the people; all checks and balances were stripped away. One of his rare marks of approval of Montesquieu's work was reserved for that paragraph of Book XI, Chapter 6 where the danger of drawing the executive from the legislative body is insisted upon.[68] In other respects the balanced constitution of Montesquieu was wholly rejected. The necessity of subjecting the legislature to any control by the executive was "an absurdity so gross as to deserve no consideration."[69] It was equally unnecessary to subject the executive to the supervision of the legislature: "If the instruments, the servants of the public offend, they are accountable, not to each other, for no fair account would be obtained, but to the community."[70] Here we are presented again with that perfect, complete separation of powers which we faced in England over a hundred years before, a rejection both of the balanced constitution and of government by an all-powerful legislature, for Williams rejected as the "most pernicious species of usurpation or tyranny" the idea that the community, or any part of it, could interfere at will with the executive, legislative, or judicial offices of government.[71]

Williams's main activities were in the fields of teaching and religious controversy, but Major John Cartwright was a very different figure. For forty years he was engaged in the forefront of the battle for parliamentary reform, earning himself the title "Father of Reform." He was a prolific, if highly repetitive, writer, who devoted enormous energies to the attack on the existing system of government. The doctrine of the separation of powers figured largely in his work, and his assertion that "the legislative and executive power ought to be totally separate and distinct" was the basis of his bitter attack on the cabinet system. In his early work Cartwright accepted the theory of mixed government to the extent of allowing the sovereign to assent to the laws, but he was insistent that the men who serve the Crown and the men who serve the people ought to "move in totally

67. Ibid., p. 165.
68. Ibid., pp. 166–7.
69. Ibid., p. 168.
70. Ibid., p. 169.
71. Ibid., p. 228.

different spheres and elements."[72] Unfortunately, said Cartwright, this was not the case in England, for there the legislative and executive functions were united in one set of hands. "We see the same men with the power of creating offices, and the power of furnishing salaries; with the power of forming schemes of expense, and the power of voting themselves the money; with the power of plunging their country into war whenever it may suit their corrupt views, and the power of granting themselves the supplies. Can faction, in the lust of dominion want more?"[73] How could de Lolme or his editors bring out further editions of his neatly divided constitutional system after such an *exposé* by the major of Northamptonshire militia? Such a curse did not exist in America or France, said Cartwright, warming to his theme. In those countries men would not be found "skipping, like harlequins, from the cabinet to the legislature, from the legislature to the cabinet; here in the shape of executive directors, there in the form of popular deputies . . . one moment issuing rash and insidious proclamations to the people; and the next, as representatives of the people, moving addresses and pronouncing panegyrics on their own performances."[74] By 1823, shortly before his death, Cartwright had come to reject all the monarchical and aristocratic elements in English government. He was wholly in favour of a "Saxon" constitution, with a unicameral legislature, an elective executive without veto, subordinate to the legislature, and both subordinate to the constitution.[75] The governments of America, particularly the first Constitution of Pennsylvania, approximated most closely to the Saxon model. "Such was the government of a Wittenagemote executed by an Alfred! Such is the government of a Congress, executed by a Monroe."[76]

The theory of the balanced constitution was under heavy attack during this period of English history, and, as in America and on the Continent, its major rival constitutional theory was the separation of powers. The alternative doctrine of parliamentary government found no inspired sup-

---

72. *An Appeal on the Subject of the English Constitution*, Boston (Lincs.), 1797, p. 45.
73. Ibid., p. 46.
74. Ibid., p. 51.
75. *The English Constitution Produced and Illustrated*, London, 1823, p. 118.
76. Ibid., p. 228.

porters in the country where it was being developed; indeed, in the first thirty years of the nineteenth century it is to France that we must look for the major advancements of a theory of government which accepts the King's Ministers as an integral part of a balanced constitutional system. Although the doctrine of the separation of powers represented an intellectual threat to the dominant constitutional ideology, the political situation never reached that boiling point where it might have become a matter of practical politics, and the passage of the Reform Act in 1832 removed whatever threat there might have been; for, interesting as the radical strain of thought was in England in the years 1770 to 1830, the doctrine of the separation of powers could never hope to reach that peak of popular acceptance and significance that it achieved first in the newly independent colonies of America, and then in revolutionary France.

SIX

The Doctrine in America

O N T H E 2 9 J U N E 1 7 7 6, twenty-eight years after the publication of the *De l'Esprit des Loix*, the "future form of government" for the State of Virginia was proclaimed in convention
at Williamsburg. It began with the resounding declaration
that the good people of Virginia ordain that "The legislative, executive
and judiciary departments shall be separate and distinct, so that neither
exercise the powers properly belonging to the other: nor shall any person
exercise the powers of more than one of them at the same time, except that
the justices of the county courts shall be eligible to either House of Assembly." This declaration, which the framers of the Constitution of Virginia
considered to be the basis of their system of government, was the clearest,
most precise statement of the doctrine which had at that time appeared
anywhere, in the works of political theorists, or in the pronouncements of
statesmen. All its major elements were set out, but of greater importance
is the fact that in the Constitution of Virginia it stood as a theory of constitutional government in its own right for the first time since the *Instrument
of Government* over one hundred and twenty years earlier. It is true that
the legislature of Virginia, and of most other revolutionary States, was
bicameral, that the division of functions between the branches of the gov-

ernments of the States was not always consistently followed through, and that in their practical operation the early State governments deviated considerably from the spirit of the doctrine; but in Virginia, and many other States, it was the separation of powers that formed the basis of the institutional structure of the government. In the same year as Virginia did, Maryland and North Carolina made similar declarations in their Constitutions, although they were less thoroughgoing than the Virginians, and in 1777 Georgia followed suit. Clearly this is an important moment in the development of the doctrine of the separation of powers. Is the "pure doctrine" to emerge again and rid itself altogether of the complexities of the balanced constitution, or is some new statement of institutional theory to be evolved? The experience of the Protectorate suggested that the pure doctrine was an inadequate basis for a system of government; would this impression be confirmed by the experience of revolutionary America? The development of political thought that led to the Federal Constitution provides one of the most fascinating spectacles of the adaptation of ideological materials to the demands of an unprecedented situation that history can offer.

The general pattern of American thought in this period provides many parallels with English developments in the mid seventeenth century. The idea of mixed and balanced government dominated the scene in America until, as in England in the 1640's, it was swept away by the democratic fervour of revolution,[1] and the dominant theory of the mixed constitution became totally inadequate to cope with a situation in which resistance to monarchical or aristocratic power was the major characteristic. In both situations the demise of the established constitution was followed by a period of government by convention in which the revolutionary legislature absorbed all power into its own hands, carrying out all the tasks of government through the medium of its committees. As a result of the demand for

1. It is not intended to adopt here a point of view in the complex dispute concerning the "democratic" or "non-democratic" character of the American Revolution, involving as it does considerations of the distribution of property, the extent of the franchise, and the power structure of colonial society. It is an inescapable fact, however, for anyone who has read the literature of the period that there was a democratic revolution in American *thought* in the 1770's. Although the aspirations of the "democrat" rarely extended as far as simple majority rule, or universal manhood suffrage, there was a rejection of monarchical and aristocratic principles that had earlier been accepted.

a return to constitutional government the revolutionary constitutions, like the *Instrument of Government,* show an adherence to the basic ideas of the separation of powers, and a determination to strip away all vestiges of royal or aristocratic power; but, as in England, there was in America a kind of "Restoration," in which the more revolutionary doctrine was modified by older ideas about the balancing and the limitation of power in governments. The parallel, however, must not be pushed too far. In revolutionary America the separation of powers was ready to hand and well understood, whereas in revolutionary England it had had to be formed and fashioned for the first time. When the Restoration came in England it all but swamped the new doctrine by assimilating it, in a subordinate role, to the complex theory of the balanced constitution; in the America of 1787 the doctrine of the separation of powers was modified, tempered, buttressed even, by the theory of checks and balances drawn from the older conception of English constitutional theory, but it remained itself firmly in the centre of men's thoughts as the essential basis of a free system of government.

A great controversy has raged around the extent to which the American colonists and the Founding Fathers were influenced by Montesquieu in their adoption of the separation of powers as a fundamental of good government. On the one hand Montesquieu has been accorded a decisive influence upon the Fathers of the Constitution,[2] whilst at the other extreme it has been argued that the American colonial experience was such that had Montesquieu never put pen to paper the results of their deliberations would hardly have differed from the actual outcome.[3] It is often an extremely difficult task to determine the "decisive influences" upon the work of a single man, let alone to attribute to a single overriding source the results of the work and thought of a large number of men, like those who were engaged upon formulating the State and Federal Constitutions. When one further reflects that the Federal Constitution resulted from a series of compromises effected in the Convention by the majority vote of State

2. P. H. Spurlin, *Montesquieu in America, 1760–1801,* Baton Rouge, 1940. In his first chapter Spurlin surveys the literature of this controversy.

3. B. F. Wright, Jr., "The Origins of the Separation of Powers in America," *Economica,* May 1933, p. 171.

delegations, themselves often internally divided in opinion, and that these majorities were often very close, and fluctuated from day to day, it becomes difficult to talk in terms of a "decisive influence." In fact both of the extreme views drastically oversimplify the actual course of events. Constitutional thought in America in the period leading up to the creation of the Federal Constitution reflects a number of interwoven influences at work. English thought, and the pattern of English institutions, inevitably provided the starting point for American development. But the structure of English constitutional theory, although it was adapted to the American environment, was potentially at variance with the social structure of the colonies. There was some strain in adapting the English form of balanced constitution to that of the colonial government. For though the former acknowledged the importance of monarch and hereditary aristocracy, with their claim to the exercise of power, the claims of the Crown, as represented by the colonial Governor, were far greater than the prerogative powers exercised in practice by the monarch in England. The growing objections of the colonists to the excessive weight attributed to the power of the governors were, therefore, expressed in terms of the need to maintain a proper balance in the constitution. "A small weight over, in either scale," a writer argued in the *Boston Gazette* of 6 June 1763, "might indeed be easily removed, but while it remains it as effectually destroys the balance, as the largest. . . ." As the conflict deepened, however, as had been the case in seventeenth-century England, the theory of the balanced constitution became more and more irrelevant, and the separation of powers emerged again as the only available basis of a *constitutional* government. Locke and Montesquieu provided the intellectual ammunition by which the separation of powers could be advanced as a principle more fundamental than that of mixed government, although the influence of the latter author was, naturally enough in view of the structure of his great work, felt and exercised on both sides of the argument, each side selecting those passages which best suited their cause. The actual outbreak of a revolution that leaned heavily upon the relatively democratic character of the American way of life rendered the old theory of government wholly inappropriate, and for a short period the pure doctrine of the separation of powers emerged in America, as it had in England over a century before, and as it was shortly to do again in France, and was incorporated in varying degrees into the institutional structure of the revolutionary State governments. With the attainment of independence, however, those leaders in America who had allied with radical forces, for the purposes of the revolution, turned back again to the old ideas of balanced government, not embracing the theory in its entirety, but grafting it on to the new basis of American constitutional thought, to provide a new, and uniquely American, combination of the separation of powers and checks and balances. These men were well aware that they faced problems which were not to be neatly solved by appeal either to experience or to the old constitutional theory. They were, necessarily, caught up in the logic of their own position as revolutionaries who wished to maintain the best of the old ways, so that they built within the general pattern of constitutional thought which they inherited, but they specifically and consciously rejected many elements of the old pattern. The remarkable achievement of the Americans was that they not only accepted and understood the constitutional theory and experience that they were heirs to, but that they took this heritage and refashioned it, effectively and successfully, to meet a new and extraordinarily difficult situation.

Until shortly before the Declaration of Independence the constitutional theory of the American colonists closely paralleled that of the mother country, with only those emendations necessary to relate it to the conditions of colonial government. Thus we find that in the mid seventeenth century the great constitutional battles of the English Civil War find a rather pale reflection in the political disputes in Massachusetts. At just the time when Herle and Hunton were grappling with the problems of adapting the age-old theory of mixed government to a rapidly changing situation, the Elders of the Church in Massachusetts were faced with the problem of adapting the same theory to the government of the "Company of Massachusetts Bay." The Elders, however, far from using the theory to justify democratic practices were concerned to use it as a weapon to defend the position of the magistrates, the Governor and Assistants, against pressures for a greater degree of democratic control. In the General Court of Massachusetts the Governor and Assistants exercised a "negative voice," and when the Court was not in session they met to deal with the business of government, making decisions over the whole range of affairs. After 1642 there was a continuous battle between the Governor and Assistants and those deputies who felt that the magistrates should be subjected to considerable restraints in the exercise of their power in the recesses of the General Court, and at the same time an attack was mounted on the "negative voice." The parallel with the course of events in England is striking. The deputies claimed the right to a continuous participation in, and oversight of, the acts of the magistrates, attacking all idea of an autonomous "standing council" free from the control of the Court. Governor John Winthrop clearly summed up the point at issue. Some of the deputies, he wrote, demanded that "all authority, both legislative, consultative, and judicial, must be exercised by the people in their body representative."[4] This claim, which the Long Parliament succeeded in making good for a while in England, was, however, successfully resisted by the elected aristocracy of New England.

In 1644 the Elders of the Church delivered an opinion upon certain constitutional questions which had been placed before them by the General Court, thus setting a theological stamp of approval upon the political theory of those who resisted the current democratic excesses. There is under the Charter, said the Elders, a threefold power of government, or "magistraticall authoritie"; these three powers are "legislative, judicative, and consultative or directive of the publique affairs of the commonwealth, for provision and protection."[5] The legislative power is given jointly to the freemen (or their deputies) and to the Governor and Assistants, as also is the directive power. As for the judicial power, however, this is to be exercised by the magistrates only, except in cases of impeachment and appeal. The government of Massachusetts is not a "pure aristocracy, but mixt of an aristocracy and democracy," in respect of the powers of the General Court, although the actual administration of justice is to be aristocratic.[6] When the General Court is not sitting the magistrates have a power of constant

4. *Winthrop's Journal*, ed. by James Savage, Boston, 1853, Vol. II, p. 282.
5. *The Records of Massachusetts*, Boston, 1853, Vol. II, p. 92.
6. Ibid., Vol. II, pp. 92–93, and 95. See also the "Small Treatise" printed in the *Proceedings of the Massachusetts Historical Society*, Vol. 46, 1913, pp. 279–85.

judicature and "counsel." The Elders even made a distinction between two types of counsel—care and action: in respect of "care" the power of the magistrates was not limited, in respect of "action" they were accountable to the General Court. Thus in 1644 we find a theory of mixed government with an essential degree of functional differentiation between the branches of the government, together with a recognition of the difference between the discretionary and "executive" duties of magistrates.[7]

The Elders in Massachusetts had evolved a constitutional theory which paralleled the seventeenth-century theory of the balanced constitution in England, and again in 1679 they set forth in another constitutional opinion the same combination of mixed government and the separation of powers.[8] Perhaps the most remarkable aspect of this period in American thought is the way in which this adaptation of English political thought to American conditions foreshadowed the eventual solution of the problems which faced the framers of the Constitution over a century later. For when the Elders in 1679 insisted that the Charter of the Massachusetts Bay Company had set up a "distribution of differing interest of power and privilege between the magistrates and freemen, and the distinct exercise of legislative and executive power,"[9] the aristocracy they had in mind was an *elective* aristocracy. The division of functions between agencies of government who will exercise a mutual check upon each other *although both are elected, directly or indirectly, by the same people,* is a unique American contribution to modern constitutional theory.

In the discussions of mixed government in early Massachusetts there was little reference to the monarch, the role of the English King being either assumed or ignored as best suited the colonists. With the establishment of royal government in Massachusetts, however, the theory in the colonies fell more into line with English thought, and by the middle of the eighteenth century the theory of the balanced constitution seemed as im-

---

7. For a discussion of the complexities of judicial administration in early Massachusetts see Mark de Wolfe Howe and Louis F. Eaton, Jr., "The Supreme Judicial Power in the Colony of Massachusetts Bay," *New England Quarterly,* Sept. 1947.

8. *Hutchinson Papers,* in *Publications of the Prince Society,* Albany, 1865, Vol. III, pp. 167–8.

9. Ibid., p. 167.

pregnably established in America as it was in England. In 1717 John Wise described the English Constitution as "an Elisium," and the mixture which it represented as the fairest in the world.[10] Jared Eliot in 1738 pictured the "respective governments in the British Plantations" as little models of that happy mixture to be found in British government, in which each branch whilst "having full power to do good" was checked and restrained by the others.[11] Conservatives, like Cadwallader Colden of New York, and the future loyalist Joseph Galloway, saw in a mixed monarchy the best possible pattern of government,[12] and the New England clergy in their election sermons thanked God for mixed government.[13] In 1753 William Livingston published in the *Independent Reflector* a eulogy of the compound British Constitution as "infinitely the best,"[14] and even as late as 1772 the British system was lauded by Joseph Warren in his Boston massacre oration, while at the same time he applied the terminology of mixed government to Governor, Council, and House of Representatives in Massachusetts.[15]

As relations with England deteriorated, the theory of mixed government as applied in England was first criticized on the grounds that corruption had so warped the Constitution that it no longer represented a truly balanced structure but was a disguised tyranny, and then was rejected altogether as inapplicable to a country where hereditary monarchy and aristocracy were unthinkable.[16] The publication of Paine's *Common Sense* in January 1776 heralded the rejection of the old theory of constitutionalism and opened a period of intense constitutional development in which all that was considered bad in the old forms would be discarded, and all that was considered good would be scrutinized and modified to suit the needs

10. *A Vindication of the Government of New England Churches*, Boston, 1717.

11. *Give Cesar His Due*, New London, 1738.

12. L. W. Labaree, *Conservatism in Early American History*, Ithaca, 1959, pp. 131–2 and 136–7.

13. Alice M. Baldwin, *The New England Clergy and the American Revolution*, Durham, N.C., 1928, pp. 83 and 175–6.

14. No. XXXIII, New York, 12 July 1753, p. 133.

15. Printed in H. Niles, *Principles and Acts of the Revolution in America*, Baltimore, 1822, p. 5.

16. See *Sullivan to Meshech Ware*, 11 December 1775, *American Archives*, ed. by Peter Force, Washington, 1843, Series IV, Vol. IV, 241–3; and *To the People of North America on the Different Types of Government*, ibid., Vol. V, 180–3.

of an independent America. The separation of powers lay ready to hand as a theoretical basis for this constitutional activity.

It has been suggested that it was one of the most curious events in the history of the United States that the colonists, after their bitter experience of divided powers in colonial governments, should have turned to the separation of powers as a fundamental principle of free government.[17] It is true, of course, that the colonial governor and the colonial assembly stood in opposition to each other as separate organs of the government in continual conflict, but it would be wrong to think that colonial governments operated in fact in a way which closely approximated to a thoroughgoing doctrine of the separation of powers, or that the colonists *at the time of the Revolution* associated the operation of these governments with such a theory of government. Undoubtedly in the earlier period of colonial development their view of the proper distribution of the functions of government closely approximated the English theory of the balanced constitution, but as the tensions of the later colonial period developed, that theory was broken down into its component parts, and the colonists criticized the colonial governments because they did not embody a thoroughgoing separation of powers. By 1776 the separation of powers was being advanced as the only coherent constitutional theory upon which an alternative to colonial forms could be based.

There were a number of reasons why the colonists could use the doctrine of the separation of powers to criticize the colonial *régimes.* First, in those royal colonies which shared a very similar structure of government we can see that the colonial government was far more in tune with the theory of mixed government than with the pure separation of powers. A most important element in these governments was the Governor's Council, which also formed the Upper House of the legislature. The Council, appointed by the Crown, except in Massachusetts, held office during pleasure, and became a stable aristocratic element in colonial government. The Council advised the Governor, was an essential part of the legislature, and, with the Governor at its head, acted as the supreme court of the colony. Although nominated

17. Wright, op. cit., p. 176.

by the Governor, the councillors could not be considered mere creatures of the Crown, for the Governor was forced to choose from among a small circle of colonial gentry, who, linked by family connections, maintained a domination on those Councils which made them a miniature replica of the great connections of the aristocracy in eighteenth-century England.[18] The colonial Council, therefore, held a crucial position between the Governor and the Lower House of the legislature, but it was usually in a spirit of rather uneasy co-operation between Governor and Council that the colony was ruled. The Council shared every type of government business, and so played a strategic role in most decisions. It is not surprising, therefore, that the idea of mixed government characterized the thought of the dominant groups in early-eighteenth-century America, for a thoroughgoing doctrine of the separation of powers would hardly have been acceptable to those "aristocratic" families through whose hands ran all the strands of government business. Nor is it surprising that in the outbreak of democratic fervour associated with the revolution there was an attack upon the whole concept of the concentration of power which these councils represented.

The second characteristic of the colonial system, which in the eyes of revolutionary Americans did not equate with a system of properly separated powers, was common to all the colonies, except Connecticut and Rhode Island. Colonial Americans saw continual infringements of the principle in the activities of the governors. Because in the earlier period the theory of the balanced constitution was dominant in men's minds, these infringements were often discussed as attempts to destroy that balance, but as the century wore on the complaints were couched more and more in terms of the vocabulary of the separation of powers, and after the publication of *De l'Esprit des Loix* the colonists gained a valuable source of intellectual ammunition. In fact, complaints that the balance of the Constitution was being perverted came from both sides of the fence. The royal governors complained that the legislature's control over finance was used to exercise undue influence in the executive sphere. In 1723 Governor Shute was led to complain that the control exercised by the House of Rep-

18. Labaree, op. cit., pp. 4 ff.

resentatives of Massachusetts over the salaries of Governor and Treasurer had given to that House "the whole legislative, and in a good measure the executive power of the province."[19] A similar complaint was made in 1754 by the Privy Council in regard to New York,[20] and Thomas Pownall, one of the most intelligent of the royal governors, indicted the colonial assemblies for having endangered "the freedom and right efficiency of the constitution," which required that the executive and judicial officers of government should be independent of the legislature.[21]

On their part the colonists saw the legislature's control over supply as the only means of maintaining their own independence in the face of the powers of the Crown. They complained of the improper exercise of power in words which reflected more and more the doctrine of the separation of powers. In 1744 the New Jersey House of Assembly protested against the appointment of the Chief Justice to the Governor's Council as inconsistent with the freedom and privilege of the people.[22] The more that the separation of powers was stressed as the tension rose in the colonies, the more clear it became that this principle, if pushed far enough, resulted in a denial of the theory of the balanced constitution. This tendency can be clearly seen in the disputes which arose in Massachusetts concerning the election of members of the judiciary to the Council of the Province, and in particular over the appointment of Lieutenant-Governor Hutchinson to the office of Chief Justice. James Otis was deeply involved in this dispute, which involved charges and counter-charges of personal interest. In 1762 Otis lauded the British Constitution as perhaps the most perfect form of government of which human nature was capable, adding that it was a fundamental maxim in such a system that the legislative and executive powers should be kept separate.[23] Two years later, however, after a bitter dispute over Hutchinson's appointment, Otis emphasized the importance of the separation of powers.[24] He now wrote passionately of the need for a proper

19. *English Historical Documents*, Vol. IX, p. 261.
20. Ibid., p. 253.
21. *The Administration of the Colonies*, 2nd edn., 1765, p. 49.
22. Spurlin, op. cit., p. 30.
23. *Boston Gazette*, 11 Jan. 1762.
24. *The Rights of the British Colonies Asserted and Proved*, Boston, 1764, p. 47.

balance between the executive and legislative powers. Drawing upon Locke and Vattel he saw these two powers as "a perpetual check and balance to each other." Using seventeenth- rather than eighteenth-century terminology, Otis argued that both the supreme legislature and the supreme executive are limited in power. If the supreme executive errs, it is "informed" by the supreme legislature in parliament. If the supreme legislature errs, it is informed by the supreme executive in the King's courts of law. He developed one of the earliest American pleas for what would today be called judicial review, by claiming that when Acts of Parliament offend against natural equity the "executive courts" will adjudge such Acts void.[25]

The dispute in Massachusetts well illustrates how the proponents of different interpretations of the best system of government appealed to the authority of Montesquieu, and how the two components of that author's theory of the constitution of liberty were torn apart. Those who were attacking plural office-holding in Massachusetts quoted him, emphasizing only those sections where Montesquieu insisted upon the separation of powers.[26] The defenders of the colonial government also quoted him, but used those passages where he supported the idea of mixed government, or where he emphasized the interdependence of the branches of government. In April 1762 a bill to exclude the judges of the Superior Court from the legislature was narrowly defeated in the House of Representatives,[27] and there ensued a lively newspaper debate in which the rival tendencies in the accepted constitutional doctrine came into conflict. Although the argument was carried on within the framework of accepted British constitutional theory, the revolutionary propensities of the separation of powers when pushed to extremes came very close to the surface. The defence of the colonial government in the *Boston Evening-Post*, signed by "J," interpreted Montesquieu to mean that liberty was sufficiently safeguarded if a *partial* separation of the personnel of government was observed. It was perfectly acceptable for one person, or a small number of people, to be members of

25. Ibid., pp. 41 and 47.
26. *Considerations on the Election of Counsellors*, [Oxenbridge Thacher?], Boston, 1761, pp. 4–6.
27. *Boston Gazette*, 26 Apr. 1762.

both the judicial and legislative branches, but it was essential that a *majority* of the legislature should have no share in judicial office. Similarly in relation to the legislative and executive powers Montesquieu had meant only that "the *whole* executive, and the *whole* legislative powers ought not to be united."[28] "J" developed in 1763 an argument very similar to that later used by Madison to defend the proposed Federal Constitution, but whereas Madison interpreted Montesquieu as propounding a partial separation of the *functions* of government in a system where the personnel of government were kept strictly separate, the writer in the *Boston Evening-Post* was concerned only with the partial separation of persons.

"J" appealed to the example of the British Constitution as a model for Massachusetts to follow, but his opponent "T.Q." in the *Boston Gazette* pushed his insistence upon the separation of powers dangerously close to a rejection of the British pattern. Although he was on occasion prepared to admit that it was the *degree* of the concentration of offices and power that mattered, "T.Q." tended to push the demand for the separation of offices to the point where no single member of the judiciary ought to be at the same time a member of the legislature. In order to support this contention he was prepared to reject the authority of British precedents as a sufficient justification for the practices of the colonial administration. "J" had argued that the colonial practice of councillors also holding judicial office was analogous to the appointment of Lord Chief Justices in England to be peers of the realm, but "T.Q." insisted that the British model was not applicable in Massachusetts. Peers were appointed by the sovereign, whereas councillors in the province were elected. Did it then follow that "because the sovereign is pleased to create a lord chief justice a peer of the realm, it is *expedient* for the people of this province to make a judge a councellor"?[29] He explicitly rejected the idea that what had happened in the past in England was necessarily "constitutional" simply because it had happened. "A practice may sometimes take place, which may interfere with and obstruct the direct end of the constitution." The arguments, drawn from British experience, which supported the combination of the offices of legislator and

28. *Boston Evening-Post*, Supplement, 23 May 1763.
29. *Boston Gazette*, 6 June 1763.

judge "with regard to this province" therefore fell to the ground. The revolutionary implications of this line of thought are very clear.[30]

Yet another indication of the way in which the eighteenth-century English constitutional theory was being broken up into its component parts can be seen in the revolutionary period itself. In 1774 the Continental Congress addressed the inhabitants of Quebec, urging them to send delegates to the next meeting of the Congress. The address contained extensive quotations from "the immortal Montesquieu," proving that the separation of powers was "the only effectual mode ever invented by the wit of men, to promote their freedom and prosperity."[31] Unfortunately for Quebec, the Congress continued, it enjoyed only the *appearance* of separated powers, for in fact all the powers of government were moved "by the nods of a Minister."[32] Two years later the Tory author of *Plain Truth*, replying to Tom Paine, used the authority of "the excellent Montesquieu" to defend the mixture of monarchy, aristocracy, and democracy which formed the basis of the "beautiful system" of the English Constitution.[33] In the bitterness of the revolutionary struggle the two potentially contradictory components of Montesquieu's theory were being rudely torn apart. His authority was invoked by those who wished to strip the separation of powers of its former association with the ideas of mixed government, but either they were very selective in their use of quotations, or they argued that in the different circumstances of the colonies, in which there was "a total absence of all nobles," Montesquieu himself would have approved the more extreme application of the principle of the separation of powers.[34]

Thus the more strongly that the principle of the separation of powers was asserted as an argument against British policy the more it became clear to the colonists that the colonial governments did not embody this principle to a sufficient degree. The Governor was not, of course, a true

30. Ellen E. Brennan tentatively identifies "T.Q." as Oxenbridge Thacher; see *Plural Office-Holding in Massachusetts, 1760–1780*, Chapel Hill, 1945.

31. *Extracts from the Votes and Proceedings of the Continental Congress*, Philadelphia, 1774, pp. 74–76.

32. Ibid., p. 77.

33. "Candidus," *Plain Truth*, Philadelphia, 1776, pp. 2–4.

34. *Pennsylvania Evening Post*, 9 Nov. 1776.

"executive officer." He did execute the decisions of the colonial legislature but his power was much greater than this. He exercised royal prerogatives, and could attempt to coerce the legislature. He played an essential role in the passage of legislation, and had powers of prorogation and dissolution. But his power was even greater than that of the King in the balanced constitution, for he claimed to exercise powers over the government of the colony which no monarch claimed any longer to exercise in Britain itself. As Jefferson observed in his *Summary View of the Rights of British America* of 1774, the royal power, exercised through the governors, to disallow laws of American legislatures was actively exercised long after the sovereign had "modestly declined the exercise of this power in that part of his empire called Great Britain." The great list of charges against the Crown in the Declaration of Independence was, of course, an indictment of the excessive powers of the royal governors as the colonists saw them. Thus the colonial Governor could never see himself, nor be seen by the colonists, as a "mere executive" in relation to the colonial legislature. These problems of fitting the ideas of "legislation" and "execution" to the colonial situation can be clearly seen in Richard Bland's *The Colonel Dismounted* of 1764.[35] Thus although in the early eighteenth century the acceptance of the balanced constitution implied an acceptance of a very modified doctrine of the separation of powers, in the tradition of Mackworth or Bolingbroke, as the century progressed the separation of powers was emphasized more and more, and became more rigid in conception. In the revolutionary period, therefore, the colonists' approach to the office of Governor was to strip it of all prerogatives, and to turn it into a purely executive position. They were not recreating the royal Governor, they were for the first time instituting an executive power in the proper sense of that term. In this respect, as in others, the Americans did not adopt the separation of powers in imitation of their colonial governments; they retained only that part of the old constitutional system which remained when the attributes of mixed government and of imperial rule were rejected.

The transfer of power from the royal governments to the revolutionary

35. Reprinted in *Pamphlets of the American Revolution, 1750–1776*, ed. by B. Bailyn, Vol. I, Cambridge, Mass., 1965, pp. 324–6.

governments was achieved by the setting up of Congresses that wrested authority from royal hands, and ruled the colonies through Committees of Safety, combining in their hands all the powers of government. This system of government by convention very quickly raised demands for a return to constitutional forms. It was at this period of his career that John Adams, who was later to defend mixed government with such passion, bent his main efforts to refuting the right of the legislature to exercise all the powers of government. The new States soon set about the business of drawing up their constitutions, and in many of them the doctrine of the separation of powers was declared to be the major criterion of constitutional government. The separation of powers had again emerged in response to democratic attacks upon the constitutional theory of privilege. Adams began his outline of a desirable form of government in 1775 with the statement: "A legislative, an executive and a judicial power comprehend the whole of what is meant and understood by government. It is by balancing each of these powers against the other two, that the efforts in human nature towards tyranny can alone be checked and restrained."[36] Adams proposed that the governor should have a veto, a proposal that few of his contemporaries were then prepared to accept, but it is his emphasis in this letter upon the separation of powers which marks it out as a piece for the times.

In 1776 eight State constitutions were written, in 1777 Georgia and New York completed theirs, and Vermont, in revolt against New York as well as Great Britain, joined in. The following year South Carolina revised her Constitution of two years earlier, in 1780 Massachusetts made her impressive contribution, and in 1784 New Hampshire, revising her Constitution of 1776, brought an end to the era of revolutionary State constitutions. Three years later the Federal Convention had at its disposal the fund of experience which these State constitutions had provided. The first two State constitutions, those of South Carolina and New Hampshire, were avowedly temporary instruments, written to cover the period until an accommodation was reached with Britain. The Constitution of New Jersey was little more than a copy of a colonial charter, although it remained in force until

36. *Letter to Richard Henry Lee, 15 Nov. 1775*, in *Works*, Boston, 1865, Vol. IV, p. 186.

1844. With the Constitution of Virginia adopted on 29 June 1776, a few days before that of New Jersey, we come to the revolutionary constitutions based upon the separation of powers. The constitutions of Virginia and of five other States that finished their labours in 1776 and early 1777 represent the height of the revolutionary acceptance of the doctrine of the separation of powers. In many respects they differed considerably: in the adoption of unicameral or bicameral legislatures, in the liberality or conservatism of the franchise, or in the experiments they made with such devices as the indirect election of the Senate in Maryland, or the institution of a Council of Censors in Pennsylvania; but they all adhered to the doctrine of the separation of powers, and they all rejected, to a greater or lesser degree, the concept of checks and balances. With the Constitution of New York in April 1777 the reaction began against the extreme rejection of checks and balances, and this movement continued until the Federal Constitution set the seal upon a new and uniquely American combination of separation of powers and checks and balances. In this the class basis of the old theory of mixed government was discarded, and some, but by no means all, of the control mechanisms of the balanced constitution were reintroduced to correct the obvious deficiencies of the early State constitutions, in which checks to the arbitrary use of power had been limited to the negative restraints of the pure separation of powers.

It has been said that the separation of powers was recognized in principle in the early State constitutions, but that this recognition "was verbal merely,"[37] and that in practice it meant little more than a prohibition on plurality of office. Even if the acceptance of the doctrine had been "limited" to this aspect it would hardly have been a matter of little consequence. The maintenance of a strict prohibition upon dual membership of the legislative and executive branches has no doubt been the most significant aspect of the doctrine in forming the special character of American government, and should by no means be underplayed. In fact the early State constitutions varied considerably in the extent to which they embodied a strict separa-

---

37. E. S. Corwin, "The Progress of Constitutional Theory, 1776 to 1787," *American Historical Review*, Vol. XXX, No. 3, 1925, p. 514.

tion of persons, although they all made great efforts in that direction. But the separation of powers meant more than that. Before the personnel of the branches of government could be kept separate the governments had to be organized along the lines of three distinct and separate branches. This was done by ensuring that the executive would have no part to play in legislation, and by abolishing the old Governor's Council, which had had a finger in every pie.

The functions of the Council were distributed between a Council of State, and the legislature, where the Upper House exercised them, except in the two unicameral States. The Governor was stripped of virtually all his prerogatives, and in the Constitutions of Virginia and Maryland it was provided that he "shall not, under any pretence, exercise any power or prerogative, by virtue of any law, statute or custom of England."[38] The Governor was given no veto power, and the only remnant of the prerogative left to any of the executives was that of pardon or reprieve, and doubt was expressed whether even this was a proper power for an executive to wield. The Governor, President, or executive council became "executive" in the strictest sense of the word, merely to enforce the rules made by the legislature. It is indeed strange to argue, as has often been done, that because the States did not provide for "strong executives," or kept the governors very "weak," they did not really intend to embody the separation of powers in their constitutions; for if one accepts the thoroughgoing view of the separation of powers the idea of a "strong executive" is a contradiction in terms. Jefferson later insisted that the basic principle of the 1776 Constitution of Virginia was that no power could be exercised that was not defined by law, and that no provision was made for circumstances where the law would not apply. Indeed, he argued, the Constitution refused even to admit that such circumstances could arise.[39] Thus was the problem of a discretionary power in government swept aside, a problem which had deeply interested John Locke, which Montesquieu had largely obscured, and which, in the

38. F. N. Thorpe, *The Federal and State Constitutions,* Washington, 1909, Vol. VII, pp. 3816–7; and Vol. III, p. 1696.

39. *Notes on the State of Virginia,* 1781, pp. 208–9. Corwin uses this source to support his contention, but it will be seen later that this is a misreading of Jefferson.

democratic mood of the American patriots, was declared no problem at all. The implications of this view for the American system of government can hardly be exaggerated; the history of the Presidency of the United States is, in large part, the history of the attempts to change this conception of the functions of a "chief executive." However, the exact importance of the separation of powers varied considerably from State to State. It would be very difficult to frame generalizations which would fit Pennsylvania, Virginia, and Connecticut in the revolutionary period. Although the major concern of all men was the dispute with Great Britain, it was the internal politics of the particular States which influenced the extent to which the doctrine played a part in their efforts at constitution-making. What can be said, however, is that the more "revolutionary" the atmosphere, the more likely it was that ideas tending towards the pure separation of powers would be in evidence. In Pennsylvania the pure doctrine played a large part in political and constitutional discussion; in Virginia, as in most of the States, it was modified and restrained by attachment to the old ways; in Connecticut the old colonial charter was not even replaced, and the revolution, together with the separation of powers, did not really arrive until 1818, when the power of an oligarchy centred in the Council was ended.[40]

The most extreme expression of the separation of powers, emerging in fact in its pure form, came in Pennsylvania, and later in Vermont. It is often stated that the Constitution of Pennsylvania did not embody the separation of powers, whereas in fact it was the basis of the whole Constitution. It is the failure to distinguish clearly between the separation of powers on the one hand, and checks and balances on the other, which leads to the confusion. The founders of the 1776 Constitution were bitterly opposed to any semblance of the checks and balances of the monarchic or aristocratic constitution. Pennsylvania in 1776 was unique among the American States in that the revolutionary movement against the authority of Great Britain was accompanied by, and was used as a cover for, a successful internal revolution in Pennsylvanian government itself. This internal revolution, whether it be seen as a regional or class movement, as

40. On Connecticut see R. J. Purcell, *Connecticut in Transition, 1775–1818*, Middletown, Conn., 1963.

an attack upon Quaker influence in government, or as a *coup d'état* by a small number of ingenious men,[41] provided in Pennsylvania a democratic revolutionary situation unlike that of any other of the rebelling colonies. In Pennsylvania the doctrines which were propounded by the radical revolutionaries were very close to those of the English Civil War period, and they rejected more whole-heartedly than other Americans any suggestion of maintaining vestiges of the mixed and balanced constitution. Paine's attack upon the English system of government had a particular success in Philadelphia, and local writers took up with enthusiasm the ideas which had in earlier years in England been associated with extreme democracy. "Demophilus" in 1776 drew upon the *Historical Essay on the English Constitution* in order to praise the "Saxon" form of government, with which he equated the separation of powers.[42] Both he and the author of some "hints" to the constitution-makers were insistent that the governor and his council should be "solely executive."[43] "Demophilus," however, was prepared to accept the idea of a bicameral legislature, whereas the most extreme expressions of the pure doctrine of the separation of powers came from those who were prepared to tolerate only a unicameral system.

The revolutionary concept of the delegation of power from the people to their agents in the various branches of government is deeply opposed to the ideas of the balanced constitution, in which important elements were independent of popular power, and able to check the representatives of that power. This idea of the direct delegation of all power had been proclaimed in the *True State of the Case of the Commonwealth* of 1654, and it was announced again in revolutionary Pennsylvania in 1776. In the *Pennsylvania Journal* of 22 May 1776 it was argued that "a charter of delegation" should be framed which would give "a clear and full description of the quantity and degree of power and authority, with which the society vests the persons in-

41. See the differing interpretations of C. H. Lincoln, *The Revolutionary Movement in Pennsylvania, 1760–1776*, Philadelphia, 1901; and D. Hawke, *In the Midst of a Revolution*, Philadelphia, 1961.

42. *The Genuine Principles of the Ancient Saxon or English Constitution*, Philadelphia, 1776, p. 5.

43. Ibid., pp. 36–37; and *The Pennsylvania Evening Post*, 16 July 1776.

trusted with the powers of the society, whether civil or military, legislative, executive or judicial." It is noticeable that the radicals did not, therefore, advocate complete legislative supremacy, or a system of *gouvernement d'assemblée.* The writer in the *Journal* proposed that a "Committee of In-quiry" should be chosen every third year to ensure that no laws had been passed which "infringed upon the Social Compact." This insistence that all power flowed from, and was delegated by, the people, and that *all* the branches of government should be limited in power, was echoed by the au-thor of *Four Letters on Interesting Subjects* printed in Philadelphia in 1776. "No country can be called *free* which is governed by an absolute power; and it matters not whether it be an absolute royal power or an absolute legislative power, as the consequences will be the same to the people."[44]

Both the author of *Four Letters* and the writer in the *Journal* were con-cerned with the distinction between, and the limitation of, the powers of government, but the former was the more radical and thoroughgoing. The notion of checking power by dividing up the legislature "has but little weight with it," for to argue for a balance in the constitution because of the existence of differing interests in society is wholly misplaced. There must be only one interest, and "that one to consist of every sort."[45] He returned to the stark simplicity of the seventeenth-century view of gov-ernment which saw only two powers of government, that of making the law, and that of carrying it out, "for the judicial power is only a branch of the executive."[46] This author also demanded a Provincial Jury which would enquire at intervals into the operation of the branches of government.

Perhaps the clearest rejection of the system of mixed government and checks and balances came in a piece entitled *The Interest of America,* which was published in the *Pennsylvania Packet* of 1 July 1776.[47] The author in-sisted that the form of government to be adopted must be *new,* not the cor-rupt mixtures of earlier governments. A "patched government, consisting of several parts," had been the disease of otherwise great systems such as those of Rome or Britain. At all costs they must avoid "several branches of

44. Op. cit., p. 19.
46. Ibid., p. 21.

45. Ibid., pp. 19–20.
47. Reprinted from *The New York Journal.*

legislature." The great absurdity of such governments was that one branch of the legislature, having a negative on the others, should be the principal executive power in the State. The mixed and balanced constitution, therefore, offended against that maxim which the author stated explicitly: "The legislative and executive power in every province, ought to be kept as distinct as possible." The same injunction was contained in a broadside put out by the revolutionary Committee of Privates of Philadelphia. Signed, among others, by James Cannon, who is credited with a large share in the authorship of the Constitution of 1776, the broadside developed again the ideas of the direct delegation of power from the people, and the keeping of the legislative and executive authority "for ever separate."[48]

The Constitution of Pennsylvania of 1776 showed clearly this extreme rejection of checks and balances, allied with the separation of powers. It established a unicameral legislature, and a plural executive, the Supreme Executive Council, directly elected by the people. No member of the Assembly could be chosen for the Council, although a joint ballot of Assembly and Council was used to select the President and Vice-President from among the twelve members of the Council. In line with the seventeenth-century inspiration of the Constitution, the judicial power was not elevated to the same level, nor given the same independence, as the "supreme" legislative and "supreme" executive powers. A Council of Censors was established to review the working of the Constitution every seven years, and to enquire "whether the legislative and executive branches of government have performed their duty as guardians of the people, or assumed to themselves, or exercised other or greater powers than they are intitled to by the constitution." If any doubt remains that this Constitution was intended to embody a thoroughgoing separation of powers, it is dispersed by the defence which was offered by its radical proponents eight years later, when its operation was being investigated by the Council of Censors. An extremely precise statement of its principles was given by "A.B." in the *Pennsylvania Gazette* of 28 April 1784. This philosophy of government, which looks back to that strain of constitutional thought to which Marchamont Ned-

48. *To the Several Battalions of Military Associators in the Province of Pennsylvania,* Philadelphia, 26 June 1776.

ham had given expression in 1654, and which contains the elements of the strict constructionist view of the Federal Constitution of later years, is stated with such felicity and economy that it cannot be bettered:

> In a government like ours, the authorities delegated by the freemen at large are distributed and lodged with three distinct branches; the legislative, the supreme executive, and the judicial: Each strongly marked and characterised. To the first belongs the right to make and alter the general rules of the society; that is to say the laws. With the second is entrusted the execution of these general rules, by itself, and the subordinate officers of the state, chiefly nominated by this body. And to the third, which is properly but a subdivision of the second, is committed the interpretation and application of the laws to controverted cases, in standing tribunals, circumscribed by solemn and settled rules of proceeding. . . . From this severance of power, essential to free and equal government, we infer, that each of these branches, of right, exercises all authority, devolved by the community, which properly belongs to it, unless the contrary be clearly expressed. And if, in any case, the constitution has assigned jurisdiction to one of these branches, which is not naturally within its resort, the power so misplaced should be construed strictly, and carried no further than barely to satisfy the words, and at the same time accord with common sense.

Two centuries of a major strand of English and American thought are summarized in these words from a Pennsylvania newspaper of 1784. This same theory was endorsed by the Radical-dominated Committee of the Council of Censors, which found the Constitution of Pennsylvania to be "clear in its principles, accurate in its form, consistent in its separate parts."[49] It was a theory that accepted no concessions to the monarchic-aristocratic idea of checks and balances. It relied for the safeguards of constitutional government upon the allocation of abstractly defined functions of government to distinct branches of government, and upon the vigilance of the people to maintain this division in practice.

The attachment to the extreme version of the doctrine of the separation of powers in revolutionary democratic situations can be seen also in the case of Vermont.[50] This area, known until 1777 as the New Hamp-

---

49. *Report of the Committee of the Council of Censors . . .* , Philadelphia, 1784, p. 4.
50. For the complicated constitutional situations in other "revolutionary" areas see John D.

shire Grants, was in revolt against the authority of New York as well as Great Britain, using the same arguments against domination by that State as the United States were using against British tyranny. The inhabitants of the Grants, opposing the land-holding oligarchy of New York, took up attitudes of extreme democracy, and when they adopted a Constitution for the State of Vermont in 1777 they based it upon that of Pennsylvania, embracing unicameralism, universal manhood suffrage, a popularly elected Council, an elected Governor (contrary to the Pennsylvania pattern), and a Council of Censors. This Constitution was in part a reaction against the recently adopted Constitution of New York, which had embodied, in the view of the Vermont democrats, an aristocratic system of government.[51] Thus we find the seventeenth-century view of the separation of powers and the delegation of power by the people expressed in the views of the proponents of the Vermont Constitution in opposition to the eighteenth-century ideas of balanced government. Thomas Young, who proposed the model of the Constitution of Pennsylvania to the people of Vermont, wrote of the people as "the supreme constituent power" and of their representatives as the "supreme delegate power,"[52] and Ira Allen, the "Founder of Vermont," succinctly expressed the principle of a twofold separation of delegated powers.[53] Their antipathy towards the rival constitutional theory was well expressed at a later date by Samuel Williams, historian of Vermont, who in describing the "American system of government" argued that "the security of the people is derived not from the nice ideal application of checks, ballances, and mechanical powers, among the different parts of the government, but from the responsibility, and dependence of each part of the government, upon the people."[54]

The other American States, not involved as were Pennsylvania and Vermont in such violent internal upheavals in their politics, did not go to the

Barnhart, "The Tennessee Constitution of 1796: A Product of the Old West," *The Journal of Southern History*, Vol. IX, 1943; and Merton E. Coulter, "Early Frontier Democracy in the First Kentucky Constitution," *Political Science Quarterly*, Vol. 39, 1924.

51. S. R. Bradley, *Vermont's Appeal to the Candid and Impartial World*, Hartford, 1780, p. 32.

52. *To the Inhabitants of Vermont*, Philadelphia, 11 Apr. 1777.

53. *Some Miscellaneous Remarks . . .* , Hartford, 1777, p. 11.

54. *The Natural and Civil History of Vermont*, Walpole, New Hampshire, 1794, p. 343.

extremes represented by the Radical constitutions of those States. Nevertheless, demands for a more democratic system of government were associated with strong assertions of the doctrine of the separation of powers and an antipathy towards checks and balances. In North Carolina the instructions of Mecklenburg and Orange to their representatives in 1776 portray much the same constitutional theory as that of the Pennsylvania Radicals, although they had little chance of acceptance.[55] Indeed the instructions of Mecklenburg to its delegates is perhaps the clearest and most effective statement of the pure doctrine of the separation of delegated powers of government to be found anywhere. Although the original draft of the instructions advocated bicameralism, it is noted that the people of Mecklenburg rejected this proposal, so leaving a statement of the doctrine in its purest form. A similar argument was developed in *The People the Best Governors*, which opposed bicameralism, and suggested a "first executive officer, without any concern in the legislature."[56] The author of this pamphlet, however, proposed the adoption of an exception to that "darling principle of freedom" that those who make the laws should not execute them: he suggested that the legislature should act as a court of appeal "in some important matters," on the grounds that interpretation of the law by a court was tantamount to a legislative act.[57]

However, most of the States retained some of the old ways, in particular bicameralism, and the separation of powers was not adopted in a stark or "pure" form. Nevertheless, in 1776, the doctrine of the separation of powers remained the only coherent principle of constitutional government upon which to build a constitution which rejected monarchy and aristocracy. The rationale of an American system of checks and balances had yet to be formulated.

The attempt to see government, in John Adams's formulation, as a system in which the whole is comprehended by a legislature, an executive,

55. *The Colonial Records of North Carolina*, Raleigh, 1890, Vol. X, pp. 870a–870h. See E. P. Douglass, *Rebels and Democrats*, Chapel Hill, 1955, pp. 125–8.

56. Printed in F. Chase, *A History of Dartmouth College*, ed. by J. K. Lord, Cambridge, Mass., 1891, Vol. I, p. 660.

57. Ibid., p. 662.

and a judiciary, exercising their proper functions, provided critical difficulties for the Americans, faced with the problem of implementing this view. Nothing in the traditional theories of government could provide simple answers to certain difficult problems. The first of these was the method of appointing the executive. The fear of executive tyranny led most of the States to provide for the election of governor, or president, by the legislature, in most cases for a term of only one year. This is perhaps the first occasion in modern history that this problem had been faced; and its relation to the separation of powers is not immediately apparent. The choice of a Protector in 1654 was hardly a matter for discussion, and the British Constitution had solved its problems of choosing an "executive" by leaving it to the chances of heredity. Yet if the executive was to be more than an errand boy he must have some independence of the legislature, and it soon became obvious that the authority of this executive official depended in large part on his method of appointment. The apparent need for independence on the part of the executive suggested, moreover, that there was more to his function than the automatic application of law, so that at once the attention of the Americans was drawn to the question of the nature of the "executive office" and of its attributes. A most important power of the royal governor had been his veto, and inevitably discussion revolved around the extent to which a legislative veto was proper to one whose function was simply to carry out the laws. The other side of the coin was the power of impeachment, which had once been a significant weapon in the hands of the British parliament, and which Montesquieu and other theorists of the balanced constitution had considered an essential check to royal power; but was this any longer necessary if, instead of a king, there was now merely an *executive* officer? Almost the only concession to the balanced constitution in these early State constitutions was the provision in some that the governor could be impeached, although in Virginia and Delaware only when he was no longer holding the office.[58]

The other remnants of the prerogative provided similar difficulties. Who

58. Thorpe, Vol. VII, p. 3818, and Vol. I, p. 566.

should exercise the appointing power? The usual revolutionary solution was to give this task as far as possible to the legislature, so further diminishing the authority of the governor. But what was the justification for seeing this as a part of the legislative power? On the other hand, to place this power in the hands of the governor would be to give him the opportunity, through patronage and influence, to make himself more than a mere executive official, and to aspire perhaps to the power which the Crown exercised in England through such dubious means. At a later stage, in the Federal Convention, the power to make treaties, and to declare war and peace, were the subject of similar uncertainty. On the treaty power it was variously argued that it was exclusively legislative, exclusively executive, or that it formed "a distinct department" of its own.[59] These were the tasks of government which an earlier theory of the constitution had comprehended but which did not fit easily into the over-simple categories of the new approach. The history of constitutional doctrine in the decade between the Constitution of Georgia and the Federal Constitution is, in part at least, the history of the search for a rationale for dealing with the former prerogatives of the Crown.

The structure of these State constitutions of 1776 and of Georgia in 1777 certainly reflects more than a mere "verbal" acceptance of the separation of powers. Most of them, however, modified the impact of the doctrine in other ways, principally by adopting bicameral legislatures and by restricting the franchise, so that the full potentialities of a system of sharply divided powers were never realized; and by making the election of the governor dependent upon the legislature they went a long way towards ameliorating the worst dangers of an extreme separation of powers. However, the abstract division of the functions of government into "legislative," "executive," and "judicial," and their attribution to three separate agencies, does not solve the problem of the control of government power, and in particular it fails to solve the problem of restricting the legislature to the mere announcement of general rules. As Corwin has pointed out, the State

59. Alexander Hamilton, *Federalist*, No. 75.

legislatures soon meddled in every type of government business, including that normally reserved to the judiciary.[60] Contemporaries also criticized this aspect of the operation of the State governments, noting the tendency for all power to gravitate to the legislature.[61] This fact, important as it is, does not allow us to conclude, however, that the doctrine of the separation of powers meant little or nothing in this period. On the contrary it is here that we reach the very core of the problem raised by an acceptance of a version of the pure doctrine, almost unalloyed with any checks or balances. It was in the realization of the shortcomings of the doctrine, standing on its own as a theory of government, that the Americans retreated from it to find a new and surer foundation for a constitutional theory. For it was the problem of placing limits on the legislative power that made this extreme doctrine unworkable. In this period the nature of the legislative power was in considerable dispute. Unrestrained legislative supremacy was clearly not intended by those who drew up constitutions in order to put an end to government by convention, or who in Pennsylvania, and later in Vermont, established constitutional councils for supervision of legislative acts. But the exact nature of the limits upon legislative power, and how to enforce them, was not clear. It is often stated that the revolutionary State constitutions embodied unrestrained legislative supremacy, but this is too simple a statement to cover such a complex situation. The view that Locke held of this matter, discussed earlier, may be seen also as the basis of the American view at this time. That is to say that the legislature must be "supreme," in the sense that its decisions cannot be gainsaid, but the power of the legislature is not unlimited. Certainly those who saw the separation of powers as a central principle of government did not accept the view that the legislature was omnipotent. Only the *people* were able to exercise an unlimited power, whereas the legislature was, in the words of the instructions of Mecklenburg County, North Carolina, to its representatives in 1776, "a derived inferior power," which was to be "restrained in all future time from

60. Op. cit., pp. 514–15.
61. See Benjamin Rush, *Observations Upon the Present Government of Pennsylvania*, Philadelphia, 1777, p. 14; and James Madison, *Federalist*, No. 47.

making any alteration in the form of government."[62] Equally certainly there were those who asserted that the legislature had unlimited power even to change the constitution, but they rarely, if ever, believed that the legislature had the power to undertake all the tasks of government, for it was, by definition, the *legislative* branch and not the embodiment of all power. As late as 1814 John Adams could write of "the *summa potestatis,* the supreme power, the legislative power, the power from which there is no appeal but, to Heaven. . . ."[63] But this view was associated, of course, with the idea of the legislative supremacy of the King-in-Parliament in Britain, and with Adams's scheme of checks and balances. Such a view, however, was not acceptable to most Americans, who saw in the people a constituent power, and in the legislature only a delegated power. Thus, for example, we find the two elements of the idea of legislative power, its "supremacy" in law-making together with its limited status under a constitution, expressed by the author of the *Observations on Government* of 1787. Like Locke's language, this author's terms seem to be contradictory. He writes that "All government necessarily requires a supreme authority lodged somewhere to superintend and direct the operations of every other part: now this office belongs exclusively to the legislature."[64] Later, however, he writes that a constitution is that original compact "whereby a certain form of government is chalked out and established unalterably, except by the people themselves."[65] Writing of the difficulties of the government of Rome he argues that "had the boundaries of the powers lodged in different parts of the government, been chalked out with precision" these difficulties would hardly have arisen. These statements were, for eighteenth-century Americans, as for seventeenth-century Englishmen, perfectly compatible, and any expression of "legislative supremacy" must be seen in this light.

Furthermore the distance between the expressed intention of the Constitutions and the actual practice of State legislatures must be seen not as a

---

62. *Colonial Records of North Carolina,* Vol. X, p. 870b.
63. *Works,* Vol. VI, p. 460.
64. Op. cit., p. 29.
65. Ibid., p. 46.

conscious rejection of the doctrine by "Americans," but as the result of the differing pressures upon politicians called upon to act both as constitution-makers and as members of a legislature. There was an inevitable conflict between the ideas of a member of a constitutional convention, even when this was also acting as a legislature, thinking in the abstract about "the best constitution" and subject to certain pressures in his work, and the ideas of the same person as a legislator under that constitution, concerned in the heat of the political battle with the gaining of a tactical advantage and subject to much more immediate and concrete considerations.

The experience of Pennsylvania illustrates this point very well. The Constitution of 1776, which embodied the separation of powers, represented the political theory of the Radicals who controlled the government for much of the time up to the election of the Council of Censors in 1783. When in control of the legislature the Radicals undoubtedly used its power to interfere in matters which, in the spirit of the separation of powers, were more appropriate for executive or judicial action. In 1783 and early 1784 the Republicans, who opposed the Constitution, were in a majority on the Council of Censors, and they used their position to attempt to put forward proposals for the amendment of the Constitution, proposals which would have restored some of the old elements of the balanced constitution and so effectively limited the power of the legislature.[66] When the Radicals gained control of the Council of Censors in June 1784, however, they too used their position to point out the abuses of power by the legislature, but only those abuses which had been committed by the Republicans when they were in control. After providing innumerable examples of the ease with which the constitutional division of power could be violated, the Radicals nevertheless concluded that there was no need to alter the Constitution, which was perfectly sound; the fault lay in the behaviour of those men who had wrongfully used their public office. Put the right men in power and all will be well![67] The duplicity of the politician who will acknowledge

66. L. H. Meader, "The Council of Censors," *The Pennsylvania Magazine*, Vol. XXII, No. 3, 1898, p. 288.

67. See R. L. Brunhouse, *The Counter-Revolution in Pennsylvania, 1776-1790*, Philadelphia, 1942, pp. 162–3.

certain constitutional principles and then act in violation of them is the very situation which constitutional structures set out to contain; and the separation of powers, like the theory of mixed government, was intended to show the way; but the pure doctrine of the separation of powers failed to do this because, unlike the theory of mixed government, which opposed power with power, the pure separation of powers depended upon an intellectual distinction between the functions of government for its safeguard and upon elections for its sanction. Once this fact was clearly grasped, the constitutionalists of America turned to their experience of the balanced constitution for the solution to their problems.

Early objections to the form of these State governments were often couched in terms of the separation of powers, arguing that the legislative, executive, and judicial powers were not properly separated. In 1777, in his *Observations on the Present Government of Pennsylvania*, Benjamin Rush used this argument.[68] He acknowledged that the Constitution of Pennsylvania "seems" to have divided up the powers of government, but in fact the executive and judicial branches, he wrote, have not been given the necessary independence of the legislature that could ensure them "the free exercise of their own judgments."[69] He strongly urged a bicameral legislature and would clearly have liked to see the governor with a veto, but his argument for the latter is confused and difficult, because he did not relate it in any obvious way to his own criticism of the Constitution. Nevertheless, he did have a basic understanding of the conflicting conceptions of government at issue. "It is one thing to understand the *principles*, and another to understand the *forms* of government," he said, and added, "Mr. Locke is an oracle as to the *principles*, Harrington and Montesquieu are oracles as to the *forms* of government."[70] The difference between Locke's seventeenth-century formulation of legislative and executive power, on the one hand, and Montesquieu's complex eighteenth-century constitution of checks and balances, on the other, was the focal point of the problems of American government in this period.

The separation of powers had emerged in 1776 as the only viable basis

68. Op. cit., p. 14. 69. Ibid., p. 13. 70. Ibid., p. 20.

for a constitutional system of limited government, finding its most extreme expression in Pennsylvania, but from the very beginning of the period of American constitution-building there were those who saw it, standing alone, as an inadequate safeguard against the abuse of power, particularly by the legislature. The author of *A Frame of Government for Pennsylvania*[71] had in 1776 urged the desirability of "vesting the supreme legislative power in three different bodies." The proponents of the pure doctrine of the separation of powers were met with strong opposition in Pennsylvania by those who "severely reprobated" the Constitution of that State because it did not contain the checks and balances necessary to a legitimate distribution of the powers of government.[72] This division of opinion formed the intellectual basis of the severe party battle between Radicals and Republicans in the early years of Pennsylvanian statehood. In other States, where the doctrine of the separation of powers had not been so fiercely adopted, there were many who wished to retain some of the checks and balances of the British Constitution. John Adams had proposed that the governor should be given a legislative veto, and Carter Braxton had proposed to Virginia a plan of government which was closely modelled after the British pattern. In 1776, however, the revolutionary situation precluded proposals that seemed designed to reintroduce monarchic or aristocratic elements into American political life. The only authority to which they could appeal was the one that was being so bitterly opposed. Nevertheless the excesses of the radicals in Pennsylvania, and the tendency of State legislatures generally to accumulate power, and to exercise it in an arbitrary way, soon effected a change of heart. In New York in 1777 the new Constitution showed a definite movement away from the extreme position of the earlier State constitutions towards some recognition of the need for checks and balances. It was in the Massachusetts Constitution of 1780, however, that the new philosophy of a system of separated powers which *depends upon* checks and balances for its effective operation was first implemented. This

71. *An Essay of a Frame of Government for Pennsylvania*, [John Dickinson], Philadelphia, 1776, Preface.

72. Alexander Graydon, *Memoirs of a Life Chiefly Passed in Pennsylvania*, Edinburgh, 1822, p. 302.

Constitution embodied the results of the ideas of John Adams, and, more important perhaps, of the *Essex Result*.

In 1774 John Adams had condemned the royal government of Massachusetts as a tyranny founded upon the concentration of legislative, executive, and judicial power in the hands of the royal officials, Bernard, Hutchinson, and Oliver,[73] and in 1775 he placed considerable emphasis upon the separation of powers in his projected form of government. However, Adams was really interested in mixed government, as became evident in his *Defence of the Constitutions of Government of the United States*, of 1787–8. Whether or not Adams deserved Paine's later gibe that "his head was as full of kings, queens and knaves as a pack of cards," his *Defence* was certainly a long, impassioned plea for a mixture of monarchy, aristocracy, and democracy. He even went so far as to say that the need for a hereditary monarchy and aristocracy might some day have to be acknowledged in America,[74] although elsewhere he denied ever having supported the idea of hereditary power.[75] However much Adams may have leaned towards mixed government in 1776 or in 1780, there was, of course, no chance of such views being accepted, otherwise than in the watered-down form of a bicameral legislature and a veto power for an elected governor. In 1776 even the latter was wholly unacceptable to his contemporaries, and although the Convention in Virginia had before it his plan, among others, it followed the lead of George Mason and adopted a scheme which showed very little concession indeed to mixed government or checks and balances. By 1779–80, however, the reaction against the earlier pattern had gone so far that a directly elected governor could be entrusted with a qualified veto as a check to the legislature. Adams drafted the Constitution of Massachusetts of 1780, and the tendency towards the reapplication of the ideas of the balanced constitution is clear, but the Convention was not prepared to go as far as Adams wished, and its amendments placed greater emphasis upon the separation of powers. The famous Article XXX of the Declaration of Rights did not come from his pen. It reads: "In the government

73. *Novanglus, or a History of the Dispute with America*, in *Works*, Vol. IV, pp. 62–63.
74. *Works*, Vol. VI, p. 67.
75. See J. T. Adams, *The Adams Family*, p. 90.

of this commonwealth, the legislative department shall never exercise the executive and judicial powers, or either of them; the executive shall never exercise the legislative and judicial powers, or either of them; the judicial shall never exercise the legislative and executive powers, or either of them, to the end it may be a government of laws and not of men."[76]

John Adams, by his consistent adherence to the theory of the balanced constitution, must be credited with having played an important part in giving direction to the retreat from the pure doctrine of the separation of powers in America. In his early plans for State governments he developed the outline of a system of separation of powers and checks and balances which was in fact later largely adopted as the solution to American problems of government.[77] But he was unable to develop a clear rationale for an American theory of constitutionalism. In his later work he proved far too enamoured of the outdated and irrelevant theory of mixed government to be the author of a truly American political theory. He pointed the way, but no more. The task of developing this theory was undertaken in Massachusetts before the Constitution of 1780 by the authors of the *Essex Result*, by Thomas Jefferson in his *Notes on the State of Virginia* in 1781, and in the discussions concerning the Federal Constitution by James Wilson and James Madison.

In 1775 Massachusetts had reverted to a form of government based upon the royal charter of 1691, in which the House of Representatives elected a council of twenty-eight members that became the executive, as well as forming the Upper House of the legislature and the supreme judicial tribunal. This system of concentrated power was even further developed by the practice of appointing members of the legislature to offices of profit, until one member held six offices at one time.[78] This so offended the current notions of constitutional government that there was continuous pressure for a new constitution. As a result a constitution was drafted in 1778 and

76. See Adams's *Works*, Vol. IV, p. 230.
77. See *Works*, Vol. IV, pp. 186–7, 196–200.
78. A. Nevins, *The American States During and After the Revolution, 1775–1789*, New York, 1924, p. 176.

submitted to the freemen, but rejected.[79] This project exhibited the same trend towards a more independent executive as was shown in New York the year before. The Governor and Lieutenant-Governor were to be directly elected, and the former was granted a limited power of prorogation, but he had no veto power, and both he and the Lieutenant-Governor were members of the Senate, each with a vote. The replies from the towns of Massachusetts to this proposal show a wide variation in opinion, one of them, Greenwich, even demanding a system of convention government by a single-chamber legislature without a separate executive.[80] The return from Essex County, however, was a most remarkable document, the precursor of the Massachusetts Constitution of 1780, and the first clear formulation of the theory which was to become the basis of the Federal Constitution. It was the work of Theophilus Parsons, then only twenty-eight years old, and later to become Chief Justice of Massachusetts.[81] With great clarity and precision the *Essex Result* formulated the problem of governmental organization and indicated the lines along which it must be solved in America. It proclaimed the freedom and equality of all men as the starting point of all political discussion, rejecting at the outset any system based upon the English pattern of mixed government. However, the author of the *Result* was a conservative who wished to restrain the exercise of government power and certainly did not wish to set up an unlimited democracy. The pattern of the old system of thought was followed, therefore, to this extent: the three qualities requisite to an effective system of government were enumerated—a concern for the interest of the whole, wisdom, and dispatch— and these were related to the need to combine democratic and aristocratic elements in the legislature with an efficient executive power. In Massachusetts at this time the aristocracy was defined as "the gentlemen of education, fortune and leisure," and although, therefore, class divisions were acknowledged, indeed welcomed, they were not the hereditary class divisions

79. Printed in *Massachusetts, Colony to Commonwealth: Documents on the Formation of the Constitution, 1775–1780*, ed. by R. J. Taylor, Chapel Hill, 1961, pp. 51–58.

80. Ibid., p. 71.

81. *Result of the Convention of Delegates . . .* , Newbury-port, 1778.

of the rejected European theories of government. This changed emphasis upon class was an essential element in the transformation of the theory of mixed and balanced government into the American theory of checks and balances. It was the inapplicability of the British pattern of thought in this respect which was repeatedly emphasized in the Federal Convention.[82]

The *Essex Result* then turned to deal with the nature of the powers of government and their distribution. The proposed constitution of 1778 was systematically analysed. All those provisions were sought out and rejected which placed powers in the wrong branch, or allowed one person to exercise authority in more than one department. A rigorous separation of the powers of government was insisted upon. However, the rigid separation of functions in different hands was not itself seen as a sufficient safeguard, and the *Result* then applied the vocabulary of the balanced constitution to this system of separated powers: "Each branch is to be independent, and further, to be so balanced, and be able to exert such checks upon the others, as will preserve it from a dependance on, or a union with them."[83] In practice this meant the direct election of an executive with effective means of checking the legislature, and with the power to appoint his subordinates, and a judiciary quite independent of the other two branches. Thus was the whole emphasis of the mid-eighteenth-century theory of the balanced constitution transformed. The ideas and vocabulary that had formerly been applied to monarchy, aristocracy, and democracy were firmly transferred to the legislative, executive, and judicial branches of government. Whereas in contemporary England the separation of powers was a necessary, but subordinate, element of a system in which three classes check and balance each other, in America the checks and balances became a necessary, but subordinate, element of a system in which the functionally divided branches of government can maintain their mutual independence. The ideas of Bolingbroke and Montesquieu emerged in another guise, all hereditary elements stripped away, and applied unequivocably to a democratic system of government.

The *Essex Result* is an indication of one trend of thought, in Massachu-

82. See for example Pinckney's remarks in the Convention: *The Records of the Federal Convention of 1787*, ed. by Max Farrand, New Haven, 1937, Vol. I, p. 398.
83. *Result*, p. 27.

setts. In 1781 Jefferson published his *Notes on the State of Virginia,* which contain substantially the same analysis of the institutional problem. The purpose of the patriots in Virginia, he said, had been to create a new system of government in which the powers should be so divided and balanced "as that no one could transcend their legal limits, without being checked and restrained by the others."[84] The Convention, therefore, had established separate and distinct departments of government, so that no person might be allowed to exercise the powers of more than one department at the same time. The Convention, however, failed in its purpose because "no barrier was provided between the several powers." As a result the executive and judicial officers were dependent upon the legislature, which could, merely by casting its decisions in legislative form, bind the other branches, even though dealing with "rights which should have been left to judicial controversy" or with "the direction of the executive."[85] Thus "all the powers of government, legislative, executive, and judiciary, result to the legislative body." Jefferson evidently saw with great clarity that the application of the principle of the separation of powers could not, in itself, achieve its object; it must, to be effective, be supplemented by "barriers" between the powers of government, and the erection of these barriers, although in a sense itself a breach of the doctrine, was necessary to its application.

The same lesson that had been learnt in Massachusetts and Virginia was driven home by the political battles in Pennsylvania which led to the dilemma of the Radicals on the Council of Censors in 1784. Whilst defending the extreme example of a constitution without "barriers," they went to considerable lengths to provide the detailed proof of its dangers. Their Republican opponents replied that without checks and balances the legislature would inevitably encroach upon the executive and judicial powers.[86] Other State legislatures, in pursuit of political advantage, continued to exercise their power in a way which clearly showed that mere exhortation to remain within their proper function was not enough. It was against the

84. Op. cit., p. 195.
85. Ibid., p. 196.
86. *Journal of the Council of Censors,* Philadelphia, 1783–4, p. 53; and *Pennsylvania Gazette,* 11 Feb. and 3 Apr. 1784.

background of this experience with the separation of powers that the Federal Convention met in Philadelphia in 1787.

Thus in revolutionary America there were those who adhered to the pure doctrine of the separation of powers, accepting no compromises with the old constitutional theory of checks and balances. But these were relatively few. At the other extreme there were those who wished to make the absolute minimum of change in the old constitution to bring it into line with new conditions. They accepted the ideas of the separation of powers, but only if that doctrine were combined with a thoroughgoing set of checks and balances comparable to those of the British system. John Adams exemplifies this latter group. The vast majority of Americans, however, fell somewhere between these extremes. For many, bicameralism was a sufficient check added to the basic separation of powers, but the various combinations of the two conceptions of government were very numerous. As the Revolution progressed, however, the extreme view of the pure separation of powers found fewer adherents, and by the time of the Federal Constitutional Convention in Philadelphia some form of a constitution of checks and balances was inevitable. The question was exactly how far it was necessary to go.

By the time that the Convention met, important sections of opinion among its members had already accepted the two central positions of modern American constitutional thought. The separation of powers was by this time, in the words of a contemporary pamphleteer, "a hackneyed principle," or a "trite maxim."[87] Now, however, the idea of checks and balances, rejected at the height of revolutionary fervour, was considered an essential constitutional weapon to keep all branches of government, and especially the legislature, within bounds. In the Convention Madison clearly stated the relationship between these two ideas. "If a constitutional discrimination of the departments on paper were a sufficient security to each against encroachments of the others, all further provisions would indeed be superfluous. But experience had taught us a distrust of that security; and that it is necessary to introduce such a balance of powers and interests, as will

---

87. *Remarks on the Proposed Plan of a Federal Government*, by "Aristides," Annapolis, 1788, pp. 13 and 40.

guarantee the provisions on paper."[88] In giving a defensive power to each department of government they were not blending them together; on the contrary, effective barriers were thus erected in order to keep them separate. The two doctrines, drawn from different sources, and as a result of the very conflict with each other, were now to become interdependent, combined into a single, essentially American doctrine, which still provides the framework of political life in the United States.

Although these two principles undoubtedly gained wide acceptance, there were many difficult problems to be solved by the Convention. Just how strong were the checks to be, and what form should they take? If the branches of the government were to be independent of each other what method of selection did this entail for the executive and judicial branches? The possibility of a hereditary executive or one appointed during good behaviour was barely mentioned.[89] The States offered two examples—election by the legislature in most of the earlier constitutions, and direct popular election in the later ones. Election by the people offered the greatest hope of an independent, though responsible, executive. However, the possibility of a real check to the exercise of power, where popular election was the ultimate source of authority in both branches, was doubted by Alexander Hamilton. "Gentlemen say we need to be rescued from the democracy. But what are the means proposed? A democratic assembly is to be checked by a democratic senate, and both these by a democratic chief magistrate."[90] Hamilton's incredulity might well have been justified had the Federal Constitution been applied to a tightly-knit homogeneous community, but in a country of such diversity the differing modes of election, and the different constituencies of the three elected branches of the government, have provided the basis for internal checks to the exercise of power of considerable strength and durability.

The reaction from the doctrine of the separation of powers, standing on its own as a theory of government, might have led the Convention towards some form of the parliamentary system which was then evolving in Brit-

88. *Records,* Vol. II, p. 77.
89. See the motion of Dr. McClurg, *Records,* Vol. II, p. 36.
90. Ibid., Vol. I, p. 310.

ain, but the Founders were not prepared to move so far away from what had now become the basis of their constitutional doctrine.

It has indeed been argued that the Founding Fathers did not "reject" parliamentary government, because in 1787 it was, after all, still very immature in England itself, and the influence of Montesquieu and Blackstone was so great that their view of the British Constitution, in which Ministers apparently played no significant role, was wholly accepted by the Americans. "As the idea never presented itself," says Lord Bryce, "we cannot say that it was rejected, nor cite the course they took as an expression of their judgment against the system under which England and her colonies have so far prospered."[91] However, as has been pointed out above, in England the understanding of the role of the cabinet was far greater than the works of Blackstone, de Lolme, and Paley would suggest, and for the best informed men in the Federal Convention there is no reason to suppose a greater degree of ignorance. George Mason in his objections to the projected constitution complained that no council of state, or constitutional body like a privy council, was provided for the President. The result might be, said Mason, that a council of state would grow out of the principal officers of the great departments, "the worst and most dangerous of all ingredients for such a council in a free country."[92] In reply, James Iredell remarked of England that "everybody knows that the whole movement of their government, where a Council is consulted at all, are directed by their *Cabinet Council,* composed entirely of the principal officers of the great departments."[93] The best evidence, however, comes in the remarkable speech made in the Convention by Gouverneur Morris. Opposing the selection of the executive by the legislature Morris showed a remarkable familiarity with the real constitutional issues in England at the time. Much has been made, he said, of the intrigues which might be practised by the executive to get into office, but what of the intrigues in the legislature to get him *out* of office? "Some leader of party will always covet his seat, will perplex his administration,

91. James Bryce, *The American Commonwealth,* New York, 1928, Vol. I, pp. 286–7.

92. *The Objections of the Hon. George Mason* . . . , 1787, reprinted by P. L. Ford, New York, 1888, p. 4.

93. *Answers to Mr. Mason's Objections* . . . , Newbern, 1788, reprinted in Ford, p. 16.

will cabal with the Legislature, till he succeeds in supplanting him." This is the way in which the King of England is "got out," for the *real* King, said Morris, is the Minister. This was the way Chatham achieved office, and Fox was for pushing the matter further still. The passage of the India Bill would almost have made the Minister King in form as well as in substance. "Our President will be the British Minister, yet we are about to make him appointable by the Legislature."[94] A clearer analysis of the situation and of the choice before the Convention could hardly be looked for. It is an interesting comment on the doctrine of the separation of powers that at the same time that it was being used in America to attack the idea of a cabinet (because the result, it was feared, would be the dominance of the legislature) it was being attacked in England as a system designed for the domination of the legislature by the executive. The use of the doctrine in these ways was quite consistent, for the crucial difference in the two situations lay in the extent of the franchise, and in the use of influence, and, therefore, in the composition of the groups which might be expected to control the legislature.

Their hatred of the corruption and influence in the British legislature, on which the Americans blamed much of the conflict between Parliament and the colonies, led the members of the Convention to accept almost automatically a complete separation of the personnel of legislative and executive branches. A few voices were raised arguing that the power to appoint legislators to office would be an important weapon in the hands of the executive, who might otherwise become a "mere phantom" of authority,[95] but the motion to make members of the legislature incapable of holding office was accepted, Madison noted, without opposition.[96] Yet the fear of legislative tyranny and the need for executive independence loomed so large in the minds of the delegates that they were prepared to move towards the partial restoration of some of the former prerogatives of the Crown, which the early State constitutions had ruthlessly stripped away. Still, they were

---

94. *Records,* Vol. II, p. 104. The discussions in the first Congress concerning the establishment of the Treasury Department also illustrate how well the cabinet system was understood in America. *Abridgment of the Debates of Congress,* New York, 1857, Vol. I, pp. 110–11.

95. *Abridgment of the Debates of Congress,* Vol. II, p. 284.

96. Ibid., Vol. I, p. 390.

hesitant about this, and adopted a half-way position on almost all issues. The veto power was restored, but only a qualified veto; the appointing power was given to the President, but subject to the power of the Senate to confirm appointments unless otherwise provided for by Congress; the power to negotiate treaties was placed in the President's hands, but confirmation was required by the Senate; and the power to declare war remained with the Congress. These were the aspects of government business that did not fit neatly into the theory of the separation of powers, and the Convention's treatment of them can be seen, in part as the application of the idea of checks and balances, and in part as compromises evolved from the uncertainty about whether these were really executive or legislative functions. The allocation of these powers was strongly criticized by those who favoured a more thoroughgoing separation. The President's veto power made him too much like the English King to pass unchallenged, and the role of the Senate in making appointments and ratifying treaties was reminiscent of the old colonial governor's council with all its overtones of aristocratic power. Thus Samuel Bryan attacked the proposed Constitution, the idea of checks and balances, and John Adams, all in the same breath, quoting Montesquieu in support of the revolutionary theory of the separation of powers as exemplified by the Constitution of Pennsylvania.[97] But the Anti-Federalist attack upon the Constitution lacked coherence and a clear alternative set of principles to oppose to the combination of separation of powers and checks and balances proposed by the Convention. The pure doctrine of the separation of powers was no longer a viable alternative, as it had seemed to be in 1776. The experience of it in operation had been a major factor in making checks and balances acceptable again. Furthermore, the opponents of the Constitution could not simply propose a pure separation of powers for the *Federal* Government, even if they did so for *State* governments, for it was by now clear that such a system of government would probably lead to an extremely powerful central legislature, and this they did not want. The suggestions of monarchic or aristocratic tendencies in the Constitution had to be refuted by its proponents by emphasizing

---

97. *To the People of Pennsylvania,* by "Centinel," Philadelphia, 1787, reprinted in J. B. McMaster and F. D. Stone, *Pennsylvania and the Federal Constitution, 1787-1788,* Philadelphia, 1888.

that it did in fact embody the separation of powers, and that the checks and balances were not in conflict with, but necessary to, the effective maintenance of a separation of the powers of government.

One of the most important consequences for American government of the development of constitutional ideas between 1776 and 1787 lay in the judicial sphere. The American doctrine of judicial review bears a complex relationship to the separation of powers. Clearly some form of separation of powers is a necessary prerequisite of judicial review. The long evolution of judicial independence in England, the development of Montesquieu's theory through the medium of Blackstone's interpretation, and the importance attached to judicial independence in the colonial period in America, are all essential steps in the development of the power of the American courts. However, the separation of powers, in itself, is not a sufficient basis for the establishment of a doctrine of judicial review: indeed, taken to its logical extreme, as in France after 1789, or by the Jeffersonian Republicans in the United States, the separation of powers is incompatible with the idea that one branch can interfere with the functions of another to the extent of invalidating its acts. Like the veto power, the establishment of judicial review depended upon the acceptance of the idea of checks and balances as essential barriers to the improper exercise of power. The idea of judicial review flows in part, of course, from the argument that the mere existence of a constitution lays a duty upon the judiciary not to enforce laws in conflict with it, but this is a view which has not been accepted in all countries with written constitutions. It was not accepted in France, and even Switzerland, with its federal constitution, has not adopted the American attitude towards judicial power. Thus although we can find indications in colonial history of the evolution of judicial review, as well as in the Council of Revision in the New York Constitution of 1777 and in the decisions of early State courts, it is in the Federal Convention, with its highly developed conception of the relation between the separation of powers and checks and balances, that we find the evidence of the belief that judges must have the power to check the legislature by limiting it to its proper functions. *Here* is the solution to the problem of the use by the legislature of "the forms of legislation" to achieve improper ends which had puzzled the early constitutionalists. Should the executive veto be insufficient to restrain the legislature then the courts would be able to declare unconstitutional acts void. The evidence of the blossoming of this view of judicial power in the Convention and in the *Federalist* is most impressive.[98]

The newly-forged American constitutional theory had now reached its practical realization, and there remained only the problem of developing that theory for the purpose of obtaining the ratification of the Constitution. The two most skilful exponents of the new doctrine were James Wilson of Pennsylvania, and Madison. Wilson, a delegate in the Convention and later to become one of the first Justices of the Supreme Court of the United States, conducted a herculean defence of the new Constitution in the ratifying Convention in Pennsylvania. His starting point was, as indeed it had to be, the sovereignty of the people. He rejected Blackstone's doctrine of parliamentary sovereignty as outmoded. The British do not understand the idea of a constitution which limits and superintends the operations of the legislature. This was an improvement in the science of government reserved to the Americans.[99] Wilson made it abundantly clear that no mere copy of the British pattern of government was intended. Mixed government as practised in Britain was inappropriate to the United States, for it was a system of government "suited to an establishment of different orders of men."[100] The Federal Convention had created a government which in principle was "purely democratical," but which applied that principle in different forms, thus obtaining all the advantages of the simple forms of government without their disadvantages.

Wilson believed that the legislature must be restrained, as must the other parts of government. However, a simple separation of powers was not enough. There must be an *active* power over the legislature, not merely a *passive* one.[101] The legislature would, therefore, be kept within its bounds

98. See for example *Records*, Vol. I, pp. 138–9; Vol. II, p. 78; and *Federalist*, No. 78. See also the arguments in *Observations on Government*, New York, 1787, pp. 27, 43–46, 50; and [Jonathan Jackson], *The Political Situation of the United States of America*, Worcester, Mass., 1788, pp. 181–3.

99. *Commentaries on the Constitution of the United States*, Philadelphia, reprinted London, 1792, p. 38, reprinted in McMaster and Stone, op. cit.

100. Ibid., p. 40.

101. Ibid., p. 51.

both by the internal check of bicameralism, and by the "interference" of the executive and judicial departments. The executive veto and the power of the courts to invalidate legislation would ensure that the legislature heeded the authority of the people.[102] It remained for Madison to complete the theoretical statement of the proposed Constitution in the *Federalist*. Madison, like Wilson, was concerned to refute the charges that the Constitution blended the powers of government too much. It would be a misunderstanding of Montesquieu, he wrote, to assert that the principle of the separation of powers did not allow of the blending of the powers of government at all.[103] Montesquieu "did not mean that these departments ought to have no *partial agency* in, or no *control* over the acts of each other." He meant no more than this, "that where the *whole* power of one department is exercised by the same hands which possess the *whole* power of another department, the fundamental principles of a free constitution are subverted."[104] The experience of Virginia and Pennsylvania proved that it was not enough to define precisely the boundaries of the power of each of the departments of government. Such "parchment barriers" are not enough. "Unless these departments be so far connected and blended, as to give to each a constitutional control over the others, the degree of separation which the maxim requires, as essential to a free government, can never in practice be duly maintained."[105]

The Americans, after a period of hesitation and experiment, had arrived at a new formulation of the doctrine of constitutionalism, which reached back over the Revolution to the theories of eighteenth- and seventeenth-century England. They had used the materials they found in English thought and in their experience of English and colonial government; nevertheless it was a new formulation, with a very different emphasis from that of the theory of the balanced constitution which had been their springboard for a jump into the new world of independence.

The Federal Constitution represented a victory for the ideas of Wilson and Madison over the principles upon which the early revolutionary State constitutions had been built. Those constitutions had been deeply influ-

102. Ibid., p. 52.
104. Ibid.

103. *Federalist*, No. 47.
105. *Federalist*, No. 48.

enced by the doctrine of the separation of powers, but there had been no real intellectual contribution made in America to the doctrine; its translation into the institutions of revolutionary governments had been the result of circumstances and of the existing tradition of English political thought. The logic of the situation had almost inevitably entailed that the subtraction of one of the two elements of English constitutional theory in the eighteenth century would leave the other component, the separation of powers, to stand upon its own feet as the basis of constitutional doctrine. The Federal Convention had returned in large part to the earlier eighteenth-century view of the proper construction of a constitution, with that vital shift of emphasis which American conditions required of the constitution-maker. There was now a new body of constitutional doctrine that justified and expounded the system of separated powers buttressed and maintained by the checks and balances built into the Constitution.

It might be thought that the ratification of the Constitution, the acceptance of the new compromise as the basis of the government of the United States, would represent the end of the pure doctrine of the separation of powers in America. Surely those who had argued that the separation of powers had not received its due from the men of Philadelphia were silenced by the success of the *Federalist?* Looking back at the success story of the Constitution and the weighty expressions of its philosophy in the work of Marshall, Kent, and Story, it might well seem that the victory of the constitutional theory of 1787 was overwhelming and complete. Yet this would be quite the reverse of the truth. In the years following 1789 the pure doctrine of the separation of powers was to battle yet again with the theory of checks and balances, and to find in America its most complete and its most impressive intellectual expression. For a short time it became the highest and most consistent expression of the philosophy of Jeffersonian Republicanism, and nowhere else in the world were the ideas of the pure doctrine of the separation of powers to be given the extended treatment that they received from John Taylor of Caroline.

Soon after the ratification of the Constitution there was a reaction against the ideas it embodied, and there developed a concerted attack upon the elements of balanced government it contained. The Jeffersonians attacked the Constitution on the grounds that it was the instrument for the reintroduction into America of the ideas of monarchy and aristocracy, and that it was constructed from materials borrowed from the despised English Constitution instead of being wholly fashioned anew upon American principles. The most "American" of these principles was undoubtedly, in their eyes, the operation of the separation of powers in a democratic system of government. The attack upon the Constitution took the form of an attack upon John Adams and his *Defence of the Constitutions of the United States*, for although it was recognized that the Constitution did not embody his vision of a mixed and balanced government, nevertheless it was a pattern which had been before the men of 1787 when they were veering away from the true State. Adams's work, extreme as it was in parts, became the ideal stalking-horse for those who wished to attack the elements of the theory of mixed and balanced government to be found in the Constitution. Once more, therefore, the constitutional debate revolved around the desire of one party to strip away the checks and balances of balanced government and to rely upon a starkly pure doctrine of the separation of powers.

There was, however, a considerable change of emphasis between this dispute and the earlier ones which had occupied English and American writers in the eighteenth century. In America at the end of the century both sides accepted the separation of powers as the *basis* of a free constitution, although at the extremes of both parties there were those who were impatient of all such constitutional checks to the exercise of power.[106] The point now at issue was the extent to which, if at all, this separation of powers should be modified by a system of checks and balances that owed its inspiration to the balanced constitution of eighteenth-century England, with all its overtones of monarchic and aristocratic power. It was a looking-glass version of the debate then going on in England, the primary and secondary assumptions of constitutional theory having changed places. As the balanced constitution had recently been rejected outright in France in

---

106. Fisher Ames described constitutional checks as "cobweb ties for lions" (quoted by David H. Fischer, "The Myth of the Essex Junto," *William and Mary Quarterly*, Vol. XXI, No. 2, Apr. 1964, p. 207); and at the other extreme Joel Barlow, "the American Jacobin," saw no dangers in democracy to be guarded against.

favour of the pure doctrine of the separation of powers, it was not surprising that the opponents of the Constitution looked to France for arguments with which to support their attack, although the hollow victory achieved by the separation of powers in that country was in many respects an embarrassment rather than a help.

An important early interpretation of the Constitution in the Anti-Federalist vein was *Sketches of the Principles of Government,* published in 1793 by Nathaniel Chipman. This work, which Jefferson later recommended, along with Locke and the *Federalist,* as a means of gaining an understanding of the principles of civil government, was by no means a mere restatement of the views of the Philadelphia Convention. Chipman, who served both on the Federal bench and as head of the Vermont judiciary, developed his own view of constitutional principles and then applied them to the new Constitution. He placed great emphasis upon the necessity of a clear definition of the powers of the departments of the government in order to limit them, and he illustrated the dangers of a system of "confusion of powers" by reference to the operation of the Ministry in Britain—another example of how well the Americans understood the system of government they had rejected.[107] Chipman maintained strongly that none of the departments of the government, including the legislature, should be allowed to encroach upon the others. He particularly opposed the aggrandizement of the executive, stating that it "ought not to have a negative, or any directing power in the passing of laws."[108] As a judge Chipman looked to the judiciary to interpret the Constitution and so keep the "interests" of the legislative and executive branches in unison with the rights and interests of the individual citizens, but he did not mean by this that the judiciary would have a veto upon legislation. Rather he saw the roles of both executive and judiciary as advisers in the process of legislation, forming them into a Council of Revision that would "give information of all difficulties, which they foresee will arise, either in the interpretation, the application, or the execution of the law." However, once having had their say, the executive and the judges

107. Op. cit., Rutland, Vermont, 1793, pp. 120–1, and 125.
108. Ibid., p. 125.

must acknowledge that the legislators are "the sole judges" of the interest of the community.[109]

Having rejected the view that checks should be applied to the legislature in the exercise of its legislative function, Chipman launched a strong attack upon the theory of balanced government, whether in a monarchy or in a political system headed by a Governor or President. To admit the necessity for such a balance, he wrote, was to admit that the laws of nature "have indulged to certain classes of men different rights," a proposition which is wholly inadmissible.[110] Like his contemporaries in France, Chipman believed that the theory of balance was based upon the principle of "a perpetual war of each against the other," which was incompatible with republican government.[111] He attacked Blackstone's *Commentaries* as inappropriate to American conditions, and lamented that it was the only treatise available to law students in the United States. The only parts of the *Commentaries* he could accept as being in accord with the universal principles of jurisprudence were those derived from the democratic part of the British system of mixed government.[112] Chipman looked back to the ideas of the early State constitutions and rejected the checks and balances of the Federal Constitution. He had, however, no clear alternative to offer which would take the place of those checks and balances as barriers to legislative encroachment upon the functions of the other branches of government. He stood on much the same ground as did Jefferson in 1781, but rejecting the solution to the problem which the Federalists presented as their means of erecting barriers to the abuse of power. To gain a clearer idea of the development of the thought of Jeffersonian Republicanism in this respect we must turn away from Chipman to the thought of Jefferson himself.

Although it is dangerous to attempt to tie down Jefferson's thought into a simple mould, if we look at the views he expressed over the years concerning the basic constitutional problem posed in his *Notes on the State of*

109. Ibid., pp. 126–7. Chipman's ideas about judicial review had altered by 1833. See his *Principles of Government*, Burlington, 1833, pp. 165a, 288 ff.

110. *Sketches of the Principles of Government*, p. 128.

111. Ibid., p. 131.

112. Ibid., p. 237.

Virginia, we can see the changing attitudes which he expressed towards the system of checks and balances. We find, in fact, that after having accepted the need for some form of a balanced system, Jefferson, towards the end of his life, turned to the pure doctrine of the separation of powers as the foundation of his constitutional thought, and, shortly before his death, he set forth the doctrine in its most rigid form. Following on his criticism of the Constitution of Virginia for having failed to place barriers between the legislative, executive, and judicial powers, and so allowing the legislature to absorb all the powers of government, Jefferson demanded the establishment of a convention which could "bind up the several branches of government by certain laws, which, when they transgress, their acts shall become nullities." Thus it would be unnecessary for the people to stage frequent rebellions in order to prevent legislative usurpation of power.[113] In the following year Jefferson commenced his proposed constitution for Virginia with a strong affirmation of the separation of powers, but at the same time he proposed the creation of a Council of Revision which would exercise a veto over legislation, and which would be overridden by a two-thirds vote of the legislature. By 1787 Jefferson seems to have accepted the philosophy of checks and balances even more whole-heartedly, for he then wrote to Madison about the proposed Federal Constitution, saying that he liked the negative given to the Executive "with a third of either house," although he would have preferred the judiciary to have been associated with the exercise of the veto, "or invested with a similar and separate power."[114] His enthusiasm for the separation of powers had not weakened, however, for at this time he expressed to John Adams his view that it is "the first principle of a good government."[115] In 1809 Jefferson seemed still to see some merit in the theory of checks and balances, indeed he argued that it was not taken far enough in the Federal Constitution, implying perhaps that the checks upon the power of the Supreme Court were not as effective as those upon the other branches.[116]

113. *The Writings of Thomas Jefferson,* ed. by P. L. Ford, 1892–9, Vol. III, p. 235.
114. Ibid., Vol. IV, pp. 475–6.
115. Ibid., Vol. IV, p. 454.
116. Ibid., Vol. IX, p. 259.

Over a long period, therefore, Jefferson seems to have tended towards some version of the checks and balances theory as the only means of preventing the abuse of power by the separated branches of the government, and in particular for preventing all power "resulting to the legislature." In 1816, however, and in the years that followed, we find a quite different point of view expressed in his letters. His antagonism towards executive power, and his hatred of the aspirations of the Supreme Court to "judicial supremacy" over the other branches of government, now led him to reject all notion of checks and balances, in favour of three separate branches of government, all quite independent of each other, and all closely responsible directly to the people; he thus came to accept the pure doctrine of the separation of powers as the only basis of a desirable constitution. His answer to the problem of preventing the encroachment of one branch of government upon the functions of another was the same as that which Sieyès had propounded in France some years earlier. If all the branches of government were equally responsible directly to the people, they would at once be equally independent of each other and equally subordinate to the true sovereign power. There would therefore be no need for checks and balances. Pure republicanism, said Jefferson, can be measured in no other way than in the complete control of the people over their organs of government.[117] The touchstone of constitutionality must be, therefore, an appeal to the people. Each department of government must have "an equal right to decide for itself what is the meaning of the Constitution in the cases submitted to its action."[118] Judicial review was "a very dangerous doctrine indeed," and incompatible with a true reading of the Constitution, which had "wisely made all the departments coequal and co-sovereign within themselves."[119] Jefferson had already, in 1815, developed this idea at some length in a letter to W. H. Torrance,[120] and had acknowledged the objection that if each branch were its own judge of the constitutionality of its decisions, then contradictions would arise "and produce inconvenience." However, he

---

117. *Letter to John Taylor*, 28 May 1816, ibid., Vol. X, p. 30.
118. *Letter to Judge Spencer Roane*, 6 Sept. 1819, ibid., Vol. X, p. 141.
119. *Letter to William C. Jarvis*, 28 Sept. 1820, ibid., Vol. X, p. 160.
120. 11 June 1815, ibid., Vol. IX, pp. 517–18.

thought that "the prudence of the public functionaries, and the authority of public opinion, will generally produce accommodation." This viewpoint had indeed long been implicit in Jefferson's Republicanism, and he had expressed it as early as November 1801 in his attack upon the Sedition Act at the beginning of his first term in the Presidency.[121] By 1816, however, his opinion on this point had hardened into a reliance upon something more than the mere prudence of public officials.

The only true corrective for the abuse of constitutional power, said Jefferson, is the elective power of the people, and he followed the logic of this statement through to its inevitable conclusion. All the departments of the government, legislative, executive, *and* judicial, must be popularly elected and subject to frequent electoral sanction. Criticizing the contemporary Constitution of Virginia, Jefferson in 1816 pointed to the fact that direct election did not govern the selection of Governor or judges. "Where then is our republicanism to be found?" he asked; "Not in our Constitution certainly, but merely in the spirit of our people."[122] If the principle of republicanism is to be adopted in Virginia, then it must be followed through inflexibly, with all government officials subjected "to approbation or rejection at short intervals." In this way the three powers of government, each drawing its authority from the only depository of the ultimate power of society, might maintain their mutual independence. Such a government might long continue, but such would certainly not be the case if any one branch could assume the authority of another.[123]

Thus at the end of his life Jefferson came to accept that extreme view of a constitutional system of government which Nedham had propounded in 1654, with "all power flowing in distinct channels" from the people. It was fundamentally the same philosophy as Sieyès had argued before the National Assembly in 1789.[124] It was the complete rejection of checks and balances, of the granting to legislature, executive, or judiciary an indepen-

121. See the passage quoted by Adrienne Koch, *Jefferson and Madison: The Great Collaboration*, New York, 1964, p. 228.

122. *Letter to Samuel Kercheval*, 12 July 1816, *Writings of Thomas Jefferson*, Vol. X, p. 39.

123. *To Jarvis*, 28 Sept. 1820, ibid., Vol. X, p. 161.

124. See Ch. 7 below.

dence of the people, or a dependence upon each other. The extreme nature of this doctrine was very clear to Jefferson, and he more than once forbad Samuel Kercheval to publish a letter in which it is set out.[125] Although Jefferson was reluctant to acknowledge the doctrine publicly through his letters, the philosophy they contained had been publicly pronounced in America at considerable length by John Taylor, who has been described as "the philosopher of Jeffersonian Republicanism." Indeed the coherence of Jefferson's views in and after 1816 must surely be due, in part at least, to the major work of John Taylor, *An Inquiry into the Principles and Policy of the Government of the United States,* which was published in 1814 and which Jefferson first read two years later.

John Taylor, of Caroline County, Virginia, United States Senator and a leader of the Jeffersonian party, was in some ways the most impressive political theorist that America has produced. He presented the essence of Republicanism in a systematic and coherent theory of politics which few can match. His style was loose and undisciplined, and the length and repetitiveness of his works was hardly designed to make him a truly popular author. Yet if the initial effort is made to overcome the barrier of his prose style, the ultimate impression is one of great clarity and consistency, together with a certain charm. Taylor represented all the major characteristics of the Jeffersonian point of view. He was an agrarian, bitterly opposed to banking and financial interests, the "aristocracy of paper and patronage" as he called them. He believed passionately in States' rights, and forcefully argued the strict constructionist view of the Constitution. It is, however, his attitude towards the separation of powers and checks and balances which most concerns us here, and it is in this respect that Taylor's achievement has been least appreciated, for the *Inquiry* is the most sustained and comprehensive defence of the extreme doctrine of the separation of powers to be found in either English or French.

Taylor's *Inquiry* takes the form of an attack upon John Adams and his *Defence of the Constitutions of the United States,* but it is far more than this. The *Inquiry* represents an attempt to define the basic principles of govern-

---

125. *Letter to Samuel Kercheval*, Vol. X, pp. 47 and 319.

ment and to apply them critically to the Constitution of the United States. It is an attempt to base a theory of government upon moral principles, rather than upon the arguments from expediency that Taylor sees in the work of Adams and the Federalists. The *Inquiry* begins with an analysis of the nature of aristocracy, which Taylor believed to be central to the whole Federalist position. As with earlier proponents of the extreme doctrine of the separation of powers, it was the role of the aristocracy in a system of mixed government that formed a central point of attack for Taylor. He argued that Adams based his whole theory upon the idea that aristocracy is "a work of nature," but this was to mistake the whole nature of government. Government, said Taylor, is founded "in moral, and not in natural or physical causes."[126] The moral qualities of man being either good or evil, every form of government must be founded in the moral principle which prevails in its construction. The "numerical analysis," as he dubbed the classification of governments into monarchy, aristocracy, and democracy, is incapable of revealing the nature of government, whereas analysis according to moral principles can do this. The acceptance of aristocracy as "natural" commits us to the acceptance also of its evil characteristics, but in America there is no reason at all to assume that society must accept the aristocratic yoke. Taylor condemned both the feudal aristocracy and the new aristocracy of "paper and patronage." Neither is inevitable or desirable. The evils of the latter far outstrip the evils of hereditary landed power, for the new aristocracy necessitates "an eternal and oppressive taxation" in order to supply it with the wealth that feudal aristocrats drew from their land. Such an aristocracy, when in control of the government, "divides a nation into two interests, and cooks one in the modes most delicious to the appetite of the other."[127] Such is the essential evil of every species of bad government, for it places a particular interest in a favoured position over the general interest.

Taylor thus summed up all the major attitudes of those who in the period between the English Civil War and the Revolution of 1848 set up the pure doctrine of the separation of powers in opposition to the ideas

126. *An Inquiry into the Principles and Policy of the Government of the United States,* Fredericksburg, 1814, p. 34.
127. Ibid., p. 51.

of the balanced constitution. It represented the constitution of a new form of State upon intellectually derived principles of the best form of government rather than upon the acceptance of the present historically determined power-structure of society. It represented an attack upon privilege and class distinction in favour of a more democratic and egalitarian distribution of power. It was the belief in a constitutional system constructed upon rational, functional criteria, rather than upon appeals to tradition and established modes of behaviour. It was this that made the pure doctrine of the separation of powers during these two centuries such a revolutionary doctrine. At the end of the eighteenth century John Cartwright in England and Sieyès in France represented this philosophy of government, and in America John Taylor pushed it to its limits. As a consequence of this he entirely rejected the view that all governments must be monarchical, aristocratic, democratic, or some mixture of these. He refused to be bound by these categories. He rejected, therefore, the very basis of the balanced constitution, by refusing to be drawn into the age-old dispute about the alternative forms of simple or mixed government. For Taylor there was no reason why America should not build entirely anew upon the basis of her own moral principles. The authors of the *Federalist*, he said, had paid too much attention to "political skeletons" constructed with fragments torn from monarchy, aristocracy, and democracy. These "rude almost savage political fabrics" could hardly be expected to provide the materials for an American system of government. To approach the problem of government in the New World in this frame of mind was like attempting to build a palace with materials taken from Indian cabins.[128]

Taylor believed that *all* the old forms of government were to be destroyed in America. Democracy was to be replaced by representative government, and the old class divisions between monarchy, aristocracy, and democracy were to give way to "the division of power." Thus he explicitly replaced the theory of the mixed constitution with the doctrine of the separation of powers; for he believed deeply that this was the major constitutional battle which was to be fought in the New World, and that only

128. Ibid., Preface, pp. v–vi.

by the triumph of the latter would a truly "American" system of government be achieved. The American system of divided powers could not be combined with mixed government; it replaced and excluded it. "Instead of balancing power, we divide it, and make it responsible."[129] In his view John Adams converted the American maxim "that legislative, executive and judicial power shall be separate and distinct," into the idea "of independent orders of men and powers. . . ."[130] Taylor saw very clearly the inconsistencies between Adams's position in the revolutionary atmosphere of 1775 when he had outlined a desirable State constitution, and the attitude he adopted in the *Defence* at the time of the making of the Federal Constitution. Taylor pointed out that in the earlier period, when the idea of the separation of powers figured more strongly in Adams's work, the latter had appealed for support to the memory of Marchamont Nedham. But a whole volume of the *Defence* was devoted to an explicit attack upon Nedham's principles. In his essay of 1775 Adams had deduced a form of government from Nedham's principle that "the people were the best guardians of their own liberties," whereas in the later work Adams based his constitutional theory upon the proposition that the people are their own worst enemies.[131] So Taylor summed up the difference between Adams and the Jeffersonians: "Our policy divides power, and unites the nation in one interest, Mr. Adams's divides a nation into several interests and unites power."[132]

Having distinguished very clearly between the two constitutional theories which had dominated Western political thought for the past century and a half, taking them to the extreme positions where their potentially contradictory nature was wholly realized, Taylor then applied this analysis to the Constitution of the United States. Human nature being a mixture of good and evil, the wise constitution, he said, preserves the good and controls the evil. Whenever reason prevails, the good moral principles of the division of power will be followed, but care must be taken to ensure that the "elements of force and fraud," which characterize the theory of balance, are not allowed to creep in. The constitution should bestow upon each officer and department only that portion of power necessary for the fulfilment

129. Ibid., p. 88.
131. Ibid., p. 531.

130. Ibid., p. 185.
132. Ibid., p. 428.

of his or its proper function, and to ensure the dependence of all of them upon the nation. The Federal Constitution fails to observe this principle in certain respects. The power of the Executive was inflated by the Convention beyond its proper limits. "The presidency, gilded with kingly powers, has been tossed into the constitution, against the publick sentiment, and gravely bound in didactick fetters, like those which in England and France have become political old junk."[133] Given the logic of the English system, in which all political power is entrusted to the government instead of being retained by the nation, it is natural to set off the parts of the government against each other, and so to "mould" the executive power by computing the force necessary to offset the numerical preponderance of Lords and Commons. Taylor saw, however, no need for such a system in America, where all political power was in the people, and where the executive officer therefore required no royal powers or prerogatives. To grant them to him was to make possible the re-creation of a monarchy. He therefore attacked the granting of these powers to the President, in particular his patronage power, his military and diplomatic powers, and his power to appoint judges.[134]

Taylor's attack upon judicial review, like that of Jefferson, was particularly bitter. It had been intended, he said, that the people should be the only source of constitutional amendment, but the Constitution was in fact open to a power of construction and interpretation not responsible to the people. "Legislative, executive and judicial powers shall be separate and distinct, yet the judges can abolish or make law by precedent."[135] The proper role of the judiciary is to enforce the law, but, "admitting that a power of construing is nearly equivalent to a power of legislating, why should construction of law be quite independent of sovereign will, when law itself is made completely subservient to it?" Thus he took the pure separation of powers to its logical conclusion, as had already been done in France, and rejected the validity of judicial review of legislation.

Taylor followed the separation of powers to its ultimate conclusion, rejecting the controlling links and balances between the branches of govern-

133. Ibid., p. 194.   134. Ibid., pp. 171-3.
135. Ibid., p. 203.

ment which had formed an essential part of the eighteenth-century theory of balanced government, and which had been partly incorporated into the Federal Constitution. He represented the philosophy of 1776 rather than that of 1787, but he was, of course, well aware of those aspects of the revolutionary State governments that had led the Americans, including his master Jefferson, to turn once again to the model of the British Constitution for methods of controlling the exercise of power, and in particular the power of the legislature. To these problems Taylor had two answers. On the one hand there was the possibility of control through the electoral process, which led him to assert that the only proper way of "exalting" the judicial power into the status of a branch of the government "which would be conformable to our principle of division" was to make the judiciary elective and so responsible to the people.[136] On the other hand, against the danger of legislative usurpation he relied upon the federal system of government. The best restraint upon legislatures, he argued, "consists of the mutual right of the general and state governments to examine and controvert before the publick each others' proceedings."[137] The separation of powers and federalism become, therefore, interlocking elements in a thoroughgoing philosophy of the division of power. Power is divided between government and people, between legislature, executive, and judiciary, and between State and Federal governments.[138] Every element of this divided system of government must be the sole judge of the rightness of its own actions, subject to the overriding power of the people. In 1822 Taylor stated this extreme view unequivocally: "As the Senate and the House of Representatives are each an independent tribunal to judge of its own constitutional powers, so the state and Federal governments are independent tribunals to judge of their respective constitutional powers. The same principle is applicable to the legislative, executive and judicial departments, both state and Federal."[139]

This fantastic picture of a fragmented governmental system has per-

136. Ibid., pp. 209 and 217.
137. Ibid., p. 649.
138. Ibid., p. 408.
139. *Tyranny Unmasked*, Washington, 1822, p. 258.

haps as its major virtue the consistency with which the Jeffersonian principles are worked out. It is an ideology of constitutionalism to oppose to the system of the Federalists. Yet in 1824, when John Taylor of Caroline died, the same year, incidentally, as John Cartwright in England, a man whom he much resembled, the basis of this battle of ideas had already slipped away. The Federalist theory of the Constitution, defended by Marshall, Kent, and Story, and the Jeffersonian theory as elaborated by Taylor, were neither of them any longer able to sustain the role of a coherent philosophy for a political movement. The emerging pattern of American politics was breaking these theories up into a number of segments, and shuffling and reshuffling them into differing patterns, determined largely by the expediencies of political life rather than by "principles." The ideas did not disappear, they were split up and scattered. The sectional forces in nineteenth-century American life made coherent philosophies like these very difficult to maintain.

Thus John C. Calhoun, who was in some ways the spiritual heir of Jefferson and Taylor, took the States' rights element in their philosophy, but combined it with ideas taken from the Federalists about the role of checks and balances. Calhoun, in his determination to limit the exercise of power, especially by the Federal Government, employed the idea of a veto power as consistently and thoroughly as Taylor had rejected it. He defended the veto power of the President, and the review of legislation by the courts, and he so far forgot the principles of his youthful Republicanism as to praise the English system of government for its balance between the King, as representative of the "tax consumers," and the Commons, as representative of the taxpayers, maintained in equilibrium by the power of the House of Lords.[140] Southern admiration for the British system of government was evidenced in a rather different way in the discussions on the Constitution of the Confederate States. Although it closely followed the pattern of the Federal Constitution, it did provide that the legislature could allow the principal executive officers to have seats in both Houses, although they were not to be members of them. This provision was never fully imple-

---

140. *A Disquisition on Government*, New York, 1854, pp. 101–2.

mented, but the Constitution did have other provisions that moved away from the idea of strictly separated powers, notably the control which the President exercised over appropriations. Alexander Stephens, who was responsible for much of this Constitution, would have preferred to see the British model, which he much admired, followed to the extent of the adoption of a fully-fledged cabinet system.[141]

Another strand of the Jeffersonian philosophy was taken up with powerful effect by President Andrew Jackson. He echoed the views of Jefferson and Taylor with regard to constitutional interpretation: "The opinion of the judges has no more authority over Congress than the opinion of Congress has over the judges, and on that point the President is independent of both."[142] In 1834 Jackson developed at some length a theory of the Constitution, which, in its strict construction of the checks and balances of the Constitution, came very close to Taylor's extreme doctrine of the separation of powers. After enumerating the checks specifically provided for in the Constitution, Jackson continued: "With these exceptions each of the three great departments is independent of the others in its sphere of action, and when it deviates from that sphere is not responsible to the others further than it is expressly made so in the Constitution. In every other respect each of them is the co-equal of the other two, and all are the servants of the American people. . . ."[143] But "King Andrew," although eager to restrict the powers of Congress or Supreme Court to check the President, used his veto power to defy Congress and to make the presidency much more than a mere executive office. Under his influence the "executive" came to assume the role of the representative of the sovereign people against an oligarchic legislature, and the veto power was transformed into "the people's tribunative prerogative."[144]

In the States the Jeffersonian philosophy was reflected in the way in

141. *A Constitutional View of the Late War Between the States*, Philadelphia, 1876, Vol. II, p. 338.

142. Bank Veto Message of 10 July 1833 in *Messages and Papers of the Presidents*, ed. by J. D. Richardson, New York, 1897, Vol. III, p. 1145.

143. The Protest of 15 Apr. 1834, *Messages . . .* , Vol. III, p. 1290.

144. Levi Woodbury in 1841, quoted by R. G. Gettell, *A History of American Political Thought*, New York, 1928, p. 257.

which executive and judicial offices were made elective, and the way in which constitutions were submitted for ratification to the people. The people of the States could now control directly all the branches of government and extract from each of them the responsibility which Republicanism demanded, but with the predictable result that responsibility was fragmented and the ability to act decisively was removed from these governments. At the same time that the agencies of State government were subjected to popular control by making them elective, they were subjected also to a variety of constitutional checks to ensure still further that they would not abuse their power. As Francis Newton Thorpe has expressed it, an effort was made to protect the State from its legislature, its governor, its judges, and its administrative officials.[145] This was yet another combination of the ideas of the separation of powers and checks and balances, and one which went much further in the division and limitation of power than either of the two schools of constitutional thought in 1787 would have considered reasonable, for it removed all semblance of the independence which the earlier theories had allowed to the parts of government. The doctrine of checks and balances had earlier been associated with the view that the departments of government were, at least to some extent, free of popular control, exerting checks upon each other, whereas the true separation of powers had subjected the agencies of government to popular control but made them independent of each other. The new philosophy in the States, however, rendered the branches of government directly dependent upon the electorate and upon each other as well. It gave rise to that strangulation of effective government action in the States that formed the focus of much of the criticism of American government in the Progressive era. The constitutional ideas that had characterized the ideological positions of an earlier age were cannibalized and ceased to have any ideological coherence.

Thus the new Whig party, an anti-Jackson coalition, claimed to represent the "revolutionary theory of checks and balances" against the monarchical usurpations of the President. They argued for legislative supremacy over the executive, quite reversing the position of 1787, for those who were

145. F. N. Thorpe, *A Constitutional History of the American People, 1776-1850*, New York, 1898, Vol. II, p. 404.

fearful of mob rule placed their faith in legislatures rather than in a strong executive. In 1847, in the Constitutional Convention in Illinois, Whigs opposed the veto power as a relic of British monarchy, whilst Democrats argued that it was a necessary check to the power of oligarchic legislatures.[146]

The period immediately before the outbreak of the Civil War might be said, therefore, to have seen a disintegration of the two theories of constitutionalism which had characterized Anglo-American thought since 1641. Both had been broken down and used as political weapons almost devoid of ideological coherence. In this period in Britain, and to a lesser extent in France, the dilemma of a continuing dispute between two constitutional theories, both of which had a purely negative approach to the exercise of power, was ended by the emergence of a theory of parliamentary government that stressed the co-operation and interdependence of the legislative and executive powers. But there was little sign of a similar development in the United States. Both of the earlier coherent approaches to government seemed to have lost their relevance, but nothing else had emerged to take their place. It was not until the Civil War had been fought and won that the dissatisfaction, both with the extreme separation of powers and with checks and balances, and also with the various combinations of the two theories that had been evolved at Federal and State level, grew into a great roar of protest against the divisive assumptions of both theories, and institutional development and constitutional theory alike turned to a new phase in which "harmony" came to be the dominant theme.

146. *The Constitutional Debates of 1847*, ed. by A. C. Cole, Springfield, 1919, pp. 409, 431, 438–9. I am indebted to C. G. Dillworth for drawing my attention to these debates.

SEVEN

The Doctrine in France

T HE PATTERN of mixed government and the separation of powers in the seventeenth and eighteenth centuries closely reflected the institutional developments of England and America, reacting to the problems those countries faced, providing the ideological materials with which they formulated solutions to those problems. The institutional development of France, however, had followed very different lines, drawing inspiration from a different set of ideas about institutions. These conflicting English and French approaches to constitutional structure were reflected in the work of Montesquieu, who attempted to integrate them into a single theoretical framework. Although Montesquieu's attempt to provide a general description of systems of government embracing both French and English thought was not altogether successful, his great achievement was to concentrate attention upon the means of containing arbitrary power, and, by writing in general terms, to suggest that those aspects of English government which were so admired in the early eighteenth century might be applied elsewhere, if the requisite physical and social conditions were to hand. The latter part of the eighteenth century in France presents, therefore, a strangely confused picture in relation to Montesquieu and his thought. On the one hand, he is in many ways more important in France than in England and America, for he represents a turning-point in the whole approach to the problems of government and their solution; on the other hand, the specific solutions he offers in his description of the constitution of liberty seem inappropriate to French conditions and the current of French thought. This dilemma is clearly portrayed in the difficulties his disciples faced in 1789, when the proposals they made, based upon the mixed and balanced constitution, were rejected as alien and irrelevant to the new France.

The separation of powers, however, upon which Montesquieu had placed so much stress, became an essential article of faith with the men of 1789, so that, in a different way from that of America, the process of rejecting mixed government and of turning instead to the separation of powers as the basis of a free constitution was followed in France, with a vital difference. In 1789 in France, both doctrines, the balanced constitution and the separation of powers, were rejected or accepted as theoretical principles which had had little or no institutional reality in pre-revolutionary experience, whereas in America the doctrines were regarded as the evolution of, and the reformulation of, a system of institutions that had been operated, had become obsolete, and were to be modernized. It is in this respect that the institutional changes in France were truly revolutionary, in a way that those of America were not.

Furthermore, the role played by the separation of powers was different in France and America. In France the pure doctrine was held fiercely as an explicit ideological position, whereas in America it had been more a matter of the logic of the revolutionary situation than a conviction of the necessity of the pure doctrine which had dominated events. When in America the political situation enabled a resurgence of the older ideas, these had quickly returned to modify the extremes of the doctrine of the separation of powers. In France, however, the pure doctrine of the separation of powers took hold of men's minds with an intensity, and a durability, not paralleled in America. Part of the explanation of this lies, as will be seen, in the complexity and intractability of the political situation, but part of the explanation must be sought further back in the past, in the particular form in which the men of 1789 came to look upon the separation of powers as a result of the development of thought after 1748. This part of the explanation of the intensity and persistence of the theory must be sought in the way in which the thought of Jean-Jacques Rousseau was overlaid upon that of Montesquieu, modified it, and gave a new direction and force to the theory of the separation of powers.

It is difficult to exaggerate Rousseau's importance in determining the particular form that the separation of powers took in France. He was himself bitterly critical of the doctrine in the form in which Montesquieu developed it, and he was supremely unconcerned with the problems most of the writers on the separation of powers had considered vitally important. Yet the form in which he cast his theory, and the vocabulary he used, when adapted to the needs of the more practical men of the late eighteenth century, combined with that part of Montesquieu's thought which seemed to them to be relevant, produced a theory of the separation of powers very different from that of England or America. Rousseau's central position in the *Social Contract,* first published in 1762, was that law can only emanate from the general will of the community; the legislative power is the exercise of the sovereign will of the people. This power cannot be alienated or delegated; any attempt to create generally applicable rules from any other source represents a usurpation of popular sovereignty and cannot result in law. Rousseau's emphatic denial of the divisibility of sovereignty was aimed at all those political theorists who in the past had divided up the sovereign powers among different persons or branches of government. Such writers, he wrote, make of the sovereign "a fantastic creature, composed of bits and pieces." Like a Japanese conjuror dismembering the body of a child and reassembling it by throwing it into the air, these writers dismember the social body and reassemble the pieces "without our knowing how."[1] For Rousseau the idea of the division of sovereignty was the central fallacy of political thought, from which flowed most of the obscurities in writings on the State. "Whenever we think we see sovereignty divided, we are mistaken . . . the rights which are taken for parts of sovereignty

1. *Social Contract,* II, ii, p. 27. Quotations are from *Rousseau: Political Writings,* ed. by F. Watkins, London, 1953.

are all subordinate to it."[2] Rousseau had, then, a boundless contempt for
the theories of equilibrium and balance that invested the parts of the State
with an independent power to check each other. It was this belief in the indivisible sovereignty of the people, adopted in the Revolution, that made
the constitutional theory of Montesquieu unacceptable, except in relation
to the separation of powers in its starkest form.

Although for Rousseau sovereignty was indivisible, the functions of
government were distinguishable, and it was here that he made his greatest
impact upon later French thought. He developed precise, abstract definitions of the legislative and executive powers, which have an immediate
appeal far greater than the confused attempts at definition made by Montesquieu. "Every free action is the effect of two concurrent causes, a moral
cause, or the will which determines the act; and a physical cause, or the
power which executes it."[3] In the political sphere this distinction between
will and *force* corresponds to the difference between the legislative and
executive powers. This intellectual distinction between the parts of any
political act was to dominate the mind of Sieyès and of other constitution-
builders for many years, as a basis for dividing the functions of government, but it did not in itself entail that the power to will and the power to
execute should be placed in separate branches of government, or in separate groups of men. On the contrary, it might well be argued, as later it was
in fact, that these faculties of willing and acting are inseparable. Yet Rousseau himself explicitly demanded their separation. The legislative power
can belong only to the people, but by definition this power can be concerned only with generalities, whereas the power to act can be concerned
only with particular cases. The executive power cannot, therefore, be placed
in the hands of the sovereign, whose province is the law, and whose acts
can consist only of laws. It is a mistake to identify the government with
the sovereign, for which the former is merely the agent or minister.[4]

It is necessary to pause here, however, and look very closely at Rousseau's usage. When he wrote of the "executive power" his meaning was
clearly something very different from that of his contemporaries. His use

2. Ibid.   3. Ibid., III, i, p. 59.
4. Ibid., III, i, p. 60.

of the term was closer to that of Marsilius than that of Locke or Montesquieu. Rousseau's *executive* denoted the whole apparatus of "the government," that part of the State which puts the law into effect. Since the law
can only be made by the people, and Rousseau refused to allow the delegation of this power to a representative assembly, then any such assembly, if
one exists, is part of the "executive." Thus a pure democracy was defined by
Rousseau as a State in which the legislative and executive powers are in the
same hands, but an aristocracy as a State in which the *executive* power is
aristocratically constituted, whether it be a natural, an elective, or a hereditary aristocracy.[5] This becomes very clear when we examine his treatment
of mixed governments. "In the distribution of executive power," he wrote,
"there is always a gradation from the greater to the lesser number"; however, "sometimes there is an equal distribution; this may occur . . . when the
constituent parts are in a condition of mutual dependence, as in the government of England."[6] Thus Rousseau subsumed all of Montesquieu's ideal
types of government under the label of "the executive power." All forms of
government, however constituted, are subject to the overriding legislative
power of the sovereign people. This was the vital principle. It was a matter
of expediency, and not of principle, to determine just how the "executive"
should be organized, and whether the branches of government should be
separated or not. The problems of institutional organization which seemed
vitally important to other theorists were of secondary importance to Rousseau. In certain states, he said, it might be desirable to divide "the executive
power." "When the executive power is not sufficiently dependent upon the
legislative, in other words when the ratio of prince to sovereign is greater
than the ratio of people to prince, this disproportion must be remedied by
dividing the government; for then its several parts have no less authority
over the subjects, and their division reduces their total power as against the
sovereign."[7] Rousseau therefore admitted the principle of the separation
of powers by the back door, but treated all the former discussions of this
problem as a matter of the organization of the "executive."

Rousseau, then, discussed the organization of the powers of government

5. Ibid., III, iv, p. 71; III, v, pp. 73–74.   6. Ibid., III, vii, p. 83.
7. Ibid.

at two levels; at the higher level he talked of the relations between the legislative and executive powers, and at the lower level he discussed the structure of the executive as he defined it. If we are to interpret Rousseau correctly, therefore, we must be careful to remember that when the discussion is at the higher level, as it almost always is, he is not using words, or conveying the same meaning, as do other theorists who write of the legislative and executive powers. Given his particular use of words, however, Rousseau had very definite views about the division of the functions of government and their separation between different bodies. It was this which led him to reject democracy. "It is not good for the makers of laws to execute them, nor for the body of the people to turn its attention from general considerations to particular objects."[8] One of the major advantages of aristocracy, including an elective aristocracy which Rousseau described as the best form of government, was that it distinguished between the sovereign and governmental powers.[9] The government has the sole duty of executing the law, and the sovereign people must not attempt to *govern*. "If the sovereign tries to govern, or if the magistrate tries to make laws, or if the subjects refuse to obey, order is succeeded by disorder, force and will no longer act in concert, and the state being dissolved, falls thereby either into despotism or anarchy."[10]

Within Rousseau's frame of reference the separation of powers is an essential characteristic of an ordered system of government, but it has nothing to do with the separation of the powers of government between an elected legislature and a king, president, or cabinet. The rejection of any possibility of delegating the legislative power made Rousseau's theory inappropriate, as it stands, to a great nation like France, and his use of terms in a way which Marsilius would have understood, but which few of his contemporaries could have accepted, made it unlikely that it would be used as Rousseau intended it. However, the emphasis upon popular sovereignty suited exactly the mood of revolutionary France, and attempts were made in 1793 to adapt the structure of the State to his theory by associating the whole people with the making of law. Most people in and after 1789,

8. Ibid., III, iv, p. 71. 9. Ibid., III, v, p. 74.
10. Ibid., III, i, p. 61.

however, accepted the necessity of a representative assembly wielding the effective legislative power, for such an assembly was the only practicable means of carrying on the business of government. Rousseau's ideas and his vocabulary were taken over and adapted to a representative system. The qualities and requirements of the "legislative and executive powers" were applied to assembly and king, or assembly and directory, in a way very different from that intended in the *Social Contract.* Indeed, when Rousseau turned to the discussion of more practical matters in the *Considerations on the Government of Poland,* he himself used the more normal vocabulary and discussed the separation of powers in the usual way. This adaptation of Rousseau's thought to the representative system had, however, serious consequences. The extremely abstract definitions of functions were applied to the activities of ordinary legislative and executive bodies; the extreme and rigid division which Rousseau insisted upon between the legislative power, that is the body of the people, and the executive power, or the whole machinery of government, was applied to the elected legislature and its corresponding executive branch. There were to be no links between these branches, whose separate functions are clear and precise; the one wills, the other acts. This is an extreme version of the separation of powers that means something very different from what Rousseau intended. He clearly meant it as a rejection of anarchy—the people cannot govern themselves, they must be governed. Applied to a representative system it means a complete, thorough, separation of the branches of government on a functional basis that is implicitly unrealizable. It is the doctrine of the separation of powers in its purest, and most unworkable, form.

Rousseau's theory of government is a direct attack upon the ideas of the mixed and balanced constitution, and its supremacy at the time of the Revolution, when the attack upon aristocratic, and later upon monarchical powers, was at its height, meant that Montesquieu's version of the English Constitution would be quite unacceptable. However, in the interpretation given to Rousseau's thought there was nothing inconsistent with what Montesquieu had to say about the separation of powers as such. Thus, once again, the attributes of the mixed and balanced constitution were stripped away, and the separation of powers remained, interpreted in the light of

Rousseau's theory as that was understood. This process of merging ideas from Montesquieu and Rousseau, and adapting them to representative government, is embodied in the work of Mably and Sieyès. Mably, well before the Revolution, evolved a version of this combination of the ideas of Montesquieu and Rousseau, although it should be mentioned that much of Mably's work predates the publication of the *Social Contract*. The Abbé de Mably died in 1785. Over a period of some forty years he had developed ideas that were to become popular with the Constituent Assembly, which met such a short time after his death. The theme of Mably's work is the equality of man, and a general feeling of dissatisfaction with all hereditary privilege.[11] Yet Mably accepted the mixed system of government as the best system that could be attained in practice. He believed that full equality was unattainable, and that unrestrained democracy would be a dangerous experiment. A representative Assembly was an essential part of this pattern, so that Mably would seem, so far, to be a disciple of Montesquieu. In fact, however, Mably's ideas were very different. He rejected all the checks and balances of the balanced constitution, and all positive links between the branches of government. The royal power of prorogation or dissolution of parliament in England, or the use of a royal veto, were indefensible because they resulted in the subordination of the legislative to the executive power. The executive, said Mably, should have no part at all in the exercise of the legislative power.[12] In fact he believed in the necessity for a strict division of the powers of government on functional lines, and for this reason he rejected the example of the English Constitution. There was no true equilibrium between the powers of the English government; it was really a disguised monarchy, for in the last analysis all power must result to the King. The King could do many things without parliament; parliament, on the contrary, could do nothing without the King.[13]

Mably, then, retained the idea of equilibrium or balance in the constitution, but it was a different balance from that of Bolingbroke or Montes-

11. Paul de Mellis, *Le principe de la séparation des pouvoirs d'après l'Abbé de Mably*, Toulouse, 1907, pp. 25 and 34.

12. *Droits et devoirs du citoyen*, 1758, *Oeuvres*, Vol. 11, p. 474.

13. *De l'étude de l'histoire*, 1778, *Oeuvres*, Vol. 12, p. 232.

quieu, for Mably emphasized the balance between the legislative and executive branches rather than a balance of estates. How did he reconcile this with mixed government? To answer this question it is necessary to look at Mably's earlier works, in which he discussed the ancient constitutions of Greece and Rome, as he interpreted them. He described these as mixed systems in which the different orders of society exercised separate and distinct functions of government, so that none could neglect their duties or abuse their power.[14] With modifications this was just the view of the Constituents of 1789. Although there was no place for an aristocracy in the new constitution, the King was to remain but only on the basis of a strict separation of the functions of government. Mably's theory is reminiscent of that of Philip Hunton; he attempted to accommodate the theory of mixed government to new conditions, and to emphasize the functional division between a hereditary monarch and an elected Assembly, although it is true that he also criticized the Constitution of Pennsylvania of 1776, because the executive was not chosen from among the legislature, a measure, he said, necessary to the attainment of harmony between the two branches.[15]

Mably's rejection of the Montesquieu version of the balanced constitution is indicative of an important aspect of French thought before and during the Revolution. The English Constitution did not lack its passionate admirers,[16] but it was under constant attack from all sides of the political spectrum. The advocates of absolute monarchy, the physiocrats, and the men of the Revolution, alike rejected the balanced constitution, either as an impossible division of sovereign power, or as an outright sham. The outbreak of the American Revolution was taken as an indication that the much-vaunted balance of powers in Britain did not result in political liberty,[17] and the observation of corruption in English politics confirmed the view that the system was a disguised monarchy or aristocracy rather than a truly mixed system. The sense of outrage against aristocratic power at

14. *Observations sur les Romains*, 1751, *Oeuvres*, Vol. 4, pp. 280–1.

15. Mellis, op. cit., pp. 113–14.

16. See E. Carcassonne, *Montesquieu et le problème de la constitution française au XVIIIe siècle*, Paris, 1927, pp. x–xii.

17. G. Bonno, *La constitution britannique devant l'opinion française de Montesquieu à Bonaparte*, Paris, 1932, pp. 142 ff.

the Revolution made a rejection of the British pattern certain, and the whole fabric of the balanced constitution was rejected along with it. In the Constituent Assembly of 1789, however, the doctrine of the separation of powers was held as an article of faith by all except the few supporters of the *ancien régime.* On all sides it was hailed as the essential basis of a good constitution; it was incorporated into the Declaration of the Rights of Man as Article 16. The Assembly staged the most intensive discussion of the doctrine of all time, testing every aspect of the proposed constitution against this touchstone. In a period when abstract principles were highly regarded it had become part of the law of nature. The limits to be set to each of the powers of government, said Mounier, were sacred.[18]

The right wing of the Assembly presented, with great ability, a version of Montesquieu's doctrine, modified somewhat to meet the views of the Assembly concerning aristocracy. In the report of the Committee on the Constitution presented by Lally-Tollendal there was set out a system of divided powers linked by the checks and balances of the English Constitution. Lally's presentation was not merely a regurgitation of Montesquieu, but drew also upon Blackstone and de Lolme, and appeal for support was also made to John Adams's *Defence of the Constitutions of the United States.* Although the idea of a hereditary Second Chamber was rejected in favour of a Senate appointed for life by the King, Lally developed the virtues of a system of perfect equilibrium, in which the three branches of the legislature would combine all the advantages of the three simple forms of government without their disadvantages. The executive power united in the hands of the King would have a veto to defend itself against encroachments by the legislature. With the power of prorogation and dissolution granted to the King and the power of impeachment vested in the Senate the structure of a free constitution was completed.[19] Thus the doctrine of the balanced constitution formed the basis of the first concrete proposal submitted to the Constituent Assembly.

Lally's proposals were based upon the mid-eighteenth-century conception of English government developed by Montesquieu, but they owed

18. *Archives parlementaires,* 1st Series, Vol. 8, p. 243.
19. Ibid., Vol. 8, pp. 514–22.

little to knowledge of the contemporary operation of English government. The links between the branches were simply to operate as checks to the encroachments of one upon the other, their function was purely negative. A few voices were raised in the Assembly, however, to put a very different point of view about the articulation of the parts of the government. Thouret, in opposing the exclusion of the King's ministers from the Assembly, argued that to do this would be to establish as a constitutional principle that there should be a constant state of antipathy and discordance between the executive and the legislature.[20] It was Mirabeau, however, who put forward most strongly the argument that although the powers of government must be separated, they must also be linked together, not merely in order that they should check each other, but so that a high degree of co-operation and co-ordination between them might be achieved. He rejected the extremes of the doctrine of the separation of powers in favour of a more pragmatic approach to the structure of government. An exact analysis of the "theory of the three powers," he argued, would perhaps demonstrate the facility with which the human mind confuses words with things, and formulae with arguments.[21] It is necessary to make the King's ministers responsible to the people through their representatives, but this could only be done effectively if ministers were in the assembly to be questioned, and could not evade responsibility. In England, said Mirabeau, the people did not consider the presence of ministers in the parliament as a danger, but as an absolute necessity if they were to be subject to control. The chief agents of the executive must be in the legislature, for they are a major source of information; laws discussed with them will be more easily shaped, more effective, and executed more faithfully. The ministers' presence will forestall incidents between legislature and executive, and will obviate the need for troublesome legislative committees.[22] In the *Courier de Provence* he wrote that the maintenance of a direct, daily intercourse between ministers and legislature was a necessity.[23] Mirabeau argued, therefore, for the recognition of a form of parliamentary government along the lines which, a few years earlier, Burke and Fox had proposed in England.

20. Ibid., Vol. 29, pp. 399–400.   21. Ibid., Vol. 8, p. 243.
22. Ibid., Vol. 9, p. 70.   23. No. 41, Sept. 1789, p. 2.

However, the majority of the Constituent Assembly was prepared to accept neither the Montesquieu scheme proposed by Lally, nor the parliamentary system of Mirabeau. They were too afraid of royal domination, too jealous of their legislative power to wish to share it, and their main impression of English politics, which formed the basis of both proposals, was of its deep corruption. They shared rather the views of one who rejected the corrupt English system, the Abbé Emmanuel Sieyès. Sieyès' thought was based upon a hatred of aristocracy and privilege that led him inevitably to reject the balanced constitution. He was as committed to the unity of the sovereign power as was Rousseau. In his *Qu'est-ce que le Tiers Etat?* published in January 1789 Sieyès had emphasized the unity and sovereignty of the nation, from which all power is derived, which establishes the constitution and determines the functions of the parts of the State. This unity precludes all privilege. The third estate *is* the nation; "*Qu'est-ce que le Tiers?*" he asked, and gave the answer "*Tout.*"[24] A single chamber is the only form of legislature which can represent this unity. At the same time, Sieyès, in 1789 at least, saw the monarchy also as a manifestation of the unity of the nation, and supported it for this reason. Thus we are presented with the simple bipolarity of a single-chamber legislature and a royal executive. Sieyès started from the same view of popular sovereignty as Rousseau, but his acceptance of the representative principle raised a number of problems about the status of the branches of the government and their relationships to each other. He attributed to the representative legislature, and to the royal executive, the same characteristics that Rousseau, with very different concepts in mind, had attributed to the sovereign people and the government. Sieyès was able to do this by inventing a fourth "power" that was solely in the nation, the constituent power. The nation exercises this power by delegating the legislative power to the assembly and the executive power to the King. Thus each of these has a "representative" character and they enjoy a certain equality of status. Each power must be limited to its proper function and prevented from interfering with the other.

Sieyès returned, therefore, to a view of the legislative and executive

24. Op. cit., p. 14.

branches more in line with that of Montesquieu than of Rousseau, and by giving to each of these branches a certain equality of status as a delegate of the people he introduced something of the idea of an equilibrium, rather like that of Malby. But Sieyès' approach to the *functions* of these branches of the government, and to the relationships between them, had nothing in common with the theorists of the balanced constitution. He took over Rousseau's definitions of the functions of government, attaching them now to the legislative and executive branches. The body politic, he said in the Constituent Assembly, must be endowed with a power to will, and a power to act; the former is the legislative power, the latter is the executive power, and these must be kept as distinct from each other, and as related to each other, as they are in the human body.[25] This rigid definition of government functions led Sieyès to strip away all semblance of links between them, and to reject all checks and balances. A royal veto is unacceptable because the executive power has no right to enter into the making of the law.[26] In England such a veto may be necessary because the English have failed to distinguish the constituent power, and the unlimited authority of parliament could therefore be used to attack the position of the monarchy if the veto were not there to protect it. In France, however, this situation could not arise, for the authority of the branches of government being drawn directly from the people, they need not fear each other, and no checks to the encroachment of one branch upon another are needed. Provided that the powers of government are divided with care, and are made independent of each other, they are then in an equally advantageous position. No veto is required, nor the power to withhold supplies, for if any part of the State should exceed its authority the people in Convention will intervene and resume the power which it has delegated.[27]

In the revolutionary conditions of 1789 we are back once again in the presence of that formula which Nedham had announced in 1654, the power of the community flowing in distinct channels, so that they may never meet. The conditions of the two periods are also similar in many respects:

25. *Archives parlementaires*, 1st Series, Vol. 8, p. 259.
26. Ibid., Vol. 8, p. 595.
27. Ibid., Vol. 8, p. 596.

we have the attack upon privilege, the determination to limit the "single person" to the execution of the law, the attempt to pick a middle path between royal absolutism and an excess of democratic government. For at no time did Sieyès advocate an all-powerful legislature. He clearly believed that the danger of arbitrary rule threatened more from the royal power than from the elected representatives of the people, but *gouvernement d'assemblée* was far from his conception of constitutional government. The French Revolution was unlike the English, however, in that the attachment to the pure doctrine of the separation of powers *preceded* the period of convention government in France, and this government by convention, when it did come, gave way again in 1795 to another constitution of divided powers, only then to succumb to the authoritarian rule of Bonaparte. Perhaps the most important difference between the ideas of the two periods in relation to the separation of powers was the determination in France to enforce strictly the separation of the personnel of government between its branches. This aspect of the doctrine, which had recently been so important to the American constitution-makers, dominated the minds of the men of the Revolution. It led to the defeat of any attempt at a parliamentary system, and it persisted well into the period of the Convention.

The Constitution of 1791 began with a sweeping abolition of all privileges, orders of nobility, and feudal or other social distinctions. It proclaimed the indivisible, inalienable sovereignty of the people, but hurriedly added that the nation could only exercise its powers by delegation through its representatives, the National Assembly, the King, and the elected judiciary. The unicameral Assembly was a permanent body, elected every two years, over which the King had no power of dissolution. The King could not initiate legislation, but he was given a suspensive veto. The idea of ministerial responsibility was rejected in favour of a process of impeachment before a National High Court.[28] Members of the National Assembly were to be incapable of appointment to ministerial office, or of accepting any place or pension in the gift of the executive, during their membership of the Assembly and for two years afterwards. Thus the legislative and ex-

28. See the discussion by L. Duguit, "La séparation des pouvoirs et l'Assemblée nationale de 1789," *Revue d'Economie Politique*, Vol. 7, 1893, pp. 364–72.

ecutive branches were strictly divided, although ministers were allowed to speak in the Assembly and to listen to the debates. The Constitution raised "the judicial power" to a level of equality with the legislature and the executive, the result, in Duguit's view, of the American example rather than a response to political theories.[29] The Assembly and the King were expressly forbidden to exercise any judicial function, and the judges were intended to be independent of the other two branches by virtue of their popular election. However, the strict separation of powers ruled out any possibility of judicial review of legislative acts like that which resulted from the theory of checks and balances in the United States. Indeed the Constituent Assembly inserted in the Constitution a specific denial of the right of judicial review; the courts were forbidden to interfere with the exercise of the legislative power or to suspend the execution of the laws. Nor were they to entertain actions against officials in respect of their administrative activities, so that the courts were prevented from exercising authority over executive or administrative, as well as legislative, actions. Thus the Assembly laid the basis for the vitally important distinction in French law between the judicial and the administrative jurisdictions. In the Constituent Assembly this was justified by the separation of powers theory,[30] but its roots went back to the practice of the *ancien régime*.[31]

The Constitution of 1791 was based, therefore, upon an extreme version of the doctrine of the separation of powers. In reality, of course, circumstances were such that there was very little likelihood of such a system of government succeeding. It assumed a degree of natural harmony between the branches of government which would be rare in the calmest of political systems, but in the turmoil of revolutionary France its chances were slender indeed. In other revolutionary situations, in England in the 1650's and America in the 1770's, it had proved unworkable. The circumstances of 1791–2 in France were even less propitious. The Assembly was determined to limit the power of the executive, and if this meant that it had to do more than merely pronounce general rules of behaviour, then an ab-

29. Ibid., pp. 571–3.
30. Ibid., pp. 601–3.
31. See A. de Tocqueville, *L'ancien régime*, Oxford, 1904, pp. 60–62.

stract doctrine like the separation of powers would not stop it. Had the King kept to the spirit of the Constitution the outcome might have been less disastrous, but even before the acceptance of the Constitution his flight to Varennes made it necessary for the Assembly to take over his authority, and to become for a time the sole source of governmental power.[32] In spite of the potential support he enjoyed in the new National Assembly of 1791 the King antagonized the Assembly by almost immediately making use of his suspensive veto. Through the medium of its committees the Assembly began to exercise an increasingly detailed control over the executive, until the further use of the veto in May and July 1792 and the insurrection of the 10 August brought an end to any pretence of divided power. The National Convention which assembled on the 20 September 1792 exercised authority in every sphere of government action, dealing with every type of government business, itself directing the everyday affairs of the State through its committees, and through the commissars it sent into the provinces or to the armies. The *régime d'assemblée* was an accomplished fact.

The deputies of the National Convention found themselves exercising a supreme, unlimited power over every type of government task, yet the extraordinary importance which they attached to the idea of the separation of powers can be seen in the way they adhered to a formal separation of persons between the "executive" and the "legislature." The Convention decreed on the 25 September 1792 that the exercise of any function of public office was incompatible with membership of the Convention.[33] It rejected the argument that with the end of royal power there was no further need for a feeling of suspicion towards the executive, and that ministers might therefore now be chosen from the Convention. It even refused to allow members of the Convention to be appointed to office if they resigned their seats, because of the possibilities for corruption that this practice would open up. Lecointe-Puyraveau carried the Convention with him when he insisted that the most important argument against the choice of ministers from within the Convention was that the deputies had been sent there to make laws for the people. If they removed a man from the Convention to

32. On this period see P. Bastid, *Le gouvernement d'assemblée*, Paris, 1956, pp. 135 ff.
33. *Archives parlementaires*, 1st Series, Vol. 52, p. 128.

the executive, would not the people be able to say "I have sent this citizen to make the laws, not to execute them"?[34]

In March 1793 Danton took much the same position that Mirabeau had taken in 1789, asking the Convention to choose the members of the executive council from among its members. There was a great need, he said, for a more direct day-to-day co-operation, a need for greater cohesion between legislature and executive. But again he was met by the same arguments. La Revellière-Lépaux argued that if men of great ambition were chosen, one day the Convention might find itself dissolved, and "these men, invested with both the legislative power and the executive power, will then exercise the most formidable dictatorship."[35] For all this formal concern with the separation of powers, the actual situation was very different. The "ministers" became little more than subordinate officials, mere clerks who submitted every decision to the Convention and its committees. Their advice was ignored, often they were not even consulted. They became mere marionettes in the hands of the deputies.[36] With the appointment of the Committee of Public Safety, first under Danton and then under Robespierre, the system bore some faint resemblance to a system of parliamentary government, but it was a system in which "ministerial responsibility" was enforced by Madame Guillotine.[37]

Finally, on the 1 April 1794 the Convention acknowledged reality and abolished the six ministerial posts, setting up twelve executive commissions, each consisting of three members, closely subordinated to the Committee of Public Safety. Carnot, in urging the Convention to take this step, developed a theory of revolutionary government. An executive council, he alleged, was an instrument of royal despotism, intended to maintain privi-

34. Ibid., Vol. 52, p. 225.
35. Ibid., Vol. 60, p. 91.
36. Bastid, *Le gouvernement d'assemblée*, pp. 153, 158.
37. See the discussion of the Convention under the Committee of Public Safety, as a system of parliamentary government, by B. Mirkine-Guetzévitch: *Le gouvernement parlementaire sous la Convention*, in *Cahiers de la Révolution française*, No. VI, 1937, pp. 66 ff. However, as Robert Villers has pointed out, neither Danton nor Robespierre exercised the power of dissolution which characterizes the classic system of parliamentary government, and gives to the parliamentary executive some degree of autonomy. "La Convention pratiqua-t-elle le gouvernement parlementaire?" *Revue du droit publique*, April–June 1951, p. 386.

lege and social distinctions; how then could it become the instrument of a representative government devoted to the principle of equality? "Government is nothing more, properly speaking, than the council of the people."[38] The people's sovereignty must be guarded by dividing up the instruments of government and restraining them within the closest limits, to prevent the accumulation of power; at the same time the closest subordination of the active agents of government to the National Assembly must be maintained.[39] This is the pure theory of *gouvernement d'assemblée,* the complete rejection of the separation of powers or any other theory which sets any sort of limit to the power of the legislature.

Whilst engaged upon a practical exercise of power which showed little concern for the spirit of the separation of powers, the Convention was also busy with schemes for the re-establishment of constitutional government. The year 1793 saw first the Girondin project for a new constitution introduced by Condorcet, then a large number of schemes presented by individual deputies, and finally the project of June 1793, the Montagnard scheme, which was accepted by the Convention but never put into operation. The *de facto* acceptance of convention government did not mean, however, that the separation of powers played no part in the thoughts of the deputies when they turned to constitution-making. Several of the projects submitted to the Convention made the doctrine the cornerstone of their proposals. Boissy d'Anglas, later to play an important role in the writing of the Constitution of 1795, rejected the idea that popular sovereignty demanded a single channel of government action as *"un blasphème politique."*[40] The existing structure of government, necessary in the circumstances, was itself evidence of the way in which a single all-powerful Assembly could subject the people to the oppressive acts of their own representatives. Daunou also strongly opposed the idea of a system of government in which the Assembly could become involved in all the operations of ministers, or exercise an immediate influence over matters purely ex-

38. *Le Moniteur Universel,* No. 194, reprinted Paris, 1841, Vol. 20, p. 114.
39. Ibid., pp. 115–16.
40. *Archives parlementaires,* 1st Series, Vol. 62, p. 288.

ecutive.[41] These men were as firmly opposed as Sieyès or Condorcet to the notion of a balance of powers, "the resort of a people half-enslaved"; they demanded only a strict division of the powers of government.[42] It is interesting to note that the project which most closely resembled *gouvernement d'assemblée* was apparently submitted by an Englishman, a "Mr. J. Smith," who argued that the executive power should reside in the legislature, to be delegated only to a legislative committee in particular circumstances and under specific and limited conditions.[43]

Condorcet, in presenting the Girondin plan to the Convention, emphatically denied any attempt to create an equilibrium of powers in the government. The new draft of the Declaration of the Rights of Man replaced the reference to the separation of powers in the 1789 Declaration by the statement that the limits of the *"fonctions publiques"* must be clearly laid down by law.[44] This was plainly a further movement away from the Montesquieu position towards that of Rousseau. The rejection of the idea of the delegation of "powers" in favour of the assignment of "functions" had been proposed by Robespierre in 1791,[45] and the Girondin project removed any suggestion of an equilibrium which had remained in the constitutional theory of Sieyès and the Constituent Assembly. The principle of the new constitution, said Condorcet, must be the unity of action and of principle between the legislature, the executive council, and the people. The system of balanced powers suggested the existence of divisions within the State, whereas in the French Republic there could be none.[46] The project gave a wide authority to the Assembly. It had not only the function of making "laws," but also of enacting measures of "general administration" over a wide range of subjects. The principle of unity required that the agent entrusted with the execution of the laws should be subordinated to the legis-

41. Ibid., Vol. 62, p. 358.
42. Ibid., Vol. 62, p. 359.
43. Ibid., Vol. 62, p. 573.
44. Art. 29.
45. *Archives parlementaires*, 1st Series, Vol. 29, pp. 326–7.
46. *Plan de constitution présenté à la Convention nationale, Oeuvres*, Paris, 1804, Vol. XVIII, pp. 185 and 201.

lature, for the executive council might not *will* but only oversee (*veiller*).[47] However, Condorcet did not wish the executive council to be the mere creatures of the legislature. They must be forced to obey, but they must also have a certain independence, and in order to accomplish this the members of the executive council were to be elected not by the legislature, but by the people whose officers they were.[48]

Thus, after strongly denouncing any attempt to erect a system of balanced powers, Condorcet arrived at a position where the executive council was directly elected by the people and was quite independent, in its origins, of the legislature. Indeed, as Saint-Just pointed out, the executive council would have been more directly representative of the people as a whole than the legislature, and might easily have assumed a position of greater prestige and importance in the eyes of the public.[49] Nor could the executive be said to be "responsible" to the legislature in any straightforward sense. The legislature could accuse the executive, or any member of it, and demand their removal, but the final decision was to be taken by an elected "national jury" to be specially convoked to hear each case. Hardly an expeditious means of parliamentary control! Condorcet, in fact, was proposing much the same sort of structure that had been established by the Constitution of Pennsylvania in 1776, a Constitution to which he had given much thought, and he was grappling with the same fundamental problem that would have faced Bentham and other English radicals had they become the Founding Fathers of a constitution. This problem, common to all three countries at the end of the eighteenth century, was the difficult one of finding a reconciliation between the desire for legislative supremacy on the one hand, and the desire to prevent government by convention on the other. How could the power of the legislature be "unlimited" at the same time that the executive was given the independence, and the power, to prevent the legislature from committing individuals to prison, issuing commands to the army, engaging and dismissing government servants, or the thousand and one other things for which it was not fitted? This basic dilemma can be

47. Ibid., p. 201.
48. Ibid., p. 205.
49. *Archives parlementaires,* 1st Series, Vol. 63, p. 203.

seen in the way Condorcet attempted to find a compromise between these two positions. Paul Bastid has suggested that Condorcet was making an explicit statement of the case for *gouvernement d'assemblée,* and the latter certainly denies to the executive council the status of a true "power."[50] But apart from the position which the Girondin project gave to the executive council by its direct election, Condorcet went out of his way to emphasize that the legislature should be given only that function in relation to the executive which was "proper" to it, that of surveillance.[51] Furthermore, the creation of a national jury to judge the shortcomings of the executive removed all suspicion, he maintained, of a possible abuse of power *by the legislature.*[52] Condorcet was in fact grappling with the problem of legislating into a constitution Rousseau's abstract notion that one set of people can *will,* and another set can *act,* without on the one hand making the latter mere automata, or on the other enabling them to interpose their own wills in such a way as to defeat the intentions of the legislature. This problem, which Rousseau had set, Condorcet attempted to solve by the introduction of the "national jury" as did the creators of the Council of Censors in Pennsylvania earlier, and Sieyès later by his *"jurie constitutionnaire."* In all cases it was hoped to avoid government by convention, to establish a rigid division of functions, and to restrict the executive exclusively to the execution of the laws. The tragedy of all these attempts was that they were based upon an unworkable and untenable definition of the functions of government, which assumed that decisions to act could be completely separated from the putting of those decisions into effect, and upon the belief that the essential discretionary powers of government had been used by kings solely to maintain their arbitrary sway.

The rejection of the Girondin project by the Assembly, and the acceptance of the Montagnard Constitution of 1793, represented a further move towards the complete subordination of the executive, and towards a constitutional system bordering on government by convention. The direct election of the executive council was rejected in favour of election by the

50. Bastid, op. cit., p. 308.
51. *Plan de constitution, Oeuvres,* Vol. XVIII, p. 201.
52. Ibid., p. 207.

legislature. This can be seen particularly in the fate of the "national jury" in the debate in the Convention. The draft submitted by the Committee of Public Safety had included provision for a national jury which would guarantee the citizens against oppression by the legislature or the executive. In this respect it retained some of the philosophical assumptions of the Girondin project. In the debate, however, Thuriot objected that it was ridiculous to raise up an authority superior to the legislature which the constitution endowed with sovereign power, and the Committee's *rapporteur*, Hérault-Séchelles, was quick to acknowledge that the national jury introduced a germ of division into the constitutional system. The national jury disappeared from the draft.[53] Although the means of bringing the executive to account were left extremely vague it is obvious that it was intended to have little prestige, and less power. Nevertheless, the Convention was seemingly not prepared to accept for a *constitution* a system which merely embodied *gouvernement d'assemblée*. In debate Barère successfully insisted that if the choice of the executive council were made at the beginning of the life of the Assembly, then the executive would simply obey in a servile fashion the men who had created it. The legislature should therefore, he proposed, renew half the executive council each year at the *end* of the Assembly's period of office, and this proposal was accepted.[54] Thus the most radical group in the Assembly was unable to obtain the incorporation into the constitution of an executive which had no independence of the legislature of any sort. The revolutionary system of Carnot could not be incorporated into a constitution which was to last for all time. As Boissy said, "We are in the day of chaos which precedes the creation, but the Creator must not restrict himself to the organization of chaos."[55]

After the experience of the revolutionary government, and the Terror, the Convention turned again, after the fall of Robespierre, to the task of establishing a constitutional system of government. The extremes of the Constitution of 1793 were no longer acceptable. The situation was again one in which men of all points of view had, each in succession, felt the

53. *Archives parlementaires*, 1st Series, Vol. 66, p. 577.
54. Ibid., Vol. 66, p. 574.
55. Ibid., Vol. 62, p. 288.

effects of unlimited power, in the hands of an absolute king or of the representatives of a faction in the legislature. Their minds turned once again towards the idea of checks to the exercise of power.[56] They moved back towards the notion of an equilibrium between executive and legislature of the sort that had prevailed in 1791, but they were still quite unprepared to consider a system of checks and balances on the English pattern. The agony of the Convention, faced with the need to create a system in which no one could exercise unlimited power, yet aware of the problems of the relationships between legislature and executive in a system of divided powers, is poignantly expressed in the attempt which Sieyès made to find a solution to this dilemma.

The report of the Constitutional Committee presented by Boissy d'Anglas was squarely based upon the absolute necessity of preventing the accumulation of the powers of government in the same hands. "Whenever they are found united, whenever they are confused, liberty is at an end, there is nothing but despotism."[57] The legislature was to be prohibited from exercising executive or judicial powers, either itself or through delegates. The executive, consisting of a Directory of five members, was to be chosen by the legislature, but not from among its own members. Members of the Directory could only be removed by impeachment before the High Court of Justice. Formal checks and balances were quite absent. The attempt by one deputy, Ehrmann, to propose a veto power copied from the American Constitution brought fierce protests, and it clearly required a good deal of courage on his part even to make the proposal.[58] The movement towards the establishment of checks to the exercise of legislative power did result, however, in the creation of a bicameral legislature. Thibaudeau, in defence of the Committee's draft, argued that the division of the legislative power was all that was necessary to maintain the necessary *rapport* between the executive and legislative branches. The Upper Chamber, the *Conseil des Anciens*, would have an interest in the maintenance of an ordered system

56. P. Duvergier de Hauranne, *Histoire du gouvernement parlementaire en France*, Paris, 1874, Vol. I, p. 338.

57. *Le Moniteur Universel*, No. 283, Vol. 25, p. 99.

58. Ibid., No. 335, Vol. 25, p. 520.

of government, and would restrain the legislature where necessary, so that there was no need for the executive to play any part in the making of law. The constitution made no provision at all for possible conflicts between the two branches of government. The same strict separation of the judicial power from the other branches of government was established as in the Constitution of 1791.

The Constitution of the year III (22 August 1795) was, therefore, another exercise in the pure doctrine of the separation of powers, with little advance over that of four years before, except in the modifications necessary to replace the King by the Directory. The most interesting aspect of this exercise in constitution-making is the attempt which Sieyès made to go beyond the constitutional pattern he had helped to create in and after 1789, and to find a solution to the problem that Condorcet and others before him had grappled with.[59] Sieyès was unsuccessful in his attempt to lead the Convention away from the pure doctrine of the separation of powers, yet his ideas are interesting, because they illustrate perfectly the dilemma into which constitutional theory had fallen in France by rejecting absolutely the theory of checks and balances. Sieyès' use of language has been described as *"metaphysico-nébuleuse,"* and his enormous conceit makes it difficult to give to his presentation the close thought that it deserves. He was concerned, however, to reconcile three positions. First, the absolute necessity of keeping the functions of government in separate hands. Second, the need to prevent the abuse of power by any branch of the government. Third, the need to ensure co-operation between the branches of government without either destroying the separation of powers or resorting to Montesquieu's system of checks and balances. His rejection of the equilibrium of checks and balances was final; it was nothing more, he said, than perpetual civil war, whereas the aim of any constitution must be to create a system of "organized unity."[60] Sieyès summed up the problem in a few

59. Sieyès' speeches before the Convention are reprinted with a commentary by P. Bastid, *Les discours de Sieyès dans les débats constitutionnels de l'An III*, Paris, 1939. See also Bastid, *Sieyès et sa pensée*, Paris, 1939.

60. *Les discours de Sieyès*, p. 26.

words: "Unity alone is despotism, division alone is anarchic."[61] It is necessary to separate those parts of the system of government that can be separated, but at the same time to reunite those parts which must co-operate if
government is not to collapse altogether. This admittedly nebulous remark
nevertheless sums up the whole problem of constitutional government at
the end of the eighteenth century, and is perhaps even more relevant at the
present time. How can the exercise of power be checked without destroying the essential harmony of the government? Sieyès' attempt to solve
this problem was, however, still dominated by Rousseau's formulation of
the nature of the functions of government. He made a distinction between
the *government* and the *executive*, and then announced that "The executive power is all action, the government is all thought."[62] Thus Rousseau's
distinction between willing and acting was still, as it was in 1789, at the
basis of Sieyès' thought. The function of the "executive" was still purely
mechanical, but Sieyès had a very much more complex approach to the
legislative power, and the limitation of the legislature to its proper function. He wished to create, in fact, *four* elected representative bodies. The
government was one of these, with the power of initiating proposals for
legislation as well as supervising the executive. The second was the *tribunat*, the function of which was to criticize the government and to propose
to the legislature measures that the government had failed to put forward.
The third was the legislature itself, which was to have no power to initiate
laws, confining itself to making decisions on the proposals submitted to it
by government and *tribunat*. The fourth was a constitutional jury, which
would consider complaints of unconstitutional action against the legislature.[63] This, then, was Sieyès' method of providing checks to the exercise
of power without the use of the hated concept of "equilibrium." The *tribunat* and the government would battle against each other, but this conflict
would provide no dangers because the legislature would act as an impartial
judge between them, without being able itself to interfere in any way with
the executive, because it could not initiate action. The constitutional jury

---

61. Ibid., p. 14.   62. Ibid., p. 22.   63. Ibid., pp. 29–30.

would ensure that the legislature did not exceed its powers. Thibaudeau remarked, rather unkindly, that for all his vehement rejection of the balancing of the powers of government, Sieyès had produced nothing more than a system of equilibrium under another name.[64] The proposals were undoubtedly too complex and too outlandish for the Convention to give them much serious consideration; nevertheless, Sieyès was grappling here with difficulties which would in future years be met with equally strange solutions, in the form of administrative tribunals, regulatory commissions, and, in the 1960's, the English equivalent of the *tribunat*, the National Economic Development Council. The Constitution of 1795, however, remained a constitution of strictly separated powers, which in a very short time became the stage for bitter conflicts between legislature and executive, soon leading to a *coup d'état* by a majority of the Directory, setting France on the road to the Empire of Napoleon Bonaparte.

A comparison of the circumstances surrounding the development of the pure doctrine of the separation of powers in France and in America at the end of the eighteenth century illustrates the interesting relationship between ideas and events. In America the pure doctrine emerged only briefly, as a result of the shattering impact of the break with traditional forms of government and the consequent rejection of monarchy and aristocracy. The institutional structure of the pure doctrine in America was the result of the logic of circumstances rather than of an ideological commitment to the pure theory, although in Pennsylvania there was a small-scale rehearsal of the French situation. In France the circumstances were also such that the pure doctrine fitted better than any other available constitutional theory the aspirations of the Revolution, but the influence of Rousseau and his interpreters gave to that doctrine a degree of intellectual precision and intensity it never could have achieved in America. Thus, in part at least, the particular quality of the doctrine in France must be attributable to the ideas of Rousseau, which had so much more of an impact there than they could have had in the American colonies, fed upon a diet of Montesquieu and Blackstone. In a few years the doctrine of the separation of powers was

64. *Le Moniteur Universel*, No. 331, Vol. 25, p. 488.

changed and modified in America by the resurgence of the theory of checks and balances, whereas in France this was not achieved until 1814, and even then the separation of powers was to burst forth again in 1848. Clearly the explanation of this is that in America the Revolution was wholly successful, monarchy and aristocracy were routed, and many of those men of wealth and status in the community who were in 1776 caught up in the onrush of democratic fervour became in a few months or years the spearhead of a movement to moderate that democracy. There was no longer anyone on the Right to fight; the only danger was from the Left, and an excess of democracy could best be combated by reintroducing a constitution of balanced powers. In France, however, the Revolution was never complete, never wholly successful, and could not be. The threat of monarchic and aristocratic privilege remained, and the theory of checks and balances must inevitably be associated with it. The doctrine of the separation of powers remained, therefore, in France, as in a very much weaker way it remained in England, a potentially revolutionary theory.

The period of the Revolution in France presents in some respects a doleful view of the development of constitutional theory, for the Constitution of 1795 provided little practical advance over the Instrument of Government of 1653 or the Constitution of Pennsylvania of 1776. Like them it was a dead-end, the institutional elaboration of an unworkable theory of government. Nevertheless, during this period a few men in France realized the basic problems of a democratic representative government in a manner unparalleled in England or America. In England the energies of those who wrote about constitutional matters were occupied with the problems of the mixed and balanced constitution, but few people were really trying to relate this constitutional structure to the need for co-operation in government other than by means of corruption. Those who looked for a unified political system hardly considered the problems of co-ordination and control that it involved; they concentrated instead upon attacking the cabinet system, which was in fact to provide a solution to this problem. In America the special circumstances of a federal system of government, and an expanding society based upon a fierce individualism, concentrated attention on the means of checking the exercise of government power, to the exclusion of all consideration of the problem of obtaining co-ordinated government action. In France, however, there were a number of men who saw the problem of obtaining both control and co-operation and attempted to fashion the necessary institutions to achieve both ends. In their different ways Mirabeau, Danton, and Sieyès all had a grasp of the deep dilemma of modern constitutional systems, which was unsurpassed in the contemporary world of thought. This fact is well illustrated by the way in which, after 1814, French writers, in attempting to create an intellectual basis for a system of parliamentary government, reached a very high order of modern political theory.

In the evolution of parliamentary government in Britain, and of the Federal Constitution in America, the theory of mixed government played an essential role in providing the basis for a system of separate and balanced "powers" of government. In France before 1814, however, the idea of mixed government had played a relatively minor role. Hotman, Montesquieu, and Mably had all championed the idea, but their views, in this respect, had had little influence. The constitutionalism of the *ancien régime* was based upon the role of the "intermediary powers" in a "legal" monarchy, but this was a very different concept from that of mixed government. The most important manifestation of the idea had been the proposals put before the Constituent Assembly by Lally-Tollendal in 1789, but this theory of constitutionalism had then been decisively rejected, and the French nation had jumped, in a few short years, from absolutism to democracy, without going through any intermediate stages. It would, of course, be rash indeed to suggest that the successful transition from absolutism to modern democracy *necessitated* a period of mixed government, yet it is certainly true that France, as if she had made a false start, emerged from the débris of Napoleon's Empire to grapple with the complexities of a system of mixed government, leaving behind, for a time, the deceptive simplicity of absolute democracy or dictatorship.

In 1814 the *Charte* of Louis XVIII ushered in a period of mixed government, which had started out as an attempt to recreate a more liberal version of the historic French Constitution, but which in fact provided the forum for a discussion of the nature and working of parliamentary government of a quality far higher than that of most English thought of the period. The role of the King's ministers was clearly faced and an attempt made to fit it into the pattern of government by King, peers, and assembly. The defeat of Napoleon brought with it a surge of admiration for British government throughout Europe, but it would be wrong to suggest that the authors of the *Charte* found their inspiration in the English system. The *Charte* was granted by Louis XVIII as an act of royal grace, not as a contract by one branch of a balanced system of government.[65] The Chamber of Deputies and the Chamber of Peers were seen rather as consultative assemblies which were to play a part not too dissimilar from the earlier role of the *parlements*,[66] although the necessary safeguards to the liberty of the individual were provided by the Constitution. The *Charte*, wrote Chateaubriand, was a treaty of peace signed between the two parties that divided France, the *ancien régime* and the Revolution. However, in practice, the political discourse of the whole period 1815 to 1848 revolved around the roles of King, ministers, and Assembly in a context similar to that of the disputes in England, and one in which the experiences of English politics were used as evidence in support of one point of view or another. The most important theorists of the period were Royer-Collard, Guizot, and Benjamin Constant. Royer-Collard and Guizot developed a theory of constitutional monarchy which was suited to the period 1814–30, whilst Constant went further and formulated a theory closely related to the *régime* established by the Revolution of 1830.

After 1814 Royer-Collard and Guizot reverted to a mid-eighteenth-century usage; when they referred to the "three powers" of government they generally meant King, peers, and deputies, and clearly had in mind a system of mixed government. But it is very clear also that they did not see this system, as had the English eulogists of mixed government, as a system of negative checks and balances. The emphasis in their work was rather upon the unity of action among the parts of government. That problem of the concerted movement of the three branches of the legislature, which Montesquieu had brushed aside as being solved by the "necessary move-

65. J. Bonnefon, *Le régime parlementaire sous la Restauration*, Paris, 1905, p. 81.
66. A. B. de Barante, *La vie politique de M. Royer-Collard*, Paris, 1863, Vol. I, p. 141.

ment of things," had become the central concern of the theorists of the Restored Monarchy in France. They accepted the separation of powers as a basis of government, but a basis only, upon which must be built a system of *concours* between the branches of the government. Royer-Collard presented a theory of the *Charte* which rejected parliamentary government, seeing ministers simply as *secrétaires du roi*.[67] In a period when ministerial responsibility to parliament was demanded by the *ultras* who had a majority in the Chamber, and who found Louis XVIII too liberal, Royer-Collard argued that parliamentary government required a stable majority in the legislature if it was to work effectively; but in France there was no means of securing the basis of a strong party system which would be able to sustain such majorities.[68] He saw clearly that a system of parliamentary responsibility was incompatible with the idea of mixed government, and that the day the government was at the discretion of a majority of the Chamber, then, to all intents and purposes a republic had been established.[69] The system of the *Charte* was, in his view, a mixed government with a strict separation of functions between King and parliament; the King governed independently of the Chambers, and their agreement with his views was only necessary for the passage of new laws and of the budget.[70]

Royer-Collard, then, presented a theory of mixed government which is more reminiscent of Philip Hunton in 1643, or of the English Constitution in 1689, than of a parliamentary system at the beginning of the nineteenth century. He insisted on the "harmony" of the powers of government, but he did not suggest how this was to be achieved other than by a simple exercise of self-restraint by the legislature. Guizot, however, took the analysis deeper. In 1816, in *Du gouvernement représentatif*, he also rejected the idea that ministers should be dependent upon a parliamentary majority as a vicious attempt to distort the whole structure of the constitution.[71] The object and tendency of a constitution must be to create unity in the sys-

---

67. R. Nesmes-Desmonets, *Les doctrines politiques de Royer-Collard,* Montpellier, 1908, pp. 168–70.
68. Ibid.
69. Ibid., p. 173.
70. Barante, Vol. I, p. 216.
71. *Du gouvernement représentatif,* pp. 21–22.

tem of government, for this unity is an overriding necessity comparable to that of the unity of society itself. Guizot interpreted English constitutional history in terms of a bitter conflict between the powers of government up to the Revolution of 1688; after that date unity between these powers was progressively established, by their reciprocal penetration, until they formed a single power, with internal limits to be sure, but able to exercise within these limits a plenitude of power without danger to the government or its adversaries.[72] When a mixed government has reached its maturity, said Guizot, there is a unity of power, and a unity of action, in which the sovereign power, fundamentally united although divided in appearance, is subjected to certain conditions by the very nature of its internal organization, which establishes within itself limits it cannot exceed without losing its force.[73] There is, therefore, in this system, "a fusion of powers," the only possible point of equilibrium for a mixed government, because it is its necessary tendency, and because in this way "the powers, far from becoming enfeebled, or being assimilated by each other, all gain equally and are equally strengthened."[74] This was to be achieved in France, as in England, by the government's entering into the Chambers, making them the centre of its activities, governing through them and by them. This did not mean government *by* the majority, but government *through* the majority. Legislative majorities, he wrote, are transient things which do not represent permanent interests, only ephemeral points of view. If indeed the King were to be faced with a stable majority in the Chambers that he could not alter or weaken, then either he must submit to it or abolish representative institutions. Fortunately this situation did not arise because majorities were shifting, and the means of management were available to the King. The government *must* obtain a majority, but it had a thousand ways of doing so, ways which, if its conduct were reasonable, and firm, would ensure its success.[75]

Du gouvernement représentatif is a first-class attempt to present the ministerial system as the peak of achievement of the ancient theory of mixed government. The unity of the divided powers of the State is achieved by government influence over a managed parliament. Guizot saw in the

72. Ibid., p. 26.
74. Ibid., p. 31.
73. Ibid., p. 29.
75. Ibid., p. 47.

English system in 1816 a "fusion of powers," just as Bagehot in 1867 also saw "fusion" rather than separation; but for Guizot it was a fusion which allowed the King to manage the deputies, whilst for Bagehot it was a fusion that subjected the executive to the control of parliament. Unlike Bagehot, however, Guizot believed that a separation of powers was the basis upon which the built-in limits to the exercise of arbitrary power depended, and, indeed, in 1849, when political circumstances had radically changed, he rewrote his thesis with a much greater emphasis upon the division of powers and the functions of government.[76]

There is no doubt that the most remarkable achievement of this period was the work of Benjamin Constant, published in 1814 and 1815. Constant accepted the need for a King and a house of peers, and so was in some sense a theorist of mixed government, but his whole approach was quite different from that of Royer-Collard or Guizot. Well to the Left of them as he was in politics, it is not surprising that the emphasis he placed upon the separation of powers was much greater, and his whole view of the relation of ministers to the King on the one hand, and to the legislature on the other, was quite different. He argued that the responsibility of ministers to the people through a majority in the assembly was an inescapable necessity in a constitutional monarchy; but if this were so how could the principle of ministerial responsibility be reconciled with the role of the King and with the separation of powers? Constant achieved this by developing a modern theory of constitutional monarchy, and by evolving a remarkable synthesis of these potentially conflicting elements. The work of Constant represents in fact a crucial turning-point in institutional theory, a turning away from the old doctrines of mixed government to a new theory of constitutional monarchy, in which the monarch assumes a new and completely different role from that assigned to him in the balanced constitution. The checks and balances of the constitution remained, but they were applied now not as checks between classes, but as checks and balances between the legislative, executive, and judicial branches of government. It is as if the approach of James Madison to the separation of powers and checks and balances in

76. *De la démocratie en France*, Paris, 1849, pp. 109–19.

the Federal Constitution were being systematically applied to a hereditary constitutional monarchy in a democracy, but with this difference, that Constant had as great a respect for harmony in the operation of government as all his contemporaries, and so he combined this Madisonian doctrine with the operation of the ministerial system. It is remarkable to see the ideas that Blackstone had advanced in mid-eighteenth-century England, and which were adapted by the Americans to a revolutionary government without King or Lords, being reinterpreted by a Frenchman to be applied to a system in which the King was no longer an equal and active branch of the legislature vested with the executive power, but was a constitutional monarch, above politics, and separated from legislature and executive alike.

Constant defined four powers of government—the executive power in the hands of the ministers, the legislative power in the representative assemblies, the judicial power in the courts, and *le pouvoir royal* in the hands of the King. Constant, therefore, made a sharp distinction between the royal power and the executive power; this distinction, which he attributed to Clermont-Tonnere during the Revolution, was, he believed, the key to all political organization.[77] A constitutional monarchy has the great advantage of creating a "neutral power" in the hands of the King; this power is to be used to maintain harmony between the other three branches of government. The legislative, executive, and judicial powers need to co-operate, each taking part in its own way in the general operations of government; but if instead they are at cross purposes then the King must step in to restore harmony. The means of doing this lies in the King's prerogatives of veto, of dissolution, of dismissal of ministers, and of pardon. These prerogatives cannot be placed in the hands of one of the potential contestants, but must remain in the hands of one who has an interest only in maintaining an equilibrium between the powers of government.[78] While insisting on the need to separate the powers of government, Constant reiterated the American argument that separation itself was not enough, barriers must be placed between them, in particular to prevent the legislature from exceeding its

---

77. *Collection complète des Ouvrages de M. Benjamin de Constant*, Paris, 1818, Vol. I, pp. 13–14.
78. Ibid., Vol. I, pp. 14–17.

---

power,[79] but at the same time he stressed the necessity of linking the legislature and the executive by allowing ministers to be members of the legislature. "By reuniting individuals, whilst still distinguishing powers, a harmonious government is constituted, instead of creating two armed camps."[80]

Constant's theory of constitutional monarchy combined those elements of constitutional theory which Sieyès had attempted to reconcile: the separation of powers, effective barriers to the abuse of power, and a harmonious and unified exercise of government authority. He did this, however, by adapting that very same theory of balance and equilibrium which Sieyès had so vehemently rejected. Constant did not write of a "fusion" of powers, as Bagehot was later to do; his view of government was rather more subtle. He realized that separation was as important as co-operation, and he emphasized that although ministers might become part of the legislature it is essential that the proportion of ministers to legislators should be very small—indeed that the number of ministers seated in the Chamber should never exceed one percent of the total membership.[81] If all the ministers and subordinate officials were to be deputies, the Chamber would no longer be the representative of the people, but would constitute a royal council. This subtle system of division, and co-operation, checks and links, is the forerunner of the classic theory of parliamentary government, and it is a theory which clearly shows the influence of its parentage in the theories of balanced government and the separation of powers. The system was to be a nice balance between executive and legislature, which were joined but not fused by the ministerial system. A few years later Jean-Denis Lanjuinais gave further expression to the essence of this theory. The two sovereign powers of government, legislative and executive, he wrote, must never be united in the same person or body of persons, being designed to balance and to supervise each other, but their separation must never be absolute.[82] Thus the *partial* separation of legislative and executive powers, which Blackstone made the cornerstone of the balanced constitution when applying it to King *and* Parliament, and which Madison used to justify the veto power of the President of the United States, was applied to the ministers

79. Ibid., Vol. I, p. 25.
81. Ibid., Vol. I, p. 90.

80. Ibid., Vol. I, p. 93.
82. *Oeuvres*, Paris, 1832, Vol. 2, pp. 202–3.

and legislature of a parliamentary democracy. The ideas and vocabulary of the theory of balanced government became the basis of a balance of legislature and executive in a system in which King and nobles found a place, but it was essentially a modern system, wherein the hereditary elements of the constitution were no longer the equal and essential powers of government that they once had been. It is important to emphasize the role of the separation of powers in this embryonic theory of parliamentary government; for, although it was recognized throughout the nineteenth century as the basis of the balance of power established in the parliamentary system, this point was to be confused and obscured when Bagehot made his indiscriminate attack upon the ideas of mixed government and the separation of powers alike.

The years 1814–48 in France were a period when the idea of mixed government shading into parliamentary government dominated the field of political thought, but, although the transition from the government of Louis XVIII and Charles X to the July Monarchy of Louis-Philippe reflected this changing pattern, it was unfortunately true that by 1848 the existing system of government was corrupt, was based upon an extremely narrow franchise, and hardly measured up, in the eyes of most Frenchmen, to the benefits that a system of "equilibrium" was supposed to bring. The demands for reform, together with the deeper social unrest that was developing, led once again to a revolutionary situation in which the trappings of monarchy, and the attributes of the system of mixed government, were rejected. In earlier revolutionary situations of this sort since the mid seventeenth century, where the mixed and balanced constitution had been under attack, the doctrine of the separation of powers surged up into a dominant position to fill the vacuum left by the rejected theory of government; and in 1848 the same pattern was repeated, except that on this occasion an attempt was made to combine the system of ministerial responsibility with a constitution which in other respects was patterned upon the pure doctrine of the separation of powers. It is hardly surprising that this last flirtation with the pure doctrine ended in the same way as others had ended in France—in absolutism.

There had been continual attacks upon the system of *contrepoids*, or equilibrium, since the restoration of the monarchy,[83] and, during the 1830's, in his lectures on constitutional law in Paris, Pellegrino Rossi had emphasized the importance of the separation of powers;[84] so it is hardly surprising that the Constituent Assembly of the Second Republic turned to the separation of powers with almost as much faith as the Constituents of 1789. The Constitution of 1848 proclaimed that "the separation of powers was the first condition of a free government," and it is clear from the debates in the Assembly that the majority of deputies saw it as the only possible basis of a system without King or nobles, which would yet avoid the ghastly spectre of the Convention. The Constitution as it stands on paper embodies a strict division of power between a unicameral legislature and a popularly elected President. Once again all the checks and balances of the balanced constitution were swept away. The President had no veto, no power of dissolution. On the other hand the attempt by Félix Pyat on the extreme Left to subordinate the executive to the Assembly and deny the validity of the separation of powers altogether was strongly rejected.[85] The proposals of Parieu and Grévy to create a purely parliamentary executive were also refused. In an impassioned speech Lamartine supported the idea of a President directly elected by popular vote. Those who wished to allow the legislature to choose the executive, he thundered, should take their ideas to their logical conclusion: "do not merely confound in yourselves the legislative and executive powers, take also the judicial power, and then call yourselves by your correct name, the Terror."[86] The fear of the Convention was enough to ensure the defeat of Grévy's proposal by 643 votes to 158.

Yet there was a great deal of confusion in the minds of the deputies on the proper structure of the government. Lamartine, for all his use of the terminology of the separation of powers to defeat a proposal of which he disapproved, did not really support the ideas behind the doctrine. Elsewhere he spoke of the division of functions rather than the division of powers,

---

83. P. Bastid, *Doctrines et institutions politiques de la Seconde République*, Paris, 1945, Vol. I, p. 183.

84. E. Fuzier-Herman, *La séparation des pouvoirs*, Paris, 1880, pp. 250–1.

85. *Compte rendu des séances de l'Assemblée Nationale*, Paris, 1850, Vol. IV, p. 651.

86. Ibid., Vol. IV, p. 679.

and during the July Monarchy he had persistently opposed attempts to exclude placemen from the Chamber. Indeed, five months after his defence of an elected presidency he told the Assembly that there was only one power of government, and this would be enfeebled by attempts to separate it into two.[87] Lamartine, whom de Tocqueville labelled the most insincere of men, no doubt modified his views to suit his ambitions, but de Tocqueville himself contributed to the confusion over the structure of the government. As one of the principal authors of the Constitution, he supported, if in a very lukewarm way, the direct election of the President, but he wished also to introduce a system of ministerial responsibility to the Assembly that would have made the President a mere constitutional figure-head. He defended this strange combination, which in a somewhat different guise was to re-emerge in the course of the life of the Fifth Republic, as a completely new system of government. Till 1848, said Tocqueville, there had been two distinct systems of constitutional government; in the one the King could do no wrong, but his ministers were responsible, in the other, as in the United States, the chief of the executive was himself directly responsible, but could "act freely." In the new Constitution a responsible President had beside him a council of ministers equally responsible without whom he could do nothing, and who could reduce him to the impotence of a constitutional monarch.[88] It seems rather unlikely that the National Assembly accepted this remarkable scheme, which one member described as a monster with two heads, in the spirit de Tocqueville intended, although it is true that after the election of Louis-Napoleon to the presidency the Assembly refused to exclude ministers from membership in the legislature because the Constitution, in Billault's words, was intended to obtain all the advantages of a republic and a constitutional monarchy.[89] The majority of republicans in the new Assembly of 1849, overawed by the popular victory of Louis-Napoleon, and out of deference to the separation of powers, tolerated a minority Ministry, and when the minority turned into a majority the President showed his independence by dismissing his ministers,

87. A. de Lamartine, *La France Parlementaire*, Paris, 1865, Vol. 6, p. 86.
88. *Compte rendu*, Vol. IV, p. 653.
89. Ibid., Vol. VIII, p. 545.

although they had not been defeated in the Assembly.[90] The Bonapartist historian, de Cassagnac, describing the ending of the system of ministerial responsibility, said, "The Constitution wished to make the President responsible; France wanted him to govern."[91]

The Revolution of 1848 brought an end to a period of development in political theory which had extended over two hundred years from the outbreak of the English Civil War. This period was one in which the two theories of constitutionalism had played out a complicated and difficult game. The proponents of both theories had rejected the absolutism of extreme Right and extreme Left, the exercise of arbitrary power by either a monarch or an all-powerful assembly. Yet they became bitterly divided whenever the attack upon hereditary privilege reached a point where it exploded into revolution, for in such an extreme situation only the separation of powers could claim to be an adequate theoretical basis for a free constitution. For two hundred years the theories of balanced government and the separation of powers were the only serious contenders in the field of rival theories of constitutionalism, but the nineteenth century was to see a fundamental change in this situation. In England and France the theory of the balanced constitution was to be transformed into a theory of parliamentary government in which most of the elements of the older theory were retained, but in which the monarchy and aristocracy of the old theory became in England merely "the dignified parts" of the constitution, or in France were wholly transformed into a republican garb. In the United States the theory of the balanced constitution had been transformed into something uniquely American, which was to follow its own rules of development. The element of mixed government in the theory of the balanced constitution was, therefore, largely suppressed, but the separation of powers continued to be an essential ingredient in the structure of Western government. The pure doctrine had finally been rejected as unworkable in favour of more complex systems, which borrowed heavily also from the theory of balanced government.

90. C. Seignobos, *Histoire de France contemporaine*, Paris, 1921, Vol. 6, pp. 130 and 145.
91. A. G. de Cassagnac, *Histoire de la charte du Roi Louis-Philippe . . .* , Paris, 1857, Vol. 2, p. 107.

The explanation of the rejection of the pure doctrine of the separation of powers is not to be found solely, however, in this development of new institutional theories of government. The Revolution of 1848 in France had revealed new social and political movements that were to change drastically the environment in which constitutional theory must operate. The year before the Revolution the publication by Marx and Engels of the *Communist Manifesto* indicated the course that political thought would now be taking, with less and less emphasis upon legal and constitutional forms, and more and more attention given to the social and economic factors in political life. In the two hundred years before 1848 the concept of political liberty which had dominated political thought was essentially a negative one, a desire for freedom from restraint, and particularly from the arbitrary restraints of government action. "Liberty is a right of doing whatever the laws permit" said Montesquieu, and the desire to gain control of the making of those laws, and to ensure that no one, including each of the elements of the government itself, could exceed the rules laid down by law, was the driving force behind the whole movement that produced the theory of the separation of powers in all its varieties during this period. But the Revolution of 1848 ushered in a new view of political liberty of a more positive kind; the right to work, Louis Blanc's conception of a fundamental duty of the State to provide its citizens with the means of livelihood, which was taken up so fiercely by the people of Paris in 1848, gave a completely new twist to the notion of "a free constitution." Freedom from restraint alone was no longer enough. The idea that the State should concern itself with creating the environment in which its people would be free to live and develop a full life (whatever that might mean) came to dominate more and more the thought of the nineteenth and twentieth centuries. Such a philosophy of freedom had, however, little in common with the motives of the pure doctrine of the separation of powers, the whole concern of which was essentially negative in its conception of a constitutional provision for liberty. The pure doctrine was, in conception, more *laissez-faire* even than its rival theory of the balanced constitution, and it was this fact that ensured that, in the long run, the pure doctrine would be rejected in favour of constitutional theories which contained strong elements of the theory of the balanced constitution, elements which could be turned to provide co-operative *links* between the parts of government rather than mere *checks*.

After 1848, then, the history of institutional thought was to become more and more concerned with the problem of creating a government machine for an age of collectivism, and the theory of the separation of powers came under fierce attack, as a barrier to the development of an efficient machine of this sort. The next step in the history of the doctrine is therefore to examine the criticisms and attacks to which it, and the institutional structures that incorporated it, were to be subjected in the nineteenth and twentieth centuries, before we may turn to a consideration of the role the theory still plays today in Western thought and institutions.

EIGHT

The Rise and Fall
of Parliamentary Government

WE HAVE SEEN that in the constitutional thought of America and France up to the mid nineteenth century the separation of powers provided the only real alternative to some variant of the balanced constitution as a basis for a system of limited government. The only other possibilities were autocracy or a system of unchecked legislative domination. In Britain, however, the situation was rather different. In spite of the enthusiasm of certain radicals for French and American models, the pure separation of powers was not, after the experiment of the Protectorate, a serious alternative to some form of a balanced constitution. It was a distant threat, but no more than that. Its major role was as a secondary hypothesis in the dominant constitutional theory. We find, in fact, that at the end of the eighteenth century the old theory of balanced government merged almost imperceptibly into a new theory of balance. The theory of mixed government gave way to the theory of parliamentary government, but the essential belief in the necessity of balance in a system of limited government remained. This new theory drew upon both of the older constitutional theories, reformulating the old concepts of checks and balances and refashioning the functional analysis of the separation of powers to suit the new balance.

The central theme of this new theory was that of "harmony"; to "ensure harmony, in place of collision, between the various powers of the state," as Lord Durham wrote in 1838,[1] was the aim of writers on politics in the first half of the nineteenth century, and Durham's formulation was echoed and re-echoed in the literature of the time. The old view of government as an equilibrium between conflicting forces was now outdated, the relic of an antiquated view of class government. The checks and balances of the constitution remained, but now they were to be applied as a means of achieving a balance between government and parliament in a system dominated by the elected representatives of the middle class. The separation of powers was still an important element in attaining this balance, as it had been under the system of mixed government, but its functional and personal elements were necessarily modified to suit the new conditions. Indeed this process of reformulation often took the form of an attack upon extreme versions of the separation of powers, and, therefore, upon French and American precedents. Taken to extremes, as in the case of Bagehot, this was represented as a complete rejection of the doctrine, but for the most part the theorists of parliamentary government had a more subtle and complex view of the part its precepts played in English constitutional theory. The result was a theory of government that seemed at last to have solved the problems of unity and control which had perplexed political writers for centuries, combining all the desirable qualities of limited and balanced government with all the requirements of harmony and co-operation between the parts of the State that modern conditions demanded. Indeed the theory of parliamentary government so dazzled observers that it has remained to this day the ideal of foreign constitutionalists, long after it has ceased to operate in its home country. Yet this system was in fact based upon a set of political conditions of such delicacy, and of such a unique quality, that it required relatively little change in the party system to put an end to it in Britain, and it is doubtful if it has ever been successfully copied elsewhere.

1. *The Report and Despatches of the Earl of Durham*, London, 1839, p. 204.

In *The English Constitution* Walter Bagehot laid claim to a twofold originality. Two obsolete doctrines had hitherto dominated English constitutional thought, he wrote; these were the theory of mixed government and the theory of the separation of powers. He defined the latter as the belief that in England the legislative, executive, and judicial powers are "quite divided—that each is entrusted to a separate person or set of persons—that no one of these can at all interfere with the work of the other."[2] This was the constitutional theory he set out to discredit, and it is of course the extreme doctrine of the separation of powers. In its place Bagehot defined the essential principle of English government in an equally extreme form; it was, he said, the "fusion" of the legislative and executive powers. The central element in this fused system was the cabinet, the role of which in parliamentary government no one had described. These claims of Bagehot have been too easily accepted, and therefore the false alternatives that he presented, of the complete separation or the complete fusion of powers in British government, have been over-influential. It is true that Bagehot's description of cabinet government was more compelling and better written than earlier discussions of British government, but it was also misleading and exaggerated. Not only was his claim to originality false, but his treatment of the central principles of the Constitution reveal a distorted and unhistorical approach to the subject he claimed to lay bare for the first time. An examination of Bagehot's claims is an essential step in the understanding of the development of English constitutional thought, for it reveals that by his particular brand of journalism Bagehot helped to destroy the very system he wished so strongly to defend.

It is a remarkable fact that very few people had characterized the Constitution in the way that Bagehot claimed was the generally accepted view of British government. The two theories Bagehot mentioned had been combined into a single theory of the balanced constitution in the eighteenth century, and this precluded acceptance of the naïve view of the separation of powers that Bagehot intended to destroy. It is true, as we have seen, that certain radical critics of the Constitution *proposed* the pure separation

2. *The English Constitution*, London, edn. of 1964, p. 59.

of powers as a basis for a remodelling of the British system, but certainly none of them for a moment thought that the existing system embodied this theory; they complained bitterly that it did not. As for the role of the cabinet as a link between the legislative and executive powers, it was just this aspect of British government that called forth, in the work of John Cartwright, for example, the loudest complaints that the doctrine was being infringed. If the critics of the Constitution at the end of the eighteenth century were well aware of the importance of the cabinet, so also were the exponents of the mid-nineteenth-century Constitution. The role of the cabinet was set forth in works well before Bagehot's that could hardly have been called *avant-garde*. Thus a political dictionary published in 1845 gives a perfectly reasonable account of the cabinet and its relation to the Commons.[3] An elementary manual on the Constitution of 1859 gives a concise picture of the role of the cabinet, "to which all the duties of the executive government are confided . . . it consists (generally without exception) of members of the houses of parliament of the same political views, and of the party at the time prevalent in the House of Commons."[4] Even one of a little series entitled "The First Class Readers" could give in 1864 a reasonable statement of the nature of the cabinet.[5] Two years before Bagehot wrote, Sir George Cornewall Lewis anticipated his most oft-quoted phrase, by referring to the idea of an executive which was "a standing committee of the supreme legislature."[6]

More important than this refusal to acknowledge the general understanding of cabinet government, however, was Bagehot's complete misrepresentation of the theory of the Constitution as it had developed in the first sixty years of the nineteenth century. The constitutional theory that he sets up, only to knock down again, does violence to the views of Fox, Burke, and Paine, but it is little short of ludicrous as a statement of the mid-nineteenth-century view of British government. It is true that one popular work did embody these naïve views, the work of Lord Brougham,

3. *Political Dictionary*, London, 1845, Vol. I, pp. 440–1.
4. David Rowland, *A Manual of the English Constitution*, London, 1859, pp. 436 ff.
5. J. S. Laurie, *Sketches of the English Constitution*, London, 1864, pp. 63–66.
6. *A Dialogue on the Best Form of Government*, London, 1863, p. 90.

and it is difficult to avoid the feeling that when Bagehot referred slight-ingly to "the literary theory" of the Constitution, it was Brougham's work, and his alone, that Bagehot had in mind. The mixed constitution and the separation of powers were indeed the main props of Brougham's treatise on British government, published in the 1840's and reissued in a more popu-lar form in 1860.[7] But his work is incredibly anachronistic, and to take it as representative of British writing on the Constitution at that date would be wholly misleading. The fact is that from the very beginning of the century, even well before the passage of the Reform Act, over which Brougham presided as Lord Chancellor, there had been a continuous process of refor-mulation of the eighteenth-century theory of balanced government, which had resulted in a subtle theory of parliamentary government.

The ideas of Fox and Burke, the attacks upon the cabinet system by Paine, Williams, and Cartwright, and the running fusillade maintained by Cobbett in the *Political Register*, had focussed attention upon the idea, in-imical to the theory of the balanced constitution, that the cabinet combined in one set of hands both legislative and executive power. The outright de-fenders of the *status quo* chose to ignore these charges and to fall back upon an idealized version of the mixed and balanced constitution such as that defended at the time of the Reform Bill. But this position was already being abandoned in the early nineteenth century in favour of a new ap-proach to the Constitution. George III's demand that a binding declaration be made by the Grenville Ministry on the Catholic emancipation issue led to a fierce discussion of the nature of ministerial responsibility. Cob-bett attacked the cabinet system and the relations between the ministry and the Commons, renewing the radical demand for an extensive place-bill, and for the exclusion of ministers from the House.[8] The reply made to Cobbett in the *Edinburgh Review* of July 1807 was not based, however, upon the eighteenth-century theory of the Constitution; rather it under-took to explain the English system of government in realistic terms, and not according to outdated ideas. The system of the balanced constitution,

7. Henry Brougham, *Political Philosophy*, 3 vols., London, 1842–3; and *The British Constitu-tion*, London, 1860.

8. *Political Register*, 1807, Vol. XI, pp. 1086–7 and 1807.

the reviewer argued, had been based upon the existence of three orders of society, and these orders still existed and were essential parts of the system of government, but they now exercised their power in a different way. The three orders of society had originally possessed distinct functions and privileges, which they "exercised separately and successively, frequently with very little concert, and sometimes with considerable hostility."[9] Now, however, the business of government had become "more complicated and operose," and some expedient had to be found in order that the three estates of the government should be able to work together with greater sympathy and more mutual contact. The principle of "harmony" was now the dominant one in the British system of government.

How was this harmony achieved? "The balance of the constitution now exists," the author continued, "in a great degree *in the House of Commons;* and that assembly possesses nearly the whole legislative authority."[10] This balance *inside* the Commons was achieved by virtue of the fact that in that body were to be found ministers with their influence over "government members," and members who were dependent upon aristocratic support, as well as independent members. The potential conflict of the three parts of the State was thus prevented or at least ameliorated, by this "early mixture of their elements," thus converting the sudden and successive checks of the old system into "one regulating and graduated pressure."[11] By this means of resolving conflicts in the Commons itself the balance of the Constitution, in danger of being lost because of the growing power of the Lower House, was preserved by being transferred into that assembly.[12] Thus, many years before Bagehot wrote, the criticisms of the idea of mixed government, which, for example, Bentham was making, were recognized by the reformulation of the idea of balanced government to meet new political conditions. The idea of government by King, Lords, and Commons was recognized by many as merely the formal theory of the Constitution; the

9. *Edinburgh Review,* Vol. X, No. XX, July 1807, p. 411. "A.B." in the *Political Register,* Vol. XII, p. 600, refers to the author as "Mr. Jeffrey," i.e. Francis Jeffrey.

10. *Edinburgh Review,* p. 413.

11. Ibid.

12. Ibid., p. 414.

reality was very different. This was recognized by Thomas Erskine in 1817 when he wrote of the entirely new character of the Constitution at that date, whereby the executive government was carried on entirely in the "popular council";[13] and James Mill in his *Essay on Government* rejected the old classification of mixed and simple forms of government altogether. The *Essay* is in fact a sustained argument for the view that the old theory of the Constitution must be replaced by one the basis of which would be the two functions of "governing" and "the control of government." Just as the idea of balanced government was being reassessed and reformulated, so the role of the separation of powers in the new system was being explored. No crude definition of the separation of powers, such as Bagehot's, would do for a system of government so complex and so delicately balanced. This concern with the relation of the separation of powers to the new theory can be clearly seen in the *Essay on the History of the English Government and Constitution*, which Lord John Russell published in 1821.

Lord John Russell believed that the highest stage in the development of civilization and the perfection of civil society was achieved by a system of government which had for its aim the union of liberty with order. The merit and value of differing systems of government are to be measured in relation to the proportions in which these two qualities are combined.[14] The function of the modern English system of government was, therefore, to produce harmony between the hitherto jarring parts of the Constitution, in order that they might act "without disturbance or convulsion."[15] This was achieved in practice by the system of ministerial responsibility, and by the mutual checks that Crown and Parliament exerted upon each other. But how could this system be reconciled with the principle of the separation of powers insisted upon by earlier writers, asked Lord John. In fact, he answered, the three powers never had been, and never could be completely separated with the exception of the judicial power, whose function was merely to apply general rules to particular cases.[16] As for the other two powers, best styled deliberative and executive, in every constitution

13. *Armata*, 1817, Vol. I, p. 67.
15. Ibid., pp. 94 and 162.
14. Op. cit., 2nd edn., 1823, Preface, p. x.
16. Ibid., pp. 148 and 157–9.

they continually influenced and acted upon each other.[17] A few years later Austin, in his lectures at University College, London, criticized the idea that the legislative and executive powers were exercised separately in the British system of government, or indeed that they could even be precisely distinguished, as "too palpably false to endure a moment's examination."[18]

It is in the work of an almost unknown author, however, that we find best represented the stage of constitutional thought transitional between the eighteenth-century theory of balanced government and the mid-nineteenth-century theory of parliamentary government. In 1831 Professor J. J. Park inaugurated a course on the theory and practice of the Constitution at King's College, London. The following year four of the lectures from this course were published under the title of *The Dogmas of the Constitution*. These lectures provide not only a survey of the development of constitutional thought at the time of the Reform Bill, but they also suggest a possible source of Bagehot's *English Constitution*. The lectures were published some ten years before Bagehot took up his studies at University College, London. Both the method and some of the content of Park's lectures are so close to those of Bagehot's essays that it is difficult to avoid the feeling that this is no mere coincidence. Park began with the assertion that for the past one hundred and fifty years there had been two constitutions in existence, the one in substance, the other only in form. The principles of the Constitution, according to Blackstone and Paley, were the division between the legislative and executive powers, and the balance of King, Lords, and Commons. But these were principles in form only. The *real* Constitution was one in which the former prerogative powers of the Crown had come to be exercised and carried on in the House of Commons, "and thence in the face of the country," which has come "to take a part, and exercise a voice, in every act of the cabinet." The supreme power, formerly supposed to reside in the three coequal elements of Crown, aristocracy, and commonalty, had settled in the Commons, and the three elements being represented in that House, their battles have been fought out there. Thus when we turn, said Park, from the *theory* of the Constitution to the *facts*, a totally different

17. Ibid., p. 151.
18. *The Province of Jurisprudence Determined*, London, 1954, p. 235.

state of affairs is found. Instead of a "chance-medley or fortuitous government" there is a highly organized system "which is not fully described in any book that I have ever met with." In fact a revolution had gone on "silently and insensibly" before the very eyes of chroniclers and Vinerian professors.[19] Over thirty years before Bagehot wrote, his argument was presented in the very same form by Professor Park. Nor was Park's attack limited to the principle of mixed government. As Bagehot was later to do, he next turned his attention to the separation of powers.

The revolution that had taken place in the British system of government, said Park, consisted in the fact that apparently "either the executive government has merged into the legislative, or the legislative has merged into the executive."[20] We find, he continued, that no sooner is an administration formed upon the basis of majority support in Parliament than it takes upon itself not merely the executive government, but also the management, control, and direction of the whole mass of political legislation.[21] Before the Revolution the functions of government had been divided into those under the direct control of the legislature, such as taxation and the making of law, and those not so directly controlled. Since the Revolution, however, the principle of English government had been to subject *all* the functions of government to the direct control of the legislature, but, by using the balance of power *within* the Commons, to prevent the democratic element from interfering too much in the government. Blackstone's warning of the dangers of uniting the legislative and executive powers had some force when the law-making power was an irresponsible one, but when the Constitution provides for the responsibility of the parts of government, and "power is effectually countervailed," then the question of the division or union of powers and functions becomes merely a matter of expediency and efficiency. It would be absurd, therefore, to deny the advantages of union "out of servile obedience to an unproved and ill-considered dogma."[22] Park's view of the Constitution before the passage of the Reform

19. *The Dogmas of the Constitution*, London, 1832, pp. 7–8, 32–33, and 38.
20. Ibid., p. 41.
21. Ibid., p. 39.
22. Ibid., pp. 98, and 115–16.

Act was, therefore, of an equilibrium between the power of the government and that of the opposition, which the structure of representation ensured in the Commons. The danger in the Reform Bill, in his eyes, was that it would upset this delicate balance. By 1832 this constitutional theory, which had started as a Whig attack upon the traditional view of the eighteenth-century Constitution, had become the standpoint of Tory resistance to reform of the franchise.[23] Once the Reform Act was passed, however, it was inevitable that this more virile view of the nineteenth-century Constitution would continue to influence thought about the British system of government, for it was a necessary stage in the development from a theory of balanced government based upon a mixture of King, Lords, and Commons to a new theory of balance in a system of parliamentary government.

The vital element of the new constitutional theory which had been inherited from the old, was, therefore, the idea of balance. This was also the central idea of constitutional thought after 1832, and, just as in Park's case, there was a determined effort to resist the idea of the pure separation of powers as inappropriate to British government. The lack of enthusiasm in the British middle classes for the doctrine of the separation of powers may well have been due to the fact that even before 1832 they realized that the extension of the franchise would give to them the control of *all* of the functions of government, so that there was no need for a revolutionary theory. Furthermore, after 1832 the idea of the separation of powers was associated in their minds with universal suffrage on the American pattern. Certainly there was an outpouring of comparisons derogatory to the United States system of government which emphasized the virtues of the greater harmony of the British system. Nevertheless, although they rejected the extreme doctrine of the separation of powers, the strong emphasis upon balanced government remained, and, therefore, the role of a separation of powers and functions continued to be an important element in constitutional thought. What were reformulated, however, were the concepts of power and function, and just how they were to be separated. The model for this reformulation was not that of Montesquieu, but that of James Mill.

23. See Corinne Comstock Weston, *English Constitutional Theory and the House of Lords, 1556-1832*, London, 1965, pp. 250–1.

The spectre of the extreme democracy of the United States was, there-fore, linked with the discrediting of extreme ideas of the separation of powers. Bagehot's comparison with the United States was the latest of a considerable number of such discourses. In 1835 de Tocqueville had pro-vided much of the material necessary for this exercise, and the greater harmony of British government compared with American government was continually stressed. In 1842, comparing the British cabinet system with the American separation of powers, P. F. Aiken wrote that in Britain "the executive and the legislature work together with fewer abuses, with more effect, and with greater harmony," whereas in America the unseemly and dangerous collision between the legislature and the executive tells its own tale,[24] and, he argued, the separation of powers had some rather surprising results. In a remarkable anticipation of the argument which Woodrow Wil-son was to use forty years later, Aiken maintained that the American sys-tem resulted in the "absorption" of the executive powers by the legislature, whereas in the English system of parliamentary government the estates of the realm were so admirably adjusted that, paradoxically, just because the executive had influence in the legislature, and the people could influence the executive through the House of Commons, the two parts of the State were able to act together in harmony *without* absorbing each other.[25] The difference in emphasis between Aiken and Park is a significant one. Park writes of the "merging" of the executive and legislative powers in England, just as Bagehot was later to write of "fusion"; but Aiken concluded that the main characteristic of the British system was that executive and legislature, though closely linked and interdependent, were not absorbed, merged, or fused. It was, in fact, just this characteristic of the balanced autonomy of interdependent and closely linked parts of the government that was central to the mid-nineteenth-century theory of parliamentary government.

By the mid nineteenth century the writers on the Constitution had re-jected any notion of an extreme separation of powers, in favour of the balance of parliamentary government. But this balance required a func-

24. *A Comparative View of the Constitutions of Great Britain and the United States of America*, London, 1842, pp. 94, 105.
25. Ibid., p. 108.

---

tional separation of powers also. There was here no crude theory of the fusion of all power in one set of hands. Perhaps the best formulation of this line of constitutional thought is Earl Grey's *Parliamentary Government*, published in 1858. Grey rejected Blackstone's legalistic view of the Constitution, replacing it with a description of the system of ministerial responsibility. It is true that the executive power and the power to formulate and initiate legislation were united in the same hands, he wrote, but both these powers were limited. The executive was limited because it must respect the law, but equally parliament was limited because of the authority that ministers of the Crown exercised over the House of Commons. The fact that ministers were responsible to the Commons did not mean that the legislature could interfere directly with the management of executive functions. A system of parliamentary government bore no resemblance to that of the Long Parliament;[26] ministers were the servants of the Crown and not of the House of Commons, and, should this position change, the system of government would become at once weak, capricious, and tyrannical. There would be all the disadvantages of American government without the checks to the exercise of arbitrary power which were to be found in that system.[27] The particular virtues of the English system of government, he believed, were due to "the peculiar character of our system of representation, which has admitted the democratic element into the House of Commons without allowing it to become predominant." The great fear of those who valued parliamentary government was, therefore, that the extension of the franchise would destroy the delicate balance of the system, and substitute a thoroughgoing democracy without restraints to its power.

The theory of parliamentary government reached a high point in constitutional thought, for it claimed, with some justification, to have attained that balance of separation and unity, of harmony and functional differentiation, of control and collaboration, which had been sought for ever since the inadequacies of the rival theories of the separation of powers and the balanced constitution had been perceived at the end of the eighteenth cen-

26. *Parliamentary Government considered with Reference to a Reform of Parliament*, London, 1858, pp. 4, 8–9.
27. Ibid., p. 94.

tury. The balance of power between cabinet and parliament depended upon a differentiation of functions, and upon a distinction also of personnel, for although ministers were also members of parliament their numbers were small, as Constant had insisted they must be, and they were swamped by the large proportion of the legislature which had no official place or interest. The functional basis of the system, however, was very different from that which had characterized the earlier theories of the Constitution. The Montesquieu categories of legislation and execution became almost, but not quite, irrelevant. The theory of parliamentary government was based upon the two functions of "governing" and "the control of government." As John Stuart Mill saw it the problem was to achieve a compromise between popular control and efficiency. This could only be achieved by "separating the functions which guarantee the one from those which essentially require the other; by disjointing the office of control and criticism from the actual conduct of affairs."[28] Thus the two parts of the government were to remain distinct and to limit themselves each to its proper function, although remaining closely linked. We see here again the difference between the English view of parliamentary supremacy and, for example, the Montagnard view of *gouvernement d'assemblée*. From a legal point of view *Parliament* is supreme, but it is the "King-in-Parliament," and not the House of Commons, which enjoys this supremacy. Neither Locke nor John Stuart Mill conceived of a legislature that would deal with every matter of government business itself. The King-in-Parliament as a legal conception consists of two parts, the Crown and the Houses of Parliament. In modern terms this means, in fact, government and Commons respectively. The prerogative powers of the Crown, in particular the power of dissolution, transferred into the hands of ministers, meant that they would not be absorbed by the legislature, but would balance it, retaining an autonomous position, but subject to removal if they failed to carry the House with them.

This delicate balance depended entirely, however, upon the operation of internal restraints; the ministers must not attempt to use their powers to coerce the Commons, and the Commons must not attempt to control the

28. *Representative Government*, Oxford, 1948, p. 174.

affairs of government directly. The breaking of these restraints would soon lead to a very different system. It was realized that this balance depended, therefore, upon a particular type of party system. Too little party discipline and coherence, and there would be nothing to prevent the meddling of a faction-ridden legislature in the day-to-day business of government, an approach towards that spectre of the Long Parliament which had long haunted English constitutional thought. On the other hand, if parties became too powerful and too cohesive the ordinary members of the legislature would be subordinated to the cabinet. Thus Earl Grey attributed the weakness of governments in the 1850's to the decline of party feeling since the Reform Act, because most of the important public questions that had divided the parties had been settled. He looked for stronger party cohesion as the only means by which the autonomy of the government could be maintained.[29] However, there were those who saw the dangers of increased party discipline for the independence of members of the House of Commons. The crucial problem was how "to define the limits of party obligations."[30] The "parties" under discussion here, were, of course, essentially parliamentary parties. Few could have foreseen the results of the introduction of the caucus system and the development of mass political parties. It was this reliance of the system of parliamentary government upon a very precise, and rare, combination of independence and party allegiance that made it so short-lived, and so difficult to imitate.

Walter Bagehot's *English Constitution*, first published in 1865 as essays in *The Fortnightly*, and as a book two years later, has undoubtedly had great influence over the course of constitutional thought during the past century. That this book is still, a century after its publication, perhaps the most oft-quoted work on the cabinet system is quite remarkable, in view of the extent to which the practice of British politics has changed during that period. No doubt the explanation of this continued popularity is that his style is so much superior to that of more academic works. As Mr. Richard Crossman pointed out in 1964, it is the journalistic quality of these essays which has made them so consistently popular. But if one of the defects of

29. *Parliamentary Government*, pp. 100–1.
30. Homersham Cox, *The Institutions of the English Government*, London, 1863, p. 256.

even the very best journalism is to exaggerate the points the writer wishes to make, then this is in fact just the major defect of Bagehot's famous book. The author wished to drive home a point, and in order to do this he misrepresented the theory he was attacking, and he exaggerated his conclusions, so as to make as clear and as great a gulf as possible between the two positions. But it is not merely Bagehot's journalism that we have to guard against. He was writing with a very strong political purpose in mind, and although this gives to his work a vehemence and a conviction which others lack, it also gives it a misleading character. Bagehot wished to warn, indeed to frighten, his middle-class readers, by pointing out to them what would be the effects of extending the franchise. He was, as he himself said in 1872, "exceedingly afraid of the ignorant multitude."[31] The American Civil War, seen in England so much in terms of a battle between the democratic North and the aristocratic South, had, in Earl Grey's words, increased "the wholesome dread" of an extreme alteration in the English Constitution.[32] If the franchise were to be extended so that the lower classes gained control of the Commons, what check would there be to their power? Bright and Forster were accused of wishing to introduce the American pattern of government into England. The result would be either an uncontrollable legislature or "Caesarism." For, as a writer in *The Quarterly Review* of January 1866 pointed out, "The feeble and pliable executive of England is wholly unsuited to such an electoral body. A government that yields and must yield to the slightest wish of the House of Commons is only possible as long as that House of Commons is the organ of an educated minority."[33] This was the point of view to which Bagehot was determined to give his utmost support. He wished to make it as clear as possible to his readers that the reform of 1832 had not, as some had argued it would, restored the balance of the Constitution. It had confirmed, in fact, that there were no longer any checks or balances in the system. Whoever controlled the Commons had absolute power. The balanced constitution was dead, and the middle class should have no illusions about it.

31. Op. cit., p. 281.
32. *Parliamentary Government*, new edn., 1864, Preface, p. vii.
33. *Quarterly Review*, Vol. 119, No. 237, Jan. 1866, pp. 278–9.

This determination to stress the absence of restraints to the exercise of power led Bagehot into considerable difficulty. He did not distinguish clearly between the Constitution as it actually worked in the hands of an educated minority, and how it *might* work in the hands of the representatives of the ignorant multitude. Nor did he, in spite of all his claims to factual realism, distinguish clearly between the legal and practical aspects of English government. As a result he presented a picture of the English system which was mangled and exaggerated. Ignoring almost everything that had been written on British government during the previous sixty years, Bagehot affirmed that the "literary theory" of the Constitution, "as it exists in all the books," was erroneously based upon the two principles of mixed government and the *entire* separation of the legislative and executive powers. In fact, wrote Bagehot, the efficient secret of the English system of government is "the close union, the nearly complete fusion" of the legislative and executive powers. Thus he represented the extreme doctrine of the separation of powers as the accepted theory of the Constitution, and then replaced it with an equally extreme principle, the fusion of powers. In order to make this point Bagehot used the comparison with the United States, and quickly proved that Britain did not have the same system of completely separate personnel for the two branches of government as the presidential system. The difference lay in the role of the cabinet, this "new word," said Bagehot, with sublime disregard of the writings on English politics from Paine to Grey. The demonstration that the complete separation of powers in all its aspects did not exist in Britain was, of course, readily established, but this did not necessarily mean that the powers of government were "fused." These alternatives were presented by Bagehot as if they represented the only possibilities. But, as we have seen, virtually the whole history of English constitutionalism has been characterized by the recognition of the need for a *partial* separation of the personnel of government, and a *partial* separation of the functions of government. Such subtleties did not exist for Bagehot, however.

Naturally enough this extreme view of the "principle" of British government did not square very well with the facts of its operation in the 1860's, and this led Bagehot into very difficult waters. On the same page as he writes of the fusion of powers, he uses expressions quite incompatible with that idea. Thus his famous metaphor of the cabinet as "a hyphen which joins, a buckle that fastens" the two parts of the State, is itself somewhat different from the idea of fusion, and elsewhere he writes of the necessity of "the constant co-operation" of the two parts of the government—a very different matter indeed![34] His most remarkable misuse of words comes in the following passage: "The chief committee of the legislature has the power of dissolving the predominant part of that legislature—that which at a crisis is the supreme legislature. The English system, therefore, is not an absorption of the executive power by the legislative power; it is a fusion of the two."[35] This might be seen as an attempt to combine the ideas of Park and Aiken, so close is the language to that used by the earlier writers, but as a piece of logic it is very difficult to follow. How does the conclusion follow from the premiss? The fact that the cabinet has the power to dissolve the Commons surely does not prove that they are fused, but that they are not. Indeed it seems that Bagehot was trapped by his own use of language. His description of the cabinet as a committee with power to destroy its parent body did not lead him, as one might expect, to discard the idea of a committee, which is entirely inappropriate here, but to insist even more strongly upon the idea of a fusion of powers. A similar confusion is found in this statement: "The regulator, as I venture to call it, of our single sovereignty, is the power of dissolving the otherwise sovereign chamber confided to the chief executive."[36] Here we are close to the root of the confusion in Bagehot's work. The legal idea of sovereignty can be attached to the King-in-Parliament, of which one part, the government, can use its power to dissolve the other, the Commons, and appeal, as Bagehot says, to the next Parliament. But the Commons alone is certainly not sovereign in the legal sense. In the political sense, if the term "sovereignty" can usefully be applied in this connection, again it is not the Commons that is sovereign, but the electorate, which judges between cabinet and Commons in case of a difference of opinion that ends in a dissolution. It is true of course

34. *The English Constitution*, London, 1964, pp. 68 and 72.
35. Ibid., p. 69.
36. Ibid., p. 221.

that the Commons must be satisfied with a cabinet if it is to continue in office, but to attribute "sovereignty" to the Commons is to misunderstand the powers the ministers exercise on the one hand, and the role of the electorate on the other. Bagehot, in fact, adopted a view of legislative sovereignty or supremacy more like that of the proponents of *gouvernement d'assemblée* than any earlier view of legislative supremacy in England; a fact which helps to explain why his ideas were so well received in extreme republican circles in France in the early years of the Third Republic.

When Bagehot turned to the description of the working of parliamentary government he dropped his preconceived framework of a "fusion" of powers, and wrote in terms of the balance between government and parliament which earlier writers had stressed. The fate of the government is determined by the debate in parliament, he wrote, but, on the other hand, "either the cabinet legislates and acts, or else it can dissolve. It is a creature, but it has the power of destroying its creators."[37] A perfect description, but not one of a fusion of powers; rather of a subtle division and interdependence of two arms of government, each with its proper function to perform. Indeed Bagehot summed up the position perfectly when he wrote "The whole life of English politics is the action and reaction between the Ministry and the Parliament."[38]

Bagehot's influence upon the study of English politics has been great. His emphasis upon the need to concern ourselves with the real working of government, and not with irrelevant "principles," has contributed to the tendency of modern students of British government to concentrate upon the day-to-day working of institutions without relating them to the over-all structure of the Constitution. Constitutional considerations became almost exclusively the domain of the lawyers, something that had never formerly been true in England. Furthermore, his characterization of the fusion of power in England seemed to become more and more relevant as the details of the system he claimed to describe changed out of all recognition. The growth of mass political parties and of party discipline in parliament created a situation in which the fusion of power seemed much

37. Ibid., pp. 69 and 73.   38. Ibid., p. 151.

more of a reality than it ever was in the period between the two Reform Acts. The concept of concentrated power that he supplied suited admirably the needs of that society, the emergence of which he had most wished to prevent. Of course, the idea of a balanced government did not die overnight. Sidgwick described the British system of government in terms of the essential balance between government and legislature, with an appeal to the electorate,[39] and Bryce wrote of "the exquisite equipoise" of parliamentary government.[40] In more recent years L. S. Amery relied upon this concept for his analysis of British government,[41] and Herbert Morrison maintained that it was the existence of a balance between cabinet and parliament which distinguished the British system of government from that of the Third and Fourth Republics.[42] But the trend of thought was against them. It was Bagehot who was read, and still is read, and who seemed to suit the mood of the age, in spite of the fact that the predominance of the Commons over the cabinet as he described it, has, in the view of present-day observers, been replaced by the predominance of the cabinet over the Commons, or indeed of the Prime Minister over both.

English constitutional thought over the past century has, therefore, been extraordinarily fragmented. The functional concepts of the theory of parliamentary government have not been jettisoned, for we still think of the function of the Commons as that of exercising control over the government, and discussion turns upon the way in which this can best be achieved, if at all. Yet the idea of a *balance* between government and parliament has almost entirely disappeared. The mechanisms of this balance as Grey saw them, dissolution and ministerial responsibility, have almost wholly ceased to play the role envisaged for them in the classical theory of parliamentary government. The tacit acceptance of Bagehot's view of a fusion of powers has not, however, entirely replaced the functional categories upon which the doctrine of the separation of powers was based. Both that theory, and the theory of the balanced constitution, had been created upon a functional

39. *Elements of Politics*, 2nd edn., London, 1897, p. 436.
40. *The American Commonwealth*, 2nd edn., London, 1890, Vol. I, p. 281.
41. *Thoughts on the Constitution*, London, 1947, pp. 15–16.
42. *Government and Parliament*, 3rd edn., London, 1964, p. 107.

analysis of the acts of government, which classified them into legislation and execution, the making of laws and the putting of these laws into effect. The idea of a rule of law was, as we have seen, closely bound up with this functional view of government acts. The theory of parliamentary government had a different functional basis, whilst Bagehot suggested that there was really no significant functional distinction to be made. These two functional analyses of the eighteenth century and the nineteenth century did not, of course, coincide. The idea of "government" and of "execution" are radically different. Yet the categories of "government" and "control" could not wholly supersede the old categories of "legislation" and "execution." For the former related only to a *theory of government*, whereas the latter had, in the seventeenth and eighteenth centuries, been part of both a theory of government *and a theory of law*. The insistence that the executive should obey the legislature was the institutional expression of the demand that the law was supreme, over King, Protector, Governor, and President alike. This view of the supremacy of the law did not come to an end with the rise of the theory of parliamentary government, and indeed it was strongly reasserted by Dicey at the end of the nineteenth century. The proponents of parliamentary government did not for a moment assert that the government was no longer subject to the restraints of the law; it was subject to the law, although it played a decisive role in the process of legislation, and in the general business of government, which bore no relation to the idea of a "mere executive." The new categories overlaid and ran parallel to the old.

It is true that the idea of a "mere executive" power had never been fully accepted in England. The King's prerogative, the discretionary powers of the Crown, had never been lost sight of in the theory of the balanced constitution, in the way in which the French and the Americans had, for a time at least, assumed that discretionary powers were unnecessary in a constitutional government. Nevertheless the insistence upon the supremacy of the law, and relegation of the royal power over legislation to a quiescent "negative voice," had made the application of the term "executive power" to the King and his ministers seem not too inappropriate. In the nineteenth century, however, the explicit recognition of the role of the government in formulating, initiating, and indeed securing the passage of legislation, made the term "executive" quite inadequate as a description of the role of ministers of the Crown. That we still use the term today is indicative of the extent to which we attach a dual role to the same body of persons.

The continued vitality of the principle of the rule of law implied also a continued adherence to the ideas which had lain behind the separation of powers. Twenty years after Bagehot's articles had been published in *The Fortnightly* A. V. Dicey restated the basis of the English theory of constitutionalism with unprecedented vigour, expounding the rule of law without any concessions, in a way which would have been acceptable to the most fervent anti-royalist of the seventeenth century. For Dicey the absolute supremacy of the regular law excluded arbitrary rule, prerogative, or even wide discretionary authority on the part of government.[43] Dicey was no advocate of the separation of powers; indeed he fired a few shots at the doctrine himself. Yet once again it was the extreme doctrine that was under attack, the doctrine "as applied by Frenchmen," the doctrine which gave birth to the dreaded *droit administratif*. Nevertheless, the whole burden of the *Law of the Constitution* was that the making of law, and the carrying out of the law, were distinct and separate functions, and that those who carry out the law must be subordinated to those who make it. On the one hand the executive might act only with the authority of the law; on the other, Parliament might not exercise direct executive power, or even appoint the officials of the executive government.[44] Dicey did not fully explore what this meant in terms of the separation of functions among different *persons*, but if the subordination of the executive to the law was the keynote of his work, it would be to reduce this principle to nonsense to assume that legislators and executives were identical, that the powers of government were "fused." Not unnaturally, therefore, an attachment to the ideas of the separation of powers in the twentieth century has been associated with lawyers rather than with students of politics, whilst the latter have preferred a point of view derived rather from an amalgam of the ideas of Grey and Bagehot. At certain points these views have come radically into conflict, and the areas in which these points of view did not overlap have

43. *The Law of the Constitution*, 8th edn., London, 1931, p. 198.
44. Ibid., p. 404.

become critical. The extreme, almost hysterical, criticisms made by Lord Hewart in the *New Despotism*, and expressed also in a more balanced way by C. K. Allen, were met, before the Second World War, with strong assertions of the need for co-ordinated, decisive government action. Since the War, however, there has been a change of tone. Lawyers are no longer so apt to think in terms of bureaucrats lusting for power, nor are students of politics so unheeding of the dangers which arise from the characteristics of modern government. There is some recognition today that there is virtue in both the theory of law and the theory of government. How to reconcile them is the great problem.

At the end of the nineteenth century the ideas of Grey, Bagehot, and Dicey seemed to run along parallel lines. The theory of parliamentary government, with its balance between government and parliament, the fusion of the legislative and executive powers, and the subordination of the executive to the law were all quite cheerfully accepted as principles of British government. They were in fact all capable of being reconciled to a considerable extent. The reconciliation between the theory of law and the theory of government was achieved through the principle of ministerial responsibility. This idea enabled the two theories to be knitted together, and the differing functional concepts they embodied to be brought into a working relationship. The "executive" must act according to the law, the "government" must exercise leadership in the development of policy; but if the government was subject to the control of parliament, and the executive to the control of the courts, then a harmony could be established between the two roles of the ministers of the Crown. Ministerial responsibility, legal and political, was thus the crux of the English system of government. Whilst it remained a reality the whole edifice of constitutionalism could be maintained; should it cease to be a workable concept the process of disintegration between the legal basis and the operation of government would begin.

At the end of the nineteenth century the view that ministers could be held responsible to Parliament for the actions of "government" and "executive" alike seemed reasonable enough. The Civil Service was seen as a passive instrument of the will of Parliament under the supervision of ministers. The tasks of government were still relatively simple and could be assumed to fit, without too much difficulty, into the categories either of policy or administration. The development of new tasks of government, however, which consisted of active intervention in the economic and social life of the country, presented a very different picture. The difference be-tween "government" and "executive" became even more marked. It was no longer possible to restrict the discretion of government by insisting upon the adherence to detailed rules laid down by Parliament. "Delegated legis-lation" and "administrative justice" were the inevitable accompaniments of the expanded role of government in society. Furthermore, the "executive" could no longer be seen to be composed of responsible ministers who de-cided "policy" and civil servants who carried it out. The new demands upon government had called into existence an extensive, complex bureaucracy, within which important decisions were taken by anonymous civil servants. The extreme critics of these new developments suggested that a nominally responsible government could, by its control over the legislative process, obtain for the so-called executive power the right to draw up its own rules and even to free itself from the control of the courts by excluding their jurisdiction. The potential power of the government, they suggested, was being used to destroy the rule of law. More important, perhaps, than these factors was the character of the twentieth-century party system. The close links which had been forged between the government and the majority in Parliament seemed to destroy all idea of balance between cabinet and legis-lature, and even to throw doubt upon the possibility of a general control of government business. The assumption underlying the system of par-liamentary government had been destroyed, and the reality of ministerial responsibility was therefore thrown in doubt. Once this essential principle was questioned the whole edifice began to show cracks.

In 1929 the Committee on Ministers' Powers was appointed, with the task of rebuilding the bridge between the two concepts of the Constitution, which had come to be represented on the one hand by politicians and ad-ministrators, and on the other by lawyers. The Committee's terms of refer-ence instructed it to consider the powers exercised by or under the direction of ministers of the Crown by way of delegated legislation and judicial or quasi-judicial decision, and to report what safeguards were desirable or necessary to secure the constitutional principles of the sovereignty of Parliament and the supremacy of the law. There was, therefore, explicit in these terms of reference the remarkable admission that it was conceivable that the decisions of responsible ministers, or of their servants, *could* operate in a way which offended the rule of law. There was a recognition, therefore, that the rule of law must mean something more than the mere formal sanction of some legal authority for every act of government, for no one suggested that ministers or civil servants had been acting *illegally*. The attempt of the less sophisticated of Dicey's critics to equate the rule of law with mere legality misses the point that the supremacy of the law in English thought since the seventeenth century has included, and must include, certain ideas about the articulation and separation of the functions of government, as well as "due process." The evidence and report of the Committee on Ministers' Powers illustrate the difficulty they had in reconciling this view of the Constitution with the needs of modern government, which seemed so much better served by the categories of the theory of parliamentary government than those inherited from the theory of the separation of powers.

The argument that the separation of powers was being destroyed by the way in which the ministers and civil servants were usurping the functions of the legislature and the courts was met by the Committee with the counter-argument that the doctrine of the separation of powers, whilst very important, had never been completely accepted in England, and that some deviation from its precepts was perfectly safe, acceptable, and indeed essential. The Committee in its Report stated: "The separation of powers is merely a rule of political wisdom, and must give way where sound reasons of public policy so require."[45] The delegation of legislative and judicial power to the executive was a necessary feature of modern government and so had to be tolerated, but it must be kept within bounds and surrounded by the necessary safeguards. With true British pragmatism the Committee concluded that the granting of judicial powers to a minister or ministerial tribunal "should be regarded as exceptional and requiring justification in each case,"[46] although of course they could not suggest what would be re-

45. *Report of the Committee on Ministers' Powers*, Cmd. 4060, 1932, p. 95.
46. Ibid., pp. 115–16.

garded as sufficient justification. Nevertheless, the Committee was quite definite in its adherence to the rule of law, and stated its belief that it was "obvious" that the separation of powers is *prima facie* the guiding principle by which Parliament when legislating should allocate the executive and judicial tasks involved in its legislative plan.[47] The problem was, therefore, to determine the criteria for distinguishing between administrative and judicial decisions.

Thus the Committee became embroiled in a discussion of the nature of the functions of government. Everyone agreed that it was impossible to draw precise boundaries, and numerous examples were cited to illustrate this difficulty. Nevertheless, the upholding of the rule of law seemed to necessitate definitions, and the Committee strove to find them. The problems they faced are well illustrated by the following excerpt from the minutes of evidence. The representatives of the Association of Municipal Corporations, W. J. Board and Sir William Hart, were discussing with members of the Committee whether or not ministers should be required to give the grounds for their decision following a public enquiry:

> *Sir Wm. Holdsworth:* Still I suppose a department where it has been given judicial powers and has been exercising those judicial powers does decide things on principle, and would it not be a help to the public to know what the principle was?
>
> *W. J. Board:* These are not judicial decisions, they are administrative. There may be certain times when they may have the appearance of a judicial decision, but we think they are of the nature, and should be of the nature of administrative decrees and should be treated as such; they are not therefore comparable with what takes place in the Law Courts.
>
> *Sir Wm. Holdsworth:* When you say "administrative decisions" you mean they must apply their minds to them and decide them justly?
>
> *W. J. Board:* Certainly.
>
> *Sir Wm. Holdsworth:* I do not see why the fact that they are administrative should be a reason why no reasons should be given. They are decisions whether administrative or judicial.

47. Ibid., p. 92.

Professor Laski: May I put it another way? The result may be administrative, but surely the process is judicial?

Sir Leslie Scott: Or to put it in another way still, if the issue is a justiciable issue, either because the facts are disputed or because the law applicable is disputed, that is essentially a matter for judicial decision.

Sir Wm. Hart: I agree.[48]

From this confusion the Committee retreated to a simple, if indefensible, criterion. Administrative decisions, they concluded, were concerned with the application of policy and therefore involved the exercise of a wide discretion, whereas judicial decisions simply applied fixed rules of law. Quasi-judicial decisions were, therefore, in the Committee's view, essentially administrative decisions which had some element of a judicial character in that they involved disputes. Such disputes, however, were not regulated by rules of law, and so remained administrative in character, and were to be determined by the minister's free choice.[49] This device enabled the Committee to solve its problem. Justiciable issues, except in exceptional circumstances, should be left to the courts, administrative and quasi-judicial decisions to the executive. Ministers should be subject to the appellate jurisdiction of the High Court in regard to judicial decisions, and subject to the control of Parliament and public opinion in the exercise of their quasi-judicial and administrative functions. Ministerial responsibility, legal and political, remained the keystone of the Constitution. As the Treasury-Solicitor, Sir Maurice Gwyer, had warned the Committee, any departure from the principle of ministerial responsibility would imply the adoption of a new theory of government.[50]

The most ardent antagonist of the Committee's view was W. A. Robson, who published his *Justice and Administrative Law* shortly before the Committee was appointed, gave evidence before them, and in later editions of the book took issue with their Report. Robson flatly rejected attacks upon administrative law and justice originating from the doctrine of the separa-

48. Committee on Ministers' Powers, *Minutes of Evidence*, 1932, Vol. II, p. 265. I am indebted to Miss S. Conwill for having drawn my attention to this discussion.

49. *Report*, pp. 74 and 81.

50. *Minutes of Evidence*, Vol. II, p. 6.

tion of powers. The doctrine, he said, was an "antique and rickety chariot . . . so long the favourite vehicle of writers on political science and constitutional law for the conveyance of fallacious ideas."[51] Like A. F. Pollard some years before, Robson demonstrated that the separation of powers had never been completely accepted in England, and that administrative and judicial functions have been mingled in the same offices since the beginning of English history. His objections to the doctrine went much deeper than those of the Committee who had accepted it as a general guide to the distribution of governmental functions. Furthermore, he objected to the distinction the Committee drew between law and policy, which, as we have seen, really stems from the dual character of English constitutional thought.

The root of Robson's attack upon the separation of powers was his antagonism to the ideas associated with Dicey's formulation of the rule of law. The implicit commitment to some form of separation of powers in Dicey's work was the basis of his rejection of *droit administratif*, and the basis also of the claim of the ordinary courts to a monopoly of judicial power. Robson, however, was interested in the creation of a system of administrative courts, similar to those in France, and his attack was, therefore, directed at a doctrine which was used to argue that judicial powers ought not to be entrusted to administrators. The most important aspect of judicial institutions, Robson believed, was the development of the "judicial mind." If a similar state of mind were to be cultivated in the minds of administrators who have to deal with judicial problems, then "we need spill no tears of regret because they do not bear the institutional characteristics of the former courts of law."[52]

Robson's attack upon the views of Dicey, and upon the conclusions of the Donoughmore Committee, might be taken as the final attack upon the separation of powers in Britain, and a rejection of it in its last stronghold, the power of the judiciary to settle judicial matters. Yet there is something of a paradox in this position, which illustrates how the *values* implicit in the doctrine have survived into the twentieth century, and how the precepts of the doctrine have doggedly refused to die. As with Duguit in France and

51. *Justice and Administrative Law*, 2nd edn., London, 1947, p. 14.
52. Ibid., p. 34.

Goodnow in America, Robson's rejection of the extreme view of the separation of powers was only one side of his argument. He was forced to fight on two fronts at the same time. Whilst attacking the vested interests of the ordinary courts in the exclusive exercise of judicial power, his attachment to the idea that there is a proper sphere of action for administrative courts forced him to adhere to the basic functional concepts which Montesquieu had enunciated. He rejected the view that the definition of government functions was logically impossible; it was only the institutional articulation of these functions that he wished to challenge. And even then, like the American opponents of the extreme separation of powers, he did not relish the idea of a single man being policeman, prosecutor, and judge on the same issue. "The exercise of judicial functions by administrative bodies can be rationalised and disciplined only by the introduction of specific institutional reforms and procedural safeguards." When it is necessary to confer legislative, administrative, and judicial powers on a single department, he wrote, it is *always* possible and desirable to separate these functions within the department.[53]

It is a remarkable fact that after the great weight of criticism that had been poured upon the Montesquieu categories of the functions of government they still remained, in the 1930's and 1940's, the basis of the discussion about the structure of government. The simple fact, of course, is that if one abandons the Montesquieu functions altogether, closely related as they are to the concept of the supremacy of law, one is left without any criteria for the orderly conduct of government business. Day-to-day expediency becomes the only guide for action, and few people would be prepared to admit that expediency alone should determine the organization and powers of government. The uncomfortable fact remains, however, that these categories have failed to provide the detailed guidance that would enable us to allocate the functions of government properly, i.e. in a way that is immediately seen to be efficient, and at the same time to safeguard the values inherent in the separation of powers. The attempt of the English

53. Ibid., pp. 333 and 473.

courts to apply these categories has led, in the opinion of one authority, to a position "riddled with ambiguities."[54] The conclusions of the Committee on Ministers' Powers were of little help in determining the later allocation of government powers. It is significant that when the Franks Committee on Administrative Tribunals came nearly thirty years later to retread some of the ground covered by the Donoughmore Committee they refused to be drawn into the discussion of the nature of the functions of government. Whilst noting that the distinctions drawn by the earlier classification of government functions were constitutionally of great importance, the Franks Committee in their Report regretted that they had been unable to fix upon a valid principle for the practical allocation of powers between ministers and administrative tribunals. The only approach that seemed to them to be useful was an empirical one, which ignored the problem of the general principles involved.[55] The difference between the approach of the two Committees is perhaps symptomatic of the more sceptical approach to political principles which had evolved during the intervening thirty years, and also reflects, possibly, the chairmanship of an Oxford-trained philosopher over the deliberations of the later one.

The "separation of powers" remains, therefore, a central problem in the English political system, for the problem of the controlled exercise of power is still, and probably always will be, the critical aspect of a system of government which hopes to combine efficiency and the greatest possible exercise of personal freedom. The basic problem remains, in spite of all the changes since the seventeenth century. If our system is to remain essentially a system of government by "law" then some form of control must be exercised over the agents of government. If we abandon this philosophy of law how do we prevent mere expediency from degenerating into arbitrary government? Not the arbitrary rule of a Charles I, a Cromwell, or a Hitler, but the arbitrariness of a great machine staffed by well-intentioned men, possessing, of necessity, a limited range of vision, and a limited ability

54. S. A. de Smith, *Judicial Review of Administrative Action*, London, 1959, p. 29.
55. *Report of the Committee on Administrative Tribunals and Enquiries*, Cmd. 218, 1957, pp. 28–30.

to judge where a succession of expedient decisions will lead. The fragmentation of constitutional thought in Britain, and the rejection, for good reasons, of older political theories, without their being replaced by any comprehensive view of the structure of our system of government and the values it is intended to safeguard, leaves us to drift before whatever wind of expediency may blow.

NINE

From the Third Republic to the Fifth

T HE CONNECTION between the doctrine of the separation of powers and the theory of parliamentary government, developed in the previous chapter, was a close and rather paradoxical one. The theory of parliamentary government, like its predecessor the theory of the balanced constitution, required a set of concepts concerning the division of the functions of government among its parts, but the categories it developed for this purpose were potentially in conflict with those which formed the basis of legal theory. As the latter depended upon a view of the nature of government closely connected with the doctrine of the separation of powers, there was a continuing love-hate relationship between the elements of these theories throughout the nineteenth century and the first half of the twentieth. When the delicately balanced party system which alone gave some semblance of coherence to these views was destroyed, the potentially conflicting elements of constitutional thought were brought into open battle. The history of France since the fall of Louis-Napoleon shows the same basic conflict between these various elements of constitutional thought, but in a more extreme and in a more complex form. Basically the last century has seen the same attempt made in France as in Britain to graft the ideas of parliamentary government onto the concepts of the rule of law and the separation of powers. But there were major differences in the French history of this attempt.

In the first place, the ideal of a balanced system of government has remained consistently as the aim of French constitutionalists from the time of the adoption of parliamentary government to the creation of the Fifth Republic; whereas in England the concept of balance has gradually dropped out of view, it has remained in France the only single constitutional ideal which had any hope of gaining wide acceptance. This ideal has persisted in spite of the fact, or perhaps because of the fact, that Frenchmen have shown little enthusiasm for putting it into practice when pursuing their own political goals. The discrepancy between theory and practice has been perhaps more significant in France than in either the United States or Britain during this period. The history of parliamentary government in France thus raises crucial questions concerning the value of constitutional structures, and the conditions in which they can or cannot achieve the aims of those who create them. Secondly, of course, the role of the party system in the operation of balanced or limited government is highlighted in the French experience. In Britain the rare and peculiar conditions necessary for a system of parliamentary government yielded gradually to the new politics of mass parties in a way which allowed the continuance of a two-party system. In France these fundamental conditions have never existed. The doctrine of the separation of powers played an important role in this situation, where constitutional ideals and political practice were so far removed from each other. As in England, the extreme form of the doctrine was attacked as far too rigid for a system of balanced parliamentary government, but the doctrine, which had been so important in French history since 1789, stayed very close to the surface of French thought. The desire to maintain a balance between the executive and legislative branches of government continually led Frenchmen to emphasize the importance of a separation of the functions of government and a division of power. The failure to maintain such a balance in practice led critics of the régime to reformulate the doctrine and to reassert it against the attempts to concentrate power in the legislature. The apparent impossibility of attaining governmental stability by means of a parliamentary constitution in France finally led these critics to doubt the compatibility of parliamentary government with an attempt to control power by constitutional methods.

The history of France from 1789 to 1958 may be seen as a long-drawn-out corollary to the developments in the United States in the years from 1776 to 1787. In revolutionary America the extreme doctrine of the separation of powers soon led in practice to legislative domination over State executive officials, and the idea of checks and balances was reintroduced into American constitutional thought as a means of maintaining a balance between the two "political" powers of the government. In France the extreme doctrine of the separation of powers also resulted in "legislative dictatorship," but then gave way to autocracy. Dissatisfaction with the results of the extreme separation of powers led to an emphasis upon the unity of power in a system of balanced government, but over the period of the history of the Third and Fourth Republics it seemed that this balance would only be maintained if a greater degree of separation of functions and personnel could be implemented in France. The Fifth Republic Constitution represented an attempt to realize this combination of separation of powers and checks and balances, but in a form which leads one to doubt the sincerity of the Founders' professions that they wished to attain a true balance between the powers of government.

The revolutionary tradition in France had embodied an outright rejection of the theory of the balance or equilibrium of powers; the theory of *contrepoids* was seen as the last resort of a people half enslaved by monarchy or aristocracy. The fierce attachment to the separation of powers as the only alternative theory of constitutional government had found its last great expression in the constitutional debates of the Second Republic. Yet the Constitution of the Second Republic had shown an important deviation from the strict revolutionary tradition. There had been a vague and grudging compromise established between the separation of powers and ministerial responsibility. With the establishment of the Third Republic, however, a new era in French constitutional theory began. The idea of a balance or equilibrium between legislature and executive, or between Parliament and government, became the keynote of constitutional discussion in the periods when the Constitutions of the Third, Fourth, and Fifth

Republics were being created. Even those who were blatantly hoping for something other than a true balance of powers were obliged to defend their proposals through the vocabulary of the equilibrium theory. This conversion to the ancient idea of the balanced constitution, in the form of parliamentary government, whilst to some extent reflecting the influence of the English example, was in fact the outcome of French experience with successive experiments in extremism. The only possible path was a middle way which attempted to avoid the misfortunes of either extreme by balancing the elements of government against each other. The experience of Louis-Napoleon, followed by that of the Paris Commune, presented once again the lessons of French history since 1789. The twin spectres of Caesarism and the Convention haunted the birth of the Third Republic. But already in the last decade of the Second Empire the almost inevitable form of the ensuing régime had been foreseen and forecast. It must be some form of balanced government. In 1861 the duc de Broglie had written: "The only choice which remains for the friends of liberty is that between a republic bordering upon a constitutional monarchy, and a constitutional monarchy bordering upon a republic . . . any other republic is the Convention; any other monarchy is the Empire."[1] In 1868 Prévost-Paradol, in *La France Nouvelle,* stated a very similar point of view.

At the time of the creation of the Third Republic the doctrine of the separation of powers still exercised a considerable influence. In the 1860's Ducrocq used it to analyse the institutions of the Second Empire, and in 1869 Eugène Poitou affirmed that the principle was no longer open to debate; it was, he wrote, everywhere seen as the prime condition of liberty.[2] Five years after the Republic came into existence Fuzier-Herman claimed the doctrine as a French invention which had now reached in the new Constitution its definitive form. He quoted from the works of contemporaries to illustrate the wide acceptance it enjoyed.[3] Yet the doctrine of the separation of powers did not play the role in the Assembly that drew up

1. *Vues sur le gouvernement de la France,* 1870.

2. *La liberté civile et le pouvoir administratif en France,* Paris, 1869, p. 20.

3. E. Fuzier-Herman, *La séparation des pouvoirs d'après l'histoire et le droit constitutionnel comparé,* Paris, 1880, pp. 290–1, and 588–93.

the constitutional instruments of the Third Republic that it had played in earlier constitutional assemblies. It was principally in connection with the administrative jurisdiction of the *Conseil d'Etat* that its arguments were deployed.[4] Discussion was now dominated by the problem of how to create a balance between executive and legislature, and, above all, by the problem of the constitution of the executive power. This latter issue so dominated men's minds, and the feeling it created was so intense, that it is difficult to give to the work of the Assembly any coherent ideological pattern. The Constitution of 1875 was not designed as a great architectural monument; it was rather, said the historian Hanotaux, a building in the design of which master-builder and plasterer's labourer alike had had a hand.[5] Nevertheless, the idea of an equilibrium between executive and legislature, the sharing of the power of government subject to the control of the electorate, was the one thread that ran through the debates. Neither the monarchists nor the extreme republicans could hope for, or indeed propose, a form of government far divorced from that which duc Victor de Broglie had foreseen in 1861. Thus de Ventavon, the *rapporteur* of the *Commission des Trente*, when he put to the Assembly the proposals which would govern the period of Macmahon's presidency, even before the form of a republic had been decided upon, insisted that the President's proposed power of dissolution was to ensure that the country might judge between the legislative and executive powers.[6] The laws of 1875 represented, on paper at least, a carefully balanced system of government, in which the power of dissolution was offset by the need to obtain the approval of the Senate for its use, together with ministerial responsibility to Parliament.

The separation of powers in its extreme form did not, therefore, play the role in the Constitution of the Third Republic that had characterized earlier constitutional thought in France, although its influence remained so strong that, in the early years of the Republic, ministers refrained from exercising their vote in the Chamber, even when defeat might result from their abstention. Yet there was, of course, implicit in this scheme of linked

4. *Journal Officiel*, 19–20 February 1872, pp. 1196–7 and 1216.
5. G. Hanotaux, *Histoire de la France contemporaine (1871–1900)*, Paris, Vol. III, pp. 322–3.
6. *Journal Officiel*, 22 Jan. 1875, p. 565.

yet divided powers of government, a strong attachment to the notion of a partial separation of powers. For the *Constitution* of the Third Republic, whatever its practical operation, emphatically did not embody a *fusion* of powers. Thus those jurists, like Léon Duguit, who expounded the Constitution as a properly balanced system of parliamentary government were forced to develop a complex and somewhat ambivalent attitude towards the separation of powers. Their problem was more difficult than that which Dicey had faced in England, for in France the liberal attachment to the Rousseauist view of the generality of the law remained very strong indeed; and this idea, closely related both in history and logic to the functional categories of the separation of powers, forced liberal jurists to maintain limits to the "proper" functions of each of the branches of government, at the same time that they were attacking the extreme doctrine of the separation of powers in defence of the parliamentary *régime.* Thus the potential incompatibility between the theory of government and the theory of law, which has characterized British thought during the past century, has been still more acutely felt in France.

A further complication arose from the need to justify and expound the French system of administrative law, which we have seen was closely related, after the Revolution, to the extreme doctrine of the separation of powers. One major justification of the existence of special administrative courts was the doctrine that the judiciary should not have the power of interfering in the functions of the administration. De Broglie and Poitou, on the other hand, had used the doctrine of the separation of powers to attack the system of administrative courts, arguing that they enabled the executive to wield judicial power. Thus the French jurists of the Third Republic conducted a complicated operation on the doctrine of the separation of powers. They rejected the strict separation of persons and functions implicit in the historical doctrine, at the same time developing a complex and detailed body of ideas concerning the intrinsic nature of the functions of government and their articulation. With much greater complexity and legalistic fervour, the same battle was fought that Grey, Bagehot, and Dicey had engaged in, with the difference that the less sophisticated English treatment of these problems had enabled much of the controversy to be glossed over in rather vague formulae, whereas in France the divisive elements in constitutional theory were made much more explicit, and battle lines were formed which still today play a significant part in French legal and political thought. Much of this discussion was legalistic in the extreme, and seemingly quite arid to anyone concerned with the understanding of the operation of working political systems. Nevertheless, the broad outlines of this strand of French legal thought help to demonstrate the dilemma of the modern constitutionalist, for these French jurists attempted to reduce to precise legal formulae the concepts which they believed to be at the very heart of Western constitutionalism. If we cannot today accept their formulation of the structure and functions of government, neither can we wholly reject the assumptions upon which they were based. The jurists of the Third Republic included a number of distinguished names, such as Esmein and Hauriou, but two who tower above the rest, and who represent the major strands of thought, are Léon Duguit and Raymond Carré de Malberg.

When Duguit and other French jurists came to consider the nature of the Constitution of the Third Republic they found to hand a useful reservoir of legal ideas which had been developed in Germany over a considerable period, and which, in spite of the rather different aim of German writers, served to illuminate their own problems. It was in Germany at the end of the eighteenth century that the abstract Rousseauist view of government functions had found its most extreme expression in the work of Immanuel Kant. The three powers in the State, Kant had written in 1796, may be compared to the three propositions in a practical syllogism: the major premiss, the legislative power, lays down the universal law as an act of will; the minor premiss, the executive power, is the making of a command applicable to an action according to the law; and the conclusion, the judicial power, contains the sentence or judgement of right in the particular case under consideration.[7] Having pushed the idea of government functions to this logical extreme Kant insisted that each function should be exercised only by the proper branch of government, and that each "power" was co-ordinate with the others, "as so many moral persons"; at the same time

7. *The Philosophy of Law*, ed. by W. Hastie, Edinburgh, 1887, pp. 165–6.

each was subordinate to the others, in that none could usurp the functions of another; each power was based upon its own principle, maintaining its authority through a particular person.[8] Kant's formulation of the doctrine of the separation of powers was therefore as "pure" and as rigid as it was possible to be, but this extreme formulation of French revolutionary doctrine was hardly likely to suit the conditions of Germany in the nineteenth century. Far from becoming the basis of German thought, Kant's formulation was rather the starting-point for the German school of legal theory which set out to discredit the idea of the separation of powers and to formulate in its place a theory of constitutional monarchy.

The German concept of constitutional monarchy, evolved in particular by Prussian writers, had little in common with the idea of constitutional monarchy in modern Britain, or indeed with that idea as it was developed by Benjamin Constant in early-nineteenth-century France. The Prussian monarch could not be a mere figure-head, or simply exercise the right to arbitrate between the powers of government; he represented the active exercise of the unified power of the State, although subject to certain constitutional restraints. Constitutional monarchy was not seen as a stage in the development towards a system of parliamentary government, but as an alternative to it, a system in its own right, a development from enlightened authoritarianism.[9] This conception was closer to that of the *Charte* of 1814, or to Tudor or Stuart government, than to the system of government in eighteenth- or nineteenth-century Britain. The impulse of the German attack upon the doctrine of the separation of powers was, therefore, that same horror of the destruction of the essential unity of State power which had characterized absolutist theories for centuries, and which had formerly been evoked by the theory of mixed government. At the same time that English liberal theorists were emphasizing the need for harmony in government, and Austin was developing the theory of indivisible sovereign power, German legal theorists were also emphasizing the unity of the State in order to maintain the power and position of the Prussian king. Von Mohl

8. Ibid., p. 170.
9. Otto Hintze, *Staat und Verfassung*, 2nd edn., 1962, p. 365.

attacked the separation of powers as logically false, and leading in practice to the destruction of the State and to anarchy.[10] Bluntschli characterized Kant's syllogism as almost childish.[11] The theorists of the Prussian State, and later of the German Empire, were concerned to reject the idea that the sovereign could be a mere executive officer, but they were also concerned to provide the judicial framework of a *constitutional*, not an arbitrary, system of government. Furthermore, they were well aware of the importance of the bureaucracy, and were interested in setting limits to its power. They therefore adapted the ancient idea of the generality of the law in order to evolve precise criteria for delimiting the proper spheres of the legislative and administrative authorities. These criteria, evolved in terms of the "formal" and the "material" conceptions of government functions, were taken up and further developed by the jurists of the Third Republic.[12]

Paradoxically enough, these two characteristics of the legal theory of monarchist Germany, the emphasis upon the unity of the State, and the means of distinguishing the proper spheres of legislative and administrative authorities, suited very well the needs of liberal French jurists expounding the constitutional law of a republican system of government. With these tools the State could achieve its aims without the possibility of deadlock implicit in earlier theories of constitutionalism, but there would be procedural limits to the exercise of power, with each act of government carried out in a controlled way. However, to these basic principles of the German constitutional monarchy there had to be added another element, drawn from an entirely different source—the concept of "balance" central to the mid-nineteenth-century English theory of parliamentary government. The attempt to combine these disparate concepts of law and government was made above all by Léon Duguit.

In 1893 Duguit attacked the "absolute separation of powers" as an artificial theory, contrary to scientific observation of the facts, and based upon

10. R. von Mohl, *Die Geschichte und Literatur der Staatswissenschaften*, Erlangen, 1855, Vol. I, p. 273.

11. *Allgemeine Staatslehre*, Stuttgart, 1875, Vol. I, p. 489.

12. R. Carré de Malberg, *Contribution à la théorie générale de l'état*, Paris, 1922, Vol. I, pp. 280–3.

a theoretical error.[13] He argued that any distinction between acts of the State will, and the putting of these acts into effect was mistaken. All the functions of the State required acts of will for their implementation, and thus necessitated "a manifestation of the personality of the state." Thus for any function to be exercised the co-operation of all the organs of government was necessary, because they were all essential parts of this corporate personality. Parliamentary government was the most satisfactory political form for a representative democracy because it was based upon the collaboration and solidarity of the powers of government, not upon their separation. In the parliamentary *régime* all the organs of the State participate in the accomplishment of each function.[14] Thus Duguit rejected the absolute separation of powers, but he rejected also the absorption of all power in one set of hands. For Duguit the separation of powers meant the distribution of the functions of the State among its various parts in a way which enabled them to co-operate, whilst dealing principally only with matters within their proper sphere. This conception, he argued, was the direct opposite of that of the separation of powers as it was applied in 1791.[15] And indeed it was, for it was the tradition of Montesquieu rather than of Sieyès which Duguit was evolving. Thus for Duguit the unity of State power did not necessitate the accumulation of this power in one set of hands. There must be some means of ensuring that all power was not absorbed by one branch of government. A parliamentary *régime* reached its proper point of equilibrium only when government and parliament were equal in prestige and influence.[16] This balance had only really been achieved in France, he asserted, during the July Monarchy of Louis-Philippe. In the Third Republic the Constitution had been "deformed," and the equilibrium destroyed, by the dominant position attained by parliament over the government.[17]

Any rigid separation of persons and functions was ruled out by Duguit's view of a balance between the organs of government in constant and

13. "La séparation des pouvoirs et l'Assemblée Nationale de 1789," *Revue d'Economie Politique*, Vol. 7, 1893, pp. 99, and 116 ff.
14. Ibid., p. 99.
15. *Traité de droit constitutionnel*, 2nd edn., Paris, 1921–3, Vol. II, p. 536.
16. Ibid., Vol. II, pp. 639–40.
17. Ibid., Vol. II, pp. 650 and 658.

intimate collaboration with each other, although he did envisage the strict separation of administrative and judicial offices, and the greatest possible independence for the judiciary. If, however, all power was not to "result to the legislature," in Jefferson's phrase, or to be usurped by a Bonaparte (the other extreme which the balanced constitution of the Third Republic was intended to avoid), then there must be some functional basis for the juridical division of powers between the organs of government. Upon what other juristic principle could the accumulation of power be resisted? It was, therefore, quite logical for Duguit to adapt to this end the distinction between the formal and the material conceptions of government functions which had been elaborated by Jellinek and Laband in Germany. The formal conception of the functions of government classifies each government act purely according to the organ of government from which it emanated. Thus any action of the legislature is "legislative," whatever its content. The material conception of government functions, however, the validity of which Duguit strongly defended, insists that the acts of government must be identified, not according to the process by which they are evolved, but by their content, according to their "intrinsic nature."[18] The criterion for distinguishing between the legislative and other functions is, once again, the idea of the generality of law. Only an abstract rule stated in general terms, and no other act of government, can claim the status of law. A decision given on a particular, concrete instance cannot be "a law" in the material sense, although if it emanates from the legislature it is "a law" in the formal sense; from the material point of view it will be, according to the circumstances, an administrative or a judicial act.[19] Thus Duguit suggested that the law passed by parliament in the Dreyfus case was an *"excès de pouvoir"* because it concerned only an individual.[20] The generality of the law becomes therefore the key to the understanding of the intrinsic nature of the functions of government. It is its generality that gives to law its sanction: *"la généralité est la raison d'être même de la loi."*[21]

18. Ibid., 1st edn., Vol. I, pp. 130–1.
19. Ibid., Vol. I, p. 135.
20. Ibid., 1921–7 edn., Vol. I, p. 196.
21. *Manuel de droit constitutionnel*, 4th edn., Paris, 1923, pp. 94–95.

The "principle of legality" remained for Duguit the central, essential, characteristic of the constitutional State. He did not imagine that the formal and the material aspects of government acts would always, or should always, coincide. The executive will sometimes exercise the power to make generally applicable rules, it will "legislate," but the existence of a recognized criterion by which such situations can be evaluated would enable a check to be kept upon the extent to which the principle of legality was being adhered to. The greater the confusion of the material functions of government, the more the system of government was likely to move away from a position of balance towards the accumulation and abuse of power. Yet although Duguit insisted that this set of constitutional concepts was embodied in the constitutional law of the Third Republic, he did not, of course, believe that the French system of government represented in practice the ideal of balance to which he aspired; it was not a system of government in which an equilibrium of powers and functions could easily be discerned. The discrepancy between the theory of law, in its fullest sense, and the practice of "parliamentary government" was only too clear.

It was Carré de Malberg who seized upon the idealistic elements in Duguit's constitutional theory and insisted that there must be a thorough-going realism in the analysis of law and State. He moved still further away from the theory of the separation of powers, rejecting the co-ordinate status which Duguit had attributed to government and parliament. Carré de Malberg might be seen as the Walter Bagehot of French jurisprudence, for he insisted upon the unity of State power organized hierarchically under the direction of the legislature. His legal theory reflected the practice of the Third Republic, whereas Duguit's had reflected the way in which the latter would have *liked* the Republic to operate. Whereas Bagehot's characterization of the British cabinet as a committee of the legislature was highly misleading, Carré de Malberg's rather similar view of the supremacy of the French legislature over the government was very much closer to the truth. The Third Republic was not a system of parliamentary government as understood by Earl Grey or Léon Duguit, nor was it a system of *gouvernement d'assemblée;* rather it was a system half-way between these two, a system of *government by delegation.* The Chamber did not itself govern, but the government had no real prerogatives; it was not the equal of the Chamber, and the latter could and did interfere with the day-to-day affairs of government.[22]

The Constitution of the Third Republic provided no safeguard for the "principle of legality," said Malberg, any more than the British Constitution safeguarded the rule of law. Thus he rejected the whole "material" view of government functions as quite baseless. There was no criterion to be found in French law for the division of the functions of government according to their content. To attempt to establish such a distinction was to confuse the *tasks* of the State with its *functions*. The science of jurisprudence was not concerned with the nature of the ends to which State action is directed, but only with its juridical effects. Legal acts of very different kinds may be employed to achieve the same ends.[23] There was thus only one tenable view of the nature of the functions of government under French law, and that was the so-called "formal" view. The legislature had the full, free, autonomous power to act, and all other governmental officers exercised their powers, however wide or narrow, in accordance with this legislative authority. There was no objective distinction to be made between the powers of the legislature and the executive or the administration; it was entirely a matter for parliament to decide.[24]

This unflinching assertion of legislative supremacy led Carré de Malberg to reject any formulation of the separation of powers, even one as weak as that of Duguit, which was intended to suggest the co-ordinate status of the organs of government, and, of course, to reject the idea of parliamentary government with its balance between parliament and government. There must be in every State, he argued, a single, unique source of power, which was by definition indivisible, but which could manifest itself in a number of forms, necessitating therefore a number of distinct agencies of government. Nevertheless, all these different forms of action, or agencies of government, contribute to a common end, the assurance of the domination of a single and indivisible will. The "separation of powers"

22. G. Burdeau, *Traité de Science Politique*, Paris, 1957, Vol. IV, p. 351; and Vol. V, pp. 743–4.
23. *Contribution à la théorie générale de l'état*, Paris, 1922, Vol. I, p. 204.
24. Ibid., Vol. I, p. 361.

can therefore mean at most only the expedient division of the work of government in a way that will ensure the predominance of this will, that is in a hierarchical fashion. A hierarchy of government powers through which parliament can obtain complete obedience from executive, administrative, or judicial officers is the only logical, acceptable structure of government.[25]

The positions represented by Duguit and Carré de Malberg are illustrative, in juristic terms, of the two main strands of thought which run throughout French history from 1875 to the present day. Duguit represented the aspiration to balanced and limited government; Carré de Malberg acknowledged the fact that there were no limits to the power of parliament and no internal checks to its exercise. Malberg did not present a crude view of the "fusion" of powers, but for him there could be no equality in their relationships, only a subordination of one to the other. These conflicting principles of balance and hierarchy constitute the dilemma of French constitutionalists in the twentieth century. The realism of Malberg's jurisprudence did not lead, however, to the eclipse of the opposing viewpoint. The disadvantages of the system of government by delegation from parliament led to continual demands for some reintroduction of the principle of balance, and the ideas which led to the Constitution of the Fifth Republic were an attempt to combine, in a somewhat uneasy alliance, the principles of Duguit and Carré de Malberg.

The work of Carré de Malberg represents a low point in the prestige of the theory of the separation of powers in French thought, yet within a few years the signs of a resurgence were already evident. The aspirations for a balanced system of government remained strong, and although it was to be some years before the importance of the separation of powers to this balance was given much weight, nevertheless the groundwork was laid in the latter part of the life of the Third Republic, and also during the Occupation, in the thought given to the future Constitution of France by some sections of the Resistance. The tendency towards *gouvernement d'assemblée*, which was feared in the governmental instability of the Third Republic, led even those who had no sympathy at all for the doctrine of the separation

---

25. Ibid., Vol. I, pp. 346–7; and Vol. II, pp. 24 and 114–22.

of powers to explore the means of restoring a degree of equilibrium into the relationships between government and parliament. Thus Léon Blum in 1918 was far from proposing any degree of separation of legislature from executive, arguing that the two must be inter-dependent, penetrating one another; nevertheless he wished to see the government strengthened to make it the master of the Chamber, not in a despotic sense, but rather in the sense of a school-master or ballet-master who would lead rather than dictate.[26] He wished to see the establishment of an equilibrium between government and parliament, but not by the use of constitutional rules so much as by the operation of trial and error. The problem of escaping from the system of government by delegation without a fundamental change in the Constitution, however, is well illustrated by this line of argument. Those proposed solutions of the problems of the Third Republic that emphasized the need to change the electoral and party systems concentrated upon the need to change political *behaviour* without changes in constitutional structure. It amounted to little more than the request for more responsible behaviour on the part of politicians and voters alike. However, the delicate conditions required for an effective balance between government and legislature in a parliamentary system could hardly be created by such appeals to good behaviour. It was the recognition of this fact in later years, during the life of the Fourth Republic, that led to the reassessment of the role of constitutional rules in order to attain this balance.

In the 1930's an appraisal of this kind was in fact made by André Tardieu. Like Blum, Tardieu wished to create a balance between government and parliament, but he placed more faith in constitutional revision as a means of achieving this aim. He deplored the influence of Bagehot, whose ideas had been taken up by Gambetta and Ferry, and who had reduced the status of the cabinet to that of the mere delegate of the parliamentary majority.[27] The consequence had been the absorption of the executive power by the legislature. The remedy was to give to the executive an untrammelled power of dissolution, and to impose constitutional limitations

26. Léon Blum, *La réforme gouvernementale*, 2nd edn., Paris, 1936, pp. 150 and 164.
27. A. Tardieu, *La réforme de l'état*, Paris, 1934, p. 29.

upon the power of the Chamber, in particular its legislative power.[28] The ideas of André Tardieu and René Capitant in the 1930's are closely related to the work of Michel Debré in the following two decades.[29] During the Occupation Debré took part in discussions concerning the future form of government for France, and the role of the separation of powers, as a means of countering left-wing tendencies towards some form of *gouvernement d'assemblée*, became more evident. In 1942–3, in the clandestine press, the "absolute confusion of powers" was blamed for the defects in the Third Republic system of government. The way in which deputies fought for ministerial office was a major cause of governmental instability. The executive power was the mere delegate of the legislature that had itself conducted the administration of the country, all because ministers were chosen from within the Assembly.[30] The legislature, this author asserted, had also encroached upon the sphere of the judiciary, and had therefore accomplished the concentration of all power in their hands. In future the President of France should be obliged to choose his ministers from outside the legislature, a requirement demanded by the "absolute necessity" of separating the legislative and executive powers.[31] It is important to note, however, that the *Comité Général d'Etudes* of the Resistance in 1944 stressed that "parliamentary government" provided the only available pattern for the future government of France, emphasizing, however, that this system necessitated a separation of the responsibilities of executive and legislature.[32] With the example of the Vichy *régime* before their eyes, a system of government based upon a strong executive seemed to provide little encouragement as a pattern for France to follow; and therefore, for the time being at least, the role of the separation of powers was seen as the means of achieving that balance in the system of parliamentary government that the Third Republic had so singularly failed to attain.

28. Ibid., pp. 29 and 44–46; also N. Wahl, "Aux origines de la nouvelle Constitution," *Revue Française de Science Politique,* Vol. IX, No. 1, 1959, pp. 59–61.

29. See Wahl, op. cit., pp. 49 and 60–61.

30. M. Blocq-Mascart, *Chroniques de la Résistance,* Paris, 1945, p. 124.

31. Ibid., pp. 128–9.

32. H. Michel and B. Mirkine-Guetzévitch, *Les idées politiques et sociales de la Résistance,* Paris, 1954, p. 291.

The resurgent interest in the separation of powers as an instrument for the forging of a true system of parliamentary government found, however, little expression in the Constituent Assemblies of the Fourth Republic. The experience of the Vichy *régime*, together with the dominant position held by the Communists and Socialists, ensured that there would be no strong independent executive power in the new Constitution. The extreme Left favoured a powerful, almost unchecked single-chamber Assembly. Yet the most striking fact about the constitutional debates of the Fourth Republic is the predominant position given to the idea of balanced government by all sides. In spite of the "unbalanced" nature of their proposed Constitution, the arguments of the Left, as presented by Pierre Cot, the *rapporteur-général* of the Committee on the Constitution, were based upon the necessity of creating a balanced constitution, an equilibrium between legislative and executive powers. The Constituent Assembly was treated to the remarkable spectacle of the spokesman of the extreme Left employing the vocabulary of the balanced constitution which had been so decisively rejected at the time of the Revolution. That Lally-Tollendal and Pierre Cot should be able, in very differing circumstances it is true, to utilize much the same arguments to very different ends, is an extreme illustration of the difficulties that face the constitutionalist. That Pierre Cot was arguing very much with his tongue in his cheek does not detract in any way from the importance that has been attached to the theory of equilibrium in modern France; rather it was an acknowledgment that no other constitutional theory was acceptable to the great body of Frenchmen. It might be seen as a victory for constitutionalism that the first draft Constitution was rejected in the referendum of May 1946, and that the main argument used against the proposals put forward by the Left was that they did not in fact embody that balanced system of government upon which they claimed to be based.

Naturally enough, the attachment which the left-wing parties publicly exhibited to the idea of balance did not extend also to the separation of powers. Indeed, Cot took the opportunity of launching an attack upon the doctrine. The revolutionary theory was no longer relevant, he argued. It was now necessary to think in terms of collaboration between organs of government entrusted with different functions.[33] The "old theory of the separation of powers," said Cot, must be seen simply as a special case of the principle of the division of labour. To isolate this special case, and to set it up as a dogma, would be to fail to recognize that it was no longer relevant to the problems of a democracy. Instead there must be established a system of *"contrepoids et d'équilibre"* which would ensure the continuity of government and the *"souplesse du pouvoir."* [34] Thus was the revolutionary tradition completely reversed, the doctrines of Sieyès replaced by those of Mirabeau as the constitutional theory of the Left. The full irony of the trend of bourgeois constitutional thought since the mid nineteenth century was realized on that day in the French Constituent Assembly. The concentration of power in the parliamentary Assembly, with only those internal checks that could be provided by the party system, previously the basis of nineteenth-century liberal democracy, was now the aim of a left wing that scented power. Pierre Cot's arguments were also those of Duguit, but Cot knew that the type of party system which alone could provide the balanced government he professed to desire did not, and could not, exist. It is hardly surprising, perhaps, that the experience of the Fourth Republic, in its inception and in its operation, led those who feared the power of the Left to turn away from the reliance upon a system of government which placed all the onus of achieving a balance upon the working of the party system, back towards a more strictly *constitutional* approach to the balance of power.

It was hotly denied by Pierre Cot that the left-wing draft Constitution embodied a system of *gouvernement d'assemblée*, but the attack made upon this draft, in particular by the M.R.P., was based upon the assertion that *gouvernement d'assemblée* was implicit, if not explicit, in the proposed Constitution.[35] The generally accepted assumption of the need for a balance between executive and legislature was not in fact realized in the Committee's proposals, it was alleged. Pierre Courant, speaking for the *républicains indépendants*, was as strongly opposed as Pierre Cot to a *régime* of separated powers, but, he argued, the checks and balances with which

33. *Journal Officiel*, 19 Apr. 1946, p. 1622.
34. Ibid., p. 1620.
35. *Journal Officiel*, 1946, pp. 1624, 1633.

nineteenth-century constitutionalists had replaced this outmoded notion were absent in the draft Constitution. Every effort must be made by the Assembly to attain that "perfect equilibrium" which alone could prevent the improper exercise of power.[36] It was left to René Capitant to argue that a separation of powers, in modern form, was *necessary* to this equilibrium. The system of parliamentary government, he insisted, was a modern version of the separation of powers, but it required an effective, powerful executive if it was to be realized in practice.[37]

The theory of equilibrium formed also the basis of Paul Coste-Floret's argument when he introduced the second draft Constitution into the Assembly, although it was little different in effect from the earlier draft, which his party had attacked as embodying a system of *gouvernement d'assemblée.* Coste-Floret rejected both the "absolute" separation of powers which characterized a presidential system of government, and the "confusion of powers" which *gouvernement d'assemblée* represented. To this extent he implied an adherence to the principle of a partial separation of powers, quoting Duguit in support of his view of a harmonious organization of the organs of government, built upon the principle of "the differentiation and the collaboration of the functions of the State."[38] But merely to denounce *gouvernement d'assemblée* and to praise "harmony" is not enough. The critical problem, as the experience of the Third Republic had shown, was to find a way of avoiding government by delegation from the Assembly, and to establish the balance between parliament and government that parliamentary government in the strict sense implied. The amendments embodied in the second draft Constitution were not sufficient to achieve this aim, and the Fourth Republic, like the Third, never achieved that balance which the constitution-makers seemed to prize so highly.

The Constitutions of the Third and Fourth Republics represented, therefore, a complete change in the constitutional theory of republicanism. The separation of powers forming the backbone of the earlier tradition was rejected, and the theory of balance took its place. However, just as the

36. Ibid., p. 1630.
37. Ibid., pp. 1669–71.
38. *Journal Officiel,* 1946, Document 350, p. 293.

separation of powers, so fiercely maintained in theory, had not been adhered to in practice in the First and Second Republics, so in the Third and
Fourth Republics the theory of equilibrium, which had loomed so large in
the constitutional debates at their inception, did not materialize in practice.
Indeed, by a strange irony of history, the practice of the Third and Fourth
Republics came close to realizing the spirit, if not the letter, of the doctrines of the separation of powers that the Constituent Assemblies had so
fiercely repudiated. For the system of government by delegation from the
Assembly lies half-way between that model of *gouvernement d'assemblée*,
in which the Assembly itself wields all the powers of government, and
the ideal of parliamentary government, in which the cabinet is more than
a mere executive, having the power to initiate and secure the passage of
legislation and the acceptance of its policies. In the system of government
by delegation from the Assembly the cabinet is drawn *from* the Assembly, but it is not *of* it. The deputies in the Third and Fourth Republics held
governments at arm's length. There was no close collaboration between
government and parliament; rather a distrust of, and a hostility towards,
the government, which set it apart even from the members of the parties
that composed it. The governments of the Third and Fourth Republics were
not *commis*, as the ministers had been under the Convention, but they
were almost in the position of the "mere executives" of the pure doctrine of
the separation of powers. The comparison with the American States after
1776 is close. There the Governor was elected by a legislature jealous of
its power, treating him as an "executive" in the narrowest sense. In both
situations there were no real limits to the power of the legislature, which
could, and did, "meddle" in matters better left to executive and judicial
officers. The Third and Fourth Republics experienced all the disadvantages
of a system of separated powers under Constitutions set up under the ban-
ners of "harmony" and "balance," whilst those who wished to escape from
this situation increasingly emphasized the importance of the separation of
powers as a means of attaining balanced government. Just as Jefferson in
his *Notes on the State of Virginia* had called for "barriers" to the exercise
of power, in the form of checks and balances that would make the separation of powers a reality, so now the critics of the Fourth Republic called for

a more formal adherence to the separation of powers in order to make the system of balanced government a reality.

The demand for more effective barriers to the power of the legislature had been expressed during the life of the Third Republic and during the German occupation, but the most powerful, if somewhat vague, expression of this point of view came from General de Gaulle in June 1946 at Bayeux, before the discussion of the second draft Constitution. The importance of some degree of separation of powers to the system of balance or equilibrium was clearly stated by the General. "Both experience and principle require that the public powers—legislative, executive, judicial—should be clearly separated and strongly balanced." If, however, the General continued, the executive were to be drawn from the legislature, there would result that confusion of powers in which government soon becomes nothing more than an assemblage of delegates. How long could unity and cohesion be maintained in government if the executive power originated from the power which it is supposed to balance?[39] Thus the two ideas of the separation and balance of powers, which had had such a complex relationship in the history of French thought, were reunited again by de Gaulle, as they had been reunited in the thoughts of the Founding Fathers at Philadelphia. This comparison between the two situations is by no means a fanciful one, for the constitutional problems of the United States and France are much more closely related than they seem at first sight. Yet already there were disturbing elements in the General's vision. In addition to balancing the legislative and executive powers he envisaged the creation of a power of arbitration, above the contingencies of day-to-day politics, which would not be derived from the political parties but be independent of them. This might mean no more than the creation of an office similar to that of the constitutional monarch in the thought of Benjamin Constant, or it might be something rather different, with a positive, active role in government. Experience was to show which of these roles the President in such a Republic would perform.

By the mid 1950's the possibility of the creation of some form of presi-

---

39. *L'année politique*, 1946, Paris, 1947, pp. 537–8.

---

dential system, ruled out in 1946, was being widely discussed. Maurice Duverger engaged in the discussion of a form of "neo-parliamentarism" in which a popularly elected prime minister would work alongside a parliament subject to automatic dissolution if it should reject his proposals.[40] A public opinion poll taken in the spring of 1956 showed a majority in favour of the direct election of the prime minister at the same time as the election of deputies.[41] It was Michel Debré, however, who developed most explicitly the combination of the separation of powers and balanced government that seemed most likely to create those conditions of stability and the controlled exercise of power which the party system had failed to provide in the context of the Constitution of the Fourth Republic. Of the necessity of the separation of the powers of government Debré was in no doubt; only in this way could the abuse of power be avoided.[42] But Debré's attitude to the separation of powers was by no means naïve. He was not an advocate of the absolute separation of powers; rather he wished to integrate this idea into a philosophy of mid-twentieth-century government which recognized all the criticisms that had been made against the pure doctrine as it had been conceived in an earlier age. Debré attempted to combine three rather different strands of constitutional thought. He was as concerned with the control of power, especially legislative power, as Montesquieu had been; the idea of balance and harmony which had infused the work of Duguit was also central to Debré's thought; finally, he was as concerned for the maintenance of the unity of the State power, and therefore of the recognition of a degree of hierarchical organization of the parts of the State, as had been Carré de Malberg.

Debré asserted the necessity of the division of power in the democratic State in terms which are almost a paraphrase of Montesquieu. The division of power in a democracy, he wrote, required that authority should not be concentrated in one set of hands. No man, no government, no assembly may freely dispose of the destiny of the nation, nor of a single citizen.[43]

40. See J. Georgel, *Critiques et réforme des constitutions de la République*, Paris, 1959.
41. Le Club Jean Moulin, *L'Etat et le citoyen*, Paris, 1961, pp. 348–9.
42. M. Debré, *La République et son pouvoir*, Paris, 1950, p. 80.
43. M. Debré, *Ces princes qui nous gouvernent . . .* , Paris, 1957, p. 20.

Some form of separation of powers was, therefore, an essential prerequisite of the democratic State. However, there was a paradox at the heart of the idea of the separation of powers, a paradox which reflected the central problem of democracy. It was necessary to divide the authority of government, yet such division carried within it the grave risk of the irresponsible exercise of power. The unity of State power was essential to the stability of the State and its effective operation. There must be, therefore, above the separate and specialized parts of the State, an authority which would ensure the coherence of government acts, and offset the weaknesses inherent in a system of separated powers.[44] This emphasis upon division and unity, which recalls the thought of Sieyès and Constant, enabled Debré to criticize the Fourth Republic, both on the ground that the powers of government were "confused" in one set of hands, and also on the ground that "power" was too divided, too broken up to enable the government to be carried on effectively. A satisfactory system of government must satisfy two conditions, he argued: first, it must allow the tasks of government to be divided up with "clarity" between the different organs of government; second, it must allow the government, wrongly termed "the executive," to attain a degree of stability and cohesion. The Fourth Republic failed on both counts. All power was concentrated in the Assembly, which intervened improperly in all fields of government action, so that the first condition was not met. At the same time the Assembly was divided into factional groups, so that power was fragmented and destroyed, and thus the second condition was not met either. "There was confusion where there should have been clarity, dispersion of power where there should have been unity."[45]

The solution to the problem of division and unity was not to be found, said Debré, in the system of the Fourth Republic, which he inaccurately described as *gouvernement d'assemblée*, nor in a system of presidential government. In the former the powers of government are confused and disintegrated; in the latter they are too rigidly separated and therefore equally disintegrated. The only alternative was to be found in a system of collaboration of powers, in a parliamentary *régime* properly so called. Thus Debré

44. *La République et son pouvoir*, pp. 38 and 81.
45. *Ces princes qui nous gouvernent*, pp. 23–24, 29.

---

returned to that theme of balanced parliamentary government which had dominated French thought for nearly a century. In defending the Consti-tution of the Fifth Republic Debré claimed to be establishing for the first time a *true* parliamentary system.[46] M. Janot, representing the government before the Constitutional Consultative Committee, referred to it as a "puri-fied" parliamentary *régime*.[47] Yet it is difficult to accept at its face value the theory that this was a completely sincere attempt to create a balanced sys-tem of the sort that Duguit had wished to see. The idea of a parliamentary *régime* in which the members of the cabinet are forbidden to be members of the legislature, although they remain responsible to that legislature, is a little difficult to grasp. This separation of personnel was necessary, accord-ing to M. Janot, to avoid the temptation, to which deputies succumbed in the Third and Fourth Republics, of defeating the government in the hope of office. The separation of cabinet and parliament might be accepted as a means of giving the former a degree of independence of the latter, but, taken together with the introduction of the referendum, and of the devices which favoured the passage of the budget and of government legislation, it would seem designed to create a degree of executive dominance compa-rable to that of modern British government, rather than to the position of a cabinet in a system of balanced parliamentary government. Critics of the Constitution have called it an Orleanist *régime*,[48] a mixture of presidential and parliamentary government,[49] or a system intended to lead to the *efface-ment* of Parliament.[50] More recent developments in the actual operation of the Fifth Republic have led to charges that, far from creating a system of balanced government, the *régime* has been turned into a system of direct government which has by-passed parliament altogether.

The Constitution of the Fifth Republic also incorporated another ele-ment of the nineteenth-century liberal view of constitutionalism, but, like the idea of balanced government, turned it into something very different in

46. "La Nouvelle Constitution," *Revue française de science politique,* March 1959, pp. 8–10.

47. Comité Consultatif Constitutionnel, *Travaux préparatoires de la Constitution,* Paris, 1960, p. 44.

48. M. Duverger, *Revue française de science politique,* 1959, p. 103.

49. Georgel, op. cit., Vol. II, pp. 120–1.

50. M. Duverger, *Institutions politiques et droit constitutionnel,* 5th edn., Paris, 1960, p. 688.

spirit and in practice. The material conception of government functions had characterized the work of Duguit and of those jurists who were not prepared to accept the thoroughgoing doctrine of parliamentary supremacy of Carré de Malberg. A set of criteria for distinguishing the law-making function of Parliament from the rule-making powers of the government was incorporated into the Constitution of the Fifth Republic, so setting up for the first time a specific, if obscure, constitutional basis for the "material" view of government functions. There was now a criterion for deciding what was, and what was not, a valid legislative act, and a Constitutional Council to apply it. Yet this was the old liberal view of the material view of government functions stood upon its head. It was true that Duguit had believed that Parliament could exceed its proper powers, as in the Dreyfus case, but his criterion of the validity of law had been its generality, whereas now the express purpose of making explicit the limits of the "legislative power" was to give to the government the power to make general rules in its own sphere of competence. On behalf of the government, Janot blamed the pure doctrine of the separation of powers as it had operated, he said, under the Third and Fourth Republics, for the system of *gouvernement d'assemblée* which had then emerged. What was needed now was a new division of powers which broke away from the old categories and which would allow the government to make general rules without the sanction of Parliament.[51]

The complex history of constitutional ideas from the Third Republic to the Fifth poses some very acute problems for the student of constitutionalism. It illustrates how the same theoretical arguments can be turned to very different uses, and how wide the gap often is between expressed aims and actual behaviour. The ideal of balanced government which has been the theme of constitutional government since 1875 has never been even closely approximated in practice. Either the Assembly has treated the government as a mere delegate, looking upon it as a committee of the legislature in the true sense of that phrase; or the realization of a strengthened executive has been the result of the desire to dominate the legislature rather than to balance it, or to accept the techniques of direct democracy rather than

51. *Travaux préparatoires*, p. 45.

accept the difficulties of governing through the representative Assembly. This disparity between theory and practice raises some important questions. If the concept of a balanced constitution is used more as a means of placing one's political opponents at a disadvantage than to effect a genuine balance, what weight can we place upon such constitutional arguments or constitutional devices? Equally important has been the question raised by the experience of the Third and Fourth Republics concerning the relationship between systems of parliamentary government and constitutionalism. Towards the end of the Fourth Republic Georges Burdeau pointed out that it was impossible to create a true parliamentary system by constitutional fiat. The basis of such a system was the party structure, not legal rules, and this necessary party structure could not be created by legislation.[52] The same point has been made more recently in publications of the Club Jean Moulin. The idea of a "constitution" comes therefore to be directly associated with a presidential system of government. It is impossible, said the *Bulletin du Club Jean Moulin* in 1962, to "decree parliamentary government," whereas it is possible to create and establish a presidential system by constitutional edict. A parliamentary system, the *Bulletin* continued, is not a body of legal rules, it is a "collection of structures," a set of given historical and sociological facts. In the last analysis there exist no parliamentary constitutions, only parliamentary structures. Thus a country can provide itself with a presidential constitution in order to realize a democratic system of government when history and sociology refuse it the conditions necessary for a parliamentary *régime*.[53] These insights into the practice and problems of constitutionalism presented by the history of France would have to be given full weight in any attempt to remodel constitutionalism for the twentieth century.

---

52. G. Burdeau, *Traité de science politique*, Vol. V, p. 745.

53. *Bulletin du Club Jean Moulin*, No. 31, juin–juillet 1962, p. 3, quoted in *Démocratie aujourd'hui*, Paris, 1963, pp. 112–13.

TEN

Progressivism and Political Science
in America

THE CONSTITUTIONAL theory of the United States down to the Civil War was dominated by the interaction between the two doctrines of the separation of powers and checks and balances, forming a complex pattern of opposition and inter-action, until they both dissolved into a number of tactical political positions with little coherence or consistency. The confused picture of constitutional thought presented in the 1840's and 1850's is indicative of the extent to which neither of these old theories of constitutionalism any longer possessed the ideological fire of an earlier age. Both represented points of view fast becoming inadequate in the face of the tasks of government in the modern world. Yet at the end of the Civil War the formal Constitution of the United States still embodied that combination of the separation of powers and checks and balances which the men of 1787 had devised, and indeed it still does so today. It seemed, therefore, that the triumph of the Union over the Confederacy was a confirmation of the constitutional system not only against the threat of secession, but in its entirety. When Cooley published his *Constitutional Limitations* in 1868 the work of the Founding Fathers seemed more secure against attack than at any time since the Convention dispersed in 1787. More important, the Constitution, with its elaborate barriers to the exercise of effective governmental power, suited very well the aims of that group of flourishing big-business men who were to dominate politics in the latter part of the nineteenth century, giving to it the character of the age of the tycoon. The high point of this philosophy of government in an industrial age was reached, perhaps, in 1918, when in the child-labour case the Supreme Court invalidated as unconstitutional the attempt by Congress to limit the hours of work for children in factories to eight hours a day. Nevertheless, the Civil War did mark a turning-point in American political thought, for it ushered in a long, intense period of criticism and attack upon the established constitutional theory, of an unprecedented ferocity, conducted alike by practical politicians, journalists, and academics.

The growth of the trusts and the concentration of economic power, the wealth and political influence of a few men, and the nature of politics in what Lippmann has called the twenty dangerous and humiliating years between the death of Lincoln and the rise of Grover Cleveland, called into existence an impressive protest, a demand for reform that built up through the Granger, Greenback, and Populist movements to its climax in Progressivism. This was another of those great democratic revolts against power and privilege which had characterized the modern world since the mid seventeenth century, but now it was a revolt with a different ideological impulse. It was no longer an attack upon oppressive arbitrary rule taking the form of demands for freedom *from* government action, but a demand *for* government to act to deal with pressing economic and social problems. It was an attack upon a constitutional system that allowed these problems to be shelved, or indeed required them to be shelved. Thus although, as on earlier occasions, this democratic onslaught was directed at the system of checks and balances which entrenched privilege, it was no longer based upon the rival principle of the pure separation of powers; on the contrary it was directed equally against that doctrine, in its extreme form at any rate, as one of the factors making for an ineffectual and weak system of government. Changing attitudes towards the nature of freedom and the role of government in society demanded a new approach and a consequent rejection of the over-simplified theories of earlier liberal constitutionalists. The need now was for a system of government that would give expression to the growing demands for government action, a system in which the unity of the "powers" of government would be as important a consideration as their separation. As early as 1864 George H. Pendleton introduced into Congress the first of a long line of bills which proposed a closer relationship between the Congress and the Administration,[1] and only fourteen years after the end of the Civil War the young Woodrow Wilson wrote his essay proposing the adoption of cabinet government in America.[2]

The attack upon the dominant constitutional theory at the end of the nineteenth and the beginning of the twentieth century fired, therefore, with both barrels. The attack upon privilege, and upon those constitutional checks and balances which, by denying majority rule, protected privilege, had something of the flavour of the Jeffersonian attacks upon the Constitution of a century earlier. They embodied demands for popular control over all the agencies of government not very different from those of John Taylor of Caroline, for they rejected entirely the concept of independent branches of government nicely balanced against each other. Franklin Pierce called the American Constitution "the most undemocratic instrument to be found in any country in the world today."[3] A Constitution containing so many checks and balances, he wrote, was a constant temptation to both President and Congress to usurp power.[4] J. Allen Smith thundered against the monarchic and aristocratic elements in the Constitution, and against the legislative role of the judiciary.[5] These undemocratic features should be replaced by an easier amending process and by the adoption of the initiative, the referendum, and the recall. Such devices would make it possible for the people to maintain their control over all the officers of government,

1. See Stephen Horn, *The Cabinet and Congress*, New York, 1960, for a full discussion of the history of these proposals.
2. "Cabinet Government in the United States," *International Review*, August 1879.
3. *Federal Usurpation*, New York, 1908, p. 389.
4. Ibid., p. 6.
5. *The Spirit of American Government*, New York, 1907.

legislative, executive, and judicial alike, as Theodore Roosevelt proclaimed to the Convention of the National Progressive Party in 1912.[6]

This aspect of the demand for constitutional reform did not, therefore, constitute a demand for the replacement of checks and balances by a straightforward system of legislative supremacy. Legislatures were more suspect in Progressive eyes than executive officers, and the best solution for the problems of modern government was seen to be the strengthening of executive power at State and Federal levels. Practical politicians like Robert La Follette were more concerned to establish popular control over all branches of government than to unite them. Thus most of the plans for the reform of State government did not propose the election of the executive by the legislature; they intended that more power should be conferred upon the executive to control and coerce the legislature.[7] The separation of the branches of government and subjecting them to popular control resembled, therefore, the old Jeffersonian tradition, but they had in reality a different aim. They did not embody the Jeffersonian philosophy of minimal government, for the popular control of the agencies of government was intended to ensure that they acted harmoniously to achieve the aims of government, not that they should be prevented from acting at all. The other line of attack upon existing constitutional thought was, therefore, upon the "negative" aspects of the separation of powers.

The demand for "harmony" between the parts of the government was now heard as often, and as strongly, in the period between the Civil War and the First World War as it had been in Britain in the early nineteenth century. It was argued that the social and economic problems of modern society required concerted action by responsible governmental authorities, whereas the separation of powers made concerted action impossible, and blurred responsibility to the point where it disappeared altogether. The nature and consequences of a system of separated powers were subjected to critical analysis like that of Henry Jones Ford in his *Rise and Growth of American Politics* of 1898. A number of influences affected the nature of these analyses. The British system of parliamentary govern-

6. Printed in G. H. Payne, *The Birth of the New Party*, 1912, p. 241.
7. See Albert M. Kales, *Unpopular Government in the United States*, Chicago, 1914.

ment, as described by Bagehot and later by Bryce, provided a new pattern of government as an alternative to the two stale philosophies of checks and balances and the pure separation of powers. The parliamentary system, as these writers depicted it, did not suffer from the disadvantages of cabinet government of the sort that the Founding Fathers had rejected in 1787; and the reformers at the turn of the century were looking for a very different performance from their government from that expected by the eighteenth-century conservatives who created the United States Constitution. The British system could be portrayed as a more modern, democratic, and effective system of government than the Federal Constitution, which a century before had been able to claim superiority in all these respects over the rejected British model. Nevertheless, there were very few Americans who were prepared wholeheartedly to accept the British pattern of parliamentary and cabinet government in its entirety. Indeed, it was in many respects incompatible with the measures of direct government and popular election that characterized Progressive constitutional theories. The importance of this influence, therefore, lay more in its embodiment of the essential qualities of co-ordination and coherence than in any direct effect upon institutional development.

Continental European influence was also of great importance at a time when French and German scholarship was much admired in America. In particular the Continental concern with administrative law seemed relevant at a time when a need was felt for new institutional developments, and when there was a growing interest in Civil Service reform and the problems of bureaucracy. The development of new patterns of government regulation through commissions, first in England and in the individual American States, and then in the form of the Interstate Commerce Commission, led to a questioning of the old triad of governmental powers. A new awareness of the importance of political parties, and the role of the political "boss" in the United States, led people to re-evaluate older constitutional theories, which had concentrated almost exclusively upon the formal legal institutions of government. All these factors led, therefore, to a searching examination of older constitutional dogmas, and so to a questioning of the separation of powers. In retrospect the over-all impression of these new approaches to the problems of government seems, at first glance, to represent an outright rejection of the doctrine. Yet the assertion, by Professor Dwight Waldo, that American reformers showed an "almost complete lack of sympathy" for the principle of the separation of powers, is rather misleading.[8] A close examination of the work of the giants of this period, Woodrow Wilson, Herbert Croly, and Frank Goodnow, does not support the view that they represent an undiscriminating rejection of the doctrine of the separation of powers and the values it set out to protect. These men certainly attacked the *pure doctrine* as intellectually indefensible and practically unworkable, as well they might, but their work can also be seen as a passionate attempt to reinterpret an earlier constitutionalism in order to protect many of its values by incorporating them into a realistic and modern philosophy of government. These men, each in his own way, were seeking for solutions *within* the great stream of Western constitutionalism, of which the separation of powers and its related ideas had for centuries formed an essential part. None of these men was a proponent of absolutism, either of a single man, or of a representative assembly, or of a political party. Almost inevitably, therefore, their work becomes a reformulation of that problem of division and unity which has perplexed Western thinkers whenever the difficulties of a controlled exercise of power have been contemplated.

The thought of Woodrow Wilson illustrates very well the complexities of that strand of American thought that was influenced by an admiration for the English system of government. Wilson was deeply affected by Bagehot's description of the English Constitution, and he used Bagehot's method and followed his analysis closely. Nevertheless he had rather different aims from those which had inspired the English writer, and his interpretation of the English political system was, in the end, rather different from Bagehot's; it was, indeed, a more balanced assessment of the working of parliamentary government than that of his master. Wilson did not describe the parliamentary system as a "fusion of powers," for his intention in appealing to the model of English government was not to further a programme of legislative supremacy but to strengthen the executive power,

---

8. D. Waldo, *The Administrative State*, New York, 1948, p. 105.

and restore the balance between Congress and Executive, which in his opinion had been lost. Although in 1879, and again in 1884, he advocated the adoption of cabinet government in the United States, in his later works he was much more hesitant. His admiration for English government still shone through, but he used its example as an indication of the values which should infuse a modern system of government rather than as a pattern to be closely followed. Wilson ended his career, of course, as a practical exponent of a strong Presidency as an alternative to parliamentary government, and as the best means of providing leadership in the American system.

In his *Congressional Government* Wilson adopted the same device as Bagehot, of distinguishing between a "literary theory" of the Constitution and its actual operation in practice. The Constitution of 1787, he wrote, is now the *form* of government rather than the reality. That Constitution had embodied a system of checks and balances, but in practice all the niceties of constitutional limitations had been over-ridden and the Founders' schemes of balance and distribution of power had been set at nought. The result of this transformation of the Constitution had been to establish "a scheme of congressional supremacy," in which "unquestionably the pre-dominant and controlling force, the centre and source of all motive and of all regulative power, is Congress."[9] He applied Bagehot's description of Parliament to the Congress: "it will enquire into everything, settle everything, meddle in everything." Congress, Wilson wrote, had entered into the details of administration, taking into its own hands all the substantial powers of government, and had emerged predominant over its "so-called co-ordinate branches."[10] So far then, Wilson paralleled Bagehot in his method and in his conclusions. Both writers believed that the constitutional barriers to the exercise of power in their countries had been destroyed, and a scheme of legislative omnipotence established in which all effective power was concentrated in the representative assembly. Yet there is a strange paradox here. In 1865 Bagehot had used the American pattern of separated powers to illustrate the complete absence of checks to the

9. *Congressional Government* (1885), New York, 1956, pp. 28 and 31.
10. Ibid., pp. 49 and 53.

power of the House of Commons in Britain; twenty years later, however, Woodrow Wilson used the pattern of English parliamentary government as an illustration of a desirable alternative to the concentration of all power in the American legislature. Why should Wilson admire a system of government which, according to his teacher Bagehot, embodied a "fusion" of the legislative and executive powers?

The answer is that Wilson did not accept the general description of the parliamentary system with which Bagehot commenced *The English Constitution;* rather he followed the description of the system in operation that Bagehot gave when describing the balance of power between Cabinet and Parliament. Wilson, that is to say, concentrated upon the elements of the system found in Earl Grey's work, rather than upon Bagehot's shaky attempts to characterize British government in general terms. The result was that Woodrow Wilson saw cabinet government as "a device for bringing the executive and legislative branches into harmony and co-operation without uniting or confusing their functions."[11] Here then was Wilson's explanation of the paradox. The American system, which is formally a system of separated and balanced powers, actually results in the concentration and confusion of all powers in Congress; the system of cabinet government is a means of ensuring that the functions of government are kept separate but co-ordinated. The "hard and fast line" separating executive and legislature in America was intended, Wilson argued, to ensure the independence of each branch of government, but it had resulted instead in their isolation.[12] The parcelling-out of power in the Constitution led to irresponsibility, and therefore enabled Congress to meddle in matters better left to the executive. On the one hand, the exclusion of the executive from all participation in the work of the legislature led to a distressing paralysis in moments of emergency, due to the lack of effective leadership; and on the other hand, rendered ineffective the attempts of Congress to exercise control over the departments.[13]

In his later work Wilson made this point even clearer. The attempt to establish checks and balances in the United States had failed, he wrote, be-

11. Ibid., p. 92.   12. Ibid., p. 109.
13. Ibid., pp. 179 and 185–6.

cause the system of separated powers had resulted in an impossible attempt to restrict the President to mere executive functions. Congress had been invested with the power of "governing," whereas the real origin and purpose of representative assemblies had been to "consult" with the government in order to apprise it of public opinion.[14] Thus the significant difference between the English and American legislatures was that the Congress had become part of the government, while in England Parliament had remained apart from it. "Parliament is still, as it was originally intended to be, the grand assize, or session of the nation, to criticize and control the Government. It is not a council to administer it. It does not originate its own bills . . . the duties of the ministers are not merely executive: the ministers are the Government."[15]

Wilson's view of the defects of the Constitution closely paralleled the views Jefferson had expressed in the *Notes on the State of Virginia*. The attempt to separate the powers of government had failed, and all power had resulted to the legislature. But whereas Jefferson, and other men in the period before the formation of the Constitution, looked to checks and balances to provide the barriers necessary against abuse of power by the legislature, Wilson believed that these checks and balances had also failed to control the exercise of power. Instead he looked to a new view of government functions; he thought in terms of the parliamentary functions of "government" and "the control of government," rather than the old legislative-executive formulation. Nevertheless for a moment even Wilson harked back to the old dialogue between the separation of powers and mixed government. The analysis of any successful system of self-government, he wrote, would show that its only effectual checks consist in a mixture of elements, in a combination of seemingly contradictory political principles. "The British government is perfect in proportion as it is unmonarchical, the American safe in proportion as it is undemocratic."[16]

Wilson's attack upon the separation of powers was, therefore, much more subtle than Bagehot's. He criticized the *extreme* separation of the

14. *Constitutional Government in the United States*, New York, 1908, pp. 14–15 and 54.
15. Ibid., p. 84.
16. *Congressional Government*, p. 154.

personnel of government in the United States, and the belief that the functions of government could be kept in watertight compartments, in order to develop a more sophisticated separation and articulation of functions, which he saw in the system of parliamentary and cabinet government. In the last analysis he rejected Bagehot's oversimplified views of the parliamentary system in favour of a combination of the virtues of harmony and balance, in much the same way as many of his contemporaries were doing in France. The insistence that the concentration of power was not the aim of reformers is to be found even more clearly in the work of Gamaliel Bradford. In *The Lesson of Popular Government* of 1899 Bradford did not advocate the adoption of cabinet government, but argued the necessity of a strong executive, which would have the function of formulating legislation and submitting it to Congress for approval; in other words, he wrote, "the veto should be applied the other way."[17] He supported the Pendleton proposals to allow members of the cabinet to speak in Congress, and used the pattern of the German Empire, with the difference, of course, that the head of government would be a popularly elected President, to illustrate the desirable relationships between the head of the government, members of the cabinet, and the legislature.[18] For Bradford the danger of the American system was that the absolute and unchecked power of Congress had reduced the executive to becoming the "blind instrument" of any order the legislature might choose to give.[19] This danger could only be met by restoring the balance of power between the branches of government. The keynote of his work, he wrote, was to further "the effective separation of the executive and legislative power," and to prevent the absorption of all power by the legislature.[20] Bradford clearly stated the view that the "proper" separation of the legislative and executive functions could only be achieved through an attack upon the particular method of separating the powers of government embodied in the Constitution. Neither Wilson nor Bradford was interested in a crude attack upon the separation of the functions of government; on the contrary, they showed a deep concern for the values the doctrine of the separation of powers had embodied, which could

17. New York, 1899, Vol. I, p. 362.
19. Ibid., Vol. II, p. 349.
18. Ibid., Vol. II, p. 354.
20. Ibid., Vol. II, p. 78.

only be safeguarded by a balanced system of government in place of the pattern of legislative domination that they abhorred.

There were, therefore, in the period before the First World War, two major objectives in the Progressive attack upon the Constitution. The main effort was directed at an attempt to ensure the responsibility of the parts of government to the people through the mechanisms of direct control; in addition an intellectual assault on the Constitution by Wilson and others stressed the need to achieve an effective, harmonious relationship between the branches of government. These two aims of democracy and harmony were by no means mutually exclusive; they were shared in varying degrees by all the reformist elements, but they embodied different approaches to institutional solutions which were to a large degree incompatible. The harmony of purpose in a system of parliamentary government resulted from the direct responsibility of the government to the elected legislature, whereas the use of the initiative, referendum, and recall, and the direct election of executive and judicial officials as well as members of the legislature, did not combine easily with the principles of the parliamentary system. The most impressive attempt to draw together and integrate these various strands of Progressive constitutional doctrine was made by Herbert Croly, journalist and, for a time, confidant of Theodore Roosevelt. Croly's concern for popular control and effective, co-ordinated government, resulted in a subtle and sensitive approach to the problems of constitutionalism. The role of the separation of powers in a modern constitutional State was one of his major concerns in his *Progressive Democracy* of 1915. In this work he was at pains to refute the charges that Progressivism was an extremist attack upon constitutionalism itself, and this led him to attempt a conscious reformulation of the doctrine of the separation of powers in the American context.

With that American genius for finding ever new combinations of the ideas of Jefferson and Hamilton, Herbert Croly had a vision of a government closely subjected to popular control, which would follow a positive national policy for the solution of pressing economic and social problems. Croly looked for direct popular control of the organs of government, which would be separated and functionally distinct, and in this respect his view was little different from that of Jefferson or Taylor, although the instruments of popular control were to be different. Croly rejected outright, just as the Jeffersonians had done, any theory of checks and balances which endowed the branches of government with an independence both of the people and of each other, and he was insistent upon the necessity of a separation of the functions of government. Yet Croly vehemently rejected Jeffersonianism in its attachment to extreme individualism, and in its insistence upon a strictly limited, negative, role for government. His was a philosophy of strong national government, opposed to the particularism of the Jeffersonians. This philosophy led him to an attack upon the extreme doctrine of the separation of powers, and to demand unity and harmony in the system of government, but he was no crude, outright opponent of all that the doctrine stood for. He understood very well that a separation of functions among the agencies of government must form the basis of any constitutional system, but he looked for a formula which would ensure that this necessary separation did not result in stagnation.

Croly's *Progressive Democracy* began with an analysis of the history of the Federal Constitution, attributing its fragmented structure to the all-pervasive fear of power in America, including the fear of the power of the people themselves. The Founders, Croly argued, had evaded the problem of rationalizing the exercise of popular power by subjecting it to rigid, effective limitations, and by dividing the government against itself. The proper way to rationalize the power of the people in his view was to accept frankly the danger of violence, and to reorganize the State so that "popular reasonableness will be developed from within rather than imposed from without."[21] Thus Croly rejected that philosophy which gave the agencies of government an independence allowing them to restrain or evade popular control, yet he certainly did not reject constitutionalism. "Constitutionalism necessarily remains," he wrote, "but the constitutions are intrusted frankly to the people instead of the people to the constitutions."[22] Thus progressive democracy did not mean that the people would assume all the functions of government, nor that they would dispense with orderly pro-

21. *Progressive Democracy*, New York, 1915, pp. 38, and 40–41.
22. Ibid., p. 225.

cedure. "Progressive democracy would cease to be progressive in case it departed for long from the use of essentially orderly methods; and excessive concentration of power in the hands of the electorate might be as dangerous to order as would any similar concentration in the hands of the executive or the legislature."[23]

Croly's belief in popular control did not lead him to an assertion of legislative supremacy. Indeed he judged the traditional American suspicion of legislative assemblies to have been fully justified by the record of history. Their "meagre powers of self-control" made it impossible to entrust them with complete legal authority over the property and lives of citizens. Legislative omnipotence, Croly believed, was far from a truly democratic form of government. The power of that many-headed monarch, "King Demos," must be divided. Popular sovereignty brings with it the necessity for the division of power, but the power is distributed, not for the purpose of its emasculation, but for the purpose of its moralization. There must be, therefore, proper provision for the co-ordination of these distributed powers, and it is here that we reach the crux of Croly's criticism of the Constitution. The Constitution provided for the separation of powers, but it did not provide for the co-operation of the powers it had divided, although their co-operation was as necessary and desirable as their separation.[24]

Thus Croly, the twentieth-century Progressive, rejected alike the checks and balances of the *Federalist* and the pure separation of powers of the later Jeffersonian critics of Federalism. The Federalist edifice of the Constitution he likened to "some elaborate masterpiece of artificial constructive genius, such as a Gothic cathedral"; on the other hand he saw the effects of the Jeffersonian philosophy as having reduced State governments "to a bed of liquid clay . . . an indiscriminate mass of sticky matter, which merely clogged the movements of every living body entangled in its midst."[25] Both these philosophies were designed to rob government of the power of positive action and were both, therefore, unacceptable. Yet Croly was by no means happy with the character of the popular Progressive movement, for he saw that the instruments of direct government it proposed were

23. Ibid., p. 226.
25. Ibid., p. 248.

24. Ibid., pp. 52, 227, 229, and 236.

too much inclined towards the "democratic" rather than the "harmonious" pole of the reform movement. In this they reflected too much the philosophy of the early nineteenth century, instead of that of the twentieth. At first glance these instruments might seem to make for the emancipation of government from the bondage of the rigid constitution of checks and balances, but, said Croly, they might from another point of view merely add one final comprehensive check to the network of personal and legal checks which had formerly reduced the States to stagnation.[26] The extreme proponents of direct government, he wrote, had the same automatic faith in their system that the Fathers had had in the checks and balances of the Constitution; they devote little attention to the problem of creating a more powerful and efficient mechanism of legislation and administration. Here, then, is the central principle of Croly's Progressivism; he did not wish, by establishing popular control of the executive and the legislature, to destroy in either of them the will and power to act effectively. On the contrary, he wished to reinforce *both* of them, to build up their power, but to render it responsible to the people.[27]

In this desire to build up both the executive and legislative powers, and to render them directly responsible to the people, Croly was therefore faced with a reformulation, not a rejection, of the separation of powers. In all three of the principal departments of government, he wrote, there are essential functions to be performed that must be delegated to selected men, under conditions which make both for efficiency and for their individual independence and self-respect. The Founding Fathers had been quite justified in keeping the powers of government distinct, and in seeking to balance one against the other, but they had been mistaken in the methods they adopted for preserving or readjusting the balance. The division of the democratic political system into three parts had the twofold role of providing for the necessary specialization of the functions of government, and of enabling the people to perform the function of recreating a unity between them. The people must themselves retain the responsibility of maintaining an ultimate unity.[28]

26. Ibid.   27. Ibid., p. 268.   28. Ibid., p. 280.

Here, then, in the demand for specialization, control, and unity without the "system of equilibrium," we have a formulation of the problem of government almost exactly in the terms Sieyès had used in 1795, but now infused with all the urgency engendered by the needs of a twentieth-century industrial democracy. Croly's answer to the institutional problem was that both the legislative and administrative branches of government should be "aggrandized" in a way that would lead neither to legislative nor executive omnipotence. The plan which most closely approximated this aim, at the State level at any rate, was, in his view, that proposed by the People's Power League in Oregon. This plan concentrated the power of effective political leadership, together with the responsibility of formulating and aiding the passage of legislation, in the Governor. This popularly elected official would have the right to sit in the single legislative assembly, to vote, to introduce bills and to advocate them on the floor of the House, although he would not possess a veto. Thus, said Croly, the administration would indeed become the government "in the English sense of the word."[29] At the same time the legislature would be reformed by a number of remarkable measures that would make it an effective balance to the great power of the Governor, who would himself be subject to recall. Thus Herbert Croly, in the most subtle and impressive of the Progressive attacks upon the existing constitutional structure, reformulated the idea of the separation of powers in order to create a "genuine" balance between an executive and a legislature subject to popular control, and to reformulate their functions. It was an attempt to bring the doctrine up to date and to avoid the sterility it had come to represent. He sought for an alternative to earlier constitutional theories, but he was well aware of the values these older theories of government had embodied, and he wished to perpetuate them without becoming committed to the negative view of government by which they had been accompanied. He summed up his view of the structure of government in this way: "Government has been divided up into parts, because no one man or group of men can be safely intrusted with the exercise of comprehensive government functions; but within the limits of a necessary and desirable

29. Ibid., p. 295.

separation of powers a partial reunion may be permissible and useful."[30] Thus towards the end of that great upsurge of criticism which was the Progressive movement its most fluent representative recognized the essential continuing content of Western constitutionalism, and the problem of how to articulate the parts of government in a system of controlled power.

Both Woodrow Wilson in his *Congressional Government* and Herbert Croly in *Progressive Democracy* had been largely concerned with a critique of the separation of powers that focused upon the allocation of the functions of government among its various parts. Another strand of thought was directed, however, specifically at the threefold formulation of the functions of government, and this eventually led to questioning the usefulness of the concept of government functions itself. This was the trend of thought associated with the growth of the study of public administration. Woodrow Wilson played a significant role in this aspect of intellectual development also, although the name most associated with the movement is that of Frank J. Goodnow. A number of influences can be seen at work in the emergence of this concern with public administration as a separate branch of study. Interest in the French and German writers of the late nineteenth century had focused, in America, upon the literature of administrative law and practice. Woodrow Wilson pointed, in 1887, to Prussia as the country in which administration had been studied and "nearly perfected."[31] The emphasis in German thought upon the twofold distinction between administration (*Verwaltung*) and government (*Regierung*), and the corresponding French formulation by Ducrocq and Duguit, provided a ready alternative to the division of functions established by Montesquieu. Second, the campaign in America to end corruption in the public services evolved into a demand that these services should be "taken out of politics." The Progressive demand for the strengthening of the executive branch of government, that it should cease to be a "mere executive" and should become a government in the English sense, associated with, if not dominant in, the field of policy-making, strengthened the feeling that only the elected members of

---

30. Ibid., pp. 364–5.
31. "The Study of Administration," *Political Science Quarterly*, June 1887, p. 204.

the "executive" should be involved in policy decisions, leaving appointed officials to put these decisions into effect with impartial, expert efficiency. Finally, the hesitant development of government regulatory commissions provided reformers with an instrument which they claimed could be an efficient method of government control free from all the disadvantages of the normal procedures of government action.

In an article on "The Study of Administration" in 1887 Woodrow Wilson drew upon the experience of Continental writers, and upon the political demands for Civil Service reform in America, to suggest that the study of administration should be developed in the United States, building upon the Continental experience, but adapted to the different environment. Administration, Wilson wrote, is "a field of business," removed from the hurry and strife of politics, a part of political life only in the sense in which machinery is a part of the manufactured product.[32] Politics sets the tasks for administration, but having set them it should not be allowed to meddle with the carrying out of those tasks; politics should not be able to "manipulate the offices" of administration. Wilson argued that, as administration was apart from politics, apart even from constitutional law, the Federal Constitution-makers had rightly ignored this sphere of government, concerning themselves only with the "political" branches, with Congress and the Presidency. Thus, consistently with his viewpoint in *Congressional Government*, he denied the existence of a strict functional division between the legislature and the "chief executive," but at the same time he laid the basis of a new and potentially rigid functional distinction between the political branches and the administrative agents of government. And, paradoxically, he employed the same criterion for the distinction of functions in this sense as had been used in the eighteenth century to make the distinction he was rejecting—the generality of law. "Public administration," he wrote, "is detailed and systematic execution of public law. Every particular application of general law is an act of administration."[33] Here, then, was a strange metamorphosis. The opponent of the separation of powers had merely shifted the spectrum a little, and the old ideas were being ap-

32. Op. cit., p. 209.   33. Ibid., p. 212.

plied in a slightly different way, in a slightly different context, but to very similar ends, to keep the exercise of power in its "proper" sphere, and operating through the "proper" channels.

The insistence that administration lies outside the sphere of politics, and that there are therefore two distinct fields of activity, the laying down of broad plans of action, and the execution of the plans by administrators, provided the basis for a new functional division. This idea fitted well into nineteenth-century psychological theories, and was consistent with the dominant trends of political thought at the end of the century. The Idealist conception of the will of the State and its expression tinged much of the thought on administration in this period. Robert La Follette described experts and commissions as "simply the executive or administrative branch of the people's will."[34] Wilson himself was by no means simple-minded on this point. He acknowledged that the administrator had a will of his own, at least in the choice of the means of accomplishing his work. Nevertheless, the distinction, between the State will and its realization in action, lay behind the whole structure of thought in this period of the development of "public administration," and it can be clearly seen in the work of Frank Goodnow, the most influential of the early writers. Thus Goodnow could write that the administrative system had been utilized wrongly by politicians for their own ends, in order to "influence the expression of the state will, and sometimes to cause the formal expression of the state will to be at variance with the real state will."[35]

The political functions of the State, said Goodnow, group themselves naturally under two heads, "which are equally applicable to the mental operations and the actions of self-conscious personalities."[36] The activities of the State consist either in operations necessary to the expression of its will, that is politics, or in the execution of that will, administration. In line with the Continental European thought upon which this distinction was based, Goodnow rejected the autonomy of the judicial function, subsuming it under the general heading of administration. Thus there was a

34. Quoted by Russell B. Nye, *Midwestern Progressive Politics*, East Lansing, 1951, p. 202.
35. *Politics and Administration*, New York, 1900, p. 43.
36. Ibid., p. 9.

return to an older theory of government functions, a duality rather than the triad of powers which had been evolved during the eighteenth century. Yet there were of course vital differences between this new formulation of politics and administration and the early modern distinction between legislation and execution. "Politics" was a much wider concept than "the legislative power," embracing the need for leadership in the formulation of policy, for securing the passage of legislation, and for the oversight of execution. The dualism between a legislating people and a ruler who executes did not fit Goodnow's twentieth-century conception of government, and indeed he attacked the categories of the old doctrine of the separation of powers which embodied it. Like Woodrow Wilson, he was concerned with the maintenance of a harmony between the parts of government, so that the idea of a sharp division between the functions of President and Congress was repugnant to him. He was also aware that, however precise and rigid the analytical distinction between the functions of government, it is impossible to be so precise about the practical division of these functions between the agencies of government.[37]

Goodnow's sophistication in the treatment of the distinction between the functions of government did not prevent him from becoming embroiled in the difficulties which flow from the attempt to draw precise lines between politics and administration. He did not wish merely to draw intellectual distinctions but also to apply them to practical political life. He was concerned to ensure that, although "politics" should oversee the execution of the State will, and therefore exercise some control over "administration," the former should not exceed the limits necessary to ensure the attainment of its legitimate purposes. To ensure this the administrator must be given the same degree of independence that judges have enjoyed.[38] This clearly involved an attempt to distinguish the "proper" area of administration in institutional terms as well as in the conceptual field of government functions, in fact to establish a form of separation of powers, and it is here that Goodnow's language becomes confused and confusing. Earlier he had defined administration as "the execution of the state will," but at this point he

37. Ibid., pp. 7, 16, and 23.   38. Ibid., pp. 26, 38, and 45.

drew a distinction between the administrative function and the executive function. Till recently, he writes, these two have been confused. The executive function must, in the nature of things, be subordinated to politics, but this is not true of an "administrative authority," which he now defined as "an authority discharging that part of the function of administration not distinctly of an executive character."[39] The confusion of vocabulary here reflects a deeper difficulty, for Goodnow's distinction between politics and administration had broken down almost as soon as he attempted to use it.

Goodnow attempted to escape from this difficulty by further defining the areas of government action which should be kept out of politics as fields of activity of a semi-scientific, quasi-judicial, and quasi-business or commercial character. These areas, together with "the function of establishing, preserving and developing the governmental organization," should be protected from the improper intervention of the political branches. Thus in effect Goodnow had shifted the emphasis of the theory of the separation of powers from a concern with the division of power between the legislature and executive, to an attempt to define distinct spheres for the political and administrative branches of government. Whilst admitting that it was impossible to draw strict boundaries between the functions of government he nevertheless wished to isolate these two areas from one another. It is not surprising, therefore, that many American students of public administration ignored Goodnow's intellectual reservations, and set about the creation of an administrative machine which was to be expert, impartial, and out of the reach of the political branches of government. The disputes which later evolved concerning the nature of the independent regulatory commissions well illustrate the problems implicit in Goodnow's ideas.

The critiques of the separation of powers generated by the reform movement in America had focused both upon the structure of legal institutions and upon the conceptual basis of the Montesquieu doctrine, but there was a third area in which this period saw a change in the treatment of this long-studied aspect of political theory. There was now a new awareness of the role of political parties and their impact upon the institutional structure. It

39. Ibid., p. 82.

is this awareness which helps to explain some of the more paradoxical aspects of the attack upon the separation of powers by men who were deeply concerned with institutional controls over the exercise of power. Those reformers who were less concerned about the problem of harmony in government nevertheless joined in the attack upon the separation of powers. They did so because they believed that such an attack was an essential prerequisite to the restoration of the desired balance in the American system of government. It was the rigid separation of powers, they argued, that had given rise to the powerful State and local party machines, that had resulted in the emergence of the "bosses" who exercised an unrestrained, irresponsible power in the political system. If the power of the bosses was to be broken then a new institutional pattern must be adopted; the party must be recognized as a part of the governmental system and subjected to popular control, or else the centre of political power must be located elsewhere in the system.

The formal separation of the powers of government had led, in their view, to a political system which was so complex, and so irresponsible, that it had necessitated the growth of strong political machines to knit together that which had been so carefully distributed by constitutional fiat. Party organization, wrote Henry Jones Ford, is the "connective tissue" which enfolds the separate organs of government and enables popular sovereignty to exercise a unified control over them.[40] Both Wilson and Goodnow made the same point. But the nature of the system of separated powers gave rise to the peculiar American party system in which power was concentrated in the hands of men who stood *outside* the formal governmental structure. "A decentralized legal government has been replaced by a centralized extra-legal government," wrote Albert Kales in 1914.[41] The fragmentation of legal power, the proliferation of elective offices, and the complication of the machinery of government reached the point where even the very intelligent elector could neither understand it, nor apportion responsibility for government action or inaction. The consequence was the rise of the "po-

40. *The Rise and Growth of American Politics*, p. 215.
41. *Unpopular Government in the United States*, Chicago, 1914, p. 23.

litocrat," the expert in politics who could "advise" the voter, and who could most effectively operate the machinery of government from a point outside it: the political boss. Both Ford and Goodnow argued that with all its faults the American party system played an essential role in government by counteracting the divisive effects of the extreme separation of powers.[42] Nevertheless, Goodnow felt that the recognition that party is an essential organ of the political system necessitated that it should be integrated into the legal structure of the State, and made responsible by means of primary elections.[43] On the other hand Woodrow Wilson wished to make legislatures and executives the *real* bodies politic, and therefore to do away with the necessity for such powerful political organizations.[44] The proper articulation of the parts of government, the proper "separation of powers," was thus bound up with the nature and characteristics of the party system.

The half-century between the Civil War and the First World War witnessed an extensive and elevated discussion of constitutional theory in the United States, of a quality and an intensity which bears comparison with the period of the great debate between Federalists and Jeffersonians. Emphasis upon reformist thought should not lead us to forget the numerous defenders of the *status quo*, of whom Lowell, Snow, and President Nicholas Murray Butler should be mentioned.[45] The various criticisms that inspired the attack upon the Constitution were given coherence by their association with an active political movement which deeply influenced American life; but when, at the end of the War, Progressivism ceased to play this important role, the coherence of the ideological attack upon accepted constitutional theory vanished with it. Criticism of the separation of powers continued unabated, of course, and the various strands of earlier reformist thought continued to exert considerable influence. But there was a disintegration in the coherence of these attacks which was comparable to the fragmenting of constitutional thought following 1825.

42. Ford, op. cit., pp. 301–2; Goodnow, op. cit., p. 106.

43. Op. cit., p. 134.

44. *Constitutional Government in the United States*, p. 221.

45. See E. R. Lewis, *A History of American Political Thought from the Civil War to the First World War*, New York, 1937, pp. 471 ff.

The coherence of the attack upon constitutional doctrine diminished for a number of reasons. The strong presidencies of Woodrow Wilson and Franklin Roosevelt changed the institutional balance of power decisively in favour of the presidency, and the functions of that office could no longer be depicted as "merely executive." The President now exercised the role of legislative leadership in domestic affairs as well as a greatly expanded role in foreign affairs and defence. The Progressive complaint of legislative omnipotence was, therefore, hardly appropriate any longer, but the problem of "harmony" between legislature and executive was not so easily solved by the "aggrandizement" of the Presidency. The demands for greater integration of the branches of government continued, in Congress through the Kefauver and Fulbright resolutions, and in the literature through a constant stream of proposals, ranging from the full acceptance of the parliamentary system, or the institution of a legislative-executive council, to the complex scheme recently put forward by Professor Herman Finer.[46] At a more practical level the attempt to improve the co-ordination between the legislative and executive branches was concentrated upon measures, beginning with the Reorganization Act of 1939, which would provide the machinery for channelling information to the President, and would enable him to supervise efficiently relations with Congress and the internal structure of the Administration. The demand, mostly in academic circles, for a more responsible party system, also reflected the continuing concern about the ability of the American political organization to satisfy the needs generated by the institutional structure.

The complexity of the institutional changes in the post-war era, reflecting both the success and the failure of Progressive ideas, was accompanied by a recognition that the ideas behind the development of public administration were over-simple. As early as 1908 Arthur F. Bentley had criticized the basis of Goodnow's politics-administration dichotomy,[47] and by 1933 the enthusiasm for Goodnow's formulation was already on the wane. It was, however, the experience of the regulatory commissions established under the New Deal that brought the problem of the separation of

46. H. Finer, *The Presidency: Crisis and Regeneration,* Chicago, 1960.
47. A. F. Bentley, *The Process of Government,* Chicago, 1908.

powers to the surface again. The commissions were attacked as a "head-less fourth branch" of government that destroyed the constitutional triad of legislature, executive, and judiciary, and, by putting much of the area of administration outside the President's control, contributed more dishar-mony to the American system of government. They were also criticized as combining legislative, executive, and judicial powers. In 1938 James M. Landis defended the "administrative process" against all these charges. It was the inability of the normal tripartite system of government to deal with the problems of an industrial society that called the administrative process into being, he argued. It enabled the government to achieve effi-ciency and responsibility whilst maintaining the traditional Anglo-Saxon balanced constitution. The commission form was an industrial pattern of organization adopted to meet the needs of an industrial society when the outmoded political divisions of Montesquieu had failed.[48] The administra-tive process required a broad grant of power of the sort normally exercised by the whole government machine, which, in a sense, it had replaced.

However, the traditional attachment to the ideas of the separation of powers was very strong. The concentration of differing types of authority in one body gave rise to considerable misgivings. Even those who were sympathetic to the commissions demanded an "internal separation of pow-ers" which would divide those officials who exercised judicial functions from those who prosecuted or those who exercised the rule-making func-tion. In 1937 the President's Committee on Administrative Management wished to incorporate all but the judicial functions of the commissions into the general structure of the executive departments.[49] The Attorney-General's Committee in 1941, however, looked rather towards a separation of function within the agencies, and the Administrative Procedure Act of 1946 largely achieved this. The development of the "administrative pro-cess," therefore, made neither the values nor the problems of the separation of powers disappear. In one respect it merely moved the discussion from the arena of presidential-congressional relations into the arena of the com-missions themselves; in another respect it made the divisive problems of

48. *The Administrative Process*, New Haven, 1938, pp. 1, 11, 13, and 15.
49. *Report*, p. 41.

the separated powers in America even greater. In the view of V. O. Key the autonomy of these "administrative" bodies mainly served to direct attention *away* from the attempt to fuse policy-forming and policy-executing functions in the same hands.[50]

Thus the various strands of thought of the Progressive era came to be rather frayed with the passage of time. In so far as the Progressive attack upon the separation of powers had been an honest attempt to reformulate it for the modern age, this doctrine also suffered from the change in the intellectual atmosphere. The burden of the Progressive attack, the negative aspects, remained, but the constructive attempts at a reformulation had little further impact. Nevertheless, the greatest threat to the reformulation of the doctrine came not so much from a direct attack upon it as from the developments in the study of politics itself, which seemed to make such a reformulation irrelevant through the impact of behaviourism upon the study of politics and administration. The consequences of this change in the approach of students of politics may be summed up as a change from an interest in "function" to an interest in "process." The old arguments about the number of government functions, or their definition, now seemed irrelevant. This was a much more fundamental challenge than any earlier threat to the doctrine, for it struck at the vital concepts upon which it was founded. The change of interest can be likened to the dispute between French jurists about the "formal" and the "material" functions of government. The whole concept that the particular content of a decision made it either legislative, executive, or judicial in nature was rejected in favour of the study of the actual processes of government as the only question worth exploring. Luther Gulick expressed this view very clearly: "Whether an act is executive or legislative or judicial in character, is purely an institutional concept, and grows out of the practical division of work which happens to exist at a given time. It does not arise from the nature of the thing done."[51] Gulick rejected both the Montesquieu and Goodnow formulations of the

<hr />

50. "Politics and Administration," in *The Future of Government in the United States*, ed. by J. D. White, Chicago, 1942, p. 146.

51. "Politics, Administration and the 'New Deal,'" *Annals of the American Academy*, Vol. 169, Sept. 1933, p. 62.

functions of government. The nature of a "political" or a "non-political" act cannot be discovered by an examination of the act itself, he declared, "but only by an examination of that act in relation to social psychology."[52] Thus the organization of the tasks of government was a matter for practical politics and not to be settled by abstract arguments about function. Pursued with the vigour of the behaviourist this point of view seemed to leave little room for the ideas or the ideals of the separation of powers. That doctrine had concentrated upon the more formal aspects of government, whereas now the attention of students was focused upon "social forces." The study of the pressure-group characterized this approach, for the pressure-group can switch its attention from legislature to "public opinion," from cabinet minister to the press, from the courts to the political party. Similarly the case-study was a natural outcome of this approach, considering a particular incident or decision in all its ramifications, legal or formal, informal or extralegal. The study of administration, freed from its earlier orthodoxy, now approached its material in "situational terms," each unique incident in government being seen as the result of a set of criss-crossing causes, with the realization that "informal organization" could be as important as, or more important than, that to be found on the organization charts.[53]

Political thought, at the academic level at any rate, had now reached a point in the United States comparable to that reached in both Britain and France in relation to constitutional theories like the separation of powers. In all three countries the view was being aired that only the day-to-day problems of government were worth investigation, that the attempts of political and constitutional theorists to make general statements about desirable systems of government were either irrelevant or incapable of giving any clear and useful guidance in practical terms. Yet we have seen that in both Britain and France, however level-headed this view might seem, it led to very serious problems, for it came into conflict with the ideas which lay at the very foundation of Western constitutionalism; to

52. Ibid.
53. G. A. Shipman, "The Policy Process: An Emerging Perspective," *Western Political Quarterly*, Vol. XII, No. 2, June 1959, p. 541.

put it in an over-simplified way, the theory of government which justified day-to-day expediency came into conflict with the ideas behind the rule of law. In the United States the nature of the Constitution, and the vitally important role which the Supreme Court continued to play in American political life, might seem to have ensured that the problems confronting Britain and France in this respect did not arise, although America had its own dramatic confrontations; but fundamentally, in spite of its very different constitutional structure, a very similar problem had to be faced in the United States. The attempts of the Supreme Court to deal with the problem of the "proper" functions of the departments of government illustrate the way in which in America also the problems of constitutionalism and the separation of powers stubbornly refused to become irrelevant.

The history of the attempts the Court has made to cope with the separation of powers between the departments of government must be seen as further proof of the difficulty, the impossibility perhaps, of applying the Montesquieu definitions of the functions of government. In 1816 Justice Story accepted the Montesquieu formulation of functions as part of American constitutional law,[54] and from time to time this general position has been reaffirmed, but the practical problems of applying these criteria were soon recognized. In 1825 Chief Justice Marshall pointed to the difficulties involved in the delegation of power from one branch to another and formulated a self-denying ordinance against "unnecessary" judicial enquiry into this problem.[55] The difficulty was also stressed in the Watkins case of 1842.[56] It is in the twentieth century, however, that the Court has come hard up against the problems of the boundaries between the functions of government. The Court invalidated the National Industrial Recovery Act, in part because in its view the Congress had attempted to bestow a rule-making power on the President so wide in scope that it was "virtually unfettered." Congress, the Chief Justice declared, was not permitted to transfer its "essential legislative functions," although the need for the dele-

---

54. *Martin v. Hunter's Lessee*, 1 Wheat. 304 (1816), 329.
55. *Wayman v. Southard*, 10 Wheat. 1 (1825), 45.
56. *Watkins v. the Lessee of Holman*, 16 Pet. 25 (1842), 60–61.

---

gation of power to deal with a host of details had long been sanctioned by the Court.[57] Yet apart from the Schechter decision it has apparently been impossible for the Court to find a formula which would enable it to distinguish "essential" from "inessential" legislative powers. In practice the grant of wide, virtually undefined powers to administrative authorities has been sanctioned. Furthermore, the Court has approved the combination of all three types of function in the regulatory commissions. American courts have retreated into the semantic maze of "quasi-legislative" and "quasi-judicial" powers, but in the opinion of one authority at least, these are merely "convenient fictions."[58] The fact is that any real attempt to apply the Montesquieu criteria would have prevented the government from meeting the demands put upon it in an efficient and effective fashion.

Judicial application of the doctrine of the separation of powers would seem, therefore, to have succumbed to the same forces as have made it seem irrelevant elsewhere. It has not been possible for the Supreme Court to apply the doctrine in any consistent way, but it would be quite wrong to suggest that the Court has abandoned the doctrine as an essential element in the American constitutional system. In recent years the Court has attempted to set limits to the power of congressional committees which try to exceed a proper legislative role, and in 1952, in the steel-seizure case, the Court reasserted the basic principle with impressive force. Denying the power of the President to seize the steel mills by Executive Order the opinion of the Court delivered by Justice Black stated: "In the framework of our Constitution, the President's power to see that the laws are faithfully executed refutes the idea that he is a lawmaker."[59] Justice Frankfurter, concurring in the Court's opinion noted that it had been fashionable in earlier years to find the system of checks and balances obstructive to effective government. "It was easy," he continued, "to ridicule that system as outmoded —too easy. The experience through which the world has passed in our own day has made vivid the realization that the Framers of our Constitution were not inexperienced doctrinaires." The dangers of the concentration and

57. *Schechter v. U.S.*, 295 U.S. 495 (1935), 529.
58. F. E. Cooper, *Administrative Agencies and the Courts*, Ann Arbor, 1951, p. 29.
59. *Youngstown Sheet and Tube Co. v. Sawyer*, 343 U.S. 579 (1952), 587.

abuse of power, though less in the United States than elsewhere, were still great. Although experience had shown that the content of the three authorities was not to be derived from "abstract analysis," the restrictions implicit in the separation of powers were real, and a price worth paying for the safeguards they provide.[60] Warning that what was at stake was the equilibrium established by the constitutional system, Justice Jackson summed up the Court's philosophy of government. "The actual art of governing under our Constitution does not and cannot conform to judicial definitions of the power of any of its branches based upon isolated clauses or even single Articles torn from context. While the Constitution diffuses power the better to secure liberty, it also contemplates that practice will integrate the dispersed powers into a workable government. It enjoins upon its branches separateness but interdependence, autonomy but reciprocity."[61]

Judicial recognition of these two apparently conflicting positions—the over-all rule of constitutionalism and the difficulty of drawing detailed boundaries—does great credit to the Supreme Court. This body, faced with the day-to-day problems of government, must make those practical compromises which circumstances seem to demand. But what has the academic student to say about this dilemma? As we have seen, the answer, in the inter-war period, seemed to be "Nothing." However, in recent years two evolving trends of thought have somewhat changed this picture. They by no means constitute a reaffirmation of older constitutional theories, at any rate in the old forms, but they do indicate the continuing strength of old ideas, and of old concepts, and the difficulty of abandoning them.

In the first place, the concept of equilibrium has come to play a leading role in discussions about the nature of the political system. This ancient concept of balance, which has been the key to discussions about the limitation of power since the time of Plato, remains, with all its disadvantages, the most fruitful concept for the understanding and investigation of democratic systems of government. It is, of course, no longer simply a matter of the balancing of the parts of government against one another. The idea is used in relation to the balancing out of social forces, of parties and groups.

60. Ibid., at pp. 593, 610, and 613.   61. Ibid., at p. 635.

These parties and groups no longer have the functional attributes that the classes had in the theory of the mixed and balanced constitution, for the triumph of the democratic ideal leaves no room for the view that particular virtues and capabilities attach to particular classes. Nevertheless the idea that power must be checked and balanced, by the pluralism of conflicting interests in a diverse society if by nothing else, remains a firm idea which the constitutionalist of the present day can grasp.

Second, in recent years a reappraisal of the concept of function in politics has been taking place. The mere investigation of "what actually happens," although a vitally important part of political study, can never tell us very much about political systems without some framework upon which to hang this information. The theoretical tool which has seemed most useful to those political scientists interested in the comparative study of political systems is the sociologists' technique of structural-functional analysis. There has been, therefore, a resurgence of interest in "function," but in a much more sophisticated way than that of the eighteenth-century thinkers who wrote about the functions of government. Governments fulfil deep social functions without which society would no longer subsist. Thus political institutions have a role to play in social integration, functions relating to the maintenance of stability, the stratification and articulation of interests, and in relation to social communication, and many other things. This is the sociologists' concept of function, and it may seem to have little to do with the categories of the separation of powers. Yet in the work of those political scientists who are most sociologically inclined we find a continuity with older ideas, which suggests that the gap between Montesquieu and modern sociology is not so great after all.

Structural-functional analysis is the technique used in the work entitled *The Politics of the Developing Areas,* edited by Gabriel Almond and James Coleman. The main theme of this study is the evolution of a framework that will enable differing political systems to be set alongside each other, through the use of analytical tools productive of meaningful comparisons. Gabriel Almond chooses as the most useful index of comparison the extent to which the structures in these varying political systems have become specialized in relation to the functions they perform.[62] It is, of course, the history of the arguments over the centuries concerning the proper extent and means of the specialization of function that we have been survey-ing. Indeed, the history of Western constitutionalism *is* the history of the emerging specialization of government functions. Almond, however, is not concerned only with the formal structures of the "constitution" or of the political system. The time is long past when a student of politics could be content with the study only of legislatures, executives, and judiciaries. He is concerned with *all* the political structures to be found in a political system. Similarly, the concept of function he employs is much wider in scope than the old Montesquieu triad of "powers." He distinguishes four "input" func-tions — political socialization and recruitment, interest articulation, inter-est aggregation, and political communication — which the structures of the political system must perform. The "output" functions, by which authori-tative decisions are taken, he labels the rule-making, the rule-application, and the rule-adjudication functions. These last three, as he readily admits, are the old categories of the separation of powers, with the labels changed in order "to free them of their structural overtones."[63] The advantage of this change of vocabulary is that it avoids the semantic difficulties in which we become involved when we discuss the extent to which courts legislate or administer, or the way in which administrators legislate. As Almond points out, a great achievement of the literature of politics in this century has been to make plain the fact that the legislature is not the only rule-making body in the political system, but that executives make rules, that courts make rules, that bureaucrats adjudicate. Particular functions are not specific to a particular structure; each political or governmental structure may perform a number of functions.

We have seen, however, that the central principle of the *pure* doctrine of the separation of powers was that government functions could, and should, be specific to particular structures on a one-to-one basis; the legislative function should be exercised only by the legislature, the executive function

62. Op. cit., Princeton, 1960, p. 11.   63. Ibid., p. 17.

should be exercised by the executive, and the judicial function only by the judges. It was the impossibility of achieving this in practice which, above all else, made the pure doctrine of the separation of powers an unrewarding doctrine to hold. But relatively few people have held to the doctrine in that form; certainly not for long once they were in a position of responsibility for the maintenance of government. The more successful varieties of the doctrine of the separation of powers have endured because they were grafted with the theory of balanced government, or one of its derivatives, to produce what Almond calls "the multifunctionality of political structures."

This change in vocabulary makes for clarity, and the analysis can be furthered by dividing the three governmental functions into sub-categories, such as the initiation, formulation, and authorization of rules, functions which again are not specific to a particular structure. But this use of a set of modified Montesquieu classifications does not in itself commit Almond and Coleman, or other political scientists who make use of it, to the positions which theorists of the separation of powers have adopted in the past, for this is merely a set of analytical categories with no necessary normative connotation. However, in so far as a general discussion of systems of government is not, and cannot be, "mere description," but entails judgements about "stages of development," or appraisals of the results political systems produce, and the values they promote, then the discussion inevitably takes on a normative content. Indeed, the interesting, and fascinating, fact about this particular, ultra-modern discussion by political scientists is that it is so clearly in the main stream of Western constitutional thought, as represented by the doctrine of the separation of powers. In fact, Almond and Coleman, in very different language, are engaged in a reformulation of constitutionalism very similar in spirit, although not in method, to that which their compatriots undertook during the Progressive era.

The comparison which they undertake of the political systems of Asia, Africa, and Latin America with Western political systems leads inevitably to a search for the distinguishing characteristic of "modern democracies," and the placing of the non-Western systems of government in a framework that makes clear the extent to which they do, or do not, approximate to the Western democracies. For Almond it is the development of specialized regulating structures, such as legislatures, which characterizes the modern democratic system, together with the "peculiar pattern of boundary maintenance" between the sub-systems of the polity, and between the polity and the society. In very different, and more precise, language Almond is stating the principle of the *partial* separation of powers, expanded to take in a wider range of political phenomena, it is true, as it has been stated again and again over the centuries. As he puts it, "What is peculiar to modern political systems is the relatively high degree of structural differentiation (i.e. the emergence of legislatures, political executives, bureaucracies, courts, electoral systems, parties, interest groups, media of communication) with each structure tending to perform a regulatory role for that function within the political system as a whole."[64] In the concluding chapter of the book James Coleman takes this aspect of the analysis even further. He sets out the characteristics of the political systems under review, in order to demonstrate the extent to which they approximate to the democratic model. The democratic model, he says, assumes that governmental and political functions are performed by specific structures; for example, that rule-making is *primarily* by parliaments, and rule-application by controlled bureaucracies.[65] The assessment of the extent to which the non-Western political systems approximate to the democratic model is made through judgements about the extent to which particular structures "over-participate" in government functions; that is the extent to which, for example, the army is involved in the rule-making function, or the executive "over-participates" in the rule-adjudication function. The more these systems approximate to the democratic model the less "over-participation" there is in the performance of governmental functions.[66] Thus a "proper" level of specificity of function is equated with modern democracy—a proposition with which Montesquieu would have been fully in agreement. Almond and Coleman spread their net much more widely than did Montesquieu, or even James Madison, but when Madison, in No. 47 of the *Federalist*, explained his interpretation of Montesquieu he was putting exactly the same general point as his two modern American

64. Ibid., p. 18.   65. Ibid., pp. 559–60.   66. Ibid., pp. 560–7.

counterparts. Given all the differences in the two levels of analysis, it is the continuities and similarities which are so striking, rather than the dissimilarities in their positions. It is, perhaps, in the further elaboration of this new statement of an old position that we must look for a modern theory of constitutionalism.

ELEVEN

Political Theory, Constitutionalism, and the Behavioural Approach

T HE TWENTIETH century is an age of cynicism and scepticism as far as political theory is concerned. It is argued that political "theory" is in fact little more than the expression of opinion or prejudice, or, to put it in another way, is the expression of an ideology which is not amenable to proof or disproof. The sceptic sees the antithesis of political theory in the strictly empirical studies which have come to be known as "the behavioural approach." At the extreme, these two approaches to political phenomena are seen as wholly unrelated and irreconcilable. Any attempt, therefore, to assess the relevance of ideas of constitutionalism in the mid twentieth century must take account of the arguments of the behaviourist, and attempt to place such ideas in a meaningful context, for the attacks which have been made upon the separation of powers over the past century have not been concerned merely with a critique of its concepts, but have been associated with the rise of the behavioural school and its philosophical forbears, whose attack has been directed towards the very foundations upon which constitutional theories of the past have been based. This is hardly surprising. A theory which has at times claimed the status of a law of nature, or which has announced universal prerequisites of good government, must expect to come under attack when, for many people, the hallmark of a meaningful proposition comes to be the extent to which it can be scientifically tested. Clearly the relevance of this criterion to theories of government like the separation of powers must be explored.

Although at times raised to higher metaphysical levels, the discussion of the separation of powers, and related theories of limited government, has usually been carried on in empirical terms. The evidence that has been summoned in their defence has been the experience of history, the assumed knowledge of human nature, or the workings of contemporary systems of government. Yet given the kind of knowledge we can have about history, human nature, and politics, exactly what would constitute "proof" or "disproof" of theories is open to considerable doubt. Propositions concerning the nature of governmental organization, as broad as those made by proponents of the separation of powers, present a rather different problem of empirical verification from that of a proposition about voting behaviour in Greenwich or Elmira at a particular point of time. Can the same criteria be applied to both types of proposition? In general, political theorists would point out that theories of constitutionalism are made up of a number of different types of proposition, not all of which could be subjected to the same rigorous treatment as studies of voting behaviour. Their antagonists argue that if this is the case, then nothing "scientific," and, therefore, they imply, nothing of value, can result from this type of theory.

The behavioural attack upon political theory has been accompanied by a related, but separate, attack upon the idea that "constitutions" play an important role in the operation of the political system. The behaviourist's concern with "social forces," and his emphasis upon the real stuff of politics, seem to lead him to the view that the behaviour which he sees as the sole content of politics is not in any significant way affected by the structure of constitutional rules, but is wholly determined by economic, racial, class, and other factors. This is not simply an attack upon an outdated legalism in the study of politics. He is not concerned simply to point out that the formal structure of a "constitution" may be a very poor indicator of the actual operation of a political system. The rejection of the significance of constitutions goes far beyond this, to encompass much of what would normally be called political "institutions." We shall examine in some detail the most distinguished work of this sort, Robert A. Dahl's *Preface to Democratic Theory*, in which the definition of "constitutional" is given as the "prescribed rules influencing the legitimate distribution, types, and methods of control among government officials." This is no mere attack upon formalism, for Dahl includes all those rules which may be prescribed "by a variety of authorities accepted as legitimate among officials: the written Constitution, if there is one; decisions of a tribunal accepted as authoritative on constitutional interpretation; respected commentaries and the like."[1]

Theories of constitutionalism are attacked, therefore, both as being incapable of rigorous proof and because they deal with insignificant factors in political life. They are further subjected to attack because of their overt normative content. This objection, however, will not detain us for long. One may *disagree* with the recommendations of the constitutionalist on the grounds that one does not share his values, or that one does not accept the logic of his arguments, but of the importance of the views of writers on political and constitutional theory in the past, and of their role in helping to shape the patterns of history, there can surely be little doubt.[2] However, it has been pointed out by J. C. Rees that political theories, which are of necessity formulated in very general terms, cannot be used to deduce unequivocal courses of action in relation to specific cases.[3] Rees has in mind such general statements as that of Sir Ernest Barker that the purpose of the State is to promote "the highest possible development of all the capacities of personality in all of its members." Although the theories of limited government, such as the separation of powers, have claimed much greater precision and much more empirical relevance than could be claimed for the above statement, nevertheless Rees's objections do impinge upon these theories, for, as we have seen, it has been found to be virtually impossible

1. Robert A. Dahl, *A Preface to Democratic Theory*, Chicago, 1956, p. 135.
2. See J. Plamenatz, "The Use of Political Theory," *Political Studies*, 1960.
3. J. C. Rees, "The Limitations of Political Theory," *Political Studies*, 1954.

in practice to deduce from the doctrine of the separation of powers any precise criteria for allocating the tasks of government to its various branches, even though jurists have striven to give such precise operative interpretations to these concepts.

Although it may be true of constitutional theories, as of political theories in general, that it is impossible to move from general propositions to unambiguous statements about particular practical issues, this does not by any means prove that such theories have no value. They can provide guiding-lines within which the solution of practical issues must be found; they help to create an intellectual atmosphere in which certain courses of action will be excluded, even though the choice between the remaining alternatives is not precisely determined; they make self-conscious the values which are to be given priority, and the choice of a means of furthering these values. Such theories have the same relation to political action as military strategy has to tactics. The strategy which has been laid down will rarely give the tactician an unequivocal course of action to be followed in a particular situation, but he does have to reconcile his tactical decisions with the ultimate aims which have been set for him by the strategist. The mere fact that there are a number of tactical courses open to him, all of which seem to be broadly consistent with the over-all strategy to be followed, does not mean that there is no relationship between strategy and tactics. Thus political theorists can set the aims, can rule out certain courses of action, can set certain limits, but like the military strategist they will be the more successful the more they keep in mind the hard facts of the terrain they survey.

The attack upon "constitutions" as significant elements in political life may be illustrated by the work of three widely separated authors—William Penn, Sir Lewis Namier, and Robert A. Dahl. It is not suggested that these men are fully representative of "the behavioural approach"; indeed, it is the extreme nature of their expression of "behaviourism" that makes them useful as a basis for discussion of the importance of constitutional structures. The traditional or institutional approach to the study of politics has at times been subjected to extreme criticism; but in recent years this has given place to a recognition that both institutional and behavioural studies are essential to a balanced approach.[4] Nevertheless, these three writers provide us with the three main characteristics of the extreme approach—the emphasis upon "human nature" to the exclusion of the mechanics of government, the underlying assumption that it is the relative power of "groups" that provides the independent variables of the political system upon which all other factors depend, and the consequent belief that institutional structures can have little or no significant effect upon the outcome of political situations.

We might begin our discussion of constitutional theory and its significance by considering the views of an early "behaviourist," William Penn, writing in 1682. Penn was himself engaged in drawing up a form of government for the province which had been granted to him the previous year by Charles II, yet he took the opportunity in the Preface to his *Frame of Government of the Province of Pennsylvania* to express an extreme scepticism about the value of constitutional restraints upon political action. He dispensed with any discussion of "particular *frames* or *models*" of government: "There is hardly one frame of government," he wrote, "so ill designed by its first founders, that in good hands will not do well enough; and story tells us the best in ill ones, can do nothing that is great or good." For Penn governments were machines that, like clocks, work according to "the motion that men give them." Thus he concluded, "Let men be good, and the government cannot be bad; if it be ill they will cure it. But if men be bad, let the government be never so good, they will endeavour to warp and spoil it to their turn."

It is interesting to find this point of view expressed by a seventeenth-century Englishman so soon after so much blood had been shed over constitutional principles, for it represents a popular view of the British system of government in the mid twentieth century—principles are unimportant, all that matters is the character of those who run the government. However, such a view leads to a dilemma which was characteristic of the government of Pennsylvania in the eighteenth century, and is perhaps *the* problem of British government in this century. That is, one either places

4. See the essay by E. M. Kirkpatrick, in A. Ranney (ed.), *Essays on the Behavioral Study of Politics,* Urbana, 1962.

one's trust in the goodness of "the people," or, if this view is considered too ingenuous, one is led to a reliance upon government by an *élite*, which, because of its internal moral code, can be trusted to govern justly and well. However, when the *élite* begins to crumble, and is replaced, the values that might have been protected by a habit of constitutional thought find no protection in a society which has been taught to despise constitutionalism.

The basic inadequacy of Penn's view of political systems is its oversimplification. Societies are not composed solely of "good" men or of "ill" men, but are complex collections of human beings most of whom are both "good" and "bad," if such simple terms can convey very much of the fine shades of morality to be found throughout the political life of society. The essential point about constitutions is not that they could restrain a society full of bad men, but that they may channel political behaviour in certain directions rather than others, that the ordinary citizen will not be subject to the whims of good or bad men, but will have some certainty of essential continuities of action when the personnel of government changes. The aspiration towards a government of laws and not of men is inherently incapable of being realized, but a government of men subject to the restraints of certain rules is not.

William Penn's over-simple view of the relation between human nature and "frames of government" is not, of course, the position adopted by modern academic behaviourists, but their attitudes may be equally extreme. The emphasis upon "social forces" may be taken to the point where "government" seems to disappear altogether. Sir Lewis Namier, whose work might be seen as the first flowering of the present-day behavioural approach, has provided us with as extreme an expression of this point of view as it is possible to imagine. Live forces, Namier wrote, break through forms, and shape results to suit requirements. "Were it decided that the 615 heaviest men in the country should constitute the House of Commons, the various interests and parties could be trusted to obtain their proportionate weight in it."[5] This is so extreme that merely to state it is for it to be seen to be absurd. Namier could hardly have believed that the failure to pass the

---

5. *England in the Age of the American Revolution*, 2nd edn., London, 1961, p. 3.

Reform Acts would have made no difference to the decisions which were actually taken in Parliament in the mid and late nineteenth century. What then was the battle over the Reform Acts about? Why should the "live forces" have bothered with such a trivial matter as the franchise? Surely the failure to reform Parliament would have led eventually to revolutions like those that took place in other European countries, yet if we accept Namier's viewpoint revolutions would never occur, for they would serve no useful purpose. "Live forces" would inevitably attain their proportionate weights. Louis XVI would have been transformed into the President of the Republic without all that messy business of the Revolution, and a Czar of Russia would now be the guiding spirit of Russian economic planning. Yet revolutions do occur, and they occur because the nature of the political machinery, the composition of the parts of government, the accepted rules by which power is allocated, do make a very great difference to the content of government decisions, and to the outcome of political situations. To capture the machinery of government and to turn it to their own ends is the aim of revolutionaries, and it is, for them, a battle worth fighting. But Namier, and the American behaviourists, lived, or live, in a society where revolutions have long ceased to occur, and have assumed therefore that the stability provided by the political system was unimportant, whereas in reality it was the political system which was the whole context for their behavioural studies. It is unlikely that their point of view would be shared in those ages, or in those parts of the world, where the machinery of government did not allow the free interplay of the groups who form the society.

Thus the basic mistake of the Namier position is the assumption that there are *absolute* "proportionate weights" for the various parties and interests in society, which exist independently of the nature of the political system, or of the channels through which they must seek expression. But what are these absolutes, and how does one measure them? This is to seek a philosopher's stone of "power" that is surely chimerical. Social forces must be seen and evaluated *within* a particular set of relationships, without which they cannot have existence or meaning. Perhaps only in a truly revolutionary period can there be a situation in which, through the exercise of naked force, a true "absolute" can be seen to emerge, and then only momentarily.

In normal circumstances the "proportionate weight" of a party or group will depend to a very considerable degree upon the institutional patterns through which it must operate, the extent to which it has freedom of manoeuvre, and the influence it has upon the decision-making process. One can see, for example, that the "weight" of the French Communist Party in French politics since 1945 has been affected deeply by the nature of the *régime*, by the electoral law, and by the extent to which it was allowed to have a direct influence upon the way in which government decisions were taken. But how would one arrive at a statement of its "true" weight in these years? A discussion of its political role, except in the context of changing *régimes* and electoral machinery, would be meaningless. On the other hand, the history of the Third and Fourth Republics illustrates the limits upon what can be achieved if one attempts to alter the behaviour of parties and groups by tinkering with the institutional machinery. It is this complex inter-relationship of groups and structures which is the very stuff of political studies, but Namier virtually dismisses it altogether.

There is clearly a sense in which *political behaviour* is the sole, exclusive content of the study of politics—there is nothing else to study. Structures, institutions are patterns of behaviour. Ideas, like art, can be studied for their own sake, but the student of *politics* will be interested in them only in so far as they have affected, or will be likely to affect, the behaviour of men in society. Equally, material things will concern the student of politics only in so far as they are objects of political action. The stones and mortar of the Palace of Westminster or of the Capitol are of political interest only in so far as they inspire awe or revulsion in those who make political decisions in their vicinity. The pieces of paper which circulate in government offices in Paris, Washington, or London have no political importance except for the reactions of men and women to the inscriptions upon them. Money, steel, land, are not in themselves subjects of political study, but only in their effects upon political behaviour; otherwise they are the concern of the economist, the metallurgist, or the agriculturalist. Thus we are all behaviourists. Political institutions are not tangible structures of steel or wood, or even of papers held together by red tape, although these materials are incidental to these institutions. The orb and the sceptre, the seal of the United States, the flag or the ballot-box are all merely the outward symbols of the things men believe in or manipulate.

A political structure then *is* behaviour, but it is not random behaviour, it has a pattern. Furthermore, it is patterned behaviour of a peculiar stability and consistency, behaviour which follows certain rules whether explicit or implicit. To emphasize the importance of these rules, and the need for stability in the patterns of behaviour they regulate, is an essential aspect of constitutionalism. This is not to equate constitutionalism with conservative attitudes in politics, it is merely the recognition of the basic requirement of order in a political system. The satisfaction of the varied wants of mankind entails a society in which the future is relatively predictable, in which plans can be made and brought to fruition. Just as the fulfilment of economic wants is dependent upon a stable economic organization that will enable the seed which is planted to become bread upon the table, so all our political needs, which include the economic ones, require a stable political organization for their satisfaction. Anarchy, the absence of all rules, and therefore of predictability, is the frustration of any hope of attaining those material and spiritual satisfactions, including that of simply staying alive, which are the ultimate aims of all political action. In anarchy none but the psychopath gains satisfaction. The *continued* satisfaction of wants, and the *expectation* of future satisfactions, demands a stable, rule-governed pattern of political organization of behaviour.

Order and the political system, therefore, are synonymous. But political systems can take many forms, and the values they embody can vary widely, so that the type of future satisfactions they hold out can also differ. The arbitrary rule of a despot *may* be preferable to the war of all against all, but once man is protected from the unpredictable behaviour of his fellow subjects, he begins to look for further stability and predictability, that is to say in the behaviour of his governors. He demands the security of knowing how decisions will be reached, who will be consulted, the procedures which will be employed, the composition of the bodies that will decide. This is not, and cannot be, a matter of the expediency of group interaction, or the casual outcome of whatever "live forces" happen to be predominant at a particular point of time. It must be a process subject to rules, as vital as, although different in character from, the laws which govern one's relations with one's neighbour. This is a "constitution," and its scope is, of course, much wider than any written constitutional law as it is usually developed by lawyers. It is the secondary layer of rules in a political system, which determine how things shall be done, how decisions are to be made.[6] Just as anarchy is the antithesis of the legal system, so are despotism and totalitarianism the antithesis of the constitutional State, for they represent an "organized anarchy" at the secondary level, unpredictable and uncontrolled.

The expression of the behavioural approach in the quotation from Namier given earlier, errs, therefore, in underestimating the requirement of order in the political system, and in taking for granted the institutionalized order of constitutional States like Britain and the United States. Behaviourists concentrate upon what actually happens *within* the ordered system provided by the constitution, ignoring the long-term stabilities which are the context of, and the prerequisite for, such behaviour. They tend to ignore the restraints that the requirement of order places upon the political situation at any one point of time. It is this set of restraints which crystallizes institutions or structures, which sets the limits within which the "live forces" or the "social forces" must operate. Indeed, it is difficult to see how behavioural methods of investigation could handle the problems presented by these structures. The student of voting behaviour, for example, in attempting to answer the question why the electorate voted in a particular way at a particular election, has developed very refined tools of investigation to deal with this narrowly defined problem. But to answer the question of why an individual voter chose candidate X rather than candidate Y is very different from trying to answer the question of how it came to be that the choice was between X and Y in the first place, and not a choice between completely different alternatives. Such a problem can only be dealt with by using the whole range of techniques available. We should not allow our devotion to certain techniques to rule out vitally important problems of political enquiry.

Robert A. Dahl has presented us, in his *Preface to Democratic Theory,*

6. This is an extension, to the political system as a whole, of the terms which Professor H. L. A. Hart has used in regard to the legal system. See *The Concept of Law,* Oxford, 1961.

with a less extreme view of the behavioural approach than Namier's, and one which, because he uses James Madison's thought as a starting-point for his analysis, deals explicitly with the doctrine of the separation of powers. Dahl's main point is that "the first and crucial variables to which political scientists must direct their attention are social and not constitutional."[7] As we have seen, Dahl's definition of "constitutional" is a fairly wide one, but he does not attempt to deal with the general structure of political institutions, except in so far as he discusses the idea of the separation of powers. Political institutions in general seem to hang in a limbo between "social" and "constitutional" factors.

Dahl takes as his starting-point a theory that he labels "Madisonian," the central thesis of which is that there must be a constitutional separation of powers if the tyranny of the one, the few, or the many is to be averted. Dahl reassembles Madison's statements to form a number of definitions and hypotheses, in order to present the theory in a more coherent form, and to be able to test its central hypotheses. The principal hypothesis is that, if unrestrained by external checks, any given individual or group of individuals will tyrannize over others, and therefore that the first condition for the establishment and maintenance of a non-tyrannical republic is that the accumulation of all powers, legislative, executive, and judiciary, in the same hands, whether of one, a few, or many, and whether hereditary, self-appointive, or elective, must be avoided.[8] Dahl's attack is directed to showing that this position is "demonstrably false," and to proving that the relative importance of constitutional rules in general is trivial compared with that of social forces. Thus in discussing the extent to which minorities are protected from oppression by governments he concludes that "if constitutional factors are not entirely irrelevant, their significance is trivial as compared with the non-constitutional."[9]

The problem of sustaining this point of view depends very much upon the level at which the discussion is conducted. If Dahl meant merely that "paper constitutions" are in themselves unimportant, we could easily accept this point, but clearly he means much more than this. Yet the "proof"

7. Op. cit., p. 83.   8. Ibid., pp. 4–11; *Federalist* No. 47.
9. *A Preface to Democratic Theory*, p. 135.

---

of the demonstrably false Madisonian position which Dahl offers is a very dubious one. So far as Madison is dealing with "constitutionally prescribed authority," the only empirical evidence which Dahl produces, in order to dismiss his hypothesis as invalid, is to argue that parliamentary systems "like that of Great Britain," which are certainly non-tyrannical, readily prove that Madison's first condition for avoiding tyranny is unnecessary to achieve that aim. But Dahl does not discuss the British example to prove, as he must do to sustain his argument, that in Britain all power, legislative, executive, and judicial is accumulated in one set of hands. He seems merely to assume that this is the case, but this is a complicated matter which can hardly be treated *a priori*. Again, it is very much a matter of levels of discussion. At a later stage it will be suggested that the practical operation of British government today does suggest doubts about undue concentration of power through the medium of the party system; but at the level of constitutionally prescribed authority, at which Dahl conducts his discussion, it is by no means clear that all power is accumulated in this way in Britain. Dahl cannot mean to equate the idea of the separation of powers with the explicit example provided by the Constitution of the United States. Certainly Madison had no such idea, and it is Madison's formulation of the doctrine that Dahl uses as a basis of discussion. If Dahl were thinking in terms only of the precise *American* formulation of the separation of powers then there could be no argument, for clearly this is not essential to the prevention of tyranny. But Madison never asserted this. Indeed, he used the British Constitution of those days as an authority to which to appeal in support of his argument that the accumulation of all power in one set of hands must be avoided. Dahl, however, seems implicitly to adopt Bagehot's view that in Britain all the powers of government are fused, and does not push the empirical approach to the point of investigating the validity of this proposition.

It is by no means clear that the *constitutional* allocation of power differs so fundamentally in Britain and the United States as Dahl suggests. Thus if we think in terms of the personnel of the branches of government, although there is not in Britain the complete separation of the United States Constitution there certainly is not a complete fusion of the personnel of the three branches, either. Indeed, in spite of recent government legislation which increased the numbers of ministers in the House of Commons, there are rigid rules preventing civil servants from being members of the legislature, and to maintain a separate judiciary except for the Lord Chancellor and the Lords of Appeal. British government would be very different if these rules did not exist. If Dahl has in mind the legislative supremacy of the "King-in-Parliament," this concept also must be treated with care. As we have seen, legislative supremacy has never meant the dictatorship of one man or of either of the Houses of Parliament, except perhaps during Tudor times, or in the reign of the Long Parliament, neither of them very good precedents for modern British government. Constitutionally the "King-in-Parliament" is composed of a number of parts, and there has always been a distribution of power among them. Thus even in the United States a legal sovereign power exists, which, however quiescent it has been over the years, is clothed with an authority equal to that of the King-in-Parliament.[10] All power, legislative, executive, and judiciary, is accumulated into the hands of this "body," although it is certainly a great deal more difficult to organize effectively than the constituent parts of the British constitutional structure.

This, of course, is a highly formal legalistic argument, which may, or may not, have relevance to political reality; but it does point to the conclusion that a useful comparison of the British and American political systems in this respect *must* be based upon a close analysis of the working of political institutions and the party systems of the two countries, rather than upon superficial comparisons of their legal structure. We shall have to consider at a later stage the relationship between the legal divisions of power in these countries and the operation of their party systems, and the extent to which the one may exercise restraints upon the other, but it is certainly not possible to discuss the significance of some form of "separation of powers" in Britain without such an investigation.

Thus far, then, the main objections to Dahl's analysis are that he does

10. Two-thirds of both Houses of Congress, together with three-quarters of the legislatures of the States, in all matters other than equal representation in the Senate, in which case the States affected by any alteration must consent.

not define the separation of powers clearly enough, nor does he apply empirical rigour in his "disproof" of Madison's hypothesis. But we must follow through Dahl's criticisms of Madisonianism, because they reveal some of the most significant problems of constitutional theory and the behavioural approach.

Dahl represents "Madisonianism" as if it were a concern merely for an abstract constitutional doctrine of the separation of powers which would of itself obviate tyrannical tendencies in government. But Madison was in fact much too aware of the importance of "social forces" to argue in this fashion. Indeed, Madison, in the *Federalist* Nos. 47–51, from which Dahl draws his "Madisonian" hypotheses, was not so much concerned with asserting the importance of the separation of powers, as with insisting upon the fact that it must be modified and buttressed with checks and balances reflecting social factors. These papers from the *Federalist* were the great climax to the campaign against a dependence upon "parchment barriers" to the exercise of power, which had begun at the very moment when the revolutionary State constitutions were being written. Madison argued forcefully, and with a good deal of empirical evidence from the experience of Pennsylvania and Virginia, in support of the view that constitutional rules not buttressed by institutionalized structures of real power, related to social reality, would be worthless. He was in fact attacking that pure doctrine of the separation of powers which Dahl attributes to him, and attacks in his turn. But, of course, Madison does not push the argument to the same extremes as Dahl does. Constitutional rules without effective sanctions are worthless in Madison's eyes, but when they are fashioned so as to correspond to the social basis of the political situation, they can and do make a considerable difference to the way in which governments operate, and the effect they in turn can have upon social forces.

Thus although Madison was wrong in detail about the way in which the institutions of the new government would work, he was right in the long run about the importance of the institutional structure as a means of channelling political activity in certain directions. He did not "deduce" checks and balances from the separation of powers as Dahl suggests,[11] he modified

11. *Preface to Democratic Theory*, p. 14.

the doctrine with ideas drawn from the balanced constitution of Britain, with its keen appreciation of the role that institutional structures could perform in a heterogeneous society. The application of the pure separation of powers in the revolutionary State constitutions had failed, because it depended purely upon an abstract formula for its effectiveness. Therefore, Madison argued, although each branch of government ought really to be invested with "a will of its own," and should ideally draw its authority direct from the people, through channels having no communication whatever with one another, this in practice would provide certain difficulties, in particular with regard to the judiciary. A better scheme would be for the legislature to be divided, with different modes of election for the two Houses, and for the separately elected President to be invested with a veto power.[12] This structure must be related to the division of power between the Federal and State governments, and to the breaking-up of the electorate into many "interests and classes of citizens." It is difficult to see how it can be asserted that this constitutional system has been of little significance in the development of the American polity. In the light of American history it is a brave man indeed who can assert that it would not have mattered very much if the President had not been given a veto, or if the Supreme Court had been forbidden, as were the French courts in 1791, to invalidate legislation.

Thus Dahl questions whether the separation of powers can provide effective external checks upon the tyrannical impulses of officials; loss of status, respect, prestige, or friendship would be ineffective, he argues, the monetary motive is ruled out, and coercive action against officials would hardly be in question.[13] What sanctions would there be? Madison, however, saw the problem more clearly. "Ambition must be made to counteract ambition," he wrote,[14] and this must surely be seen as the key to the antagonisms between President and Congress, between Senate and House of Representatives, between Congress and the bureaucracy, and even between all of these and the Supreme Court. Ambition, whether it be simply to wield power, to serve the people, to make money, or to make history, this has been the continuing dividing force that has operated through the various

12. *Federalist*, No. 51.   13. *Preface to Democratic Theory*, p. 20.
14. *Federalist*, No. 51.

337

channels which the Founding Fathers provided, in order that no matter how tall one man's ambitions became, there would always be an institutional basis upon which other ambitious men could oppose him. At times one feels that Dahl believes these institutionally-supported ambitions to have been all too successful in directions of which he disapproves,[15] whilst his main argument is directed towards showing that they could not have been significant. But if it *is* his intention to argue against the results produced by the American system of government, then this is inconsistent with his general argument that the nature of the system does not really matter.

We arrive, therefore, at the central issue between Dahl and Madison— whether a particular type of constitutional structure is, or is not, a prerequisite of a non-tyrannical republic. The definition of "tyranny" is in Dahl's view a crucial problem of the Madisonian argument. As he points out, Madison does not give a precise and specific meaning to this concept, so that the validity of hypotheses which relate to "the prevention of tyranny" cannot be established by rigorous empirical tests. He concludes, therefore, that Madisonianism is an "ideology" rather than a "political theory," a significant and important ideology, which has played, and will continue to play, a role in politics, but which has no contribution to make to political science.[16] Yet surely the inability to make precise a definition of tyranny that will be operationally effective does not dispose of the problem with which Madison was concerned. The concept of tyranny, or the rather less dramatic idea of "the abuse of power," may not be susceptible of very precise definition: yet of the historical fact of the existence of tyranny or abuse of power there can hardly be much doubt. The existence of tyranny cannot be denied because we are unable to say precisely where it begins and where it ends. It is a fact, of course, that there can be no absolute definition of these terms, for they are relative to the particular period and the particular culture being considered. There are inescapable value-judgements here, and we must accept that a discussion of constitutionalism can begin only by pointing to certain specific examples of societies which are asserted to

15. See for example his remarks p. 81, op. cit., about the role of checks and balances in depriving the unpropertied masses of political equality.

16. Op. cit., pp. 30–31.

be non-tyrannical, and to attempt to elucidate their major characteristics. This, in fact, was the procedure Madison followed, and, it will be contended, is the only one that can be followed.

Thus the insistence of the behavioural approach upon what its proponents consider to be strict empirical verification is taken to the point where the most important questions of the study of politics are excluded from consideration. Yet the behaviourist himself rarely appreciates the extent to which his own criteria, if strictly applied, would prohibit him from discussing even those things he considers appropriate for investigation. For the theoretical demands of the behaviourist for precision and empirical verification are not always reflected in his statements about the real world. This is simply a result of the fact that it is impossible to subject the discussion of political systems to the criteria of verifiability which the behaviourist espouses. This point cannot be illustrated more effectively than by an examination of Dahl's work itself.

He points out that in some nations powerful minorities have not refrained from the excessive exercise of power, whereas in others they have refrained. He argues that "whether or not powerful minorities or mass-based dictatorial leaders have refrained from establishing tyranny is clearly not related to the presence or absence of constitutional separation of powers. Many variables are involved in such a situation, but the constitutional separation of powers cannot be established as one of them." Again Dahl does not attempt to give any empirical evidence for this assertion, but a brief attempt to repair this deficiency in his argument will help to illustrate the problems of the strict behavioural approach.

We can formulate two hypotheses that the doctrinaire separation of powers theorist might adopt, and consider the problems of testing them, leaving aside for the moment the problems of definition. They are as follows:

(i) *No non-tyrannical republic can exist without a constitutional separation of powers.*

(ii) *Any republic which has a constitutional separation of powers will avoid tyranny.*

Now these hypotheses have one characteristic of which Dahl should approve—they are strictly empirical and capable of being falsified by empirical evidence. Find any one example of a non-tyrannical republic in which there is no constitutional separation of powers and (i) is false. Find any one example of a republic with a constitutional separation of powers which lapsed into tyranny, and (ii) is false. We have already referred to Dahl's attempt to disprove (i) by a simple reference to Great Britain. Such a disproof does not work, yet it might well be that if history were scoured such an example might be found—in the ancient world with small city-States, or in the town-meetings of New England, if local government be admitted here for discussion. In such small face-to-face societies the requirements of political organization are likely to be different from those of modern nation-States. Such a conclusion would hardly be surprising. The main point is that proposition (i) could in principle be shown to be false.

Proposition (ii) is a much easier nut to crack. There must be many States that embodied some form of separation of powers—not necessarily on the American model—which have later succumbed to tyranny, or the abuse of power, by almost any definition. The Weimar Republic, Republican Spain, the Kingdom of Italy—all had constitutions that incorporated some form of separation of functions among distinct, though not completely separate, branches of government. South America provides examples of constitutions much closer to the American pattern which have not been able to stem the advance of tyranny. There is, therefore, a wealth of evidence to dispose of (ii).

A more subtle hypothesis, however, would be as follows:

(iii) *A constitutional separation of powers is an important factor in maintaining certain types of political systems in which abuses of power are checked.*

This is, in fact, the antithesis of the assertion Dahl makes that the separation of powers is "clearly not related" to the question of tyranny. Now to establish either hypothesis, (iii) or Dahl's, presents problems of great complexity. Certainly neither can be asserted as self-evident, and it is impossible to test either of them in the strict terms which Dahl himself advocates. Such an hypothesis can be examined only by looking at the examples of non-tyrannical political systems which exist, and attempting to form a judgement about their operation. Thus we can consider the role of the separation of powers in the history of the United States, but to do so we must employ a whole range of historical and philosophical techniques, concerning ourselves with modes of thought, indeed, which Dahl rejects as merely "ideological." Indeed Dahl's proposition is, in his own terms, an expression of an "ideology" and not a conclusion of political science, for he is asserting that the separation of powers is *not a significant variable in the United States,* and this is a proposition it would be impossible to substantiate through strict empirical "tests." To apply his own strict criteria to the proof of this statement he would have to compare the United States with a society like the United States in every respect over the past two centuries, except that in the latter all powers were accumulated in one set of hands, and to show that, as regards tyranny or the abuse of power, there were no significant differences between the two societies. The impossibility of adopting this procedure indicates the limits of the behavioural approach in politics.

This limitation upon the nature of proof in history and politics must be accepted. There is no way round it. This does not mean that strict empirical verification should not be applied wherever possible, nor that the examination of propositions, like that which Dahl contends for, should be conducted as a metaphysical enquiry, and without the closest possible reference to all known facts. It simply means that if we wish to consider the most interesting, and the most important, propositions about politics we cannot afford to restrict ourselves to techniques that will allow of the investigation only of matters of secondary importance.

That Dahl himself is really aware of this can be seen by a comparison of the later chapters of the work in question with its earlier ones. He adopts very different methods when developing his own views about American government from those he wishes to apply to Madison's thought. Thus after a close criticism of the separation of powers doctrine, as applied by Madison, Dahl ends by acknowledging that there is a sense in which every "polyarchy" is characterized by a separation of powers. He talks in terms of the need for a "more or less representative body to legitimize basic decisions by some process of assent," of a need for bureaucracies of permanent experts, of the need for "a specialized bureaucracy" to pass judgements upon appeals from decisions of bureaucratic officials and to adjudicate conflicts among individuals, and of the need for leaders to co-ordinate bureaucratic, judicial, and legislative decisions.[17] Dahl suggests that this is a matter of the division of labour, but this, of course, is only partly true. The division of labour requires specialization, but not necessarily of this precise type. Indeed the extent to which Western society has followed the dictates of the division of labour is itself an expression of a value-judgement, for if we follow its prescription we are pursuing a value, i.e. efficiency measured in terms of output or technical effectiveness. But this type of efficiency can be, and has been, sacrificed if other values predominate. Totalitarianism and theocracy, each in its own way, sacrifice technical efficiency in order to achieve other aims. The division of labour has been emphasized in Western societies *because* of the values we place upon technical efficiency, and also because, happily, the requirements of the division of labour have tended to match fairly well the other requirements of these societies. Yet where "fairness" or "justice" has been considered more important than speed or the expediency of policy-makers, complex time-consuming procedures have been evolved in an attempt to give priority to the desired values.

In fact the whole section where Dahl develops this point is shot through with the values and concepts of the writers who have related democracy and the separation of powers down through the centuries. Dahl is very clearly a Madisonian. He notes indeed that all polyarchies have "strikingly similar constitutions," but his conclusion is that this means "the constitutional variable" is even more limited than would be thought at first glance.[18] Others might consider this to be a highly significant correlation.

The fundamental error of all three of our "behaviourists," William Penn, Sir Lewis Namier, and Robert A. Dahl, is that they draw a false dichotomy between "constitutions" and "social forces." This suggestion, that social forces and constitutional structures are quite distinct entities, is a result of, and a reaction against, the legalism and formalism which once domi-

17. Op. cit., p. 136.   18. Ibid., pp. 135–6.

nated the study of politics. But it leaves the whole question of the nature of "political institutions" in an awkward limbo. The Congress of the United States is surely an important subject of study for political scientists, but is it "constitution" or is it "social forces"? Merely to pose the question is to reveal its absurdity. Of course, it is neither, but it involves both. The problem arises from the attempt to reduce the material of politics to one set of "independent," and one set of "dependent," variables, in a way that will give a specious mathematical neatness to what is in fact an enormously complex situation. Yet the inter-relationships of this material can be seen once again by taking an illustration from Dahl's own work. In his discussion of "polyarchy," Dahl hypothesizes that polyarchy is a function of the consensus on the norms which are its definitional characteristics, and further that the extent of this consensus is dependent upon the extent of social training in these norms. The concluding hypothesis is: "Polyarchy is a function of the total social training in all the norms." Now Dahl conceives of "social training" as carried on by the family, schools, churches, clubs, literature, newspapers, "and the like." Yet social training in most societies, and not least in America, may also be carried on by governments, and all the above-mentioned media of social training may to a considerable extent consciously or unconsciously direct their activities towards training in the constitutional rules, and in the operation of the political institutions, of the country concerned. "Social training" is not an "independent variable" which gives rise to a particular constitutional structure; it is itself the result of the historical evolution of the political system and knowledge of its operation. Dahl acknowledges this "hen–egg" relationship in regard to "consensus" and "social-training," but still doggedly removes constitutional factors from the realm of "significant variables."[19]

The role of "constitutions" and of the study of "constitutions" is, then, much more complex and much more important than the behaviourists suggest. But do not let us seem to be claiming too much. We must accept the view that much of the Madisonian approach is inadequate to an understanding of the role of constitutions and political institutions in the

19. Ibid., pp. 76–78; 83.

twentieth century, although not for the reasons Dahl gives. The concepts of the eighteenth-century theorists were too crude to cope with the complexity of modern government.

Furthermore we have accepted that what was labelled (ii) above was an untenable hypothesis, and that (i) was unlikely to be true if applied to all societies at all times. There clearly are limits to what constitutional rules can achieve, however broadly we conceive of constitutionalism. In 1892 Jowett criticized Plato and Aristotle for having entertained a dream of a mixed State which would escape the evils and secure the advantages of both aristocracy and democracy. Such a creation he believed was beyond the legislator's art. "No system of checks and balances, such as Plato has devised in the *Laws,* could have given equipoise and stability to an ancient state, any more than the skill of the legislator could have withstood the tide of democracy in England or France during the last hundred years, or have given life to India or China."[20] The primacy of "social forces" in this sense of the great movements of social life can hardly be questioned. Constitutions, or political systems, are not iron-clad structures which can withstand the transformation of the social assumptions on which they are based, resulting from great technological or ideological developments. But this is not to say that even in such situations constitutions are insignificant or unimportant. The Constitution of the United States is today a very different structure from that of 1789, but it is still a Constitution, possessing a recognizable continuity with that of the earlier age, and it would be very difficult to prove that it had had a negligible part in creating the present political structure of the United States.

Jowett's objection was an aversion to constitution-building, rather than to constitutions, and it illustrates the difference between an abstract constitution on paper, and the operation of a set of political institutions which has been evolving slowly over centuries. Even so, we do live in an age that provides a veritable storehouse of political experience with new constitutions, offering an opportunity to study the circumstances in which they can and cannot have a significant effect. Jowett's reference in 1892 to India is

20. *The Dialogues of Plato,* 3rd edn., Oxford, 1892, Vol. V, pp. ccxvii–ccxviii.

of great interest, for seventy years later we do find a constitutional democracy in existence in India, although it is one the stability of which is still not very certain. The life that has been given to India must surely in part be due to the history of the development of constitutionalism in that country during the present century. The study of politics must, therefore, very largely consist of the examination of the ways in which constitutional and political institutions, and the social forces and movements in a particular society, interact with each other; of the limits upon the extent to which stable constitutional modes of behaviour can be developed and maintained; and of the effects they can have in moulding behaviour. To do this we shall have to adopt all the techniques of study which are relevant to the solution of such complex problems, but however much we learn about politics in this way we shall never, and can never, have final and completely "verified" answers to any of these questions.

TWELVE

A Model of a Theory of Constitutionalism

P OSSIBLY the dominant impression left by this survey of three centuries of Western constitutional thought is that we of the middle of the twentieth century live in an age which has inherited a number of different traditions, without being able ourselves to knit these varied strands into a coherent pattern, to derive a unified reconciling theory of constitutional government. Some prevailing intellectual modes, indeed, are hostile to any attempt at it. The demands made upon modern governments, the complexity of their aims, demand new techniques, new procedures, new forms: it is not surprising that the relevance of older theories and traditional systems of thought are doubted, and certain modern students of government have adopted a narrowly conceived "scientific" approach to the study of politics which is intended as a fresh start. Yet their own work, as we have tried to show, betrays the impossibility of rejecting centuries of discussion on a subject as purposive as the pursuit of political aims. Their value-patterns and aspirations show through the superficial detachment, and they reveal themselves as the children of Locke, of Montesquieu, and of Madison.

For the functional categories of the doctrine of the separation of powers with their intimate relationship to the rule of law, the concept of balance which was the essential element of theories of limited government, and the central ideas of representation and responsibility underlying theories of parliamentary government—all these continue to be important parts of our intellectual apparatus. We still appreciate the ideal of a moderate government, one which will avoid the extremes of any "simple" form of State—an ideal to which the ancient world first gave expression. The demand for freedom from arbitrary rule, which dominated the minds of the men of the post-Renaissance era, is also our demand. The nineteenth-century middle-class aspiration towards a "harmonious" polity is, in the conditions of universal suffrage, transmuted into an increasingly insistent search for co-ordinated and efficient government.

The persistence of these values—justice, "democracy," efficiency—in our constitutional thinking does not, of course, demonstrate that the old functional and structural conceptions, which earlier writers found satisfactory, are still adequate to explain modern government. New trends in the institutional development of advanced Western countries in the last hundred years are somewhat difficult to fit into the older categories, and new concepts have to be found. Account must be taken of the concept of *process*, which has so illumined modern sociological thought, and which can now be put alongside the older concepts of function and structure.

These, then, are the three elements of the model which it is proposed to develop: to approach the constitutional system from these three related view-points of function, structure, and process; to show how they are interdependent, mutually interacting, and how they are intimately related to certain value-patterns; and to emphasize that the character of constitutionality lies in this inter-penetration of function, structure, and process.

In the history of constitutional theory the most persistently used concept has been that of function. It finds its roots in Greek political thought, it is the basis of the idea of a government of laws, and it has been the most used tool of analysis for purposes of articulating the parts of government. Yet it has been subjected to a vast amount of criticism, and by many writers has been rejected as a useless concept. Perhaps the most serious aspect of these criticisms is that they strike at the basis of the rule of law, not merely in the sense of the particular formulation that Dicey developed, but in the sense in which a primary rule-making function is the basis of any constitutional theory.

The nature of the "functions" of government thus requires considerable clarification. The long discussion of the powers of government has been conducted largely in terms of the legislative, executive, and judicial functions. These abstract concepts emerged after a long period in which men thought mainly in terms of the "tasks" which government had to perform, such as conducting war and diplomacy, and maintaining order. The emergence of the idea of legislative and executive powers, or functions, had in itself little to do with an analysis of the essential nature of government; it was concerned more with the desire, by delimiting certain functional areas, to be able to restrict the ruler to a particular aspect of government and so to exercise limits on his power. This "purposive" quality of the traditional classification of government is important, for it makes the discussion of functional analysis much more than simply an attempt at description; it inevitably carries a normative connotation as well. The very use of these terms assumes a commitment to some form of constitutional government.

Let us, for a moment, accept the traditional triad of "government functions" in order to consider the problems of adopting a functional analysis. However, we shall think in terms of the functions of the *political system* rather than the government, for the problem of the control of government action which lies at the heart of constitutional thought necessitates an over-all view of function, rather than a concern merely with the relationship between government and citizens implied in the earlier usage. This emphasis upon the political system, rather than upon the machinery of government alone, is a characteristic of a recent functional analysis of government, that of Gabriel Almond in *The Politics of the Developing Areas*. Almond attempts to incorporate into the functional concepts developed by political theorists the rather different type of functional analysis of the sociologist. He distinguishes the "input" functions of the political system from the governmental "output" functions. The former include political socialization and recruitment, interest articulation and aggregation, and political communication. The latter consist of the rule-making, rule-application, and rule-adjudication functions;[1] Almond attempts to rid these concepts of their attachment to particular structures of government by adopting these terms instead of the more familiar legislative, executive, and judicial categories. This usage helps to make clear the often-emphasized fact that the structures of government are, in Almond's term, "multi-functional." That is to say that rules are made by civil servants and by judges as well as by legislatures; rules are applied by the courts as well as by "the executive"; and judgements are made by civil servants and ministers as well as by judges. Thus the purposive nature of the older concepts is removed and the scientific generality of these tools for the analysis of systems of government is established. Yet, as we have seen, the values of earlier centuries persist strongly, and the insistence upon rules being made by legislatures remains for Almond and Coleman a distinguishing characteristic of democratic political systems. The fact that a particular task of government is regulated by "legislation" rather than by some other procedure reflects the determination that certain values shall predominate in the ordering of society rather than others. It is in fact the procedures of government which are "purposive," for they are chosen or rejected to perform certain tasks because of the values they embody. It is this connection between functions, procedures, and values which we must explore.

The pure doctrine of the separation of powers implied that the functions of government could be uniquely divided up between the branches of government in such a way that no branch need ever exercise the function of another. In practice such a division of function has never been achieved, nor indeed is it desirable that it should be, for it would involve a disjuncture in the actions of government which would be intolerable. But the criticism of the threefold conception of government functions can be taken much further than pointing out that it has never been wholly achieved in practice. It can be suggested that the "multifunctionality" of political structures can, and perhaps must, be carried to the point where any attempt at a division of functions is quite impossible.

1. G. A. Almond and J. S. Coleman, *The Politics of the Developing Areas,* Princeton, 1960, pp. 16–17.

Let us take two examples, the first from the courts. A judge when dealing with a case, at any rate in a common-law country, is applying the law to a particular instance, is "judging" or determining the nature of the rule to be applied, and is at the same time creating a precedent to be followed by other courts. He, therefore, *of necessity*, exercises all three functions, and cannot be prevented from doing so if he is to perform the tasks which he is set. To take a more extreme case, let us consider the work of the administrator. The most extreme theorists of the policy-administration dichotomy suggest that the civil servant merely exercises a technical skill which is directed towards the execution of rules laid down for him by the political branches of the government. Thus they think in terms of an "administrative function." But in fact civil servants, without any intention of abusing their powers, inevitably make rules, interpret them, and apply them. Nor is this limited to the formal cases of delegated legislation, or administrative jurisdiction, which have received so much attention. As in the case of the judge, it seems to be inherent in the tasks which the administrator must perform. The administration of any complex governmental programme involves the taking of many decisions at all stages of its operation, many of which will become precedents for later administrative decisions. These "rules," though not always formulated as such will govern the decisions of other civil servants, and will be applied to the clients of the government department, the public, who are affected by its decisions. This situation arises from the fact that statutes or other policy decisions can never present a rigid plan to be followed exactly by civil servants, who must be allowed a certain discretion, often very wide, in the administration of government programmes. Furthermore, administrative action demands a high degree of consistent, patterned behaviour, and the administrative machine generates the rules and precedents which will ensure this consistency. They will not be "authoritative" in the sense in which a court ruling is authoritative, for they could in principle be invalidated by judicial review. Yet as far as the ordinary citizen is concerned they will for the most part represent "the law." Often these rules will be matters on which a court would refuse to adjudicate, and the overwhelming majority will never be brought before the courts.

The misconception of the functional categories of the separation of powers, therefore, stemmed from the naive view that there were distinct actions of willing and execution that could be isolated and kept in separate compartments. Such a distinction *might* possibly be applied to extremely simple actions. A decision to open the door, and then opening it, might be treated in this way. But most operations of government are much too complex, requiring a whole stream of decisions to be taken, such that it is impossible to divide them up into acts of will and acts of execution. In the same way the later distinction between "policy" and "administration," which was intended to replace the legislative-executive dichotomy, also breaks down. An important decision about "policy" will often be the climax of much administrative activity, rather than the initiation of it.[2]

Thus if we pursue the analysis to its limits we see that the exclusive allocation of rule-making, rule-application, or rule-adjudication to particular organs of government is not only inconvenient, it is probably quite impossible. Every act of every official, except perhaps the most routine and trivial operations, embodies all three types of activity. The policeman on the beat creates precedents in his actions, even if only for the people in his vicinity; he determines in which cases he will apply the rules, and when he does apply them his decision is subject to appeal; but when he decides *not* to apply the rules, as he interprets them, his interpretation will usually be final. Thus within his sphere of competence he will make rules by interpretation of other rules, and apply them. Such a view might seem to put an end to functional analysis of the kind which has in the past been the basis of attempts to confine parts of the government to specified types of behaviour.

Can we then save the idea of functionalism in the sense in which it has traditionally been used in the analysis of political systems? The first idea which we might use is that of a hierarchy or structure of rules, so that even if we accept that judges and administrators *must* also make rules these will be subordinated to those made by the legislature. This is, of course, the extension of the idea of law which has for centuries been the sheet-anchor of the concept of constitutionalism; the idea of a hierarchy of norms that will

2. In this discussion I am greatly indebted to an unpublished manuscript on administration by Andrew Dunsire of the University of York.

enable each of the decisions of an official to be tested against a higher rule. This ultimate rule-making authority in a democratic system is entrusted to a body representative of the people, or to a constitution ultimately subject to popular control. The history of Western constitutionalism has been the history of the constant pressure to maintain the ultimate authority of "the legislature."

However, there are considerable difficulties with this seemingly essential element of the theory of the constitutional State. To argue that rules must be arranged in a hierarchical fashion so that they can be tested suggests an ability always to apply the logical criteria of deduction to the material of government decisions. It can easily be shown from the material of judicial opinions that the discretion in the hands of a judge to place one interpretation rather than another upon the relationship between "higher" and "subordinate" decisions is often very great indeed. Yet the very fabric of the constitutional State would seem to depend upon the willingness of courts to undertake and to operate successfully this "semi-logical" procedure. The success of the Supreme Court of the United States in exercising this discretion has been considerable, and in spite of the highly-charged political character of many of its decisions it has retained the ability and the prestige to enable it to perform this function. In the field of administrative law, in which so many of these decisions fall, the *Conseil d'Etat* in France has been equally successful. In Britain, however, one of the most marked governmental trends has been the continued decline of judicial power—a refusal on the part of the judges to exercise this discretion and a readiness to acquiesce in governmental and administrative acts. Discredited in their attempts at defending privilege against government action, the courts have not followed the line the American courts took in the same situation, and become the defenders of "the individual," or "the people," against a government which might be representing interests rather than the community. Part of this failure has undoubtedly been a failure of nerve, but partly also it is due to the operation of party politics, which has increasingly threatened the judges with the use of the rule-making power of Parliament if they attempted to restrain administrative actions. There have been a number of instances since the Second World War where decisions of the courts which went against the administration have been quickly reversed by Parliament, sometimes with incredible rapidity. The case of the War Damage Act of 1965 in Britain is an extreme one, for it had retroactive effect, and so offended against the basic rule of constitutionalism, the predictability of action.

Thus even if we accept "the rule of law" in the sense of a hierarchy of rules which can ultimately be tested against the final statutory or constitutional authority, we have to face the fact that this may become merely a matter of form. The outward forms of legality are retained, but they may be manipulated by the party leaders in a way which makes a mockery of them. The twentieth-century concern with the solution of practical problems can be taken to the point where the desire to deal with particular issues overrides all consideration of the way in which these issues are dealt with. Yet so long as the procedures for changing the law, or for making new laws, retain their vitality, and represent a genuine check upon the bureaucracy and its political chiefs, the dangers of the abuse of power in this way are minimized.

Thus, although dangers exist, it would be wrong to argue that *at the present time* all powers in Britain are accumulated in the same hands. There are two reasons for taking this view. The first lies in the nature of the ultimate rule-making power. It is obvious that neither in France, in the United States, nor in Britain does "the legislature" any longer *exclusively* exercise a rule-making, or legislative power. In Britain, of course, the "King-in-Parliament" legislates in the formal sense, but the House of Commons does not, either alone or in combination with the "upper" house, actively make law. "Legislative supremacy" is guarded, but the "legislature," in the sense of the assembled representatives of the people, does not write the laws. The overwhelming proportion of legislation is written in the government departments and is presented to Parliament by ministers and accepted by the House with only minor amendments. In the United States the trend towards Presidential legislation is also marked, although it has not, of course, developed to the same extent that it has in Britain. Most major measures are prepared by the Administration, and although a particular session of Congress may exercise its prerogatives and substantially amend or even reject Administration proposals, it seems to be true that constant pressure by Administrations over a number of years will gradually wear down Congressional opposition. We are perhaps entering a period when the most significant difference between the British and American systems of government is that in Britain consultation about proposed legislation takes place almost exclusively *before* its introduction into Parliament, whereas in America it still takes place *within* Congress. But the ultimate result is still that the major initiative for, and the largest share in the framing of, legislation is in the hands of civil servants, ministers, and presidents or their advisors. In Fifth Republic France the need for rules to be made other than in the "legislature" has been recognized by the granting of a constitutional rule-making power to the government.

But have we really described how rules are *made* in Britain? What does rule-*making* mean? Are rules made by the person who drafts them, by the body which formally approves them, or by the leaders who instruct the draftsmen and who organize the approving body? The answer in Britain today is, surely, that the rules are made by all three elements in the process. We should not forget that ministers and civil servants are different bodies of men, differently composed, differently recruited, with a different tenure, with different skills, and with different interests. The number of important decisions taken by government is so great that ministers cannot possibly hope to give their attention to, or even to understand, all of them. There is also a division of power and of interest between ministers and the members of Parliament who compose the legislature. If the functions of the House of Commons were truly formal, if it were a rubber-stamp, then it could hardly be said to share in rule-making. But this is surely not yet the case. The existence of an opposition party in the House of Commons, and its role of making a constant appeal, with the next election in mind, to the public, imposes upon the government the necessity of defending its measures in Parliament not as a mere formality but as a genuine attempt to convince; not to convince the Opposition—that could hardly be hoped for—but to convince interested groups, the more perceptive elements in the electorate, and, most important of all, its own supporters in the House. Thus, although governments do not expect, and very rarely meet, defeat in the legislature, they do not do so largely because the political problems have been ironed out as far as is possible in the consultations, before the introduction of legislation, in the party, with interested groups, in the departments, in the government itself, and in a few cases in the cabinet, or between the Prime Minister and a few close colleagues. Yet this whole complex process of consultation is dependent upon the structure and constitutional powers of the House of Commons. It is the ultimate reality of that body which imposes this whole process upon the government. Let us not decry that institution because it no longer *makes* laws, for it imposes great restraints upon the way in which they are drafted. Not the least important part of its structure is the rule which excludes holders of offices-of-profit (principally civil servants) from membership of the House. To take this point to extremes, it would be a very different system of government if *all* members of the House were ministers or civil servants; then truly the function of the House in regard to rule-making would be purely formal. It is this consideration that makes the further increase in the number of ministers in the House of Commons inimical to our constitutional traditions and interests. There is thus a real sense in which the ministers, the civil servants, and the House of Commons *share* the rule-making power; furthermore, this is a body of men which is, by law, differentiated into three distinct but overlapping groups, and it is legal rules which, by helping to minimize the importance of party among the civil servants, and by helping to ensure a two-party system in the Commons, place limits upon the ultimate power of a single political party or its leaders in the exercise of the rule-making function. It is in this sense that a "partial separation of powers" is still the central principle of the British system of government today. This should not lead to complacency, for, as will be argued later, it is the balance between these elements which should concern us.

Thus there are rules, in this case formal legal rules, which ensure some basis for a functional view of the rule-making power in Britain. These formal rules, however, need support; for, as we have seen, it is very difficult to ensure the primacy of the formal rule-making function when all elements of the government make rules in one sense or another. In Britain this support has been provided by a second set of informal, extra-legal rules of behaviour. Among the bureaucrats, the judges, and also among ministers, there has been a *conscious* attempt to maintain a distinction between what they have been taught to regard as their own *primary* functions and the primary functions of other officials, although they might agree, if pressed, that they exercised *subordinate* rule-making functions as an essential ingredient of their primary function. Thus judges would argue that their main function is the *interpretation* of statutes, and that although this involves rule-making they will normally attempt to subordinate this rule-making function to that of Parliament. Civil servants *could* apply policies in such a way that the reverse effect is produced from that which was intended by Parliament, but it is normally assumed that they will subordinate their activities to the statutory intent. Thus professional loyalty, or integrity, the acknowledgment that a certain "function" is their primary concern, is an essential ingredient in the attitudes of ministers, judges, and administrators in the constitutional State. Certain rules of behaviour, *internal* to the group concerned, are as essential as the external rules imposed by law. The "internal" rules are not, of course, internal in the sense that they are secret, or that they are known only to the group concerned. On the contrary, they are more likely to persist if they are publicly upheld as a "code of behaviour" which distinguishes the group from the common herd. The exemplification of this attitude is to be found in the office of Lord Chancellor in Britain. This office is often quoted to prove that there is no separation of powers in Britain, because this official performs functions in the legislative, executive, and judicial branches of government. This is not, however, a very strong argument, for the Lord Chancellor holds a unique office. It does nevertheless illustrate the importance of internal rules, for this man, when acting as a judge, is expected to show impartiality, and that expectation is enforced by the attitudes of the members of the legal profession, who would quickly denounce any attempt to use the office for purely party ends. Again, there is no fusion of power here, for the "internal" restraints upon the Lord Chancellor are dependent upon his position in a profession the vast majority of the members of which operate *outside* the government machine.

In the United States the more rigid application of rules to attempt, however imperfectly, to maintain a distinction between those who make, those who apply, and those who interpret the rules, has produced considerable difficulty in the working of that system of government, and many Americans are today impatient with the restraints it imposes. In Britain the partial separation of the personnel of government has been reinforced and buttressed by the sets of internal rules which govern the behaviour of politicians and officials. This comparison is interesting. Americans who find the externalized rules over-restrictive tend to look to Britain as an example of what can be achieved without such rigid rules. But do they, even the behaviourists among them, realize how vital these internal codes of behaviour are, and how far they have in the past depended upon the *élitist* character of British public life? Without the formal restraints of the Constitution would America have developed, or indeed has she yet done so, a set of internal checks? America has never been a society which was truly run by an *élite* except perhaps during the years immediately following the adoption of the Constitution in 1789. It was the democratic nature of American society, when compared with that of Europe, that concerned Madison and his friends in the Convention. There was a difference, in their view, between an *élite* with certain standards and a democratically maintained oligarchy. On the other hand, those who in Britain deny the importance of constitutional rules, or internalized codes of conduct, forget how significant these have been in a country which has always been governed by an *élite*. If Britain is moving into a more democratic age, one in which the old *élite* which dominated civil service, judiciary, and ministerial positions alike, is coming to the end of its period of dominance, it may well be that the assumption that rules can be further slackened will prove a danger. The main point of this comparison is that formal rules and internal codes of behaviour may be in part alternatives and in part necessary counterparts.

The usefulness of functional analysis in these terms, it is suggested, is that only by this means can the reality, in some form, of a government by law be maintained. Once the external and internal restraints of the idea of functions and the rules they imply have gone, what else remains? Nevertheless, this does not imply the outright acceptance of the functional categories of Montesquieu or of Almond. The idea of a *rule-making function* developed above is considerably different from the older idea of the legislative power. But dissatisfaction with the old triad of "powers" goes further than this. In the first place we suggest that there are two levels of the functions of the political system, the primary and the secondary;[3] furthermore that at the primary level there are four, not three, basic governmental functions. There is a primary level of functions, which is concerned with the relations between the government and citizens or other governments. Then there is a second level which is a matter of the internal relationships of the parts of government. These two levels are by no means discrete, and it would be difficult to delineate their boundaries in practice. Yet for analytical purposes it is clear that there is, for example, a considerable difference between a legislature concerning itself with a law for licensing dogs and the same legislature engaged in creating an independent judicial system. The *forms* of legislation may be the same, but the realities are very different.

At the primary level there would seem to be four major functions embodied in the working of Western systems over the centuries—rule-making, a discretionary function, rule-application, and rule-interpretation. The importance of rules, and, therefore, of the rule-making function, to a constitutional State has been sufficiently stressed above, but it must be made clear that in the *most* constitutional of States there must be a discretionary function which is largely free of pre-determined rules. The threefold formulation of the functions of government left no room for the prerogative or discretionary powers, and in the historical application of the extreme theory of the separation of powers the "rule of law" was so strongly asserted that no discretion could be left to governments. But this was an extremely unrealistic view of government both in the eighteenth century and the twentieth. Today in democratic Britain the importance of the prerogative powers of the Crown, especially in the fields of foreign affairs and defence, control of aliens, and internal order, is still recognized. That these powers, exercised by ministers, often provoke the most heated controversy, is a reflection of the fact that such powers are not, and cannot easily be, subjected to prior rules. Of the Constitution of Virginia of 1776 Jefferson said it was not conceived that any power could be exercised that

3. This terminology again is taken over from the rather different usage of Professor H. L. A. Hart.

was not subject to law, and the President of the United States was given no "prerogatives" in the Federal Constitution. Yet Jefferson, himself so concerned with the purity of the functional division of governmental power, when in office soon acknowledged the importance of a reserve of discretionary power. The President of the United States has, over the years, developed powers, particularly in the field of foreign affairs, which make him far more than an official who proposes and executes laws, and the courts have been either unable or unwilling to check the evolution of this powerful discretionary authority. The acknowledgement that such a function exists gives added weight to the discussion of control in constitutional systems.

Almond uses the term *rule-adjudication,* instead of the older *judicial power,* and this is a most valuable step away from the confusions implicit in the older term, but he does not expand on the nature of this function, and implies that, except for its structural connotation it is co-extensive with the earlier usage. However, the confusions which have surrounded this concept in the past need to be explored and if possible cleared away. The history of this question has consisted of a constant dialogue about whether the judicial power is a distinct and separate power or whether it forms a part of the executive power. On the one hand it has been argued that the judiciary *applies* the law equally with civil servants, but through a different procedure. On the other hand it has been argued that the distinctive function of the judges is that they decide disputes, whereas civil servants simply "administer." Thus Montesquieu wrote of "the power of judging." The longevity of this dispute is explained by the fact that, although both sides of the argument seem to have some validity, the language used in the discussion has never been clear enough to reconcile the two points of view.

There are two elements here—the functional element and the structural. If we study the work of the courts we can see that in the general sense they are applying the rules made by the legislature or by other courts. At the same time, by the creation of precedents they also make rules, which in normal circumstances they consider to be subordinate to, or consequent upon, other broader rules. They do, of course, settle disputes, but this really is a *task* of government, as is that of punishing criminals, an end product, such as making roads or fighting wars. Thus we can say that the courts apply the law, but they do so in a special way, through a special procedure. The institution of a jury which determines matters of fact is a specific procedural way of safeguarding certain values in the application of the law, for these judgements of fact *could* be determined by a clerk in an administrative office; but the matters under consideration are thought to be so important to the individuals concerned that there must be a special procedure to determine them. The idea of a "dispute," which is often said to characterize the exercise of judicial power, is hardly very important. Many of the "disputes" which come before the courts are not really disputes at all, but are arranged to look like disputes in order that the judicial procedure may be applied to them. On the other hand, many matters which are decided in administrative offices are just as much disputes between parties as are the matters decided in court, or at least could be formulated in this way. There has thus been a continuous sifting-out over the course of history of matters which it is considered should be decided by one procedure rather than another. The gradual evolution of the King's "courts" can be seen as the movement from the position where all business was dealt with in a judicial fashion to one involving a "division of labour" and "specialization," but not a specialization concerned merely with "efficiency"—rather one concerned with placing emphasis upon different values.

Thus far, then, it seems that the courts do indeed merely perform the rule-application function, but in a different way from administrators. However, this is to ignore an essential aspect of the history of judicial machinery in Western constitutionalism. The courts also perform the function of stating *authoritatively* what the law is. Whenever the meaning of a rule is called in question the judge must make a binding interpretation of it. Interpretation is an essential step in the application of any rule. It is performed also by policemen, prosecutors, and civil servants at every stage of their work. Each of them interprets the law and then applies it as he understands it, although these two stages will not always be consciously distinguished from each other. The difference between these interpretations and those of the judge, however, is the authoritative quality of the judicial interpretation, whereas those of other officials, although usually accepted as valid, are in principle subject to review. The importance of this distinction cannot be lost sight of in the constitutional system of government, for unless we are prepared to allow the administrator to have the last word on the meaning of the law, some independent check must be maintained upon the interpretations he places upon it. If we were to lose sight of this fact we should indeed live in a society in which the bureaucrat, however benevolent, had the last word.

The judicial procedure, therefore, encompasses the application of the law in two major ways which are different from that of the Civil Service—the facts are ascertained by a special procedure, the law is announced in an authoritative way, and, of course, a single judge may be entrusted with both these functions when a jury is not considered necessary. The reason for the independence of the judiciary, therefore, and incidentally of juries, is not that they perform a judicial function, an expression to which it is very difficult to give a precise meaning. The argument for the independence of the judge is that in performing his function of rule-interpretation he should not be subject to pressure that would cause him to vary the meaning of the rules to suit the views of the persons affected by them, and that in ascertaining "facts" he will not be influenced by considerations of expediency. It is an essential element in the maintenance of that stability and predictability of the rules which is the core of constitutionalism.

We may therefore sum up the primary functions of government as rule-making, a discretionary function, rule-application, and authoritative rule-interpretation. These functions are not closely tied to particular structures in the constitutional State, but the history of constitutional development is the history of the attempt, often hesitant and vague, to articulate government in such a way that a particular structure plays a dominant or important, but not exclusive, role in the performance of a given function. There has been, therefore, a conscious and deliberate attempt to articulate structure and function in a way which would reflect certain values in the operation of government. Although it is impossible to develop a thoroughgoing separation of functions of the kind that the pure doctrine of the separation of powers demanded (and if it were possible it would be undesirable), this does not mean that there is no importance in the attempt to assign the primary or dominant concern with the performance of a particular function to one agency of government rather than another. The whole history of the doctrine of the separation of powers and its related constitutional theories is indicative of the fact that neither a complete separation nor a complete fusion of the functions of government, nor of the procedures which are used to implement these functions, is acceptable to men who wish to see an effective yet controlled use of the power of governments.

At the secondary level the functions of the political system in the constitutional State are even more different from the traditional functional categories. At this level attention has focused upon two functional requirements, *control* and *co-ordination*. Men have concerned themselves with these concepts, particularly the former, since the beginning of recorded history. In earlier centuries great emphasis was placed upon the control function, and the whole panoply of mixed government, the separation of powers, the balanced constitution, and checks and balances, was devised in order to ensure the discharge of this function. However, there were differing emphases in the approach made to the problem. The theory of the balanced constitution and its derivatives embodied the concept of the *internal* checks to power obtained by balancing the parts of the government against each other, whilst the more democratic expression of the pure separation of powers looked for the *external* control of the various parts of the government by the people. It was considered necessary to divide government to weaken it, and to ensure fairness in its operation, but to subject all its parts to direct popular control. There were many combinations of these philosophies of balance and of popular control, and the vocabulary of one was sometimes transferred over to the other, but they represented the two logical extremes of the approaches to this problem.

Yet why should there be a problem of control in the mass democracies of the mid twentieth century? Does not the establishment of universal suffrage, and of free elections, remove the need for these elaborate ideas about the control of government? It would certainly seem that the electoral system should be a prime means of control in such a State, and clearly it is of the first importance, but is it an adequate, a sufficient means of control? There are, of course, certain technical deficiencies in particular electoral systems, such as the fact that the party gaining the most votes in a British election may quite easily lose that election, but presumably these are matters which could quite easily be put right if the machinery were properly adjusted. Such problems aside, however, it is rare for even the most democratic of thinkers to place his faith in a thoroughly democratic electoral system. Thus in Britain the argument, of all parties, against a thoroughgoing system of proportional representation is that "democracy" is only one of the values, although an extremely important one, which must be taken into consideration. There is also a need for strong, effective, and stable government, and this would be endangered if "the people" were to be represented in their infinite variety. Furthermore governments must have a degree of independence of popular control, they must be given the chance to exercise leadership rather than, merely passively, to follow public opinion. Thus elections must not be too frequent, the electoral system must be tailored to fit the needs of governments as well as of electors, and governments cannot be fully representative, for this would destroy their unity and effectiveness. It becomes obvious, therefore, that the electoral system is not, and cannot be, the sole means of control in a democratic system. It is a spasmodic, and a rather crude, mechanism for the control of government, although obviously its over-all psychological impact upon politicians and officials is enormous.

Are these deficiencies in the electoral system counterbalanced by the structure of political parties and pressure-groups? These organizations are also representative, they exercise an influence upon the government and the decisions it takes. They are the link between the people, who clearly cannot govern directly, and the government, and therefore an essential channel of control. They serve to select leaders and formulate choices in a way which the electoral machinery itself cannot be expected to do. They are a means by which popular views about the aims of government are gathered and registered. The organizational apparatus of the party structure is an essential part of the political system, for it is difficult to see how the necessary choices that must be made could be formulated in an intelligible way without the channels of communication between electorate and government which the parties provide. Political parties, therefore, in a mass society, are an essential part of the machinery of government and a prerequisite of control in a democratic society. The argument for not having a fully "efficient" electoral system is the obverse of the argument for having an effective party system.

Yet, like the electoral system, the party system is by no means a perfect instrument for the control of government. The electoral system, for good reasons and for bad, can and does distort the expression of electoral opinion, for example by preventing the proliferation of parties, or by gerrymandering. But by comparison with the party system the electoral system is an extremely neutral instrument of popular control. Political parties are not merely channels through which opinions are expressed and co-ordinated into simplified choices between men and ideas. They are also organizations through which individuals and groups hope to change opinion, to use popular support for their own ends, to create situations, or to wield power rather than to control its exercise. Political parties, by their very nature, not only *link* electorate and government, they get between the electorate and the government, and they use the authority of government to attain sectional aims. The studies of leadership and oligarchy in political parties demonstrate that political parties are not neutral instruments of control, and that at the extremes they can be most effective instruments for the abuse of power rather than its control. They must, therefore, themselves be subjected to control, as indeed has been the case in this century with the various laws relating to party finances, and to primary elections.

The argument for interest or pressure-groups is basically the same as that for parties. Through their representative and informative roles they perform an essential control function, but the sectional nature of their membership and aims makes them very suspect as an instrument of control. Nor has it been demonstrated that, although a particular party or group may be only a partial and biased channel for the expression of opinion, the sum of party and group interactions produces an equilibrium in which all points of view and all interests are given adequate weights. This hypothesis, which is the basis of the behaviourist philosophy of democratic government, of which their rejection of the significance of political institutions is taken to be a corollary, is based upon a number of implicit assumptions which cannot be examined at this point; suffice it to say that it does not seem to the present writer that they make out a case, or that it can be shown that the resulting equilibrium is not in large part dependent upon institutional controls.

There are other important structures in the modern State which perform control functions. The press, in the widest sense, radio, and television, are, like parties and groups, essential to the dissemination of information and the collation and expression of opinion. The influence they exert over the formulation of government decisions is undoubtedly a matter of great and growing importance. Yet again, however, we have the two-edged nature of this instrument of control. It is not, and cannot be, a wholly representative or neutral channel. If publicly-owned, the media of communication may become the organs of particular parties or groups who dominate the government; if privately-owned, these media will never be merely the channels for the expression of opinion, but will be used by groups or individuals to shape that opinion. Here too there will, in a free society, be in operation a system of countervailing power, in which the existence of one strongly representative section of communication calls into existence an opposing section. But again, the inequalities of wealth, and organizational power, will ensure that the representative character of these media is by no means perfect.

Thus the argument that the advent of universal suffrage has removed the necessity for control of governmental agencies is certainly not acceptable. There have grown up new and powerful means of controlling government, but like the earlier mechanisms of control they are not neutral instruments, but organizations which must themselves be subject to control. Indeed, there can *never* be a "neutral" control system, for we must never lose sight of the fact that these "controls" are not pieces of machinery in the mechanical sense. The mechanical analogy is a dangerous one. They are all, without exception, patterns of behaviour, they are all procedures operated by human beings, and they can never be neutral. This, in the last analysis, is the justification of the idea of balance, of setting organizations, government agencies, and groups against each other to provide a means of preventing the control mechanism from taking over and becoming the controller. Control of government can never be a one-way channel, for this will always mean that one group of persons will gain control over others. We can echo Madison here: "If men were angels, no government would be necessary. If angels were to govern men, neither external nor internal controls on government would be necessary."[4] This fact has been increasingly recognized in this century, with movements being instituted to establish a degree of governmental control over political parties, pressure-groups, and the media of communication.

The function of control, therefore, requires in some fashion a notion of balance, whether this balance is expressed within the government machinery, between government and people, or between the media of control themselves. The historic notion of balance cannot be jettisoned at the present stage of development of human institutions. We must reformulate the earlier theories so that they no longer seek a balance merely between executive, legislature, and judiciary, but so that they encompass also those essential parts of modern government, political parties, pressure groups, press, radio, and television.

Thus the historic problem of the control of government remains, in spite of the transformation of the forms of government from monarchical or aristocratic or mixed systems to the modern systems based upon universal suffrage. Yet it would clearly be impossible to leave our analysis of government functions at this point unless we ignored the whole development of political theory since the early nineteenth century. At the secondary level of the political system there is another function, that of *co-ordination*. It might be thought that this function could be subsumed under *control*, as it is in fact the function of ensuring that the government works in an effective, coherent way towards the achievement of the goals set it by society. By integrating this conception into that of control we might rid the latter concept of its negative qualities, and forge a new concept of control with positive aims in view. It would be very difficult, probably impossible, to prove either that there was, or that there ought to be, only one secondary function in the modern Western political system, that of "positive control," rather than the two functions of control and co-ordination. In the

4. *Federalist*, No. 51.

last analysis the choice between these alternative formulations is a value judgement—one either places great emphasis upon, and perhaps fears, the tendency towards the abuse of power in political man, and seeks to check it, or one believes that the divisive elements in society can gradually be eliminated, either by "totalitarian" methods or by arriving at a version of the consensus society in which brotherly love rules all. Without being unduly pessimistic the former view of human nature is the one which seems to the present writer to be nearer the truth, and therefore the twin concepts of control and co-ordination, with their potentially conflicting aims, seem more useful than a rather forced view of the unity of purpose in society.

Furthermore, the function of co-ordination might be described as the twentieth-century function of the political system *par excellence.* The concern of government with new aims has made this the essential function for attaining the ends of modern society, and has often reduced the primary functional mechanisms to mere tools for the attainment of ends other than those they were originally intended to serve. This function has largely been performed by political parties, and by those specialized mechanisms which have grown up in this century—the Executive Office of the President, the modern cabinet system in Britain, with its committees and secretariat. The great importance of this function and its relation to the nature of modern government will be taken up again at a later stage.

The very success of this adaptation of the structure of government to emphasize the importance of a function which is supremely important in the technological, social, and international context of modern government helps to point-up the problem of control as distinct from co-ordination. For the view, associated with writers of the Progressive era, that in the last analysis it is the "people" who must exercise the function of ensuring unity among the parts of government, is wholly unrealistic. The "people," through the electoral machinery, may set the general pattern of aims for government, but the combination of aims which they choose will have been "assembled" for them by a political party, and even this party programme will normally have relatively little coherence, nor will it give a clear picture of the way in which the tasks of the government will fit, or be fitted, together. In Britain, where party programmes are relatively coherent and are intended to offer the voters a co-ordinated set of programmes, governments, whether Labour or Conservative, have made clear that the actual pattern of government action is a matter for their decision and not that of the party or its members as such.

The differing balance that is struck between the functions of control and co-ordination constitutes the essential difference between the American and British systems of government today. At this point of time, in spite of the pressing problems of the modern world, it seems inconceivable that Americans would ever tolerate that degree of continuously co-ordinated action that the British system today makes possible, or that they would relinquish the control processes that have been given up in Britain. This is not merely a matter of history, it is in large part the reflection of the fact that Americans still do not have an instinctive trust of other Americans. America is still only self-consciously a nation; one part of the country is still unsure of what another part will do, and still has interests which distinguish it sharply from the others. Undoubtedly, as American self-confidence as a nation increases, there will be a greater demand for co-ordination, and consequently a lesser emphasis upon control. In Britain the danger is that the emphasis upon co-ordination will be taken to the point where effective control disappears altogether.

Thus again we return to the idea of balance, a balance between the functions of control and co-ordination. It is important that particular structures should combine the performance of both functions, and that no single structure should be solely responsible for one or the other of them. It is impossible to state any absolute values for either of these, or to set unchanging boundaries between them, only to say that they must be "in balance" and that neither should ever eclipse the other, unless and until that view of the brotherhood of man of which we wrote earlier becomes a reality.

This functional analysis has represented both an attempt to describe and an attempt to draw out the implications of Western constitutional thought and institutions. It illustrates the complex interaction of purposive intentions in the history of constitutionalism with the cold hard facts of organizational needs. Thus the desire to establish the primacy of a rule-making function comes up against, but is not wholly defeated by, the necessity of giving government a wide discretion in certain areas. Furthermore, the functional analysis we have presented here, important though it may be for understanding the over-all character of Western systems of government, does not, *prima facie*, have very much to say about actual institutions or structures. There are intimations, no more. Clearly a monolithic structure is ruled out, for the idea of balance, and the very concepts of control and co-ordination, in the sense used here, would be meaningless. But if the analysis suggests that there should be a number of structures, it does not say how many, and it certainly does not suggest that each structure should perform only a single function, for the one thread which runs throughout it is the insistence upon the necessity of the performance of more than one function by each structure. Let us turn, therefore, from the analysis of function to look at the organizational structure of modern Western democracies, and their evolution, for further clues to the solution of our central problem.

In general it would be correct to characterize the history of Western institutions to the end of the nineteenth century as a gradual evolution into three great branches or departments of government. It would be impossible here to justify this statement in detail, or to make all the necessary qualifications of it. Furthermore, in the present century this evolution seems to have ceased, or, rather, institutional development has taken on a new and more complex pattern. It is sometimes argued, by Dahl for example, that this development was really a matter of division of labour and had nothing to do with the separation of powers, and certainly the division of labour has had a great deal to do with it. It has been found that certain things can be done more efficiently in certain ways—but what does "efficiently" mean in this context? We have no single criterion, such as output, or profitability, that the economist can apply to this concept. Division of labour has in fact very complex roots when applied to the development of political institutions. It always begs the question "division for what?" and although the answer involves certain technical questions of how things may be done most expeditiously, or more cheaply, it involves a great deal more than this, in particular the recognition of the importance of certain *values* in the development of Western political institutions.

Let us begin by looking at the building-blocks of organization, in order to suggest some of the factors involved in this institutional development and its relation to function. Any organizational structure is composed of two elements—hierarchy and collegium. At the extreme there is the concept of a perfect hierarchy, best typified in practice, perhaps, by the military organization of a regiment. At the other extreme there is the collegiate body, in which, apart from a presiding officer, the organization is wholly horizontal in character, and perfectly democratic. Perhaps the governing body of an Oxford College is a good example of this type of organization, and so is the prototype Western parliamentary assembly. In practice, of course, these extremes are rarely realized; most organizations are a combination of hierarchical and collegiate elements, with so many possible variants and combinations that the potentialities for experiment are almost limitless. Nevertheless, these two basic structures exist as the poles of organizational structure, embodying very differing characteristics, which in turn lend themselves to the furthering of very different value-patterns. The hierarchical structure has as its major characteristics an authoritative chain of command, unity, and expedition, whereas the collegiate structure involves lengthy debate, divided views which may prevent the taking of decisions, and leads almost inevitably to compromise solutions. These characteristics are, of course, the characteristics one might attribute to the "ideal types" of hierarchy and collegium; undoubtedly collegiate authorities do on occasion act speedily and effectively, whereas hierarchies can in practice become incapable of producing an effective decision; but these are the attributes which the two types of organization in their pure state may be expected to display. Furthermore, the two structures, again in their pristine types, embody very different possibilities of representation. At the one extreme the hierarchical structure is wholly devoid of representative content, for the head of the hierarchy, organizationally at least, is a complete despot, whilst at the other extreme all views can be represented, all arguments aired, all interests can be given their due weight. These characteristics of the two poles of organizational structure come to represent differing value-patterns, and in organizational terms to represent the aspiration towards different ways of taking decisions. The most spectacular confrontations of these ideas, divine right versus parliamentary supremacy, totalitarianism versus representative democracy, involve issues of the greatest ideological and historical significance; but it is also true that at a less spectacular, but nevertheless very important level, the day-to-day operations of Western systems of government can be seen in terms of the tensions between these two organizational types, the continual choice between the values of the one and the values of the other, the attempt to combine the speed and efficiency of the hierarchy with the information and consent which are to be obtained from the collegium.

There is thus a built-in tension between these two types of organizational structure which, however they are modified, can never be wholly removed. This "tension" is the organizational basis of control in government, and it forms the natural and obvious peg on which to attempt to hang functional and procedural distinctions.

The progressive evolution of the great branches of government can be seen, therefore, both as the evolving conflict between differing value-patterns in the way in which decisions are taken, and as a result of the evolving conceptions of functions of government. That is to say that, even if these functional classifications, with their connection with the idea of the rule of law, had not developed, a conflict between the making of effective decisions, by one man or by many men, is built in to the nature of human organizational structure. In fact, these two factors seem to a considerable extent to coincide—that is to say the collegiate organization and the making of general rules seem *a priori* to be closely correlated, and the hierarchical organization and the application of law seem to be well suited to each other. Certainly most Western theorists have agreed, no matter how sharply they have disagreed on other subjects, that all decisions should not be made by a single man whose word is law, and that all the tasks of government should not be performed by a representative assembly. Except in revolutionary periods these extremes have been excluded from the range of possibilities, so that there must, in some sense, be a functional division at the root of government organization. It is this connection, however difficult it may be to make it precise, between organizational structure, functions, and values, that gives to the separation of powers or rather to its central theme, that indestructible quality we found throughout its history.

It is a crucial relationship, to which we continually return, no matter how complex the political and governmental machinery becomes, no matter how intricate the tasks of government. It is here that we reach the abiding core of truth in the idea of the separation of powers, and we can understand also why, throughout the history of Western thought, from Marsilius to the present day, there has been the continual tendency for writers to insist that there are only two functions of government, functions which seem to correspond so neatly with the "natural" tendencies of organizational structure. In fact each of these structures came to perform not one overriding task, but a number of them. Thus the "legislature" is associated in separation of powers theory with the "legislative power," but its representative nature ensured that it would in fact be associated with all those tasks, such as control of finance, administrative oversight, redress of grievances, and deliberation upon matters of general significance even if legislation was not involved, which seemed relevant to a body with this particular representative structure rather than another. The older term "parliament" better represents the nature of this body than the more modern "legislature."

The structure of judicial organization, however, has never seemed to fit very neatly into the simple functional classification of those who wished to see all actions of government in terms of a simple psychological theory of willing and acting, for this left no room for the complexities of judicial organization. The judicial system is in fact the clearest indication of the impact of purposive procedures upon organizational structure. It is the expression of the determination to ensure that certain values are given priority at the expense of expediency or speed in the performance of certain types of governmental tasks. It represents the conscious effort to combine the values of different types of organization in order to achieve particular aims. Historically, English institutions have never approximated very closely to either of the extreme poles of organizational structure, although Tudor government on the one hand, and the Long Parliament on the other, have perhaps come fairly close. They have always been a combination of the two types of organization—the King in Council, the King in Parliament—and the tension between those hierarchical and collegiate principles has been a great theme of British constitutional history. Although this clash of the two basic organizational types has been a dominant note of Western constitutional development, perhaps the most interesting, and the most successful, developments have been the attempts to create new structures which combined the advantages (and of course the disadvantages also) of both the extremes. The evolution of the judicial system, with its combination of the King's judge and a people's jury, was considered by many English and American writers up to the end of the eighteenth century as perhaps the most important institutional development that safeguarded the liberty of the individual. The parliamentary system, in its mid-nineteenth-century heyday, was seen as the great achievement of a harmonious relationship between the two potentially opposed principles formerly embodied in the ideal types of absolute monarchy and Long Parliament. For the middle-class proponents of harmony in the nineteenth century this system, with its delicate balance, and its internal compensating mechanisms, was the final answer to the centuries of strife between two apparently incompatible forms of organization.

The late nineteenth century and the present century have seen, however, the destruction of this dream of perfect balance and perfect harmony, for harmony suggested an equal, not a subordinate, relationship between the parts of the system. The mid twentieth century has attempted to evolve its own answer to this ever present tension, replacing that harmony of the system of parliamentary government with new forms. To understand this we must look briefly at the main trends of government organization in the past eighty years.

In the first place the twentieth century has seen the re-emergence of the hierarchical principle to a dominant position in government organization. In Britain, first the cabinet rose from a position of rough equality with the House of Commons till it led and dominated it, and then the growth of the power of the Prime Minister lifted him up far above his cabinet colleagues in power and prestige. At the extreme this has been labelled "government by Prime Minister," and it has been argued that the cabinet as an institution has joined the monarchy and the House of Lords as a "dignified" rather than an "efficient" part of the Constitution. The English system is now portrayed as the Prime Minister, supported by a few close associates, directing his ministers, controlling Parliament, and through the whole hierarchy of cabinet committees and sub-committees maintaining a grasp upon the administrative machine: an elective monarchy, in fact. This, no doubt, is an exaggeration. The limits upon the Prime Minister's power clearly vary very much according to circumstances, and the usual exemplifications of his great power are drawn from the field of foreign affairs and defence rather than from domestic politics, where he has much less freedom of manoeuvre. Still, the general picture is nevertheless one of the growing dominance of the hierarchical principle. This is the result of the greater demand for emphasis upon co-ordination noted earlier, and for the speed, despatch, and relatively purposeful activity of a single man rather than a committee or assembly. The delicate mechanisms of the nineteenth-century theory of parliamentary government have been transformed into very different instruments. Ministerial responsibility is now little more than a formal principle used by ministers to deter parliamentary interference in their affairs, and the power of dissolution has become simply a tactical weapon in the hands of the Prime Minister to enable him to choose as favourable a date as possible to fight an election. The enormous growth of presidential power in this century in the United States, and the Constitution of the Fifth Republic in France, reflect the same tendencies, with the same basic forces at work, although the different political structures of those countries have modified the methods adopted and the detail of their application.

At the same time that this emergence of the hierarchical organization as the major force for initiation and co-ordination was taking place, another, contradictory, development was in process. There was a fragmentation of the structure of government in an attempt to combat the growing importance of the hierarchical principle, an attempt to modify its force. This was most marked in the United States, where the development of the independent regulatory commissions took a large area of administration out of the direct control of the President, and thus provided some form of compensation against his growing power. The wide use of these independent or semi-independent agencies in the United States illustrates the emphasis placed upon the control function in that country. It was an almost automatic response to the relative decline of Congressional power. Although in Great Britain we find some tendencies towards this type of fragmentation—in the semi-independent status of the National Assistance Board for example—the emphasis upon the co-ordination function has been so strong that the fragmentation of structure we find in the United States has not occurred to the same extent.

The growing dominance of the hierarchical structure has met with a rather different reaction in Britain. Instead of attempting to frustrate the hierarchy by imposing external checks upon it, there has been an increasing tendency to build in internal restraints upon its action, and to create in fact a new combination of the hierarchical and collegiate forms which might achieve some of the same ends that were implicit in parliamentary government, without the dispersion of effective decision-making power that the initiative of rule-making power in the legislature implied. In the early part of the century the relative decline in the importance of Parliament led to proposals which suggested the creation of some form of corporative parliament in which interests would be represented rather than geographic areas. This formal proposal never gained acceptance in Britain, but much of its spirit has been realized in other ways. In the first place, the hierarchy of ministers and civil servants was encrusted with an enormous outgrowth of advisory and consultative committees, which provided information and expressed opinions of interest groups. The practice of formally consulting interested parties before important decisions are taken has virtually become one of the new "conventions" of the Constitution. In 1962 this attempt to democratize the administration advanced an important step further. The problem of obtaining consent for government programmes that planned to maintain restraints upon wages, salaries, and prices led to the creation of the National Economic Development Council, which was a formal attempt to integrate administrative and representative organizations and procedures, so that at least part of the control of the government's policy that it refused to surrender to Parliament was entrusted to a body representative of only certain sections of the community. This type of development has gone even further in France, where the planning machinery encompasses a much wider consultative apparatus. Indeed, M. Mendès-France has proposed this as a pattern for the evolution of a modern structure of government for France.

Thus there has been an attempt to infuse the administration with representative structures, and to find some sort of balance between expeditious government and representative control *within* a single structure. At the same time there has also been an attempt to infuse the judicial values of fairness and due process into the administrative procedure. Thus the growth of administrative tribunals, and the use of "quasi-judicial" procedures, represents an attempt to give due weight to the interests of the individual, without destroying the speed and effectiveness of government action. There has, therefore, been a twofold attempt to dilute the hierarchical form rather than to exert an external check upon it, by building collegiate organizations and judicial procedures into the very structure of administration itself. This is a reflection of the continuing desire for the performance of an effective control function, but it also represents a determination to maintain the advantages of the hierarchical form of organization.

It is doubtful, however, if these attempts could be said to be successful. The dissatisfaction with the way in which the control function is being performed has produced the Council on Tribunals to attempt to give some independent supervision of administrative justice, has led to demands for the reform of Parliament to make control of the administration more effective, and to the proposals for a Parliamentary Commissioner to investigate grievances. There has thus been a resurgence of demands for more effective external checks to be applied to the hierarchy of ministers and civil servants, and a suspicion that bodies, which are representative of outside interests, but which work for long periods with the hierarchy, become identified with it in the minds of the ordinary people, and perhaps in their own minds as well. There is the awful fact that a decision which you have helped to make must in part at least be defended by you, and it becomes, in the eyes of other people, your responsibility. This fact has always been recognized by parliamentary oppositions, who have consistently refused to accept any responsibility for, or even to enter into private discussions on, government policy. The need for an external check of some description seems continually to emerge from these situations. It is this fact which, above all else, suggests the need for a Parliament with effective control functions. Parliament has given up any attempt to initiate or even amend rules which are to be made. It must, therefore, control the means by which government is carried on. Only in this way can an external check be applied. We should not allow one-sided appeals to the out-dated vocabulary of the separation of powers to prevent this; to talk of interference in executive functions by Parliament is today the most cynical use of terms that no longer have any real meaning.

The final way of looking at our material is summed up in the term "process." This is a term which has as many meanings in the literature of the study of politics as has "function,"[5] and undoubtedly it is often used simply to give the impression of being modern and up-to-date. It has value in the sense that it stresses a concern with the whole complex of political activity rather than with merely formal elements, for the term "institution" has come to take on the connotation in the study of politics, unlike sociology, of a set of lifeless forms, with perhaps little relevance to what actually goes on in the hurly-burly of everyday politics. The term *process* can, however, be helpful in ways other than merely demonstrating our up-to-date attitudes. In particular it can point attention to the importance of the dynamic elements in the study of politics. A. F. Bentley used *process* simply to mean that in politics all is movement, all is flux.[6] It is true that the political system is in a constant state of change, nothing ever stands still, patterns never repeat themselves exactly. Yet, as has been argued above, this does not mean that there is no stability in political life, for the political system and the idea of order are inseparable. If all were flux, there would be no possibility of foreseeing the outcomes of political actions, no basis for rational behaviour—in fact, no politics.

Thus, if the concept of process means anything in politics, it does not mean that all is flux. It can help to focus our attention, however, upon the problem of how events move from point A to point B, of how the situation at the end of a period of time is different from, but clearly related to, the situation at the beginning of the period. We have to take into account

5. See the discussion by W. Harrison, *Political Studies*, Oct. 1958, p. 243.
6. See Norman Jacobson, *A.P.S.R.*, Mar. 1964, p. 15.

time sequences when discussing the nature of political institutions; thus institutions, or structures, are patterns of behaviour that persist over time, but they are never exactly the same after the passage of time. What makes them recognizable as institutions is the fact that they show a basic stability and continuity, which allows them to adapt to changing circumstances without losing their identity. At any particular point of time we must concern ourselves with how people are behaving in relation to past patterns of behaviour, and take note of their expectation of how other people will behave in the future. At any point of time the rules explicit or implicit in past patterns of behaviour will be influencing people to continue broadly as they have done in the past, but there will also be an infinite number of variations in behaviour from past patterns, many of them minor and ephemeral, some of them important for future patterns of behaviour. There will thus be a constant potential for change, which will normally be marginal, but which can over a long period alter the general structure very considerably.

If we think of this whole complex of political behaviour as the political process, it becomes in fact coextensive with politics. "Process" really becomes redundant. However, in so far as we divide up the study of the political system into a number of areas, the idea of the legislative process does convey something of the combination of stable, continuing activity which forms the core of the operations of a legislature together with the innumerable ephemeral political acts of those interested in the particular events that are its concern. The stable institutional pattern will operate, must operate, in terms of a set of rules implicit in the behaviour of those who are involved in it, or which may be made explicit in a set of formal constitutional or legal rules, or explained by observers as "conventions" or usages. The more formal, written rules may, of course, become out-of-date, so that they are no longer in practice regulating, or influencing, the behaviour of the actors in the situation. In this case, they will be modified, or superseded, by unwritten codes of behaviour more relevant to what actually happens. It is the unfortunate tendency of revisionists in history or politics, having demonstrated that the old written rules or unwritten conventions no longer have relevance to the practice of a political institution, to assume that such rules never were important, and that no such rules are important today.

Yet what has usually happened in fact is that a new set of rules, different from, but usually clearly related to, the older set, is now in operation.

In this wide sense, therefore, there must be a procedure at the heart of every political process. Procedure, which is just another name for these rules, is the distillation of the institutional pattern; not an unchanging, rigid set of rules, but rather a flexible body of precepts which contain the provision for their own amendment. Viewed in this light the political system will reveal many processes and their related procedures—certainly not merely the three, legislative, executive, and judicial, of the earlier writers. There will be a political party process, and an electoral process. There will be a tendency to create new procedures to meet new needs, just as the gradual evolution of three distinct procedures in earlier centuries reflected the changing aspirations of the peoples of England and France, and as the development of such new procedures as those of the independent regulatory commissions, or administrative tribunals, reflected newly emerging problems and the desire for their solution. There is nothing sacred, or divine, about the trinity of legislative, executive, and judicial powers in earlier theory. It is a matter of the procedures which are felt to be necessary to meet current needs.

We have seen, however, that although historically and logically there is no justification for the view that there must be three and only three "powers" of government, there is a remarkable stability in the general articulation of the parts of the constitutional State and of the procedures they adopt. It is here that we may begin to see some of the inter-relationships between function, organization, and procedure.

In the first place the functional characteristics of the constitutional State exercise great influence upon the number of different procedures adopted. The constant pressure to ensure that the rules governing behaviour are explicit and formalized, so that each person is aware, so far as possible, of the consequences of his actions, that is to say the ancient demand that people shall be governed, in Locke's phrase, by "promulgated establish'd laws, not to be varied in particular cases," will inevitably tend towards the creation of a hierarchical system of rules, with a single final source of authority and a procedure for testing their legality. The demands for a balance between the co-ordination and control functions will inevitably lead to a limited number of structures and procedures, but a number greater than one. Thus we find continual attempts, throughout the twentieth century in Britain and the United States, to keep the evolving structures of government in a pattern which will ensure that they are co-ordinated and subject to control. The reports of the various commissions of enquiry into government organization in these countries illustrate the pressures which operate to bring about the consolidation of these structures into a single hierarchical structure, subject to the control of representative institutions, with only those exceptions considered necessary because of the values they represent. On the one hand, no means of checking the exercise of power without some form of external restraint has yet been evolved; on the other hand, the pressure in the modern state towards a set of co-ordinated harmonious government policies is such that the integrative tendencies will always be at work. The nature of the basic forms of organization, hierarchy, and collegium will also tend always towards two or more, but not many more, organizations and procedures. There are characteristics of those two forms which make them suitable to certain tasks and to certain modes of proceeding. As we have seen, the most interesting and significant developments have been in terms of the attempt to create new combinations from these basic forms, yet the organizational pressures that tend to polarize institutions remain very great.

Second, it cannot be too strongly stressed that procedures, the rules governing behaviour, reflect certain value-patterns. The way in which things are done makes a very great difference. Men could be condemned to death, and in some countries are, by an administrative procedure. Roads could be built by a collegium determining by vote, after discussion, where every stroke of the pick should be made. The judicial method involving open discussion and an adversary procedure before a jury could be used to determine important questions of foreign policy and diplomacy. The results of allocating these tasks of government to be decided in this way would undoubtedly be disastrous. The present-day procedures in Britain and the United States, and the matters decided by them, have not been evolved by chance; they represent the collective judgement of centuries concerning the way in which certain things should be decided. This is not an argument against all innovation, but it should lead us to enquire into, and to examine the values which these procedures embody, and to look very closely at new procedures, and at the allocation of tasks to them, in order to be sure what we are doing.

Thus procedures, which form the heart and core of every political process, may be seen as the institutional expression of the value-patterns of particular societies. These value-patterns are extremely complex, but broadly speaking the evolution in modern times of three major procedures of government reflected the importance attached to three dominant values in the Western World—efficiency, democracy, and justice. Over the past hundred years, however, a new value emerged which could not be subordinated to these—social justice. It is the concern with social justice which above all else has disrupted the earlier triad of government functions and agencies, and has added a new dimension to modern government. It has resulted in the creation of new structures, and the evolution of new procedures, but its implications go beyond the mere multiplication of values, structures, and procedures; for, with all the difficulties which the functional classification of government that dominated the years 1640–1848 presented in detail, the broad correlation of the three concepts of government function with three structures was a reality. The three values of efficiency, democracy, and justice did, of course, come into sharp conflict, but this conflict could be institutionalized and controlled; it was this conflict that gave the fundamental impulse to the concept of the separation of powers. Thus functional intentions, organizational structure, and the values implicit in procedures combined to give a meaning to this constitutional doctrine. There was a logic behind the apparent illogicality of much of the writing about the separation of powers.

The growing importance of social justice, however, threatened to destroy this logic. This new value cut across the other three in new ways, and it could not result simply in the construction of new structures and new procedures to form a new fourfold separation of powers, although the fragmentation of government structure which took place in the twentieth century reflected in part an attempt to do this. To a considerable extent this was due to the fact that the aims of social justice had to be achieved largely through the same machinery which in earlier ages had been concerned almost exclusively with maintaining order, conducting war, and diplomacy, or dealing with the minimum routine needs of society. But also it was because the achievement of social justice meant more than the distribution of new goods and services; it meant also the control of the economy to ensure full employment, the attempt to secure the incomes of farmers and wage-earners, the control of monopolies, the maintenance of a certain level of public expenditure, the control of the balance of payments, and so forth. The measures needed to achieve these aims cut across the older values; in particular they entrenched upon democratic controls and judicial procedures, and they demanded far more co-ordination of government action than in the past.

Indeed, it could be argued that this new value had not been added to the earlier ones, but had become *the* value, an overriding factor which did not have to be articulated with the others, but superseded them; to the extent that they could be accommodated to it, they would survive, but no further. The rise of the modern mass-based political party is closely connected with this emphasis upon the value of social justice. In fact the twentieth-century political party is the structure through which this value has been realized, just as in an earlier age the representative assembly was the structure through which democracy was realized. By performing, above all else, the function of co-ordination, by using the primary functions as mere tools, with little concern for the ends they had been fashioned to pursue, and by ensuring the creation of new co-ordinating instruments of government to further their aims, political parties have become governmental structures *par excellence*. Of course, the other structures of government also perform this function—they are no less multifunctional in this respect than in others—yet it has become the prime function of the political party. Thus the analysis of the correlation of value, function, and structure remains complete, but the picture has changed because this value is seen as superior to the others, because the main purpose of this new structure is to co-ordinate the older structures, and therefore to some extent to subordinate them. The political party process has come to encompass the electoral, legislative, and executive processes, and indeed the judicial process as well. The rise of this new value and the structures which ensure its realization must mean that any facile view of "the separation of powers" is dead.

It is natural that the emphasis upon one value, social justice, and the functions and the structures it entails, should have been so great in a period when the realization of the shortcomings of earlier ages in this respect had become so intense. We have witnessed a revolutionary change in attitudes, and there has been a consequent extreme emphasis upon the new value, and its institutional expression, of the kind which has accompanied earlier revolutions. The overriding importance attached to "democracy" in revolutionary situations at the end of the eighteenth century led to an extreme emphasis upon the power of representative assemblies, only to give way to a compromise between the old and the new when the dangers were seen of erecting a single criterion, a single value, to this dominating position.

In the mid 1960's it cannot be said that social justice has been accomplished completely in Britain or the United States, any more than it could be said that democracy had been completely achieved at the end of the nineteenth century, or justice completely achieved at the end of the eighteenth. Yet we have perhaps come to the point where we must pause, and turn again, as earlier ages have turned, to the reconciliation of the new values with the old; to question whether one value, however important, can be allowed to exclude others. Human beings are much too complex to be dominated for long by one overriding consideration; they demand a number of satisfactions, usually potentially contradictory ones, if pursued to extremes. A system of government which is to meet these demands, which will respond to a variety of values and their functional and structural requirements, must attempt to reconcile the old structures and procedures with new ones. Control will be important alongside the function of co-ordination, to maintain a balance between differing views of the nature of government; the primary functions will be considered important in order to give expression to older values that we cannot relinquish; even the old concept of the separation of persons in government will be important where it is seen, not as an end in itself, but as a means of maintaining this balance. The task of the twentieth-century political theorist is to place these values in perspective, and to suggest the institutional means by which they can be reconciled.

THIRTEEN

Epilogue: The Separation of Powers and the Administrative State

The Separation of Powers and Political Theory

WHEN THE FIRST edition of this book was published in 1967 it was extremely unfashionable. The history and analysis of an institutional theory concerned with the limitation of the power of government clashed with the dominant intellectual trends of the time. There were then three powerful streams of thought, all of which, from very different standpoints, were hostile to the idea that there could be a coherent tradition of political thought about the institutional structure of government that had something useful to say about the way in which government impacted upon the liberty of the citizen.

The first, Marxism, saw political institutions as the instruments of the domination of the proletariat by the bourgeoisie, a mere reflection of the economic relations of production, the differing details of the structure of which in different capitalist countries could have no more than a trivial effect upon political outcomes. Thirty years on, this line of thought has little to tell us about the study of politics. The utopian assumptions of

Marxist thought about human nature, so far from the realism of Montesquieu or Madison, can provide no viable basis for political analysis.

There were, however, two other intellectual tendencies, one predominantly American, the other predominantly British, in origin, each equally dismissive of constitutional or institutional theory. Behaviourism was then at its high watermark and is dealt with at some length in Chapter 11. Essentially behaviourism propounded a demand for empirical verification in terms which were impossible to realize. But the problems which had for centuries been the concern of theorists dealing with the separation of powers and other institutional safeguards did not go away and became in some respects more acute. The inability of behaviourists to address these problems effectively has now become fully apparent.

The other attack came from the work of those whom, for want of a better term, I shall describe as the sceptics. The sceptics found it impossible to see how theories could be framed in a manner which could generate valid propositions across space and time. On the one hand, Peter Winch attacked the concept of social science as a comparative study.[1] On the other hand, Quentin Skinner denied the very possibility of writing a meaningful history of a concept such as the separation of powers.[2] Skinner went so far as to say that "it must be a mistake even to try either to write intellectual biographies concentrating on the works of a given writer, or to write histories of ideas tracing the morphology of a given concept over time. Both these types of study . . . are necessarily misconceived."[3] He argued that "the classic texts are concerned with their own quite alien problems. . . ."[4] Because, according to this view, it was impossible for us to understand properly the meaning of texts from earlier periods of history, he concluded that "any statement . . . is inescapably the embodiment of a particular intention, on a particular occasion, addressed to the solution of a particular problem, and thus specific to its situation in a way that it can only be naive to try to transcend."[5]

1. Peter Winch, *The Idea of a Social Science and Its Relation to Philosophy*, London, 1958.

2. Quentin Skinner, "Meaning and Understanding in the History of Ideas," *History and Theory*, Vol. VIII, No. 1, 1969. See also John Dunn, review of *The Meaning of the Separation of Powers*, by William B. Gwyn, *The Historical Journal*, 1967, pp. 472–4.

3. Skinner, op. cit., p. 48.

4. Ibid., p. 52.

5. Ibid., p. 50.

Ten years later Skinner had abandoned this untenable line of argument. In a book on the history of political thought he wrote, "I have thus tried to write a history centred less on the classic texts and more on the history of ideologies, my aim being to construct a general framework within which the writings of the more prominent theorists can be situated."[6] The importance of the mistake made by Skinner in his earlier work is that he misunderstood the essential continuity of human thought, the extent to which one writer builds upon the work of another, even if only by reacting against it. It is impossible to draw hard and fast divisions between periods of thought and to put them into watertight compartments. Earlier thinkers were not a series of different species, they were human, as we are. The contextual details were different, to be sure, a fact we must always be aware of; but the problems, the concerns, and the dilemmas were essentially the same as those we face today.

These attacks upon a tradition of thought stretching back to Aristotle were perhaps doomed to fail; but the reason that the theory of the separation of powers remains significant, however, is because the problem it addresses is as salient now as it was in the seventeenth or eighteenth century. Far from its central issue having changed fundamentally, the nature of the political problem that concerned earlier writers on the separation of powers has remained exactly the same: how to control the power of government. The rise of the administrative state, the weakening of the effective power of legislatures, and the problem of democratic control—these are the new concerns, but they are variations on an old theme. The theory of the separation of powers is an empirical theory. It embodies values, but in a hypothetical sense. "If you wish to safeguard liberty, then. . . ." The object of this Epilogue must therefore be to ask where political thought stands today in relation to the theory of the separation of powers. We shall survey the main areas of interest that have evolved over the past thirty years in Britain and the United States and then attempt to draw together the threads of the argument into a credible theory of political institutions consonant with the model developed in Chapter 12, above.

6. Quentin Skinner, *The Foundations of Modern Political Thought*, Vol. 1, *The Renaissance*, Cambridge, 1978, p. xi.

The Problem of Government: The United States

In both the United States and Great Britain the concern with the practical problems of the articulation of government and its impact upon the rights and liberties of the individual have been prominent themes in public life and academic literature alike over the past thirty years. Since the 1970's the problem of the separation of powers has exercised the American courts more than at any time in their history. This concern was evidenced in a wide variety of fields, and the issues involved were not trivial; they went to the heart of the problems of modern government. The output of books and articles on the separation of powers during this period bears witness to the importance attached to the issues that are at stake.[7]

The court order requiring President Nixon to produce the Watergate tapes in evidence raised in a stark form the question of the extent to which the Chief Executive was entitled to the privilege of confidentiality for his communications with his advisers. In *United States* v. *Nixon* the Supreme Court accepted, some would say invented,[8] the right of the President to withhold information from Congress, holding this privilege to be "fundamental to the operation of Government and inextricably rooted in the separation of powers under the Constitution."[9] Nevertheless, the claim of confidentiality could not "prevail over the fundamental demands of due process of law in the fair administration of criminal justice."[10] The Court ordered the tapes to be produced, and the resignation of the President became inevitable.

Another decision of the Court, less dramatic perhaps but potentially more wide-ranging, invalidated the use of the "legislative veto," a device which had been developed to enable Congress to control the way in which the Administration carried out the laws which the Congress had enacted. By 1983 Congress had inserted nearly two hundred legislative vetoes into statutes, making it possible to strike down specific actions of the execu-

7. See the section of the Bibliography on Modern American Constitutional Law and Theory, pp. 436–40 below.

8. Philip B. Kurland, *Watergate and the Constitution*, Chicago, 1978, p. 34.

9. *United States* v. *Nixon*, 418 U.S. 683 (1974), at p. 708.

10. Ibid., p. 713. See also *Nixon* v. *Administrator of General Services*, 433 U.S. 425 (1977).

tive branch. When legislation was passed delegating power to the executive, provisions were included in the legislation which allowed vetoes by one House of Congress, by both Houses, by a congressional committee, or even by a committee chair of decisions made by executive departments or independent agencies.[11] In this way Congress could intervene in the administrative process to reverse decisions of which Congress, or in reality some congressmen or senators, disapproved. In the *Chadha Case*, in 1983,[12] the Court considered the constitutionality of a legislative veto exercised by the House of Representatives reversing a decision of the Attorney General, which would have allowed Chadha, a student whose visa had expired, to remain in the United States. The Chief Justice, delivering the opinion of the Court declaring the legislative veto unconstitutional, argued that the Constitution had erected checks to the exercise of power by each branch of government, and that "to preserve those checks, and maintain the separation of powers, the carefully defined limits on the power of each Branch must not be eroded."[13] Although this case did not prevent Congress from making further use of the legislative veto,[14] it did raise vitally important issues to which we will return.

In 1985 Congress passed the Gramm-Rudman-Hollings Act, the Balanced Budget and Emergency Control Act. The intention of the Act was to reduce the federal budget deficit to zero in the fiscal year 1991. Part of the process of achieving this aim was to give to the Comptroller General, an official appointed by the President with the approval of the Senate but removable only by a joint resolution of Congress or impeachment, the duty of reporting to the President his conclusions on the measures necessary to give effect to the legislation. The Supreme Court, in considering the validity of this legislation, based its decision on the doctrine of the separation of powers. "That this system of division and separation of powers produces conflicts, confusion, and discordance at times is inherent, but it was

11. K. A. Kirwan, "The Use and Abuse of Power: The Supreme Court and Separation of Powers," *The Annals of the American Academy*, Vol. 537, 1995, p. 78.

12. *Immigration and Naturalization Service* v. *Chadha*, 462 U.S. 919 (1983).

13. Ibid., pp. 957–8.

14. Louis Fisher, "The Legislative Veto: Invalidated It Survives," *Law and Contemporary Problems*, Vol. 56, No. 4, autumn 1993.

deliberately so structured to assure full, vigorous, and open debate on the great issues affecting the people and to provide avenues for the operation of checks on the exercise of governmental power."[15] The Court found that the Act charged the Comptroller General, an officer subject to removal by Congress, with making "executive" decisions, and that therefore the Congress "in effect has retained control over the execution of the Act and has intruded into the executive function. The Constitution does not permit such intrusion."[16]

As a reaction to Richard Nixon's dismissal of Watergate Special Prosecutor Archibald Cox, Congress passed the Ethics in Government Act of 1978, which was intended to limit the President's control over such investigations. The Act provided for the judicial appointment of Independent Counsel to investigate alleged misdeeds of senior members of the executive branch.[17] It had been argued before the Court that the Act infringed upon the separation of powers, because the function of prosecution, being essentially executive in nature, should not be entrusted to an officer with a degree of independence of the President. The Court rejected this view and upheld the constitutionality of the Act. The dissent of Justice Scalia in this case, however, and in *Mistretta* v. *U.S.* demands further examination.[18]

The question of the circumstances in which individuals can sue public bodies for redress, and therefore involve the courts in the detail of the regulatory process, provided another occasion for the Supreme Court to appeal to the doctrine of the separation of powers. In 1984 the Court refused standing to sue to a group of parents of black children who complained that tax exemptions granted by the IRS to racially discriminatory private schools impaired their ability to have public schools in their area desegregated.[19] The Court argued that

> the Government has traditionally been granted the widest latitude in the "dispatch of its own internal affairs. . . ." That principle, grounded as it is in

15. *Bowsher* v. *Synar*, 478 U.S. 714 (1986), at p. 722.
16. Ibid., p. 734.
17. K. J. Harriger, "Separation of Powers and the Politics of Independent Counsels," *Political Science Quarterly*, Vol. 109, No. 2, summer 1994.
18. *Morrison* v. *Olson*, 108 S.Ct. 2597 (1988). See below, p. 402.
19. *Allen* v. *Wright*, 468 U.S. 737 (1984).

the idea of separation of powers, counsels against recognizing standing in a case brought, not to enforce specific legal obligations whose violation works a direct harm, but to seek a restructuring of the apparatus established by the Executive Branch to fulfill its legal duties. The Constitution, after all, assigns to the Executive Branch, and not to the Judicial Branch, the duty to "take Care that the Laws be faithfully executed."[20]

Professor Sunstein has remarked that the Court's attitude in this case reflects "a form of judicial skepticism about both government regulation and court entanglement in executive functions."[21] This scepticism lies "in the belief that administrative regulation, grounded as it is in technocratic expertise and political accountability, is incompatible with judicial oversight."[22]

In a number of other cases the federal courts have used the separation of powers to resolve issues before them: the constitutionality of the Sentencing Reform Act of 1984;[23] the use by the President of advisory committees,[24] including his wife's membership of one of them;[25] the jurisdiction of the courts in international law[26] and extradition cases;[27] and in 1995 the Supreme Court's invalidation of a section of a federal statute which required the courts to reopen certain cases on which final judgements had already been made.[28]

Clearly the Supreme Court has pursued its own agenda in trying to rec-

20. Ibid., at p. 761.

21. Cass R. Sunstein, "Standing and the Privatization of Public Law," *Columbia Law Review*, Vol. 88, No. 6, October 1988, pp. 1460–1. See also C. J. Sprigman, "Standing on Firmer Ground—Separation of Powers and Deference to Congressional Findings in the Standings Analysis," *University of Chicago Law Review*, Vol. 59, No. 4, 1992.

22. Sunstein, op. cit., p. 1461.

23. *Mistretta v. U.S.*, 109 S.Ct. 647 (1989).

24. *Public Citizen v. U.S. Department of Justice*, 491 U.S. 440 (1989).

25. *Association of American Physicians and Surgeons v. Clinton*, 997 F.2d 898 (D.C. Cir. 1993). See J. S. Bybee, "Advising the President: Separation of Powers and the Federal Advisory Committee Act," *Yale Law Journal*, Vol. 104, No. 1, Oct. 1994.

26. *Filartiga v. Peña-Irala*, 630 F.2d 876. (2d Cir. 1980). See H. H. Koh, "Transnational Public Law Litigation," *Yale Law Journal*, Vol. 100, No. 8, 1991, pp. 2362–8.

27. *Ahmad v. Wigen*, 726 F. Supp. 389 (EDNY 1989).

28. *Plaut v. Spendthrift Farm, Inc.*, 115 S.Ct. 1447 (1995). See also *Franklin v. Massachusetts*, 112 S.Ct. 2767 (1992); *Touby v. United States*, 500 U.S. 160 (1991); and *Metropolitan Washington Airports Authority v. Citizens for the Abatement of Aircraft Noise, Inc.* (1991).

oncile the problems of the modern State with its view of the intentions of the Founding Fathers. But whether one agrees with the Court's decisions in individual cases, the over-all problem remains: the balance between the control that each branch of government exercises over the others and the degree of co-ordination among them necessary to the effective operation of government.[29] The almost feverish activity of the American judiciary in recent years in attempting to draw this line reflects, in part at least, the political reality of "gridlock," the fact that in only six of the thirty years from 1969 to 1998 will the presidency and a majority of both Houses of Congress have been in the hands of the same political party. Although the significance of party allegiance in the American system of government is not as great as in European states, this record of split control of the executive and legislative branches, culminating in the capture of both Houses by the Republicans in 1994 and the continuation of this situation in 1996, does reflect an important consequence of the American version of the separation of powers.[30] The precise reasons why divided government became so significant after 1968 are not clear, and as the constitutional separation of powers existed both before and after this watershed it cannot be blamed, or credited, with the whole responsibility for this situation. However, as the mechanism which facilitates this American form of "coalition government" it is clearly a very significant factor.

For some this disjunction is simply the desirable realization of the Founders' prescription of "weak government,"[31] for others it is the cause of "the structural inability of our government to propose, legislate and administer a balanced program for governing."[32] There is little point in retracing in detail the outworn controversy over the proposals that have been made for the United States to adopt parliamentary government, but we

29. For a very different view of the "balance" between the branches of government see Ralph Rossum, *Congressional Control of the Judiciary: The Article III Option*, Center for Judicial Studies, Cumberland, Va., 1988.

30. David McKay, "Review Article: Divided and Governed? Recent Research on Divided Government in the United States," *British Journal of Political Science*, Vol. 24, No. 4, 1994.

31. James Q. Wilson, "Does the Separation of Powers Still Work?" *The Public Interest*, Vol. 86, winter 1987, p. 43.

32. Lloyd N. Cutler, "To Form a Government," *Foreign Affairs*, fall 1980, pp. 126–7.

shall return later to the implications for the United States of divided government.[33] Although the British model of parliamentary government is by no means the sole version on offer,[34] it is the one which has been promoted since Woodrow Wilson advocated it in 1879. The attractions of the "Westminster model," however, have to be judged in terms of its performance in the last decade of the twentieth century, and it is to this issue we now turn.

Government by Party in Britain

In Chapter 12, above, the argument was developed that, although Britain did not have the kind of separation of powers that the Founding Fathers adopted in the United States, nevertheless the branches of government were not "fused" and there were still important boundaries between them. Today much of that argument still stands, but a number of factors have further eroded the values which lie behind the doctrine of the separation of powers and which have therefore led to the emasculation of the checks and balances that still, even after the Second World War, had some significance. In the mid-nineteenth century it was possible to see a balance between Parliament and Government such that neither dominated the other. Parliamentary government meant that the legislature could exercise control over the government by the use of the vote of confidence, or the vote of censure, and the government could restrain the excesses of the House of Commons by the threat of dissolution. In the period from 1832 to 1868, eight governments were defeated in the House of Commons and resigned immediately or obtained a dissolution and then were either beaten in the ensuing election or failed to win the confidence of the House after the election. Even when a government had a nominal majority in the House, the bonds of party were too weak to enable it to discipline its "supporters" if they disliked the party's policies. This was a balanced system of government, operating within the framework of a very limited franchise and

33. See M. J. C. Vile, "Presidential and Parliamentary Systems," in Albert Lepawsky (ed.), *The Prospect for Presidential-Congressional Government*, Berkeley, 1977.

34. William B. Gwyn, "The Separation of Powers and Modern Forms of Democratic Government," in Robert A. Goldwin and Art Kaufman (eds.), *Separation of Powers—Does It Still Work?* Washington, D.C., 1986.

reflecting the views of a middle-class electorate still dominated by a land-owning aristocracy. It was the model of parliamentary government which became so admired in other countries, but the "balance" of legislative and executive powers it represented rested upon a very special set of social and political conditions which were soon to change.

The extensions of the franchise in 1867 and 1884 ushered in a period of cabinet government in which the executive, because of the strengthening of party ties, began to dominate the legislature, and the likelihood of a government defeat in the House of Commons (except when a minority government was in office) grew smaller and smaller.[35] The rise of the Labour Party, with its strong ideological basis, accelerated these tendencies, and with the Labour victory of 1945, Parliament became the forum for set battles between Government and Opposition, in which, because of the tight discipline exercised by the party leaders, there was no real possibility that the legislature, as such, would have a role to play. Whilst a government with even a slender majority in the House of Commons was in office decision-making was not carried on in the legislature. Policy decisions were made in government departments, in cabinet committees, in the offices of cabinet ministers, and above all in the office of the Prime Minister. The legislature retained its importance, because its procedures imposed upon the government the necessity of presenting and defending its measures in public. During the legislative process, however, no more than marginal changes in government proposals were made, and then usually because the government had become aware of faults in its own drafting or changed its mind on some point of detail on which its own party members felt particularly strongly. The justification of the system depended on the concept of the united party, sustained by an ideology and a sense of loyalty to its principles. If a united party had a majority in the Commons, the fact that the Opposition could make little or no difference to policy outcomes did not of itself destroy the concept of rule by the majority of the legislature. The major parties connived, and still do connive, in the maintenance

35. Since 1895 no government with an over-all majority in the House of Commons has been forced to resign by losing a vote in the House.

of this fiction, for it was assumed that each would get its turn, and none wanted to spoil its future exercise of power. In reality there have always been internal party divisions on policy, which are resolved by discussion or by the threat of the exercise of party discipline, or both. In fact it is within the ruling party that decisions are taken, *by the party,* and not by the legislature. This then is the system of "government by party," which although subject to certain restraints, in particular the concern with the outcome of the next election, can no longer be described, by any stretch of the imagination, as "parliamentary government."[36]

Under the prime ministership of John Major government by party took a new twist which effectively made the workings of the system quite apparent. Under previous regimes, both Conservative and Labour, the constitutional myths of the system, ministerial responsibility and the collective responsibility of government to Parliament, which were the basis of the "accountability" of government, had been sedulously maintained. However, the long period of office of the Conservative Party, since 1979, and the looser style of leadership of John Major made it very apparent that the locus of decision-taking was well outside Parliament. Mr. Major's perceived weakness compared with his predecessor, Margaret Thatcher, well-publicised differences within his cabinet, and the intensification of divisions within the Conservative Party over European integration led to the emergence of a large group of dissidents in the Conservative parliamentary party who were prepared to challenge Major's leadership to the point of voting against him in the House of Commons, provided that they did not actually bring down the Government.

Faced with defeat on a number of issues the Government made it clear that it did not consider resignation necessary if defeated in the Commons, even on an important matter of policy. The Government would resign only if defeated on a formal vote of confidence.[37] Thus party dissidents felt rela-

36. The House of Lords can exercise a check upon governments, and in a number of cases caused the government to change its policy, but the extent to which governments accept changes in policy rather than over-ruling the Lords depends in the last resort on the internal politics of the government party in the Commons.

37. This attitude is perfectly compatible with the (very flexible) conventions of the British

tively free to harass their leaders in the Commons, openly fighting battles over policy, voting against government measures, going to the brink with threats to bring down the Government, but drawing back at the last moment.

In 1995 Britain was subjected to the ultimate expression of the operation of government by party. The Prime Minister, beset by Europhobe rebels, both in the cabinet and more generally in the parliamentary party, continually threatening to destroy him if he did not accede to their demands, resigned as leader of his party and stood for re-election as leader, as a means of reasserting his authority. There followed the amazing spectacle of a contest between two candidates for the leadership of the Conservative Party, one of whom happened to be the Prime Minister of the United Kingdom. That one political party, by its internal discussions and political manoeuvering, should determine government policy on vital national issues and decide who should hold the highest office in the land, while the rest of the country stood by powerless to intervene, was surely a travesty of "parliamentary government." John Major won the contest, a personal triumph for him perhaps, but a death-knell for any concept of parliamentary government in Britain, for, if he had lost, the country would have had a new Prime Minister and a new set of policies, without a general election, as a result of a decision of the majority of the majority party, and without Parliament, as such, having had any say in the outcome.[38]

It has now become clear that the myths which sustain the constitutional theory of governmental accountability to the electorate are in fact the greatest obstacle to genuine accountability. The formal theory of ministerial responsibility, the requirement of the accountability of the executive to the legislature, in practice makes real accountability impossible

---

Constitution. "What the Government will treat as a matter of sufficient importance to demand resignation or dissolution is, primarily, a question for the Government." Sir Ivor Jennings, *Cabinet Government*, Cambridge, 1947, p. 381.

38. Similar palace revolutions occurred in 1976 when James Callaghan succeeded Harold Wilson and in 1990 when John Major replaced Margaret Thatcher. Formerly appointments of new Prime Ministers had taken place without reference to Parliament or without a general election, but that was before the Conservative Party moved to elections for its Leader and in an age when the role of the monarch was still seen as significant in the choice of Prime Minister.

to achieve. The reason is that criticism of the process of administration amounts to criticism of the government, of the ministers, and of their ability to govern. Therefore ministers resist any kind of investigation of alleged maladministration, they maintain a pall of secrecy over what goes on in the administrative machine, and because they are technically responsible for all that goes on in their departments, they defend the indefensible. The situation is made worse by the need of the majority party in the House to support the government, so that informed criticism is further suppressed. The Select Committee on the Public Service recognized this in 1996. "A Minister's survival in his job depends primarily on the satisfaction of his ministerial colleagues—particularly the Prime Minister—and of his fellow Members of Parliament . . . so long as his ministerial and party colleagues are prepared to defend him, the chances of obtaining his removal are minimal."[39]

To some extent this situation has changed in recent years. The government has in part privatised the administrative machine, and as a result refuses to accept responsibility for errors, as in the case of the Home Secretary and the Prison Service Agency. Without adequate controls over the privatised functions, however, and without clear boundaries between the responsibilities of ministers and agency heads, the minister is still seen as responsible, and indeed it remains open for ministers to intervene when it suits them to do so. The secrecy and impenetrability of the British system of government can therefore be clearly attributed to the limited extent of the application of the separation of powers in Britain. In the United States the absence of formal "responsible government," the separation of powers, in fact, has made investigation and criticism of the administration much easier and more acceptable, making it possible to pass the Freedom of Information Act and to have regulatory authorities with teeth.

The complete failure of parliamentary control over the administrative machine in Britain is witnessed by the amazing proliferation of regulators and "ombudsmen" that has characterized the past thirty years. The

---

39. Select Committee on the Public Service, House of Commons, *Ministerial Accountability and Responsibility*, Second Report, 1996, p. xvi.

CONSTITUTIONALISM AND THE SEPARATION OF POWERS

privatization of public utilities has resulted in the creation of a series of pale imitations of the American regulatory commissions, in an attempt to give the impression that the interests of consumers were being protected. These bodies include the Director General of Telecommunications, the Director General of Gas Supply, the Director General of Water Supply, the Director General of Electricity Supply, the Director General of Fair Trading, and the Ombudsman for Legal Services. In the public sector there is the Parliamentary Commissioner for Administration, the Health Service Commissioner, the Northern Ireland Parliamentary Commissioner for Administration and Commissioner for Complaints, the Police Complaints Authority, the Independent Commission for Police Complaints in Northern Ireland, the Broadcast Complaints Commission, the Data Protection Registrar, the Council on Tribunals, the Local Government Ombudsman, the Prisons Ombudsman, among others. Nothing could be a clearer acknowledgment of the inability of Parliament to control the administrative machine than this plethora of independent regulatory officials, but the government's acceptance of this fact for the purposes of public relations did not lead them to set up an effective control over administrative agencies. The powers of the ombudsmen, at any rate those who deal with the public sector, are inadequate. They have little power to enforce their decisions, and their work is effectively advisory rather than regulatory. Another indicator of the failure of the traditional mechanisms of control has been the appointment of extra-parliamentary committees, chaired by senior judges, to look into standards of public life (the Nolan Committee), and arms sales to Iraq (the Scott Committee).

Furthermore in Britain we have recently seen a most extraordinary misuse of the executive power over the legislature. In the Deregulation and Contracting Out Act of 1994, in the words of one commentator, "Part I . . . conferred upon Ministers a power to suspend any provision of an Act of Parliament if they were of the opinion that the effect of the provision in question was to impose a burden affecting any person in the carrying on of any trade. Part II of the Act provided for the transfer of statutory functions from the Ministers to which they were entrusted to private sector contractors at the discretion of the Minister in question."[40] This was not a delegation of legislative power, it was an abdication of the power of the legislature. This domination of government by party, however, is becoming increasingly out of step with trends in public opinion which reflect a loosening of old party allegiances and a greater independence of electoral behaviour.

The Administrative State

The modern world is characterized by the development of what has been described as the "administrative state." Bureaucracy has been with us, of course, for more than two hundred years, but the modern administrative state exhibits such complexity of structures and such a proliferation of rules that the earlier conception of an "executive" consisting of a body of civil servants putting into effect, under the direction of ministers, the commands of the legislature is no longer tenable. The distinction between political leaders and bureaucrats has simultaneously become sharper and more confused. Sharper because the administrative state has taken on an autonomy of its own—it is only marginally under the control of its political masters at any point in time. A large proportion of a country's budget is committed by existing legislation so that even a government determined on change can achieve very little in the short run, and the complexity of the rules governing economic and social life is such that even small changes can produce quite unexpected results. Thus the so-called executive, the political leaders nominally responsible to the legislature for the conduct of government, may in practice have little real control over the government machine, a fact which is only too obvious if we examine the attempts which have been made to develop new procedures for the control of the administration. The confusion arises because the political leaders spend a great deal of their time attempting to manage the administrative machinery for which they are ostensibly responsible but which they are invariably unable to control.

40. Mark Freedland, "Privatising *Carltona:* Part II of the Deregulation and Contracting Out Act 1994," *Public Law,* spring 1995, p. 21.

The reality of the working of government provides a difficulty for the traditional theory of the separation of powers, which divides the powers and functions of government into three, for, in effect, there are now four major sections of the political institutions of the democratic state: the legislature, the government, the administrative machine, and the judiciary. The term "executive" long ago lost its original connotation, because the political leaders at the head of the state machinery, whether the presidency or a cabinet in a parliamentary system, became deeply involved in the formulation and initiation of policy and legislation as well as their implementation. Now the label "executive" is even less appropriate, because it is the administrative machine, influenced but not controlled by the political leadership, which carries the laws into effect. It would be less confusing if we were able to drop the term "executive" altogether, a solution relatively easy in Britain, where the term "government" is normally used, but a very difficult solution in the United States, where the "Executive Power" is embedded in the Constitution. For analytical purposes, however, it would be more satisfactory to avoid using the term "executive," and we will attempt to do so. Equally the term "government" is ambiguous, and we will therefore designate the political leadership as the "policy branch."

The logic of the present situation, therefore, is to accept that there are now four branches of government, each with its own structures and processes, and to provide the control mechanisms necessary to prevent the abuse of power by any of them. Thus the attempt by the Supreme Court of the United States to define only three branches of government and to distribute functions among them is an impossible task, particularly, as we will argue, when their functional analysis is inadequate. This leaves open the question of the appropriate methods by which to control each branch, but does not, of course, imply that any one branch of government can be exclusively entrusted with only one function.

It is increasingly clear that the problem of administering the modern State is made more and more difficult by the assumption that the administrative machine should be under the direct control of the "government," the policy branch. Politicians are in general incompetent to control that machinery, and indeed, by their meddling in the day-to-day working of the administration they create enormous problems, reacting to the political pressures of the moment. In Britain the uncertainty and confusion caused in this way, in such fields as education, transport, and health, are only too obvious. Almost weekly changes in policy imposed by weak and ineffectual ministers leave the administrative machine in chaos. Only too often in past years universities, schools, or hospitals have not been told the size of their annual budget until the financial year is already well advanced, because the policy branch could not resolve its internal conflicts.

In this respect the earlier advocates of administrative autonomy were correct.[41] Unless the administrative state is abolished altogether—an unlikely eventuality—in some sense politics will have to be taken out of administration. This does not mean, however, that the administrative machine should be left to get on with the job uncontrolled, as some of those writers would suggest. It means that effective methods of control must be established to safeguard the rights of the individual to prevent the abuse of power by administrators, as much as by the legislature or the policy branch.

Judicial Review and the Administrative State

The failure of legislatures to exercise adequate controls over the administration has led, both in the United States and in Britain, to attempts by the judiciaries to fill this gap. The rise of the administrative state and the "Death of the Separation of Powers," among other things, lead Gary Lawson to argue that the processes of judicial review since 1789 have created a situation in which "one cannot have allegiance both to the administrative state and to the Constitution." If one then chooses the administrative state over the Constitution "all constitutional discourse is rendered problematic. . . . What is left of the Constitution after excision of its structural provisions, however interesting it may be as a matter of normative political theory, simply is not the Constitution."[42] It is not exactly clear what the practical results would be of accepting this "originalist" view, which pre-

41. See pp. 304–8 above.

42. Gary Lawson, "The Rise and Rise of the Administrative State," *Harvard Law Review,* Vol. 107, 1994, p. 1253.

sumably would return the American system of government to its position in 1789, but it does lead one to consider the way in which the Supreme Court has attempted to deal with the problem of the separation of powers, particularly over the past thirty years.

Professor William Gwyn has set out very clearly the major ideological rift between the Justices in the cases that came before the Supreme Court in the Reagan era.[43] On the one hand, the "formalists" would wish to limit each branch of government to the exercise of a "power" given to it by the Constitution. On the other hand, the "functionalists" take a more flexible view, examining each situation where one branch is accused of having intruded on the "primary function" of another branch. One problem of this classification is that the so-called formalists, in order to maintain their position, have to attempt to define the nature of the "legislative power," the "executive power," and the "judicial power." The ambiguity of the term "power" leads them in fact into a dependence on establishing the essential *function* of a particular branch of government. Thus Justice Scalia, the arch-formalist, declares that "governmental investigation and prosecution of crimes is a quintessentially executive function,"[44] and that "all purely executive power must be under the control of the President."[45] It is not revealed how we are to determine the purity of the power in question. In fact problems met by the Supreme Court in attempting to define the "powers" or functions of government reflect very closely the chaotic discussion of this subject by the Committee on Ministers' Powers in Britain in the 1930's. It was clear many years ago that attempts to allocate particular functions precisely to particular branches of government must fail. It is possible to define four *abstract* functions—rule-making, a discretionary function, rule-application, and rule-adjudication[46]—but quite impossible to allocate them exclusively to different branches of government, because all human behaviour involves all four functions to some degree. A partial

43. William B. Gwyn, "The Indeterminacy of the Separation of Powers and the Federal Courts," *George Washington Law Review,* Vol. 57, No. 3, 1989, pp. 474–5.

44. Dissenting opinion in *Morrison v. Olson,* 108 S.Ct. 2597 (1988) at p. 2627.

45. Ibid., p. 2641.

46. See above pp. 358–9.

resolution of this dilemma comes from Jesse Choper, who argues that the federal judiciary ought not to "decide constitutional questions concerning the respective powers of Congress and the President *vis-à-vis* one another," but that the determination of these issues should be left to "the interplay of the national political process."[47] While this view would make many of the post-war issues that have come before the Supreme Court in the area of the separation of powers non-justiciable, it would still leave in place the problem of the role of the judiciary in regulating the administrative state, which is concerned more with the impact of administrative action upon individual rights and liberties than with the grand issues of "legislative-executive relations." Certainly those who advocate judicial restraint in disputes between government and legislature have logic on their side, if for no other reason than that no sound functional basis can be found for making decisions in this area. In the absence of any other effective control over the administrative machine, however, the role of the courts in defending individual rights must remain. It is therefore very important to distinguish between actions of "the policy branch" and actions of the "administration," if this control is to be exercised effectively.

In Britain the role of the judiciary has also been changing. The first edition of this work included a rather harsh judgement on the British judiciary and its "failure of nerve." Traditionally the British courts have been extremely tolerant of the power of the "executive," reflecting the dominant mythology of a government's executing the will of a sovereign Parliament and aware that a government with a secure parliamentary majority could quickly reverse any decisions of the courts which were distasteful to it. In recent years, however, there has been a change in the attitude of the courts to the power of government and administrative decisions taken under its auspices. The earlier rejection of the idea of a body of administrative law has given way to an acceptance of the need for a set of rules which

47. Jesse H. Choper, *Judicial Review and the National Political Process: A Functional Reconsideration of the Role of the Supreme Court*, Chicago, 1980, p. 263. See also Gwyn, op. cit., pp. 504–5. For an extended discussion of this aspect of the problem see Thomas W. Merrill, "The Constitutional Principle of the Separation of Powers," *The Supreme Court Review, 1991*, Chicago, 1992, especially pages 226–9.

restrains the exercise of administrative power. In part this change can be traced to the influence of the European Convention on Human Rights and to the fact that the Treaty of Rome has become part of English law.

An English judge has declared that "we have now a developed set of distinct public law principles which are of general application, independent of private law and comparable to those in civil jurisdictions."[48] The High Court is now "exercising a quite separate jurisdiction: its inherent power to review administrative action."[49] He continued, "There are . . . situations where already, in upholding the rule of law, the courts have had to take a stand. The example that springs to mind is the *Anisminic* case [1969] 2 A.C. 147. In that case even the statement in an Act of Parliament that the Foreign Compensation Commission's decision 'shall not be called in question in any court of law' did not succeed in excluding the jurisdiction of the Court. Since that case Parliament has not again mounted such a challenge to the reviewing power of the High Court. There has been, and I am confident there will continue to be, mutual respect for each other's roles."[50] Another judge has said, "Thus, save as regards the Queen in Parliament, there is in principle always jurisdiction in the court to review the decisions of public bodies."[51]

This assertion of judicial power has been felt in a number of ways. The courts have been ready to declare acts of ministers, usually in reality the actions of civil servants under the cover of formal ministerial powers, to be illegal, and not simply on the grounds that these acts are *ultra vires* but also that the courts exert a power of judicial review over administrative acts which "even the sovereign Parliament cannot abolish."[52]

48. Lord Woolf of Barnes, "Droit Public—English Style," *Public Law,* spring 1995, p. 57.
49. Ibid.
50. Ibid., p. 69.
51. Sir John Laws, "Law and Democracy," *Public Law,* spring 1995, p. 72.
52. Sir William Wade and Christopher Forsyth, *Administrative Law,* 7th edn., Oxford, 1994, p. 737. See also Richard Gordon, "The New Sovereigns?" *New Law Journal,* Vol. 145, Apr. 14, 1995, p. 529.

The Theory of Constitutionalism

Two main conclusions flow from the argument so far, conclusions which can be stated in a way which is valid both for Britain and the United States. First, there exists an entity, the "administration" (with a small *a*), which can be distinguished from the "policy branch." In practice the administration already has a great deal of autonomy, is only marginally under the control of the policy branch, and could be more efficient if the existing, unsatisfactory link with "the government" were to be modified. Second, the present controls operated by the judiciary and the ombudsmen over the administration are inadequate to safeguard the rights of the individual. There needs, therefore, to be a new approach to the way government is articulated, and this in turn entails a quite different approach to the mechanisms by which control is exercised over the administration.

The traditional theory of the separation of powers sought to divide the functions of government between three branches of government and to keep the personnel of the three branches separate. The evident inability of this arrangement to control abuses by government led to the modification of the theory by grafting on to it checks and balances derived from the mixed constitution of eighteenth-century Britain. Although this institutional structure was explicitly embodied in the Constitution of the United States, the values it was intended to safeguard, democracy, efficiency, and justice, were just as important in nineteenth- and twentieth-century Britain, and the institutional structure of British government showed, and still shows, the influence of these values, particularly in the way in which particular processes characterize the operations of the differing branches of government. Although many commentators have rejected the idea that British government embodies a separation of powers, none would argue that laws should be made by civil servants, that members of the government should have the power to commit people to prison at will, or that the House of Commons or its committees should run the Health Service on a day-to-day basis. The development during the twentieth century of political parties that threatened the degree to which in reality the functions and branches of government were separated was not an overt attack upon the historic values they embodied, except by a small group of now discredited ideologues who rejected the whole basis of the system, but rather was a response to the introduction of a fourth value, social justice, which seemed to demand new structures and a new emphasis upon the co-ordination of the machinery of government, instead of the earlier emphasis on control. The consequence was the rise of the administrative state and the attack by its champions upon the separation of powers, an attack which as we have seen still characterizes those who yearn after an integrated, cohesive theory of administration.

Before beginning to develop the implications of these conclusions in detail, it would be as well to set out the general background approach to the view which I am adopting. First, the past fifty years have, to a considerable extent, been characterized by an optimistic, not to say utopian, view of human nature. On the Left, the assumption was that the abolition of property, and therefore the end of capitalism, would usher in a period in which, in the words of Karl Marx, communist society would make it possible for one to "do one thing today and another tomorrow, to hunt in the morning, fish in the afternoon, rear cattle in the evening, criticize after dinner, just as I have a mind, without ever becoming hunter, fisherman, shepherd or critic."[53] On the Right, extreme libertarians seem to believe that if government were abolished, the unrestrained free market would produce a universal harmony. Others seem to believe that if the administrators, the experts, were given free rein, without interference by politicians or judges, total efficiency would be achieved. There is no empirical evidence for any of these assertions, all of which derive presumably from the Victorian belief in the inevitability of the progress of man. In fact, the evidence suggests that human beings are characterized by ambition, by the desire for power, and by the search after ever greater satisfaction of wants. Human beings may be capable of improvement, but even if we make the assumption that they are perfectible, we are so far from realizing such a condition that to base political structures on the assumption of the perfectibility of man is just sheer foolishness. The world has not progressed very greatly since James

53. *The German Ideology,* quoted in Erich Fromm, *Marx's Concept of Man,* New York, 1961, p. 42.

Madison wrote, "in every political institution, a power to advance the public happiness involves a discretion which may be misapplied and abused."[54] Whether human nature is perfectible is an almost irrelevant consideration. We can agree that human nature is capable of being *improved*—Britain is a better society today than it was in the Middle Ages—but a glance at the circumstances of the world today is evidence enough that it would take a lot more than the abolition of property to produce utopia. Given this assumption of the frailty of human nature, it is surely wise to assume that those who hold power in government will be likely to abuse that power, not necessarily to the extent of a Hitler or a Stalin, although there are examples in the world today not far removed from those horrors, but in a thousand different ways.[55]

Second, institutions do make a difference. Institutions are well-established, rule-governed patterns of behaviour. If there were no institutionalized patterns of behaviour, there would be no predictability, all would be random, the true war of all against all. Institutions are not irrelevancies as Marxists and behaviourists would have us believe. It makes a great deal of difference to the individual accused of a crime whether he is tried in public, in court before a jury, rather than in secret by a member of the security police.

Third, if we need to guard constantly against the abuse of power, then we must heed the admonition of Montesquieu to oppose power with power. The recent history of British politics, with its revelations of corruption, mild perhaps in comparison with many other countries but there nevertheless in the legislature and in the government, confirms the continuing necessity for control mechanisms.

Fourth, it is important to emphasize that a commitment to constitution-

---

54. *Federalist*, No. 41.

55. Any theory of politics must begin with a discussion of human nature. The "public choice" school of political science has entered into the discussion of the separation of powers. See G. Brennan and A. Hamlin, "A Revisionist View of the Separation of Powers," *Journal of Theoretical Politics*, Vol. 6, No. 3, July 1994. The assumptions on which they base their analysis are so far removed from reality as to make their conclusions of limited value. An attempt to overcome these limitations is the development of models based on more complex assumptions. See M. C. Jensen and W. H. Meckling, "The Nature of Man," *Journal of Applied Corporate Finance*, Vol. 7, No. 2, 1994.

alism does not consist in trying to increase the power of that particular part of the government machine or that political party or movement, which for the time being is following policies of which one happens to approve. The switch of conservative support to a strong presidency during the Reagan era is an example of this kind of misjudgement, based on the assumption that the presidency would remain under Republican control indefinitely. Thatcherite governments in Britain pursued policies which cast off traditional attitudes towards those constitutional conventions intended to limit the power of government.[56] Thus they saw Friedrich Hayek simply as an economic guru but did not share his respect for constitutional principles.[57] Constitutionalism is not a matter of seizing a short-term advantage; it is a belief in the need to establish and support those values in the political system which provide for stability and to maintain the procedures which protect the liberty of the individual in a democratic society. Thus it is important that opponents of the administrative state should not assume that it can be abolished. There is no way to predict how large, or how important, the administration will be in five or fifty years' time: it may be larger, or it may be smaller, but it will be there. The priority, therefore, is to control it.

Equally, it should be accepted that the abuse of power can be perceived to arise from the actions of any branch of government—the policy branch, the legislature, the bureaucracy, or the judiciary. The exercise of presidential power to commit American troops abroad without congressional approval, from Theodore Roosevelt to Richard Nixon, resulted in passage of the War Powers Act of 1973. In recent years decisions of the United States Supreme Court have called forth many proposals to curb its power,[58] and the recent challenges that the British judiciary has made to the power of both the policy branch and the bureaucracy have initiated charges of judicial usurpation.

56. See Cosmo Graham and Tony Prosser (eds.), *Waiving the Rules: The Constitution Under Thatcherism*, Milton Keynes, 1988.

57. F. A. Hayek, *Law, Legislation and Liberty*, London, 1989. See also Graham and Prosser, op. cit., pp. 17–18; and Richard Bellamy, " 'Dethroning Politics': Liberalism, Constitutionalism and Democracy in the Thought of F. A. Hayek," *British Journal of Political Science*, Vol. 24, No. 4, 1994.

58. See Ralph Rossum, *Congressional Control of the Judiciary: The Article III Option*, Cumberland, Va., 1988.

It is equally important, however, to recognize the need for co-ordination of government as for control over government. The theory of the separation of powers and checks and balances emphasizes the element of control. The demand for co-ordination must be met largely through the mechanisms of politics — the political parties and pressure-groups — in other words through the interaction of the legislature and the policy branch.

The Control of the Administrative State

There have been two major developments in the nature of the political systems of America and Britain in the twentieth century. First, the structure of government has undergone fundamental change: administrative structures have developed to the extent that their impact upon the life of the ordinary citizen is more significant, and potentially more oppressive, than the actions of the traditional triad of governmental powers. The administration sits like a great cuckoo in the nest, elbowing out the historic actors in the drama of government. But this does not invalidate the analysis of the separation-of-powers theorist. It means that the analysis has to be brought up to date and applied to the new situation. The concern which always lay behind the doctrine of the separation of powers is still valid, namely, the concern to protect the individual against the overbearing power of government. Both models we have examined have failed to cope with the problem of the administrative state: in Britain the system of administrative government goes largely unchecked because of the pretence of ministerial responsibility; in the United States the separation of powers has allowed a greater degree of control over the administration, but "divided government" is a cause of deep concern to many political scientists, and it is asserted, the cause of public disquiet about the system of government.

Second, in the latter half of the twentieth century another fundamental change in the political systems of America and Britain has been taking place, a change which is gathering pace in the last decade of the century. There has been a decline in the importance of ideology in politics and consequently in the relevance of party organization to the conduct of government. It is true that there was a resurgence of ideology in the 1980's at the elite levels of the party activists—Thatcherism and Reaganism dominated the headlines—but at the level of the electorate there has been a steady decline in the strength of party identification, and in the United States there has been the phenomenal development of split-ticket voting.

What is needed therefore is an analysis of government appropriate to an era in which the electorate is more concerned with outcomes than with party ideologies and government structures which reflect this concern. Students of administrative theory have bewailed the fact that "American public administration has been unable to develop a satisfying and enduring conception of democratic administration,"[59] and have blamed this on the separation of powers, which built conflicting sets of values into the constitutional system, which pervade the administrative machine, and which could not be synthesized without "violating values deeply ingrained in the United States political culture."[60] It should not be assumed that the fact that these values, democracy, efficiency, and justice, are deeply ingrained is necessarily dysfunctional, even though they continually conflict. These values are there for good reasons, and they conflict because in practical situations it is rarely possible to hold that one or another of them is an absolute which must be maintained at all costs. Certainly one would not see administrative efficiency as an absolute which would override in all circumstances the considerations of justice. We have, therefore, to devise means, as best we can, which will reconcile these values within a viable institutional framework.

In the first half of the twentieth century administrative theorists argued for a system of government based on two functions—policy and administration.[61] These writers were generally hostile to the traditional tripartite theory of the separation of powers.[62] The politics-administration dichotomy does not work, because it is founded on an inadequate functional

59. Robert S. Kravchuk, "Liberalism and the American Administrative State," *Public Administration Review*, Vol. 52, No. 4, July/Aug. 1992, p. 374.

60. David H. Rosenbloom, "Public Administrative Theory and the Separation of Powers," *Public Administration Review*, Vol. 43, May/June 1983, p. 219.

61. See pp. 304–8 above.

62. See Laurence J. O'Toole, "Doctrines and Developments: Separation of Powers, the Politics-Administration Dichotomy, and the Rise of the Administrative State," *Public Administration Review*, Vol. 47, Jan./Feb. 1987, pp. 17–19.

analysis, but some of the ideas these writers developed illuminate the possibilities of an administrative machine which would be relatively free of constant political interference but subject to external controls. It is the intention here, therefore, to attempt to synthesize these ideas into a more comprehensive analysis of the political system in the light of the nature of politics today.

As we have seen, there are four abstract functions of government and effectively four branches of government, although two of these, the policy branch and the administration, are still closely linked in terms of law, even if the reality is rather different. In the modern State we need a more effective control over the administrative machine, and the ending of the pretence of "accountability," as we now understand it, would contribute towards this end. The autonomy of the administration should be recognized, but at the same time it should be subject to effective control. The administration needs to be independent to the extent that it is given a task to do and must carry it out. The policy branch should not be able to give direct instructions to the administration nor be responsible for the appointment, promotion, or dismissal of its members. What is being proposed here is a further extension of the process which was begun in Britain by the so-called Next Steps Report of 1988, produced by the Efficiency Unit of the Cabinet Office.[63] The Report asserted that the responsibilities for management at the top of government departments were unclear; a few government ministers were even prepared to admit that they did not have the skills to manage their departments.[64] Some top civil servants spent 90 percent of their time dealing with policy and "political support tasks" and only 10 percent managing their organizations. The Report recommended that agencies should be established "to carry out the executive functions of government within a policy and resources framework set by a department."[65] The Report made an attempt to deal with the question of the accountability

63. *Improving Management in Government: The Next Steps.* Report to the Prime Minister, The Efficiency Unit, HMSO, London, 1988. See E. C. S. Wade and A. W. Bradley, *Constitutional and Administrative Law,* 11th edn., London, 1993, pp. 294–5.

64. *Improving Management in Government,* op. cit., p. 25.

65. Ibid., p. 9.

of these agencies to Parliament, but it could not break away from the accepted theory of the Constitution: "It is axiomatic that Ministers should
remain fully and clearly accountable for policy. For agencies which are government departments or parts of departments ultimate accountability for
operations must also rest with Ministers."[66] Nevertheless the authors of
the Report hoped that a convention could be established so that heads of
agencies could have delegated authority from Ministers for the operation
of their agencies. "There is nothing new in the suggestion that Ministers
should not be held answerable for many day-to-day decisions involving the
public and public services." This deliberate blurring of the issue of accountability in order to pay lip-service to the doctrine of ministerial responsibility, typical of much of the way in which the unwritten British "Constitution" now operates, was further compounded by the Prime Minister,
Margaret Thatcher, when she introduced the Report to the House of Commons. She assured the House that "there will be no change in the arrangements for accountability. Ministers will continue to account to Parliament
for all the work of their Departments, including the work of the agencies."[67]
The Efficiency Unit, however, which was attempting to drive forward the
agency concept, returned to the task of reducing the interference of ministers in the administrative process. The terms of reference of a study set up
in 1990 to assess the progress of the "Next Steps" initiative proclaimed that
"Ministers and Departments should to the greatest extent practicable stand
back and leave Agency managers free to manage. Intervention, planned or
unplanned, in the day-to-day managements of Agencies should be exceptional and positively justified in each case."[68] The study group concluded
that "Chief Executives are directly accountable to a Minister in a 'quasi-
contractual' relationship. In any such relationship it is important that the
responsibilities of both sides are clearly defined and both are in a position
to deliver their side of the bargain." Thus a typical British compromise was

66. Ibid., p. 17.
67. *Hansard,* 18 Feb. 1988, Col. 1151.
68. *Making the Most of Next Steps: The Management of Ministers' Departments and Their
Executive Agencies,* Report to the Prime Minister, The Efficiency Unit, HMSO, 1991, p. 30.

evolved, blurring the issues at stake. The minister remained accountable to Parliament, but it was *hoped* that the minister would behave reasonably and not interfere in the day-to-day administration of agencies.[69] This hope was shattered in October 1995 when the Home Secretary dismissed the Director General of the Prison Services Agency for his failure to administer the Prison Service efficiently. This dismissal occurred amidst accusations that the minister had intervened in the day-to-day operations of the Agency, without being prepared to accept responsibility for the failure of its actions.

Thus we have arrived at a point where either the government must accept full responsibility for every action of the administration, however trivial, which is unrealistic, or it must be detached altogether from its operation. The middle ground is unacceptable and unworkable. True we must accept that it would not be possible for the administration to carry out its tasks without exercising judgement and discretion and that "politics" would characterize its operation just as it does in any large organization. For that reason it is vital that the administration should be subject to effective checks. The policy branch would be required to report to the legislature about how the administration was working and to propose reforms or policy changes. The administration would report to the legislature annually and would be subject to all the normal procedures for control of finance, and the committees of the legislature would scrutinize its operation. This process of committee scrutiny could certainly be much more effective in Britain than it is at present, because committee investigations would no longer be seen as direct criticism of ministers. The policy branch would make recommendations to the legislature both for changes in policy and in administrative procedures, and the administration would be subject to review by the courts, as suggested below.

The sphere of the "administration" would exclude those activities of government where what I have called the discretionary function is dominant. It would be impossible to include all the activities of government within the framework here proposed. Foreign affairs, defence, and the macroeco-

69. Ibid., p. 7.

nomic control of the economy necessitate government action which cannot be subject to the restraints which are necessary in the fields of domestic regulation and social policy, and these activities would remain under the direct control of the policy branch.

There are two problems with this approach. If policy-makers are divorced from those who will have to put the policies into effect the results will be unrealistic and uninformed by the requirements of implementation, and when these policies result in failure, the electorate will not know whom to blame. But accountability is already unsatisfactory in both the United States and Britain, in spite of the differing extent to which the separation of powers is embodied in their respective institutional structures. In the United States the President blames Congress for failing to legislate his programmes, and Congress blames the President for failing to implement legislation effectively. In Britain, as we have seen, the close alliance of government ministers and government members of the House of Commons makes effective control impossible. Thus what is required is a clear and open procedure for taking policy decisions so that responsibility can be unambiguously allocated. For this reason it is essential that the "policy branch" consults the "administration" before proposing legislation, obtains its views in writing, and is required to publish them with all draft legislation. It would be a mark of the existence of a mature society that policy decisions, other than those affecting foreign affairs and defence, should be taken only after public scrutiny of all the considerations involved, including the opinions of those administrators who would be charged with the implementation of the policy and who would have the independence that would evoke an honest opinion.

The second problem lies in the apparent assumption that the administrative machine does not have policy aims of its own and will faithfully implement the policies laid down by the legislature. Thus although the checks to the abuse of power by the administration set out above are important at a general level, if individual rights are to be safeguarded there must be a much more detailed case-by-case control. One solution to the problem would be to follow the continental system of administrative courts, the model of the French *Conseil d'Etat*, which is quite separate from the general courts.[70] The danger, however, would be that such a court would seem totally alien to the Common Law tradition. Another solution is possible. Both the British and American courts have shown a readiness to develop the kind of public law which could fill the gap left in our system of jurisprudence. At present administrative cases come piecemeal to the United States Federal District Court, or to the English High Court, are subject to all the corresponding problems of delay and expense and are dealt with by judges who are not specialists in administrative law. Yet our systems of courts already include specialist divisions, which because of their differing subject material have differing procedures. It would be perfectly possible to set up an Administrative Division with the tasks of overseeing the administration's activities, hearing complaints from the public, and providing remedies. It ought not to operate through the adversary system, which characterizes our current judicial system, and it could have very different methods of gathering evidence, accepting documents and written submissions where possible. The Division could in fact learn a great deal from the procedures of the *Conseil d'Etat* but still be integrated into the body of the judicial system. Appeals could lie to the Common Law courts, but the grounds of appeal, particularly by the administration, could be severely limited to important questions of law.

It is not possible to allocate particular functions exclusively to each branch of government (and in the United States this is not merely because the Constitution makes specific exceptions to the overall distribution of power), but it is possible to say that there is a function which is more appropriate to a particular procedure, to attempt to restrict each branch to particular *procedures*, and therefore to make one function the dominant concern of that branch. In a sense this is the aim of those who have espoused the "functionalist" tendency on the Supreme Court in recent years, but they have attempted to achieve it without setting out a clear basis for their decisions.

Thus we can accept that the rule-making function is exercised in some degree by all branches of government but nevertheless assert that the legis-

70. See pp. 258–9 above.

lature should be concerned only with rule-making of a general kind and that the rules it makes should be binding on both the policy branch and the administration and subject to being over-ruled by the judiciary only on the grounds of their having offended against certain basic constitutional principles. That the legislative branch should restrict its rule-making to general rules, not dealing with specific individuals, is an essential part of the Rule of Law, a major tenet of constitutionalism for 350 years. Thus those legislative vetoes of the United States Congress which, as in the *Chadha Case*, dealt with specific individuals should have been invalidated because they dealt with particular cases. The Supreme Court invalidated the legislative veto on the grounds that one part of the legislature was exercising a "legislative function" which should have been exercised only by both Houses and with the approval of the President. On the contrary, what the House of Representatives did in exercising a "veto" over the granting of resident status to Chadha was to engage in rule-application.

Justice Powell in his concurring opinion in *Chadha* made this point clearly, although he thought the use of the veto in this case constituted rule-adjudication. "On its face, the House's action appears clearly judicatory. The House did not enact a general rule. . . . It thus undertook the type of decision that traditionally has been left to other branches."[71] He quoted John Marshall in *Fletcher* v. *Peck*, "It is the peculiar province of the legislature to prescribe general rules for the government of society; the application of those rules to individuals in society would seem to be the duty of other departments."[72] Powell made reference to the constitutional prohibition on Bills of Attainder and quoted *United States* v. *Brown*, to the effect that the separation of powers was intended as a safeguard against "trial by legislature."[73] In other words this was an inappropriate procedure for making such a decision. This surely is the basis of the Rule of Law. It is the consideration which led to the rejection of the exercise of the unlimited power of the Long Parliament and of the American revolutionary state legislatures. There can be no Rule of Law if the legislature intervenes

71. *Chadha*, op. cit., at pp. 964–5.
72. *Fletcher* v. *Peck*, 6 Cranch 87 (1810), p. 136.
73. *Chadha*, op. cit., at p. 962.

arbitrarily in the administrative or judicial process to favour or disadvantage an individual, as in the *Chadha Case*.[74]

Conclusion

Compared with the parliamentary system the weakness of the American version of the separation of powers lies in its apparent inability to deliver a satisfactory degree of co-ordination between the legislative branch and the policy branch, even to the extent that government can be on the edge of collapse, as in 1995. The American system does, however, provide the possibility of an effective control over the policy branch and the administration, which the Westminster model of parliamentary government has signally failed to achieve. The problem at the centre of constitutional government today, as has been for the past 350 years, is how to achieve a balance between co-ordination and control in the relationships among the branches of government which will safeguard individual freedom but which will also ensure that government can deliver to its citizens those essential services without which modern society cannot survive.

A major function of the legislative branch is to exercise control over the policy branch and the administration. The effectiveness of this control is hampered by the partisanship of members of the legislature, a partisanship which is artificial, not reflecting the needs or attitudes of the electorate at large. Separating the policy branch from the main body of the administrative machine would tend to diminish the effect of partisanship in the legislature's attitudes towards the administration. This arrangement would decrease very considerably the size of the overblown ranks of the present governments in Britain, where almost one-third of the government members of the House of Commons may hold an office of profit under the Crown. The growth in the number of members of the Commons in the government has, of course, been a consequence of the growth of the ad-

---

74. The importance of art. 1, sec. 9, of the Constitution, the Bill of Attainder prohibition, was fully discussed in *Nixon* v. *Administrator of General Services*. The Court distinguished the legislation under consideration, The Presidential Recordings and Materials Act of 1974, from a Bill of Attainder, arguing that the Act did not inflict a "legislative punishment" on Mr. Nixon. 97 S.Ct. 2777 (1977), pp. 2803–11.

ministrative state, and inevitably the need to find such a large proportion of the governing party in the Commons to run the administration has led to second-rate people being put into posts for which they do not have the necessary competence. To return many of these people to the back benches would reduce the government's power of patronage and would therefore be likely to increase the independence of government back-bench members. The problems faced by an incoming President, when control of the presidency changes from one party to another, involving the filling of thousands of positions, would also be alleviated by separating the administration off, consequently making more posts into civil-service positions.

To hive off a major part of the administration from the direct control of political leaders would transform the character of the British "Government" and the American "Administration." It would remove from them the day-to-day routines of the administrative machine, which they are in general ill-equipped to supervise, and allow them to concentrate upon those vital functions which only the "policy branch" can perform: the planning of legislative policy and the formulation and implementation of policy concerning foreign affairs, defence, and macroeconomics.

Another major responsibility of the policy branch is co-ordination, working through the party system and pressure-groups. The problem of co-ordination may be seen at two levels—the over-all co-ordination of legislative and administrative policy, for example, through the budget, or the co-ordination of the activities of the different departments of the administration. The problem of co-ordinating the policies of the presidency and the Congress has in recent years concentrated attention on the phenomenon of divided government and on the desirability, in the eyes of some commentators, of strengthening the party system in order to prevent this from occurring. Divided government may be the result of purposive voting or an "accidental" result of the separation of powers in a period of weak party government.[75] "Purposeful voting advocates put their faith in the will of the majority: as long as the people want (divided government),

75. James L. Sundquist, "Needed: A Political Theory for the New Era of Coalition Government in the United States," *Political Science Quarterly*, Vol. 103, 1988, p. 527.

that's fine,"[76] but in the opinion of its critics the problems of the American system are not always the product of divided government: "The separation of powers operating in an age of weak parties is as likely a culprit."[77] But if this is the case it is important to ask why the political parties are so weak. The root cause of the weakness of American political parties is the increasing fragmentation of the electorate. America has experienced increasing diversity in the electorate, of a number of different kinds, since the Second World War. Ethnic groups previously excluded from the political process are now important electoral forces. The multi-cultural society has replaced the old system of positive Americanization, which from the time of Jefferson has been the all-embracing ideology of the United States. It was not until the Vietnam experience that it became impossible to impose this positive Americanization through the processes of socialization that had previously operated. The resulting fragmentation has made coalition government inevitable, and it is unlikely that such deeply embedded social factors can be overcome by tinkering with the electoral system. Coalition government everywhere reflects potentially irreconcilable conflicts in society; why should it be different in the United States? A parliamentary system with weak parties would be no better. The great benefit that the Constitution has given to the United States is stability, and this becomes even more important in an era when the electorate is increasingly fragmented.

Unless divided government can be eliminated, which seems very unlikely, then the less coherent the parties are, the better. In the long run President and Congress must live together by compromise, and the more coherent and ideological the parties become, the more difficult this will be. The "great" periods of united control, such as the New Deal period, actually worked only because party unity was not complete, allowing the President to find support where he could. To adopt the system of a quadruple separation of powers advocated here should make it easier to live with a fragmented political system and at the same time keep the powers of government from abusing their position.

There are two dangers in giving the administration a greater degree

76. McKay, op. cit., p. 533.   77. Ibid., p. 534.

---

of autonomy. First, the danger that pressure-groups would turn their attention to the administrative machine to an even greater extent than at present.[78] The second is that the "directors-general" of the administrative departments, meeting together to co-ordinate their operations, would become the unelected government of the country. These dangers could be offset if the legislature, freed from the sense of partisanship in relation to the administration, exercised a genuine control over that administration and would be able to work more closely and effectively with the President. Equally, the convergence of the political parties that is taking place in Britain in the second half of the 1990's offers the possibility of a system of government in which genuine accountability to the legislature, and ultimately to the electorate, may make the control of government more of a reality than has been the case since the rise of the administrative state.

78. See Terry M. Moe and Scott A. Wilson, "Presidents and the Politics of Structure," *Law and Contemporary Problems*, Vol. 57, No. 2, 1994, p. 7.

BIBLIOGRAPHY

This bibliography, although not claiming to be exhaustive, includes works not referred to in the text, drawn from a number of sources. Good sources for further bibliographical material are William B. Gwyn, *The Meaning of the Separation of Powers;* and Michel Troper, *La séparation des pouvoirs et l'histoire constitutionnelle française.*

1. General Works
2. The Precursors
3. Seventeenth-Century England: The Birth of the Doctrine
4. The Balanced Constitution of the Eighteenth Century and Its Critics
5. Montesquieu
6. The Colonial Period in America
7. The American Revolution and the State Constitutions
8. The Federal Constitution and Its Critics
9. The French Revolution
10. Post-Revolutionary France
11. The Nineteenth-Century British Constitution
12. The United States: 1850–1945
13. The Twentieth-Century British Political System
14. From the Third Republic to the Fifth
15. Modern American Constitutional Law and Theory
16. General References
17. Political Theory and the Separation of Powers

1. General Works

Bluntschli, J. C. *Allgemeine Staatslehre.* Stuttgart, 1875.
Bondy, William. *The Separation of Governmental Powers: In History, in Theory,*

and in the Constitutions. Studies in History, Economics and Public Law, Vol. V, No. 2. New York, 1896.

Burdeau, G. *Traité de science politique.* Paris, 1957.

Fuzier-Herman, E. *La séparation des pouvoirs d'après l'histoire et le droit constitutionnel comparé.* Paris, 1880.

Gwyn, William B. *The Meaning of the Separation of Powers: An Analysis of the Doctrine from Its Origin to the Adoption of the United States Constitution. Tulane Studies in Political Science,* Vol. IX. New Orleans, 1965.

Kant, Immanuel. *The Philosophy of Law* (1796). Translated by W. Hastie. Edinburgh, 1887.

Mohl, R. von. *Die Geschichte und Literatur der Staatswissenschaften.* Erlangen, 1855.

Sartori, Giovanni. "Constitutionalism: A Preliminary Discussion." *The American Political Science Review,* Vol. LVI, No. 4, December 1962.

Troper, Michel. *La séparation des pouvoirs et l'histoire constitutionnelle française.* Paris, 1973.

Wormuth, F. D. *The Origins of Modern Constitutionalism.* New York, 1949.

Wright, B. F. Jr. "The Origins of the Separation of Powers in America." *Economica,* May 1933.

2. The Precursors

Aristotle. *The Constitution of Athens.* Edited by Kurt von Fritz and E. Kapp. New York, 1950.

———. *Ethics.* Translated by J. A. K. Thomson. London, 1955.

———. *Politics.* Edited by Sir Ernest Barker. New York, 1958.

Bodin, Jean. *The Six Bookes of a Commonweale.* Knolles edition, 1606. Edited by K. D. McRae. Cambridge, Mass., 1962.

Church, W. F. *Constitutional Thought in Sixteenth-Century France.* Cambridge, Mass., 1941.

Fortescue, Sir John. *The Governance of England: The Difference between Absolute and Limited Monarchy.* Edited by C. Plummer. Oxford, 1885.

Gewirth, A. *Marsilius of Padua: The Defender of Peace.* New York, 1951.

Hinton, R. W. K. "English Constitutional Theories from Sir John Fortesque to Sir John Elliott." *English Historical Review,* Vol. LXXV, July 1960.

Hotman, François. *Franco-Gallia* (1573). Second English edition. London, 1721.

Levin, M. L. *The Political Doctrine of Montesquieu's* Esprit des Lois: *Its Classical Background.* New York, 1936.

McIlwain, C. H. *The High Court of Parliament and Its Supremacy.* New Haven, Conn., 1910.

————. *Constitutionalism, Ancient and Modern.* Ithaca, N.Y., 1947.

Nippel, Wilfrid. *Mischverfassungstheorie und Verfassungsrealität in Antike und früher Neuzeit.* Stuttgart, 1980.

————. "Ancient and Modern Republicanism: 'Mixed Constitution' and 'Ephors.' " In *The Invention of the Modern Republic,* edited by Biancamaria Fontana. Cambridge, 1994.

Plucknett, T. F. T. *Statutes and Their Interpretation in the First Half of the Fourteenth Century.* Cambridge, 1922.

Pocock, J. G. A. *The Machiavellian Moment: Florentine Political Thought and the Atlantic Republican Tradition.* Princeton, N.J., 1975.

Poynet, Bishop John. *Short Treatise of Politicke Power.* Strasbourg, 1556.

Previté-Orton, C. W. "Marsiglio of Padua, Part II. Doctrines." *English Historical Review,* Vol. XXXVIII, No. 149, January 1923.

Pufendorf, Samuel. *Le droit de la nature et des gens.* Translated by J. Barbeyrac. Amsterdam, 1712.

Smith, Sir Thomas. *De Republica Anglorum* (1583). Edited by L. Alston. Cambridge, 1906.

Ullmann, W. *Principles of Government and Politics in the Middle Ages.* London, 1961.

Vindiciae Contra Tyrannos. English edition. London, 1648.

Von Fritz, Kurt. *The Theory of the Mixed Constitution in Antiquity.* New York, 1954.

Von Mehren, A. "The Judicial Concept of Legislation in Tudor England." In *Interpretations of Modern Legal Philosophies,* edited by P. Sayre. New York, 1947.

3. Seventeenth-Century England: The Birth of the Doctrine

Buchanan, George. *De Jure Regni apud Scotos.* English edition. 1680.

Charles I, King of England. *His Majesties Answer to the XIX Propositions Of Both Houses of Parliament.* London, 1642.

Condren, C. *George Lawson's* Politica *and the English Revolution.* Cambridge, 1989.

Dallison, Charles. *The Royalists Defence.* 1648.

Ferne, Dr. H. *Conscience Satisfied. That there is no Warrant for the Armes now taken up by Subjects.* Oxford, 1643.

Filmer, Sir Robert. *The Anarchy of a Limited or Mixed Monarchy.* London, 1648.

Fink, Z. S. *The Classical Republicans: An Essay in the Recovery of a Pattern of Thought in Seventeenth-Century England.* Evanston, Ill., 1945.

Foundations of Freedom: or an Agreement of the People. London, 1648.

Frank, J. *The Levellers. A History of the Writings of Three Seventeenth-Century*

Social Democrats: John Lilburne, Richard Overton, William Walwyn. Cambridge, Mass., 1955.

Gibb, M. A. *John Lilburne: The Leveller, A Christian Democrat.* London, 1947.

Gooch, G. P. *English Democratic Ideas in the Seventeenth Century.* New York, 1959.

[Hall, John]. *Confusion Confounded: or a Firm Way of Settlement Settled and Confirmed.* London, 1654.

Haller, W. *Liberty and Reformation in the Puritan Revolution.* New York, 1944.

Harrington, James. *The Commonwealth of Oceana.* London, 1656.

[————]. *The Humble Petition of Divers Well-affected Persons.* . . . London, 1659.

Herle, Charles. *A Fuller Answer to a Treatise Written by Dr. Ferne.* . . . London, 1642.

————. *An Answer to Dr. Ferne's Reply.* London, 1643.

Hunton, Philip. *A Treatise of Monarchy.* London, 1643.

————. *A Vindication of the Treatise of Monarchy.* London, 1644.

Jenks, E. *The Constitutional Experiments of the Commonwealth.* Cambridge, 1890.

Judson, Margaret A. *The Crisis of the Constitution: An Essay in Constitutional Thought in England, 1603-1645.* New Brunswick, N.J., 1949.

Kliger, Samuel. *The Goths in England: A Study in Seventeenth- and Eighteenth-Century Thought.* Cambridge, Mass., 1952.

Lawson, George. *An Examination of the Political Part of Mr. Hobbs his Leviathan.* London, 1657.

————. *Politica Sacra et Civilis.* London, 1660.

L'Estrange, Sir Roger. *A Plea for a Limited Monarchy.* London, 1660. In *Harleian Miscellany,* Vol. 1, pp. 17–23.

Lilburne, John. *The Earnest Petition of Many Free-born People.* London, 1648.

————. *The Picture of the Councel of State.* London, 1649.

Locke, John. *Two Treatises of Government* (1690). A Critical Edition. Edited by Peter Laslett. London, 1960.

Maclean, A. H. "George Lawson and John Locke," *The Cambridge Historical Journal,* Vol. IX, 1947.

Milton, John. *Eikonoklastes.* London, 1649.

————. *Character of the Long Parliament.* London, 1681.

————. *The Ready and Easy way to Establish a Free Commonwealth.* In *Works,* Vol. II. Amsterdam, 1698.

Nedham, Marchamont. *A True State of the Case of the Commonwealth.* London, 1654.

————. *The Excellencie of a Free State.* London, 1656.

Pease, T. C. *The Leveller Movement: A Study in the History and Political Theory of the English Great Civil War.* Washington, D.C., 1916.

Penington, Isaac the Younger. *A Word for the Commonweale. . . .* London, 1650.

――――. *The Fundamental Right, Safety and Liberty of the People. . . .* London, 1651.

――――. *A Considerable Question about Government. . . .* London, 1653.

Pole, J. R. *The Seventeenth Century: The Sources of Legislative Power.* Charlottesville, Va., 1969.

The Priviledges and Practice of Parliaments in England. 1628.

Sadler, John. *Rights of the Kingdom.* London, 1649.

Sidney, Algernon. *Discourses Concerning Government.* London, 1698.

Vane, Sir Henry. *A Healing Question. . . .* London, 1655.

Weston, Corinne Comstock. "Beginnings of the Classical Theory of the English Constitution." *Proceedings of the American Philosophical Society,* April 1956.

――――. "The Theory of Mixed Monarchy Under Charles I and After." *English Historical Review,* Vol. LXXV, July 1960.

――――. *English Constitutional Theory and the House of Lords, 1556-1832.* London, 1965.

Weston, Corinne Comstock, and J. R. Greenberg. *Subjects and Sovereigns: The Grand Controversy over Legal Sovereignty in Stuart England.* Cambridge, 1981.

Wildman, John. *Truths, Tryumph, or Treachery Anatomised.* London, 1648.

Wolfe, Don M. *Leveller Manifestoes of the Puritan Revolution.* New York, 1944.

4. The Balanced Constitution of the Eighteenth Century and Its Critics

Acherley, R. *The Britannic Constitution.* London, 1727.

Bentham, Jeremy. *A Fragment on Government.* London, 1776.

――――. *A General View of a Complete Code of Laws* (1802). In *The Works of Jeremy Bentham,* Vol. 3. New York, 1962.

――――. *The Elements of the Art of Packing.* London, 1821.

――――. *The Book of Fallacies.* London, 1824.

――――. *The Constitutional Code.* London, 1825.

The Black Book: An Exposition of Abuses in Church and State. London, 1835.

Blackstone, Sir William. *Commentaries on the Laws of England.* London, 1765-9.

Bolingbroke, Henry St. John. *A Dissertation on Parties.* Second edition. London, 1735.

――――. *Remarks on the History of England.* London, 1743.

――――. *Of the Constitution of Great Britain.* In *A Collection of Political Tracts.* London, 1748.

Carpenter, W. S. "The Separation of Powers in the Eighteenth Century." *The American Political Science Review,* Vol. XXII, February 1928.

Cartwright, John. *An Appeal on the Subject of the English Constitution.* Boston, Lincolnshire, 1797.

———. *The English Constitution Produced and Illustrated.* London, 1823.

Grenville, George. *The Speech of a Right Honourable Gentleman.* London, 1769.

An Historical Essay on the English Constitution. 1771.

Klimowsky, E. *Die englische Gewaltenteilungslehre bis zu Montesquieu.* Berlin, 1927.

Lolme, Jean Louis de. *Constitution of England.* . . . London, 1775.

Mackworth, Sir Humphrey. *A Vindication of the Rights of the Commons of England.* London, 1701.

Nares, R. *Principles of Government Deduced from Reason.* London, 1792.

The Old Whig, No. 1. London, 1719.

On the Peerage. 1719.

Paine, Tom. *Common Sense.* 1776.

———. *The Rights of Man.* London, 1791.

Paley, William. *The Principles of Moral and Political Philosophy.* London, 1785.

[Payne, Sir Peter]. *Defence of the Constitution.* Birmingham, 1822.

Peacock, Rev. D. M. *Considerations on the Structure of the House of Commons.* London, 1794.

Plowden, F. *A Short History of the British Empire.* London, 1794.

Reflections on the Formation of a Regency. London, 1788.

Robbins, Caroline. *The Eighteenth-Century Commonwealthman: Studies in the Transmission, Development, and Circumstance of English Liberal Thought from the Restoration of Charles II Until the War with the Thirteen Colonies.* New York, 1968.

Rous, G. *A Candid Investigation.* . . . London, 1784.

———. *The Claim of the House of Commons.* . . . London, 1784.

———. *A Letter to the Right Honourable Edmund Burke.* London, 1791.

Ruff, Edith. *Jean Louis de Lolme und sein Werk über die Verfassung Englands.* In *Historische Studien,* Vol. 240. Berlin, 1934.

Steele, Sir Richard. *The Plebian,* No. II. London, 1719.

Stephens, William. *A Letter to His Most Excellent Majesty King William III.* Third edition. London, 1699.

Swift, Jonathan. *A Discourse of the Contests and Dissentions between the Nobles and Commons in Athens and Rome.* 1701. In *Works,* Vol. III. London, 1766.

Toland, John. *The Art of Governing by Partys.* London, 1701.

Turner, E. R. "The Peerage Bill of 1719." *English Historical Review,* Vol. 28, 1913.

Walpole, Sir Robert. *Some Reflections on a Pamphlet called the Old Whig.* London, 1719.

————. *The Thoughts of a Member of the Lower House, etc.* London, 1719.

Williams, David. *Letters on Political Liberty.* 1782.

————. *Lectures on Political Principles.* London, 1789.

Yate, Walter. *Political and Historical Arguments Proving the Necessity of Parliamentary Reform.* London, 1812.

5. Montesquieu

Barckhausen, M. *Montesquieu, ses idées et ses oeuvres.* Paris, 1907.

Bonno, G. *La constitution britannique devant l'opinion française de Montesquieu à Bonaparte.* Paris, 1932.

Carcassonne, E. *Montesquieu et le problème de la constitution française au XVIIIe siècle.* Paris, 1927.

Condorcet, Marie-Jean. *La pensée politique de Montesquieu.* Caen, 1985.

Courteney, C. P. *Montesquieu and Burke.* Oxford, 1963.

Dedieu, J. *Montesquieu et la tradition politique anglaise en France.* Paris, 1902.

Eisenmann, Charles. "*L'Esprit des Lois* et la séparation des pouvoirs." In *Mélanges R. Carré de Malberg.* Paris, 1933.

Fletcher, F. T. H. *Montesquieu and English Politics (1750–1800).* London, 1939.

Granpré Molière, Jean-Jacques. *La théorie de la constitution anglaise chez Montesquieu.* Leiden, 1972.

Merry, Henry J. *Montesquieu's System of Natural Government.* West Lafayette, Ind., 1970.

Mirkine-Guetzévitch, B., and Henri Puget, eds. *La pensée politique et constitutionnelle de Montesquieu.* Paris, 1952.

Montesquieu, Baron Louis de Secondat. *De l'Esprit des Lois.* Edited by J. Brette de la Gressaye. Paris, 1950.

Raumer, K. von. "Absoluter Staat, korporative Libertät, persönliche Freiheit." *Historische Zeitschrift*, Vol. 183. Munich, 1957.

Schönfeld, K. M. *Montesquieu en "La bouche de la loi."* Leiden, 1979.

Shackleton, Robert. "Montesquieu, Bolingbroke and the Separation of Powers." *French Studies*, Vol. III, 1949.

————. *Montesquieu: A Critical Biography.* Oxford, 1961.

Shklar, Judith. *Montesquieu.* Oxford, 1987.

Sorel, Albert. *Montesquieu.* London, 1887.

Stark, W. *Montesquieu: Pioneer of the Sociology of Knowledge.* London, 1960.

Struck, W. *Montesquieu als Politiker.* Berlin, 1933.

6. The Colonial Period in America

Bland, Richard. *The Colonel Dismounted*. Williamsburg, Va., 1764. In *Pamphlets of the American Revolution, 1750–1776*, edited by B. Bailyn. Cambridge, Mass., 1965.

Eliot, Jared. *Give Cesar His Due*. New London, 1738.

Howe, Mark de Wolfe, and Louis F. Eaton, Jr. "The Supreme Judicial Power in the Colony of Massachusetts Bay." *New England Quarterly*, September 1947.

Labaree, L. W. *Conservatism in Early American History*. Ithaca, N.Y., 1959.

Otis, James. *Boston Gazette*, 11 January 1762.

————. *The Rights of the British Colonies Asserted and Proved*. Boston, 1764.

Penn, William. *The Frame of Government of the Province of Pennsylvania*. 1682.

Pownall, Thomas. *The Administration of the Colonies*. Second edition. London, 1765.

"Small Treatise." *The Proceedings of the Massachusetts Historical Society*, Vol. 46, 1913.

Spurlin, P. H. *Montesquieu in America, 1760–1801*. Baton Rouge, La., 1940.

[Thacher, Oxenbridge]. *Considerations on the Election of Counsellors*. Boston, 1761.

"T.Q." [Oxenbridge Thacher]. *Boston Gazette*, 6 June 1763.

Winthrop's Journal. Edited by James Savage. Boston, 1853.

Wise, John. *A Vindication of the Government of New England Churches*. Boston, 1717.

7. The American Revolution and the State Constitutions

"A.B." *The Pennsylvania Gazette*, 28 April 1784.

Adams, John. *Letter to Richard Henry Lee, 15 Nov. 1775*. In *Works*, Vol. IV. Boston, 1865, p. 186.

————. *Novanglus, or a History of the Dispute with America*. In *Works*, Vol. IV. Boston, 1865.

Allen, Ira. *Some Miscellaneous Remarks*. Hartford, Conn., 1777.

Baldwin, Alice M. *The New England Clergy and the American Revolution*. Durham, N.C., 1928.

Barnhart, John D. "The Tennessee Constitution of 1796: A Product of the Old West." *The Journal of Southern History*, Vol. IX, 1943.

Bradley, S. R. *Vermont's Appeal to the Candid and Impartial World*. Hartford, Conn., 1780.

Brennan, Ellen E. *Plural Office-Holding in Massachusetts, 1760–1780*. Chapel Hill, N.C., 1945.

Brunhouse, R. L. *The Counter-Revolution in Pennsylvania, 1776–1790.* Philadelphia, 1942.

"Candidus." *Plain Truth.* Philadelphia, 1776.

The Committee of Privates of Philadelphia. *To the Several Battalions of Military Associators in the Province of Pennsylvania.* Philadelphia, June 1776.

Coulter, Merton E. "Early Frontier Democracy in the First Kentucky Constitution." *Political Science Quarterly,* Vol. 39, 1924.

The Council of Censors. *Journal of the Council of Censors.* Philadelphia, 1783–4.

———. *Report of the Committee of the Council of Censors.* Philadelphia, 1784.

"Demophilus." *The Genuine Principles of the Ancient Saxon or English Constitution.* Philadelphia, 1776.

[John Dickinson]. *An Essay of a Frame of Government for Pennsylvania.* Philadelphia, 1776.

Douglass, E. P. *Rebels and Democrats.* Chapel Hill, N.C., 1955.

Fischer, David H. "The Myth of the Essex Junto." *William and Mary Quarterly,* Vol. XXI, No. 2, April 1964.

Four letters on Interesting Subjects. Philadelphia, 1776.

Graydon, Alexander. *Memoirs of a Life Chiefly Passed in Pennsylvania.* Edinburgh, 1822.

Hawke, D. *In the Midst of a Revolution.* Philadelphia, 1961.

"The Interest of America." In *The Pennsylvania Packet,* 1 July 1776.

"J." *Boston Evening Post,* Supplement, 23 May 1763.

Jefferson, Thomas. *Summary View of the Rights of British America.* Williamsburg, Va., 1774.

———. *Notes on the State of Virginia.* Philadelphia, 1781.

Lincoln, C. H. *The Revolutionary Movement in Pennsylvania, 1760–1776.* Philadelphia, 1901.

McMaster, J. B., and F. D. Stone. *Pennsylvania and the Federal Constitution, 1787–1788.* Philadelphia, 1888.

Manin, Bernard. "Frontières, freins et contrepoids: La séparation des pouvoirs dans le débat constitutionnel Américain de 1787." *Revue française de science politique,* Vol. 44, No. 2, April 1994.

Marcus, Maeva. "Separation of Powers in the Early National Period." *William and Mary Law Review,* Vol. 30, 1989.

Meader, L. H. "The Council of Censors." *The Pennsylvania Magazine,* Vol. XXII, No. 3, 1898.

Nevins, A. *The American States During and After the Revolution, 1775–1789.* New York, 1924.

Niles, H. *Principles and Acts of the Revolution in America.* Baltimore, 1822.

[Parsons, Theophilus]. *Result of the Convention of Delegates . . . (The Essex Result)*. Newbury-port, Mass., 1778.

The People the Best Governors. In F. Chase, *A History of Dartmouth College*, Vol. I, edited by J. K. Lord. Cambridge, Mass., 1891.

Pocock, J. G. A. *Three British Revolutions: 1641, 1688, 1776*. Princeton, N.J., 1980.

Purcell, R. J. *Connecticut in Transition, 1775–1818*. Middletown, Conn., 1963.

Rush, Benjamin. *Observations on the Present Government of Pennsylvania*. Philadelphia, 1777.

Taylor, R. J., ed. *Massachusetts, Colony to Commonwealth: Documents on the Formation of the Constitution, 1775–1780*. Chapel Hill, N.C., 1961.

Thorpe, F. N. *A Constitutional History of the American People, 1776–1850*. New York, 1898.

——. *The Federal and State Constitutions*. Washington, D.C., 1909.

To the People of North America on the Different Types of Government. In *American Archives*, edited by Peter Force. Washington, 1843.

Williams, Samuel. *The Natural and Civil History of Vermont*. Walpole, N.H., 1794.

Young, Thomas. *To the Inhabitants of Vermont*. Philadelphia, 1777.

8. The Federal Constitution and Its Critics

Adams, John. *Defence Of the Constitutions of Government of the United States of America, 1787*. Boston, 1865.

"Aristides." *Remarks on the Proposed Plan of a Federal Government*. Annapolis, Md., 1788.

Blumoff, Theodore Y. "Separation of Powers and the Origins of the Appointment Clause." *Syracuse Law Review*, Vol. 37, 1987.

Carey, George W. "Separation of Powers and the Madisonian Model: A Reply to the Critics." *The American Political Science Review*, Vol. 72, 1978.

Casper, Gerhard. "An Essay in Separation of Powers: Some Early Versions and Practices." *William and Mary Law Review*, Vol. 30, 1989.

"Centinel." *To the People of Pennsylvania*. Philadelphia, 1787. In J. B. McMaster and F. D. Stone, *Pennsylvania and the Federal Constitution, 1787–1788*. Philadelphia, 1888.

Chipman, Nathaniel. *Sketches of the Principles of Government*. Rutland, Vt., 1793.

——. *Principles of Government*. Burlington, Vt., 1833.

Conkin, P. K. *Self-Evident Truths: Being a Discourse on the Origins and Development of the First Principles of American Government—Popular Sovereignty, Natural Rights, and Balance and Separation of Powers*. Bloomington, Ind., 1974.

Corwin, E. S. "The Progress of Constitutional Theory, 1776 to 1787." *American Historical Review*, Vol. XXX, No. 3, 1925.

Farrand, Max, ed. *The Records of the Federal Convention of 1787*. New Haven, Conn., 1937.

Ford, P. L., ed. *The Writings of Thomas Jefferson*. New York, 1892–9.

Gwyn, William B. "The Indeterminacy of the Separation of Powers in the Age of the Framers." *William and Mary Law Review*, Vol. 30, No. 2, winter 1989.

Hamilton, A., J. Madison, and J. Jay. *The Federalist Papers*. Edited by Clinton Rossiter. New York, 1961.

Iredell, James. *Answers to Mr. Mason's Objections*. Newbern, N.C., 1788.

[Jackson, Johnathan]. *The Political Situation of the United States of America*. Worcester, Mass., 1788.

Koch, Adrienne. *Jefferson and Madison: The Great Collaboration*. New York, 1964.

Manin, Bernard. "Checks, Balances and Boundaries: The Separation of Powers in the Constitutional Debate of 1787." In *The Invention of the Modern Republic*, edited by Biancamaria Fontana. Cambridge, 1994.

Mason, George. *The Objections of the Hon. George Mason . . . 1787*. In P. L. Ford, *Pamphlets on the Constitution of the United States*. New York, 1888.

Morgan, Robert J. "Madison's Theory of Representation in the Tenth Federalist." *The Journal of Politics*, Vol. 37, 1974.

Observations on Government. 1787.

Sharp, M. P. "The Classical American Doctrine of the Separation of Powers." *University of Chicago Law Review*, Vol. 2, April 1935.

Storing, H. J. *The Complete Anti-Federalist*. 7 vols. Chicago, 1981.

Stromberg, Joseph R. "Country Ideology, Republicanism, and Libertarianism: The Thought of John Taylor of Caroline." *The Journal of Libertarian Studies*, Vol. VI, No. 1, winter 1982.

Taylor, John of Caroline. *An Inquiry into the Principles and Policy of the Government of the United States*. Fredericksburg, Va., 1814.

———. *Construction Construed and Constitutions Vindicated*. Richmond, Va., 1820.

———. *Tyranny Unmasked*. Washington, 1822.

———. *New Views of the Constitution of the United States*. Washington, 1823.

Walsh, Correa M. *The Political Science of John Adams: A Study in the Theory of Mixed Government and the Bicameral System*. New York, 1915.

Wilson, James. *Commentaries on the Constitution of the United States*. London, 1792.

———. *The Works of the Hon. James Wilson*. 3 vols. Philadelphia, 1804.

9. The French Revolution

Bastid, P. *Les discours de Sieyès dans les débats constitutionnels de l'An III.* Paris, 1939.

———. *Sieyès et sa pensée.* Paris, 1939.

Boissy d'Anglas, François Antoine. *Le Moniteur Universel,* No. 283, Vol. 25. Paris, 1840–7.

Carnot, Lazare. *Le Moniteur Universel,* No. 194, Vol. 20. Paris, 1840–7.

Condorcet, Marie-Jean. *Plan de constitution présenté à la Convention Nationale.* In *Oeuvres,* Vol. XVIII. Paris, 1804.

Duguit, Léon. "La séparation des pouvoirs et l'assemblée nationale de 1789." *Revue d'Economie Politique,* Vol. 7, 1893.

Mably, Gabriel Bonnot, l'Abbé de. *Observations sur les Romains.* 1751.

———. *Droits et devoirs du citoyen.* 1758.

———. *De l'étude de l'histoire.* 1778.

Mellis, Paul de. *Le principe de la séparation des pouvoirs d'après l'Abbé de Mably.* Toulouse, 1907.

Mirabeau, Honoré-Gabriel, comte de. *Courier de Provence,* No. 41, September 1789.

Mirkine-Guetzévitch, B. *Le gouvernement parlementaire sous la Convention.* In *Cahiers de la Révolution française,* No. VI, 1937.

Pasquino, Pasquale. "The Constitutional Republicanism of Emmanuel Sieyès." In *The Invention of the Modern Republic,* edited by Biancamaria Fontana. Cambridge, 1994.

Rousseau, Jean-Jacques. *The Social Contract* (1762). Edited by F. Watkins. London, 1953.

———. *Considérations sur le gouvernement de Pologne et sur sa réformation projettée.* London, 1782.

Sieyès, l'Abbé Emmanuel. *Qu'est-ce que le Tiers Etat?* 1789.

Villers, Robert. "La Convention pratiqua-t-elle le gouvernement parlementaire?" *Revue du droit publique,* April–June 1951.

10. Post-Revolutionary France

Barante, A. B. de. *La vie politique de M. Royer-Collard.* Paris, 1863.

Bastid, P. *Doctrines et institutions politiques de la Seconde République.* Paris, 1945.

———. *Le gouvernement d'assemblée.* Paris, 1956.

Bonnefon, J. *Le régime parlementaire sous la Restauration.* Paris, 1905.

Broglie, Victor, duc de. *Vues sur le gouvernement de la France.* Paris, 1870.

Constant, Benjamin. *Collection complète des ouvrages de M. Benjamin de Constant.* Paris, 1818.

Guizot, François. *Du gouvernement représentatif et de l'état actuel de la France.* Paris, 1816.

————. *De la démocratie en France.* Paris, 1849.

Lamartine, A. de. *La France parlementaire.* Paris, 1865.

Nesmes-Desmonets, R. *Les doctrines politiques de Royer-Collard.* Montpellier, 1908.

11. *The Nineteenth-Century British Constitution*

Aiken, P. F. *A Comparative View of the Constitutions of Great Britain and the United States of America.* London, 1842.

Austin, John. *The Province of Jurisprudence Determined.* Second edition. London, 1861.

Bagehot, Walter. *The British Constitution* (1867). Introduction by R. H. S. Crossman. London, 1964.

Brougham, Henry. *Political Philosophy.* 3 vols. London, 1842–3.

————. *The British Constitution.* London, 1860.

Bryce, James. *The American Commonwealth.* Second edition. London, 1890.

Cox, Homersham. *The Institutions of the English Government.* London, 1863.

Dicey, A. V. *The Law of the Constitution.* Eighth edition. London, 1931.

Erskine, Thomas. *Armata: A Fragment.* Second edition. London, 1817.

Grey, Earl Henry George. *Parliamentary Government considered with Reference to a Reform of Parliament.* London, 1858.

[Jeffrey, Francis]. *Edinburgh Review,* Vol. X, No. XX, July 1897.

Laurie, J. S. *Sketches of the English Constitution.* London, 1864.

Lewis, Sir George Cornewall. *A Dialogue on the Best Form of Government.* London, 1863.

Mill, John Stuart. *Representative Government.* London, 1865.

Park, J. J. *The Dogmas of the Constitution.* London, 1832.

A Political Dictionary. London, 1845.

Rowland, David. *A Manual of the English Constitution.* London, 1859.

Russell, Lord John. *Essay on the History of the English Government and Constitution.* London, 1821.

Sidgwick, Henry. *The Elements of Politics.* Second edition. London, 1897.

12. The United States: 1850–1945

Bradford, Gamaliel. *The Lesson of Popular Government.* New York, 1899.

Calhoun, John C. *A Disquisition on Government.* New York, 1854.

Cole, A. C., ed. *The Constitutional Debates of 1847.* Springfield, Mass., 1919.

Cooper, F. E. *Administrative Agencies and the Courts.* Ann Arbor, Mich., 1951.

Croly, Herbert. *Progressive Democracy.* New York, 1915.

Ford, Henry Jones. *Rise and Growth of American Politics.* New York, 1898.

Goodnow, Frank. *Politics and Administration.* New York, 1900.

Gulick, Luther. "Politics, Administration and the 'New Deal.'" *Annals of the American Academy,* Vol. 169, September 1933.

Horn, Stephen. *The Cabinet and Congress.* New York, 1960.

Kales, M. *Unpopular Government in the United States.* Chicago, 1914.

Key, V. O., Jr. "Politics and Administration." In *The Future of Government in the United States,* edited by J. D. White. Chicago, 1942.

Landis, James. *The Administrative Process.* New Haven, Conn., 1938.

Payne, G. H. *The Birth of the New Party: Or Progressive Democracy.* New York, 1912.

Pierce, Franklin. *Federal Usurpation.* New York, 1908.

Report of the President's Committee on Administrative Management. Washington, D.C., 1937.

Smith, J. Allen. *The Spirit of American Government.* New York, 1907.

Stephens, Alexander H. *A Constitutional View of the Late War Between the States.* Philadelphia, 1876.

Vanderbilt, Arthur T. *The Doctrine of the Separation of Powers and Its Present-Day Significance.* Lincoln, Neb., 1953.

Waldo, D. *The Administrative State.* New York, 1948.

Willoughby, W. F. *An Introduction to the Study of the Government of Modern States.* New York, 1919.

Wilson, Woodrow. "Cabinet Government in the United States." *International Review,* August 1879.

———. *Congressional Government.* New York, 1885.

———. "The Study of Administration." *Political Science Quarterly,* June 1887.

———. *Constitutional Government in the United States.* New York, 1908.

13. The Twentieth-Century British Political System

Amery, L. S. *Thoughts on the Constitution.* London, 1947.

Committee on Ministers' Powers. *Minutes of Evidence,* HMSO. London, 1932.

The Financing and Accountability of Next Steps Agencies. H.M. Treasury. Cm 914, HMSO. London, 1989.

Galligan, D. J. *Discretionary Powers: A Legal Study of Official Discretion.* Oxford, 1986.

Gordon, Richard. "The New Sovereigns?" *New Law Journal,* Vol. 145, April 14, 1995, p. 529.

Graham, C., and T. Prosser. *Waiving the Rules: The Constitution Under Thatcherism.* Milton Keynes, 1988.

Harden, Ian, and Norman Lewis. *The Noble Lie: The British Constitution and the Rule of Law.* London, 1986.

Improving Management in Government: The Next Steps. Report to the Prime Minister. The Efficiency Unit, HMSO. London, 1988.

Making the Most of Next Steps: The Management of Ministers' Departments and Their Executive Agencies. Report to the Prime Minister. The Efficiency Unit, HMSO. London, 1991.

Morrison, Herbert. *Government and Parliament.* Third edition. London, 1964.

Mount, F. *The British Constitution Now.* London, 1992.

Norton, Philip. *The Constitution in Flux.* Oxford, 1982.

Report of the Committee on Administrative Tribunals and Enquiries. Cmd. 218, HMSO. London, 1957.

Report of the Committee on Ministers' Powers. Cmd. 4060, HMSO. London, 1932.

Ridley, F. "Using Power to Keep Power: The Need for Constitutional Checks." *Parliamentary Affairs,* Vol. 44, October 1991.

Robson, W. A. *Justice and Administrative Law.* Second edition. London, 1947.

Vile, M. J. C. "Unbuckling Bagehot." *The Times Higher Educational Supplement,* No. 814, June 10, 1988, p. 17.

———. "Parliament and Government: Unbuckling the Powers." *Social Studies Review,* Vol. 4, No. 3, January 1989, pp. 100–3.

14. From the Third Republic to the Fifth

Bacot, G. "L'Esprit des Lois, la séparation des pouvoirs et Charles Eisenmann." *Revue du droit publique,* No. 3, May–June 1992.

Blocq-Mascart, M. *Chroniques de la Résistance.* Paris, 1945.

Blum, Léon. *La réforme gouvernementale.* Second edition. Paris, 1936.

Carré de Malberg, R. *Contribution à la théorie générale de l'état.* Paris, 1922.

Chorin, J. "Les entreprises publiques: statut, le code du travail et le principe de séparation des pouvoirs." *Droit social,* No. 12, December 1993.

Club Jean Moulin. *L'Etat et le citoyen.* Paris, 1961.

————. *Bulletin du Club Jean Moulin*, No. 31, juin–juillet 1962.

Comité Consultatif Constitutionnel. *Travaux préparatoires de la Constitution*. Paris, 1960.

Debré, Michel. *La République et son pouvoir*. Paris, 1950.

————. *Ces princes qui nous gouvernent*. Paris, 1957.

————. "La Nouvelle Constitution." *Revue française de science politique*, Vol. 9, March 1959.

Duguit, Léon. *Traité de droit constitutionnel*. Second edition. Paris, 1921–3.

————. *Manuel de droit constitutionnel*. Fourth edition. Paris, 1923.

Duvergier de Hauranne, Prosper. *Histoire du gouvernement parlementaire en France*. Paris, 1874.

Gooch, G. P. "Modern French Views on the Separation of Powers." *Political Science Quarterly*, Vol. XXXVIII, December 1923.

Mény, Y. "Le cumul des mandats ou l'impossible séparation des pouvoirs?" *Pouvoirs*, Vol. 64, 1993.

Michel, H., and B. Mirkine-Guetzévitch. *Les idées politiques et sociales de la Résistance*. Paris, 1954.

Poitou, Eugène. *La liberté civile et le pouvoir administratif en France*. Paris, 1869.

Tardieu, André. *La réforme de l'état*. Paris, 1934.

Troper, Michel. "The Development of the Notion of Separation of Powers." *Israel Law Review*, Vol. 26, No. 1, winter 1992.

Wahl, N. "Aux origines de la nouvelle Constitution." *Revue française de science politique*, Vol. IX, No. 1, 1959.

15. Modern American Constitutional Law and Theory

Berger, Raoul. *Impeachment: The Constitutional Problems*. Cambridge, Mass., 1973.

————. *Executive Privilege: A Constitutional Myth*. Cambridge, Mass., 1974.

Berlin, E. P. "The Federal Sentencing Guidelines' Failure to Eliminate Sentencing Disparity—Governmental Manipulations Before Arrest." *Wisconsin Law Review*, No. 1, 1993.

Brennan, G., and A. Hamlin. "A Revisionist View of the Separation of Powers." *Journal of Theoretical Politics*, Vol. 6, No. 3, July 1994.

Bybee, J. S. "Advising the President: Separation of Powers and the Federal Advisory Committee Act." *Yale Law Journal*, Vol. 104, No. 1, October 1994.

Calabresi, S. G., and J. L. Larsen. "One Person, One Office—Separation of Powers or Separation of Personnel?" *Cornell Law Review*, Vol. 79, No. 5, 1994.

Carey, George W. *In Defense of the Constitution.* Revised edition. Indianapolis, Ind., 1995.

Choper, Jesse H. *Judicial Review and the National Political Process: A Functional Reconsideration of the Role of the Supreme Court.* Chicago, 1980.

Cooper, S. W. "Considering Power in Separation of Powers." *Stanford Law Review,* Vol. 46, No. 2, 1994.

Curlin, J. W. "Science and Technology Under Constitutional Separation of Powers." *Technology in Society,* Vol. 14, No. 1, 1992.

Cutler, Lloyd N. "To Form a Government." *Foreign Affairs,* fall 1980.

Doidge, J. R. "Is Purely Retroactive Legislation Limited by the Separation of Powers?—Rethinking *United States v. Klein.*" *Cornell Law Review,* Vol. 79, No. 4, 1994.

Dolan, Michael W. "Congress, the Executive, and the Court: The Great Resale Price Maintenance Affair of 1983." *Public Administration Review,* Vol. 45, November 1985.

Essayian, Lisa G. "Separation of Powers—The Federal Sentencing Commission: Unconstitutional Delegation and Threat to Judicial Impartiality?" *The Journal of Criminal Law and Criminology,* Vol. 80, winter 1990.

Fisher, Louis. "Judicial Misjudgments About the Lawmaking Process: The Legislative Veto Case." *Public Administration Review,* Vol. 45, November 1985.

———. "The Legislative Veto: Invalidated, It Survives." *Law and Contemporary Problems,* Vol. 56, No. 4, autumn 1993.

———. *The Politics of Shared Power: Congress and the Executive.* Third edition. Washington, D.C., 1993.

Fitzgerald, John L. *Congress and the Separation of Powers.* New York, 1986.

Fletcher, George P. "The Separation of Powers: A Critique of Some Utilitarian Justifications." *Nomos,* No. XX. New York, 1979.

Freedman, J. *Crisis and Legitimacy.* New York, 1978.

Goldwin, R. A., and A. Kaufman, eds. *The Separation of Powers—Does It Still Work?* Washington, D.C., 1986.

Gwyn, William B. "The Indeterminacy of the Separation of Powers and the Federal Courts." *George Washington Law Review,* Vol. 57, No. 3, January 1989.

Halton, William. "Separating Powers: Dialectical Sense and Positive Nonsense." In *Judging the Constitution,* edited by Michael W. McCann and Gerald L. Houseman. Glenview, Ill., 1989.

Hardin, Charles M. "A Challenge to Political Science." *PS, Washington, D.C.,* September 1989.

Harriger, K. J. "Separation of Powers and the Politics of Independent Counsels." *Political Science Quarterly,* Vol. 109, No. 2, summer 1994.

Kirwan, K. A. "The Use and Abuse of Power: The Supreme Court and Separation of Powers." *Annals of the American Academy of Political and Social Science*, Vol. 537, 1995.

Koh, H. H. "Transnational Public Law Litigation." *Yale Law Journal*, Vol. 100, No. 8, 1991.

Korn, J. "Improving the Policy-Making Process by Protecting the Separation of Powers—*Chadha* and the Legislative Vetoes in Education Statutes." *Polity*, Vol. 26, No. 4, 1994.

Kravchuk, R. S. "Liberalism and the American Administrative State." *Public Administration Review*, Vol. 52, No. 4, July/August 1992.

Kurland, Philip B. *Watergate and the Constitution*. Chicago, 1978.

Lawson, Gary. "The Rise and Rise of the Administrative State." *Harvard Law Review*, Vol. 107, 1994.

Levi, Edward H. "Some Aspects of Separation of Powers." *Columbia Law Review*, Vol. 76, 1976.

McClellan, James. *The Constitution from a Conservative Perspective*. Washington, D.C., 1988.

———. *Liberty, Order and Justice—An Introduction to the Constitutional Principles of American Government*. Cumberland, Va., 1989.

Macey, Jonathan R. "Separated Powers and Positive Political Theory: The Tug of War over Administrative Agencies." *Georgetown Law Journal*, Vol. 80, 1992.

McGinnis, J. O. "Constitutional Review by the Executive in Foreign Affairs and War Powers—A Consequence of Rational Choice in the Separation of Powers." *Law and Contemporary Problems*, Vol. 56, No. 4, 1993.

McKay, David. "Review Article: Divided and Governed? Recent Research on Divided Government in the United States." *British Journal of Political Science*, Vol. 24, No. 4, 1994.

Merrill, Thomas W. "The Constitutional Principle of the Separation of Powers." *Supreme Court Review, 1991*, Chicago, 1992.

Miller, A. S. "An Inquiry into the Relevance of the Intentions of the Founding Fathers with Special Emphasis upon the Doctrine of the Separation of Powers." *27 Arkansas Law Review, 583*, 1974.

Miller, Geoffrey P. "The President's Power of Interpretation: Implications of a Unified Theory of Constitutional Law." *Law and Contemporary Problems*, Vol. 56, No. 4, 1993.

Moe, Terry M., and Scott A. Wilson. "Presidents and the Politics of Structure." *Law and Contemporary Problems*, Vol. 57, No. 2, 1994.

Montgomery, B. P. "Nixon Legal Legacy—White House Papers and the Constitution." *American Archivist*, Vol. 56, No. 4, 1993.

Mullenix, L. S. "Unconstitutional Rulemaking—The Civil Justice Reform Act and Separation of Powers." *Minnesota Law Review,* Vol. 77, No. 6, 1993.

O'Toole, Laurence J. "Doctrines and Developments: Separation of Powers, the Politics-Administration Dichotomy, and the Rise of the Administrative State." *Public Administration Review,* Vol. 47, January/February 1987.

Peterson, T. D. "The Role of the Executive Branch in the Discipline and Removal of Federal Judges." *University of Illinois Law Review,* No. 4, 1993.

Rakove, Jack, and Susan Zlomke. "James Madison and the Independent Executive." *Presidential Studies Quarterly,* Vol. 17, spring 1987.

Redish, M. H., and E. J. Cesar. "If Angels Were to Govern—The Need for Pragmatic Formalism in Separation of Powers Theory." *Duke Law Journal,* Vol. 41, No. 3, 1991.

Rosenbloom, David H. "Public Administrative Theory and the Separation of Powers." *Public Administration Review,* Vol. 43, May/June 1983.

Rossum, Ralph. *Congressional Control of the Judiciary: The Article III Option.* Cumberland, Va., 1988.

Sargentich, Thomas O. "The Contemporary Debate About Legislative-Executive Separation of Powers." 72 *Cornell Law Review,* 1987.

Scheiber, H. N. "Constitutional Structure and the Protection of Rights—Federalism and the Separation of Powers." In *The United States Constitution—Roots, Rights, and Responsibilities,* edited by A. Howard. Washington, D.C., 1992.

Shuman, Howard E. *Politics and the Budget: The Struggle Between the President and Congress.* Englewood Cliffs, N.J., 1984.

Siegan, B. H. "Separation of Powers and Economic Liberties." *Notre Dame Law Review,* Vol. 70, No. 3, 1995.

Smentkowski, B. "Legal Reasoning and the Separation of Powers: A State-Level Analysis of Disputes Involving Federal Funds Appropriations. *Law and Policy,* Vol. 16, No. 4, October 1944.

Sprigman, C. J. "Standing on Firmer Ground—Separation of Powers and Deference to Congressional Findings in the Standings Analysis." *University of Chicago Law Review,* Vol. 59, No. 4, 1992.

Stover, C. P. "The Old Public Administration is the New Jurisprudence." *Administration and Society,* Vol. 27, No. 1, 1995.

Strauss, Peter. "The Place of Agencies in Government: Separation of Powers and the Fourth Branch." *Columbia Law Review,* Vol. 84, 1984.

———. "Formal and Functionalist Approaches to Separation of Powers Questions—A Foolish Inconsistency." *Cornell Law Review,* Vol. 72, 1987.

Sundquist, James L. "Needed: A Political Theory for the New Era of Coalition Government in the United States." *Political Science Quarterly,* Vol. 103, 1988.

Sunstein, Cass R. "Constitutionalism After the New Deal." *Harvard Law Review,* Vol. 101, 1987.

———. "Standing and the Privatization of Public Law." *Columbia Law Review,* Vol. 88, No. 6, October 1988.

Thomas, Richard M. "Formalism and Functionalism: From *Northern Pipeline* to *Thomas v. Union Carbide Agricultural Products Co.*" *Syracuse Law Review,* Vol. 37, 1987.

Tomaszczuk, A. D., and J. E. Jensen. "The Adjudicatory Arm of Congress—The GAO's Sixty-Year Role in Deciding Government Contract Bid Protests Comes Under Renewed Attack by the Department of Justice." *Harvard Journal on Legislation,* Vol. 29, No. 2, 1992.

Treister, D. S. "Standing to Sue the Government—Are Separation of Powers Principles Being Served?" *Southern California Law Review,* Vol. 67, No. 3, 1994.

Tushnet, M. "The Sentencing Commission and Constitutional Theory—Bowls and Plateaus in Separation of Powers Theory." *Southern California Law Review,* Vol. 66, No. 1, 1992.

Verkuil, Paul R. "Separation of Powers, the Rule of Law and the Idea of Independence." *William and Mary Law Review,* Vol. 30, 1989.

Vile, M. J. C. "Presidential and Parliamentary Systems." In *The Prospect for Presidential-Congressional Government,* edited by Albert Lepawsky. Berkeley, 1977.

Vincent, J. C., and T. H. Roback. "Dilemmas of Legitimacy—The Supreme Court, Patronage, and the Public Interest." *Administration and Society,* Vol. 26, No. 4, 1994.

Wilson, James Q. "Does the Separation of Powers Still Work?" *The Public Interest,* Vol. 86, winter 1987.

16. General References

Amissah, A. N. E. *The Contribution of the Courts to Government: A West African View.* Oxford, 1981.

Aznam, Suhaini. "Separating the Powers (Malaysia)." *Far Eastern Economic Review,* Vol. 34, December 1986.

Ceterchi, I. "Institutional Problems of Transition in Romania." *Revue d'études comparatives est-ouest,* Vol. 23, No. 4, 1992.

Chiu, H. D. "Constitutional Development and Reform in the Republic of China on Taiwan." *Issues and Studies,* Vol. 29, No. 1, 1993.

Currie, D. P. "Separation of Powers in the Federal Republic of Germany." *American Journal of Comparative Law,* Vol. 41, No. 2, 1993.

Ding, A. S. "The Debate on the Supervisory Powers of the People's Congresses (1986–9)." *Issues and Studies,* Vol. 28, No. 5, 1992.

Ebeku, K. S. A. "The Separation of Powers in Local Government in Nigeria." *Journal of African Law,* Vol. 36, No. 1, spring 1992.

Pokstefl, Josef. *The Revival of the Theory of Division and Supervision of Power During the Prague Spring.* Frankfurt, 1980.

Resnick, Philip. "Montesquieu Revisited, or the Mixed Constitution and the Separation of Powers in Canada." *Canadian Journal of Political Science,* Vol. 20, March 1987.

Stark, A. "Public Sector Conflict of Interest at the Federal Level in Canada and the United States—Differences of Understanding and Approach." *Public Administration Review,* Vol. 52, No. 5, 1992.

Tate, C. N. "The Judicialization of Politics in the Philippines and Southeast Asia." *International Political Science Review,* Vol. 15, No. 2, 1994.

Winterton, George. *Parliament, the Executive, and the Governor-General.* Carlton, Victoria, 1983.

Zafrullah, H. M. *Sri Lanka's Hybrid Presidential Parliamentary System and the Separation of Powers Doctrine.* Kuala Lumpur, 1981.

17. Political Theory and the Separation of Powers

Almond, G. A., and James Coleman, eds. *The Politics of the Developing Areas.* Princeton, N.J., 1960.

Ball, Terence, and J. G. A. Pocock. *Conceptual Change and the Constitution.* London, 1988.

Bellamy, Richard. " 'Dethroning Politics': Liberalism, Constitutionalism and Democracy in the Thought of F. A. Hayek." *British Journal of Political Science,* Vol. 24, No. 4, 1994.

Dahl, Robert A. *A Preface to Democratic Theory.* Chicago, 1956.

Dry, Murray. "The Separation of Powers and Representative Government." *The Political Science Reviewer,* Vol. III, fall 1973.

Dunn, John. "The Identity of the History of Ideas." In *Political Obligation in Its Historical Context: Essays in Political Theory.* Cambridge, 1980.

Fisher, Louis. "The Efficiency Side of the Separation of Powers." *American Studies,* Vol. 5, August 1971.

Hayek, F. A. "The Constitution of a Liberal State." *Il Politico,* Vol. XXXII, 1967.

———. *Law, Legislation and Liberty.* London, 1982.

Pargellis, Stanley M. "The Theory of Balanced Government." In *The Constitution Reconsidered,* edited by Conyers Read. New York, 1938.

Roelofs, H. Mark. "The American Polity: A Systematic Ambiguity." *The Review of Politics,* Vol. 48, summer 1986.

Skinner, Quentin. "Meaning and Understanding in the History of Ideas." *History and Theory,* Vol. VIII, No. 1, 1969.

Sorenson, L. R. "Madison on Sympathy, Virtue, and Ambition in the Federalist Papers." *Polity,* Vol. 27, No. 3, 1995.

Wilson, Francis G. "The Mixed Constitution and the Separation of Powers." *Southwestern Social Science Quarterly,* Vol. XV, June 1934.

INDEX

Act of Settlement, 1701, 73, 81, 114, 122
Adams, John: and Nedham, 56; on legislative power, 146, 159; in revolutionary period, 146, 162; and Constitution of Massachusetts, 163–6; checks and balances, 168; and Bryan, 172; and Taylor, 177, 183–6; and France, 202
Adams, J. T., 163n.
Addison, Joseph, 77
administration, study of, 304–8; and politics, 304–5, 348–9; and representation, 375–6
administrative jurisdiction, 267–9, 271
Administrative Procedure Act, 1946, 312
administrative state, 399ff.; and machine, 400, 401, 414, 418; autonomy of, 400–1; judicial review of, 401–4; control of, 409–17; four branches, 411
Agreement of the People, 48
Aiken, P. F., 243, 249
Allen, C. K., 254
Allen, Ira, 154
Allen, J. W., 42n.
Almond, G. A., 9n., 318–21, 348–9, 359
American colonies: and Blackstone, 112; and balanced constitution, 133–45; and separation of powers, 139ff.
American Revolution, 109; democratic nature, 132–3; convention govern-

ment, 146; effect in France, 201; cf. Third and Fourth Republics, 282–3
Amery, L. S., 251
Ames, Fisher, 177n.
Anisminic case, 404
Answer to the Nineteen Propositions, 43. *See also* Charles I
Aquinas, St. Thomas, 29, 41
Aristides, 168n.
Aristotle, 387; definition of political science, 24; and separation of persons, 24–5; and generality of law, 26; parts of the State, 29–31; and mixed government, 39, 344
Austin, John, 5, 240, 270

Bagehot, Walter, 5, 224, 226, 253–5; originality, 234–43; on English Constitution, 246–51; and functions of government, 251–2; and Woodrow Wilson, 294–6, 297–8
Balanced Budget and Emergency Control Act, 389
balanced constitution, theory of: and mixed government, 43, 108, 109–10; development of, 58ff., and 107ff.; Locke on, 71–3; and division of functions, 74, 80–1; and parts of sovereignty, 74; and separation of powers,

443

This book is set in Aldus, which was designed in 1953 by the prolific type designer Hermann Zapf. Aldus was designed as a Linotype companion to Zapf's Palatino. It is a compact, narrow face in the Renaissance scribal tradition.

Printed on paper that is acid-free and meets the requirements of the American National Standard for Permanence of Paper for Printed Library Materials, z39.48-1992. ∞

Book design by Louise OFarrell, Gainesville, Florida
Typography by Tseng Information Systems, Inc.,
Durham, North Carolina
Printed and bound by Worzalla Publishing Co., Stevens Point,
Wisconsin